Getting Started

WITH
THE INTERNET

Floyd Fuller

William Manning

Portland State University

THE DRYDEN PRESS

HARCOURT BRACE COLLEGE PUBLISHERS

Fort Worth   Philadelphia   San Diego   New York   Orlando   Austin   San Antonio
Toronto   Montreal   London   Sydney   Tokyo

PUBLISHER	*George Provol*
EXECUTIVE EDITOR	*Wesley Lawton*
ASSOCIATE EDITOR	*Elizabeth Hayes*
PRODUCT MANAGER	*Federico Arrietta*
PROJECT EDITOR	*Charles J. Dierker*
ART DIRECTOR	*Scott Baker*
PRODUCTION MANAGER	*Darryl King*
ELECTRONIC PUBLISHING COORDINATOR	*Lisa Rawlinson*
PERMISSIONS EDITOR	*Adele Krause*

ISBN: 0-03-025077-3

Library of Congress Catalog Card Number: 98-84608

Many of the products designated in this book are trademarked. Their use has been respected through appropriate capitalization and spelling.

Copyright © 1999 by Harcourt Brace & Company

Requests for permission to make copies of any part of the work should be mailed to:
Permissions Department, Harcourt Brace & Company, 6277 Sea Harbor Drive, Orlando, FL 32887-6777

Copyright acknowledgments appear on page 285 and constitute a continuation of this page.

Address for Editorial Correspondence:
The Dryden Press, 301 Commerce Street, Suite 3700, Fort Worth, TX 76102

Address for Orders:
The Dryden Press, 6277 Sea Harbor Drive, Orlando, FL 32887-6777. 1-800-782-4479

Web site address:
http://www.hbcollege.com

Harcourt Brace College Publishers may provide complimentary instructional aids and supplements or supplement packages to those adopters qualified under our adoption policy. Please contact your sales representative for more information. If as an adopter or potential user you receive supplements you do not need, please return them to your sales representative or send them to:

Attention: Returns Department, Troy Warehouse, 465 South Lincoln Drive, Troy, MO 63379

Printed in the United States of America
8 9 0 1 2 3 4 5 6 7 048 10 9 8 7 6 5 4 3 2 1

The Dryden Press
Harcourt Brace College Publishers

For who he was and for all that he did, for his devotion to his family and friends, and because he was always there to help guide me along the right path of life's journey, I dedicate this book to the loving memory of my brother, Johnny Irby Fuller

Floyd Fuller

I would like to dedicate this book to my family. My wife, Norma, has been my inspiration and companion for 35 years. There is no one finer. My daughters, Toni, Kelly, and Andee, have been a source of continual joy to me. Thanks for being such great people and a blessing to your father and mother.

Bill Manning

The Dryden Press Series in Information Systems

Coorough
Getting Started: The New Multimedia User

Fenrich
*Practical Guidelines for Creating Instructional Multimedia
Applications*

Fuller/Manning
Getting Started with the Internet

Gordon and Gordon
Information Systems: A Management Approach

Gray, King, McLean, and Watson
Management of Information Systems
Second Edition

Harrington
*Database Management for Microcomputers: Design and
Implementation*
Second Edition

Harris
Systems Analysis and Design: A Project Approach

Head
An Introduction to Programming with QuickBASIC

Larsen/Marold
*Using Microsoft Works 4.0 for Windows 95: An Introduction to
Computing*

Laudon and Laudon
Information Systems and the Internet: A Problem-Solving Approach
Fourth Edition

Laudon and Laudon
Information Systems: A Problem-Solving Approach
(A CD-ROM interactive version)

Licker
Management Information Systems: A Strategic Leadership Approach

Lorents and Morgan
Database Systems: Concepts, Management, Applications

Martin
Discovering Microsoft Office 97

Martin/Parker
PC Concepts

Mason
Using Microsoft Access 97 in Business

Mason
Using Microsoft Excel 97 in Business

McKeown
Living with Computers
Fifth Edition

McKeown
Working with Computers
Second Edition

Morley
Getting Started with Computers

Morley
Getting Started: Web Page Design with Microsoft FrontPage 97

Morley
Introduction to the World Wide Web and Web Pages

Parker
Understanding Computers: Today and Tomorrow
98 Edition

Parker
Understanding Networking and the Internet

Spear
Introduction to Computer Programming in Visual Basic 4.0

Spear
Visual Basic 3.0: A Brief Introduction
Visual Basic 4.0: A Brief Introduction

Sullivan
The New Computer User
Second Edition

Martin and Parker
Mastering Today's Software Series

Texts available in any combination of the following:

Disk Operating System 5.0 (DOS 5.0)	*Lotus 1-2-3 for Windows (5.0)*
Disk Operating System 6.0 (DOS 6.0)	*Lotus 1-2-3 97*
Windows 3.1	*Excel 5.0 for Windows*
Windows 95	*Excel 7.0 for Windows 95*
Microsoft Office 97	*Excel 97*
Microsoft Office for Windows 95 Professional Edition	*Quattro Pro 4.0*
WordPerfect 5.1	*Quattro Pro 6.0 for Windows*
WordPerfect 5.2 for Windows	*dBASE III PLUS*
WordPerfect 6.0 for DOS	*dBASE IV (1.5/2.0)*
WordPerfect 6.0 for Windows	*dBASE 5 for Windows*
WordPerfect 6.1 for Windows	*Paradox 4.0*
Corel WordPerfect 7.0 for Windows 95	*Paradox 5.0 for Windows*
Word 6.0 for Windows	*Access 2.0 for Windows*
Word 7.0 for Windows 95	*Access 7.0 for Windows 95*
Word 97	*Access 97*
Lotus 1-2-3 (2.2/2.3)	*PowerPoint 7.0 for Windows 95*
Lotus 1-2-3 (2.4)	*PowerPoint 97*
Lotus 1-2-3 for Windows (4.01)	*A Beginner's Guide to BASIC*
	A Beginner's Guide to QBASIC
	Netscape Communicator

The Harcourt Brace College Outline Series

Kreitzberg
Introduction to Fortran

Introduction

Perhaps no field is more influential today than computer technology. It affects how we live, learn, play, and work. The Internet and World Wide Web have become a daily part of our society that is impacting youngsters to the elderly.

Development and growth of the Internet and World Wide Web could prove to be the most important phenomenon since computers were introduced. Recent estimates suggest that there are currently more than 60 million users in the United States alone. Projections put the number of users worldwide at more than 90 million by the year 2000.

Despite the explosive increase in Internet use, few textbooks address the total needs of students. *Getting Started with the Internet* will help students develop an extensive understanding of the Internet in both their personal and professional lives.

The goal of *Getting Started with the Internet* is to immerse students in this field of changing technology—to show the processes, opportunities, and implications for the future. We hope to increase student interest, broaden abilities, develop resourcefulness, and enhance self-confidence in harnessing today's newest, cutting-edge technology for personal and professional use.

Three overall themes converge in *Getting Started with the Internet:*

- Personal and organizational productivity are the keys to success. Communications and computer technologies support that productivity.
- Computer technology and the work environment are continuously evolving. This book covers current communication issues as well as creating an anticipation and understanding of changes in the future.
- The Internet and the Web increase the richness and enjoyment of life.

The text is organized broadly into three sections. The first introduces students to the Internet and the World Wide Web and explains how students can get connected. The second provides basic information and guidelines for using electronic mail, navigating the Internet and World Wide Web, searching for and finding useful information, visiting Web sites, and establishing a personal presence on the Web. The third covers Internet issues, problems, and concerns that are encountered by individual users and organizations. Also covered is the emerging activity of conducting business on the Web, a practice known as electronic commerce.

Key Features

CHAPTER OUTLINES AND OBJECTIVES

Each chapter begins with an outline and a set of learning objectives to guide students as they read through the material.

FULL-COLOR ILLUSTRATIONS

The text contains more than 200 photos, screen shots, and illustrations. Numerous screen captures throughout the text illustrate today's most current Internet applications.

THEME BOXES

Each chapter contains special theme boxes that highlight Internet topics of interest to students. Typically, feature boxes such as *Industry Updates, The Internet in the Future,* and *The Internet and You: Careers and Opportunities* appear in each chapter.

END-OF-CHAPTER REVIEW MATERIAL

Each chapter concludes with a summary and list of key terms. Students can also use an accompanying series of short-answer and matching questions to review the chapter's concepts.

INDIVIDUAL AND GROUP ACTIVITIES

Student activities at the end of the chapter are intended to help students delve into their environments and see how the Internet is being used by others. Students are encouraged to conduct interviews, visit local organizations, talk to school administrators, visit sites on the Web, and discuss Internet opportunities with their family, friends, and classmates. They are also urged to be creative and find Web opportunities and applications that are related to work, school, life, and leisure.

STUDENT CYBERTEAM ACTIVITIES

On occasion, students are asked to work in cyberteams, using the Web to collect information and to communicate with their team members. Here the goal is to prepare the students for future Web collaborations in the workplace.

INTERNET EXPLORER AND NAVIGATOR APPENDIXES

The end of the book contains two appendixes that cover tips on getting started using Netscape Navigator and Microsoft's Internet Explorer.

Supplements

WEB SITE

Books in dynamic fields quickly become dated. To keep this book as current as possible, we have created a Web site at http://www.dryden.com/infosys that contains extensive corresponding information. Here instructors and students can stay informed about current Web information and issues. New sites and information about new breakthroughs will be posted here as well as useful links to Web sites that are mentioned in the book. In addition, instructors can download the book's Instructor's Manual, which includes lecture outlines, teaching tips, answers to the end-of-chapter questions, and additional activities for assignment.

DRYDEN RESOURCE CD-ROM

A Resource CD-ROM that accompanies the textbook contains a variety of freeware and shareware programs, including the two most popular browsers, Netscape Navigator and Microsoft Internet Explorer. A useful tool for the beginning Internet user, this CD-ROM also includes FTP programs, file compression programs, image viewers and editors, and more.

INTRODUCTION TO THE INTERNET & WORLD WIDE WEB SKILL BUILDER CD-ROM

This optional CD-ROM from the DrydenOnline.com courseware series presents an effective skills-based instructional design combined with a user-friendly interface, hands-on practice exercises, audio prompting, and preassessment testing that creates a learner-defined training path by utilizing simulations. This CD-ROM may be bundled with the text or ordered separately. See your local Dryden sales representative for more information or e-mail the Dryden product manager at **farrieta@harbrace.com.**

Acknowledgments

Reviewers prove the wisdom of the old adage, "More heads are better than one." Our reviewers added reality and fresh insights to this project. We would like to especially thank them for their interest, valuable comments, and overall support of this project. They have helped us build a better book.

Lynda Armbruster, Santiago Canyon College

Wade Graves, Grayson County College

Betty A. Dalton, Tarrant County Junior College

Barbara M. Jaffari, College of the Redwoods

Anthony J. Nowakowski, Buffalo State College

Philip Whitney, Bakersfield College

We have thoroughly enjoyed writing this book. The professionals at The Dryden Press have been outstanding in their contributions and support. A special thanks is due to our publishers, editors, and staff. They are: George Provol, publisher; Wesley Lawton, executive editor; Elizabeth Hayes, associate editor; Federico Arrieta, product manager; Charles Dierker, project editor; Darryl King, production manager; Scott Baker, art director; Lisa Rawlinson, electronic publishing coordinator; and Adele Krause, permissions editor.

A Final Thought

We need your help. We are all sincerely committed to serving the needs of our adopters and readers. Like the Internet itself, the writing and publishing process is evolutionary and participatory. We encourage you to join us in bringing you the best educational resources in this field. Toward that end, please write us with your ideas, suggestions, and criticisms. We will consider each of them as we prepare for the next edition of this book. Address your correspondence to:

Floyd Fuller and Bill Manning
c/o the Dryden Press
301 Commerce Street, Suite 3700
Fort Worth, TX 76102

Thank you, in advance, for your contributions.

CONTENTS IN BRIEF

Chapter 1:   **Introduction to the Internet and World Wide Web**   1

Chapter 2:   **Getting Connected**   31

Chapter 3:   **Navigating the Internet and the World Wide Web**   57

Chapter 4:   **Searching the Web**   87

Chapter 5:   **Web Resources and Applications**   113

Chapter 6:   **Building a Web Presence**   147

Chapter 7:   **Issues, Problems, and Concerns**   183

Chapter 8:   **Internet Commerce: Doing Business on the Internet**   205

Appendix A: **Getting Started with Netscape Navigator 4.0**   233

Appendix B: **Getting Started with Microsoft Internet Explorer 4.0**   249

Glossary   267

Index   281

CONTENTS

Chapter 1:   Introduction to the Internet and World Wide Web   1

Our Information Society   2

The Communications Process   3

    Communication Components   3

    The Evolution of Communications   3

    Communications Today   4

Introduction to the Internet   4

    The Scope of the Internet   5

    History of the Internet   5

    The Internet Today   6

INTERNET INDUSTRY UPDATES

    America's Top Business Leaders Learning to "Surf the Net"   8

Getting Connected to the Internet   8

THE INTERNET IN THE FUTURE

    The Next Step: "Internet in the Sky"   12

Internet Applications   11

    Electronic Mail   11

    Information Retrieval   11

    File Transfer   11

    Chat Lines and Newsgroups   15

    Entertainment   15

    Home Shopping   16

The World Wide Web   16

    Improvements on the Web   19

Who Uses the Web and Why   20

    User Demographics   21

    Web Uses   21

    Issues and Concerns   21

    Implications   21

How the World Wide Web Works   23

Hypertext and Hypermedia   23

An Example   23

Internet and Web Opportunities for Students   25

THE INTERNET IN THE FUTURE

    Distance Learning: The Classroom of the Future   26

Summary   28

Key Terms   29

End-of-Chapter Activities   29

    Matching   29

    Review Questions   30

    Activities   30

Chapter 2:   Getting Connected   31

    Your Commitment As an Internet User   32

    Getting Started: First Steps   33

Establish Your Objectives   33

Determine Your Needs   34

Gather Information   34

Compare Costs and Services   34

Make Your Decision   34

Hardware You Need   34

A Basic Computer System   35

INTERNET INDUSTRY UPDATES

Utility Companies and the Internet   36

Modem   36

RAM and Secondary Storage   37

Compatibility   37

Add-ons and Plug-ins   37

Upgrades   38

Software You Need   39

Communications Software   40

Navigational Software   40

Fuctions   42

Ease of Use   42

Speed   42

Framing Capability   43

Multimedia Support   43

Publishing Capability   44

Security   45

Search Engines   45

THE INTERNET AND YOU: CAREERS & OPPORTUNITIES

Internet Service Representative   47

Connecting Your Computer to the Internet   47

Service Providers   47

Commercial Online Services   47

Internet Service Providers   48

Internet Access Providers   48

Choosing a Service Provider   48

Cost   49

Speed   49

Support and Service   49

Ease of Use   49

Setting Up Your Computer   50

Summary   51

Key Terms   52

End-of-Chapter Activities   53

Matching   53

Review Questions   53

Activities   54

Chapter 3:   Navigating the Internet and the World Wide Web   57

The World Wide Web: Growth and Popularity   58

The Art of Navigating   59

INTERNET INDUSTRY UPDATES
  The New Netscape Navigator 4.0   *61*
How the World Wide Web Works: An Overview   61
Using a Keyboard and Mouse   62
Protocols: Standards for Communications   63
Internet Addresses: What They Are and How They Work   64
    Uniform Resource Locators (URLs)   66
    Domains   67
    Examples of Addresses   67
Navigational Software   67
Starting Your Browser   69
THE INTERNET AND YOU: CAREERS & OPPORTUNITIES
  Web Page Designer   *70*
Browser Windows   71
    The Netscape Navigator Window   71
    The Internet Explorer Window   74
How a Browser Works   75
Using a Browser   76
Web Sites   76
    Home Pages   76
    Web Pages   77
    Hypertext Links   77
Bookmarks   77
Structure of Web Sites   77
Hypertext Markup Language (HTML)   78
Virtual Reality Modeling Language (VRML)   78
Some Popular Web Browsers   79
Other Internet and Web Activities   80
    Electronic Mail   80
    Internet Relay Chat   81
    Internet Telephone   81
Summary   82
Key Terms   83
End-of-Chapter Activities   83
    Matching   83
    Review Questions   84
    Activities   84

Chapter 4:   Searching the Web   87
The Art of Searching the Web   88
The Internet and the World Wide Web: Storehouses of Information   89
What You Can Find and Do on the Web   89
Reasons for Searching   89
    Curiosity   89
    Need   90
    Research   90
    Work   91
    Business   92

THE INTERNET AND YOU: CAREERS & OPPORTUNITIES
Data Communications Specialist   *93*
Some Popular Search Engines   95
    Searching the Web Using AltaVista   95
    Searching the Web Using Excite   97
    Searching the Web Using Lycos   99
    Searching the Web Using Infoseek   101
    Searching the Web Using WebCrawler   101
    Searching the Web Using NetFind   103
    Searching the Web Using Yahoo!   104
Using Keywords and Symbols to Search   105
Search Programs   105
Accessing Files with File Transfer Protocol (FTP)   106
Accessing Files with Telnet   107
Potential Internet and Web Perils   108
Summary   109
Key Terms   110
End-of-Chapter Activities   111
    Matching   111
    Review Questions   111
    Activities   112

Chapter 5:   Web Resources and Applications   113
Decision Making, Problem Solving, and the Web   114
The Internet, the Web, and the National Information Superhighway   115
    Computer Power   116
    Digital Communications and Content   116
INTERNET INDUSTRY UPDATES
The Fiber Frenzy   *114*
    Information Terminals   118
Web Applications and Their Impact on Us   119
    Work   120
    Life   122
    Learning   122
THE INTERNET AND YOU: CAREERS & OPPORTUNITIES
Growing Internet Use: Senior Citizens and Women   *123*
    Leisure   124
Web Applications for Students   124
    Art and Leisure   125
    Government   126
    Home Shopping   126
    Sports   128
    Travel   128
Teams, Collaboration, and the Web   130
    Collaborative Tools   130
    Collaboration Opportunities   131
    Building a Cyberteam: Designing for Success   132
Improving Web Efficiency   134
    Push/Pull Web Technologies   134

Spam Mail   135
Two Sample Internet Case Studies   136
Preparing for Your Career While Still in School   136
How to Buy a Car Using the Internet   139
Summary   141
Key Terms   142
End-of-Chapter Activities   142
Matching   142
Review Questions   143
Activities   143
Two Collaborative Team Projects   143

Chapter 6:   Building a Web Presence   147
Why Build a Web Site?   148
Personal Sites   148
Organizational Sites   149
Building a Cyber Portfolio: A Student Project   150
Steps in Web Page Creation: What Makes a Great Web Site   151
Step One: Ideate   153
Step Two: Formulate   154
Step Three: Construct   154
Designing Sites for Success   155
The Customer   156
Content   156
Site Structure   157
Color and Emotion   159
Web Media Types   160
Text   160
Graphics   160
Clip art   162
Schematics   162
Sound   163
3-D Virtual Reality   164
Media Considerations   165
Bandwidth   165
Different PC Capabilities   166
Specialized Media Hardware Devices   166
Digital Cameras   167
Scanners   167
Video Cameras   167
Web Site Builders   168
Web Site Hosts   171
Registering and Promoting Your Site in Cyberspace   173
Registration Process   173
Promotion Options   175
THE INTERNET IN THE FUTURE
Online Learning on the Internet Blossoms   177
Maintaining the Site   178
Timely/Current Information   178

Continuous Refinement   178

INTERNET INDUSTRY UPDATES

Grocery Shopping on the Web   *179*

Summary   180

Key Terms   180

End-of-Chapter Activities   181

Matching   181

Activities   181

Chapter 7:   Issues, Problems, and Concerns   183

Introduction   184

Control of the Internet   184

Internet Behavior   184

Web Ethics and Etiquette   185

Mailing Lists   186

Privacy and Cryptology   187

Viruses on the Internet   188

THE INTERNET IN THE FUTURE

Education Going Online   *189*

Internet Fraud   190

Pornography and Obscenity   190

Security   191

INTERNET INDUSTRY UPDATES

Reading e-mail by Phone   *192*

Information Theft   192

Hackers and Crackers   193

Espionage and Sabotage   193

The Year 2000 Dilemma   194

Useless Web Sites   194

Advertising on the Internet   195

Misinformation   195

Overburdened Internet   196

Online Games   197

Software Piracy   197

Issues and User Responsibility   199

Summary   199

Key Terms   200

End-of-Chapter Activities   201

Review Questions   201

Matching   201

Activities   202

Chapter 8:   Internet Commerce: Doing Business on the Internet   205

What Is Internet Commerce?   206

Foundations of Internet Commerce   206

Information and Competitive Advantage   206

A Growth Projection   207

Internet Commerce and the Organizational Value Chain   208

Building Blocks and Connectivity   209

INTERNET INDUSTRY UPDATES
Online World Goes AOL   *211*
Internet Commerce System Configurations   212
    People-to-People Systems (PPSs)   213
    People-to-System-to-People Systems (PSPSs)   213
    System-to-System Systems (SSSs)   214
Internets within an Organization: Intranets   215
    Definition   215
    Applications   215
    Intranet Benefits   216
THE INTERNET AND YOU: CAREERS & OPPORTUNITIES
The Internet Creates Shortage of Qualified People   217
Internet Commerce between Organizations: Extranets   217
    Definition   217
    Combining Internets and Intranets to Form Extranets   218
    Two Extranet Examples   219
        The Automotive Network Exchange (ANX)   219
        Boeing's Customer Inventory System   219
    Extranet Pitfalls and Security Issues   220
Internet Commerce between an Organization and Consumers   220
    The Customer Is King   220
    Electronic Marketplaces   221
INTERNET INDUSTRY UPDATES
Schwab Discount Brokers Increase Online Presence   222
    Intelligent Shopping Agents   223
    Web Financial Systems and Electronic Payments   224
    Local Web Shopping   225
In Closing   226
Summary   228
Key Terms   228
End-of-Chapter Activities   229
    Matching   229
    Review Questions   230
    Activities   230

Appendix A: Getting Started with Netscape Navigator 4.0   233
Introduction   234
Starting Netscape Communicator   235
The Netscape Home Page   236
Browsing the Web   239
Using a History List   240
Using Bookmarks   241
    Bookmarks   241
    Adding a Bookmark   241
    Deleting a Bookmark   242
    Retrieving a Web Page with a Bookmark   242
Saving Information with Navigator   242
    Saving a Web Page   243

Saving an Image   243
Inserting a Picture   244
Printing a Web Page or Document   244
Using Navigator's Electronic Mail   244
Accessing Netscape's Electronic Mail   245
Preparing and Sending Mail Messages   245
Reading Mail Messages   246
Saving a Mail Message   246
Printing a Mail Message   246
Deleting a Mail Message   247
Using Netscape's Address Book   247
Exiting Electronic Mail   248
Exiting Netscape   248
Conclusion   248

Appendix B: Getting Started with Microsoft Internet Explorer 4.0   249
Introduction   250
Starting Internet Explorer   251
The Internet Explorer Start Page   253
Browsing the Web   254
Using a History List   255
Saving and Using Favorite Web Pages   255
Adding a Favorite Web Page   256
Deleting a Favorite   256
Retrieving a Favorite Web Page   257
Saving Information with Explorer   257
Saving a Web Page   258
Saving a Picture   258
Inserting a Picture   259
Printing a Web Page or Document   260
Using Internet Explorer for Searches   260
Getting Stared with MSN Mail   261
Accessing MSN Mail   262
Preparing and Sending Mail Messages   263
Using the Personalized Address Book   264
Reading Mail Messages   265
Saving a Mail Message on a Floppy Disk   265
Deleting a Mail Message   265
Printing a Mail Message   265
Exiting Electronic Mail   266
Exiting the Microsoft Network   266

Glossary   267

Index   281

CHAPTER ONE

Introduction to the Internet and World Wide Web

Our Information Society
The Communications Process
   Communication Components
   The Evolution of Communications
   Communications Today
Introduction to the Internet
   The Scope of the Internet
   History of the Internet
   The Internet Today
Getting Connected to the Internet
Internet Applications
   Electronic Mail

Information Retrieval
File Transfer
Chat Lines and Newsgroups
Entertainment
Home Shopping
The World Wide Web
   Improvements on the Web
Who Uses the Web and Why
   User Demographics
   Web Uses
   Issues and Concerns
   Implications

How the World Wide Web Works
   Hypertext and Hypermedia
   An Example
Internet and Web Opportunities
  for Students
Summary
Key Terms
End-of-Chapter Activities
   Matching
   Review Questions
   Activities

AFTER COMPLETING THIS CHAPTER, YOU WILL:

1. Discuss how computers contribute to our information society and their impact on personal and organizational productivity.

2. Describe the communications process and the three elements that define it.

3. Define the term Internet.

4. Briefly explain how Internet evolved.

5. Discuss four different ways users can connect to the Internet today and the popularity of each.

6. Explain the nature of the World Wide Web (WWW).

7. List ten applications or situations where you might use the Web.

8. Describe the typical profile of a Web user.

9. Explain how the Web and Internet have affected communications and the social behaviors of our global society.

10. Discuss how Web and Internet advancements will affect our future.

Our Information Society

A revolution suggests fundamental change. Since the introduction of the personal computer by IBM in 1981, our global society has experienced a computer revolution. As computer capabilities have grown, so too have the ways computers affect how we work, live, learn, and play. The computer has become the primary productivity tool for many workers in today's information society.

Computers are used to automate manufacturing processes. Auto and airline manufacturing industries use computers to run manufacturing and assembly processes. Workers take on a supervisory role, intervening only in exceptional cases. With more powerful supercomputers, scientists now delve into microgenetics and the origin of the universe. Using powerful microcomputers, it is possible to shop, invest, bank, and even work at home. Our cars and appliances carry onboard computers to control functions and improve performance. In 1996, for the first time in history, the sales of personal computers exceeded the sales of television sets.

Truly we are experiencing the results of an information society. Computers are increasing personal and organizational productivity. In the future, Bill Gates, founder and chairman of Microsoft, foresees **personalized computers** that recognize their user, talk to the user, and are even able to recognize and react to moods and unusual user behaviors. (See Figure 1.1).

FIGURE 1.1

Personalized Computers

In the future, personal computers will truly become "personal." Acting much like pets, this new breed of computers will recognize their users, identify their moods, talk to the users, and react smartly to their current mental state and needs. Technology in the future will create a stronger bond between humans and computers, tailoring that bond to the moment.

The Communications Process

What is communications? When does communication occur? What is needed for successful communications processes? Individuals, groups, and organizations need to communicate. Typically, when organizational surveys are done, the number one problem identified by its members is communications—or the lack of it! "We need better communications" is the common complaint. How do computers contribute to improved communications in our society?

Communication Components

To have a **communications system,** you need a sender, medium, and receiver. Figure 1.2 depicts these three elements in an early communications system. Have you ever heard the hypothetical story about the large tree that fell in the forest? Did the falling tree make a noise? Were there a sender (the tree), medium (air), and a receiver? Who or what was the receiver, or was the receiver missing and therefore there was no noise? These questions always elicit a spirited debate.

The Evolution of Communications

Throughout history, people have worked on improving the communications process. Egyptians used homing pigeons to deliver messages. Native Americans used

FIGURE 1.2

An Early Communications Process

Even in the early days, poor communications caused problems for people. Technology can help.

smoke signals and mirrors to transmit warnings of advancing intruders. American pioneers used the Pony Express as their communications medium. With the invention of the telegraph, communications technology took a giant step forward and, in its wake, made the Pony Express obsolete.

Since then, new technology breakthroughs have accelerated the speed and lowered the costs of global communications. The telephone, movies, television—all have had an effect. But the greatest impact on personal and organizational communications occurred in 1981 when IBM introduced its PC computer and joined the Apple Corporation in the race for the personal computer market.

Communications Today

Today, we have a proliferation of communications options. Simply listen to radio and television commercials or read newspaper and magazine advertisements. When a powerful personal computer operated by a knowledgeable user is connected via phone lines to the information-rich resources available today, almost anything is possible. Truly, we are limited only by our understanding and imagination. But, to be knowledgeable users in today's information society, we must understand the Internet.

Introduction to the Internet

History is framed by major events. Wars, space travel, famous personalities, and technologies all anchor history to specific points in time. Today, we are all living through an evolution in technology that is changing the entire world and the way we live. It is called the **Internet**. The word *Internet* literally means "a collection or network of networks." The Internet is comprised of thousands of small regional computer networks scattered throughout the globe. It connects millions of users in hundreds of countries. The Internet affects the way we live, work, learn, play, and communicate. The Internet today is virtually ubiquitous. It is everywhere. It is shaping our world, our future, and our lives with the opportunities it offers.

Recent history gave us the Industrial Revolution and then the Information Age. For you to be an integral part of the current revolution, the "Internet Revolution," it is essential that you understand its mission, scope, elements, operations, and implications. That is the purpose of our book.

In the following chapters, we want to share with you our ideas and frameworks about the Internet. We want to give you trends, theories, applications, implications, and activities to make you an expert driver on today's Information Superhighway. We want you to be effective and efficient in the way you use this resource at work, at home, and at school. Never before in the history of the world have so many had so valuable a resource. It is your responsibility to use it. Treat this book as your opportunity to learn more about the Internet, to enhance your personal skills in using it, and to pursue your dreams by utilizing it.

This chapter defines the scope and magnitude of the Internet. It profiles the users, the applications, and the trends for future use. It lays the foundation for the chapters that follow. All of this is intended to convince you of the Internet's value and to capture your time and attention for our orientation. And, as with any developing revolution, the terrain is constantly changing—new technologies, new applications, new users, and new partners are continuously discovered. Learning about the Internet is an ongoing, continuous process. This book is the first step. Your own personal needs and interests will steer you in the future.

Everyone is talking about the Internet today. In offices, elevators, on street corners, and in restaurants, people share their latest experiences on the Net. Creative new Internet sites are springing up daily. Age or gender is no barrier. Recently, one of the authors of this text helped a lady shopper in her mid-seventies load her Costco purchases into her car. Her most exciting purchase was a book on the Internet. She had recently gone online and was "going home to surf the Web" and write e-mail to her granddaughter. Yet for many others, the Internet still remains a mystery.

The Scope of the Internet

The Internet is a worldwide network of computers linked together via various communications channels. Local networks are connected to other local networks via some communications vehicle—typically a combination of normal telephone lines and more high-speed channels. No one knows the Internet's actual size. No one group or organization has control over the Internet. It is self-regulated. The Internet is expanding so rapidly that it is virtually impossible to keep track of the number of networks, information services, databases, hardware and software packages, and information being made available to users on an almost daily basis.

The International Telecom conference is held every four years. At its last conference, held in 1995 in Geneva, Switzerland, the organization presented its estimates about the size of the Internet. They included the following:

1. 100,000 networks
2. 35,000,000 users worldwide
3. 3,000,000 computers connected to the Internet
4. 21,500 organizations connected to the Internet
5. Users located in over 110 countries

Since 1989, the Internet has grown exponentially, doubling in size every year. By the year 2000, the Internet is projected to serve 60 million to 70 million users worldwide.

Where did this new and powerful resource come from? Who built it? Who owns it? What does it consist of? These questions are answered next.

History of the Internet

For brevity's sake, we will say that the Net started in 1969. Figure 1.3 shows a time line of key Internet and Web events. In that year, the Advanced Research Projects Agency (ARPA), part of the U.S. Department of Defense, formed **ARPANET.** ARPANET's main function was to link leading researchers in four universities who were working on specialized government projects. Military scientists could "talk" to each other and to university research professors via computers, sharing data files and research findings. Its second purpose was to create a backup national communications system in case of war or natural disaster. The first node on the Net was at UCLA, then Stanford Research Institute (SRI), University of California at Santa Barbara, and the University of Utah. Each node had to be able to send, receive, and pass data and messages to the other nodes in the network.

Slowly but quietly, other colleges and universities and private sites were added. By 1971, the Net had grown to a remarkable fifteen nodes with the addition of schools such as Harvard and MIT. The first international connections to

Time Line for Evolution of the Internet and the World Wide Web

In just a few short years, the Internet and the Web have grown to become a major source of connectivity and communications in our global society.

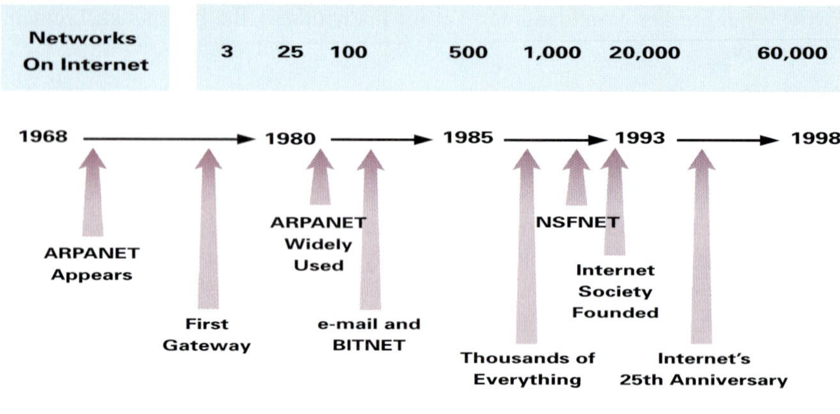

ARPANET occurred in 1973 with the addition of England and Norway. The creation of **e-mail,** or **electronic mail,** in 1981 enabled users to send personal electronic messages to other specified users on the network. It was carried on a new network called **BITNET** ("Because It's Time NETwork"). By 1984, over 1,000 host computers were on the Net. Many people felt it had reached its limit! They were wrong. Five years later, in 1989, there were 100,000 host computers.

At the end of the last decade and throughout this decade the network's communications languages and processes were improved. In 1989, the National Science Foundation chose to share its net, called **NSFNET,** and joined the Internet. NSFNET connected the Internet to various supercomputers located throughout the United States, giving Net users extensive computing power. As more networks joined, the term *Internet* was coined to represent the interlinking of these nets. Later, the two founding networks withdrew: ARPANET disappeared in 1990, and NSF exited in 1995. In October of 1992, host computers exceeded one million. In 1994, the Internet celebrated its twenty-fifth anniversary. The rest is history.

The Internet Today

The experiment has been a huge success. Today the Internet is a worldwide computer network linking individuals, organizations, and countries in a vast blanket of connections. It is filled with vendors, information sources, databases, libraries, multimedia, and software. Some resources are protected from general use. Others are free.

The Internet offers the user immediate information search and retrieval capabilities. It also offers global communications at little or no cost. These two features make it a strong competitor to the U.S. Postal System and to companies such as Federal Express. In addition, the user is in control of the medium through determining the content of the message and who receives it. Most correspondence

Recent Internet Articles in *USA Today*

Look at the variety of Internet stories and applications discussed in recent articles in the *USA Today* newspaper. This is only a small sample of the stories that actually occurred in this paper.

Political Action on the Web Offers a Boost to President

Weeding through the CD-ROM Selection

TV Makers Using Internet to Fend Off PCs

State of the Web: Once Obscure, Now Mainstream

Coming to a Screen Near You: A Guerrilla War in Cyberspace

Cyberphone Reality Falling into Place

Internet Regulating Body Takes First Action in Singapore

Reaching into Cyberspace Makes Calls Cheaper

Singapore Sets Internet Rules

TV Set Could Become Channel to the Internet

Ann Landers Missing a Connection?

Internet-Only Mutual Fund Coming to a Site Near You

Cancer Support in Cyberspace

Wired Up or Beamed In, It's Coming Cheaper, Faster

Microsoft Deal Expands Reach of CompuServe

Fidelity Plans 401(k) Link on the Internet

On the Internet, Virtually no Privacy

Apple to Put Sales Focus on Internet

Cyberporn Law Isn't Censorship, Government Says

is done so quickly it can almost be considered real time. Figure 1.4 shows a list of recent *USA Today* newspaper articles about the Internet.

Think of the applications and implications of a global communications system. Medical expertise in the finest research hospitals can be immediately available for consultation by doctors working in the most remote regions of Africa, India, or South America. Students can correspond with professors at their school or with other students across the world. Shopping can be done without ever leaving your home.

America's Top Business Leaders Learning to "Surf the Net"

A recent poll of 300 American business leaders found:

70 percent believe Internet access improves their company's business abilities

33 percent say the Internet is the most important technological development of this decade

49 percent say Internet increases worker productivity

72 percent either have or will have a company Web site within one year

The primary uses of Web sites are to display company products, services, and new developments

78 percent of the executives spend at least one hour per day on their computer

20 percent of future capital expenses will be on computing. Primary justifications include information transfer, worker productivity, and product sales.

Truly, today's successful business executives are weaving the Web into the fabric of their organizations.

Getting Connected to the Internet

How many ways can you connect to the Internet, and what should you consider when connecting? There are a number of new alternatives. Historically, Internet communications have been limited to telephone wires: Users hook them to personal computers and then typically pay about $20 a month to send and receive electronic mail and browse the Web.

For many, that expense is too great. In addition, Internet connections on phone lines are still slow. Today's conventional modems can take half a minute or more to receive a single page filled with color pictures from the Web. About 19 million homes in the United States (about 19 percent of the total households) use this type of connection to the Internet. That still leaves almost 80 percent of the homes unconnected.

New connections are here or on the way. With lower costs and faster transmission speeds, companies are experimenting with broadcasting Internet data via TV signals, microwaves, and satellites. If successful, Internet growth will accelerate rapidly, with major impacts on entertainment, communications, and commerce.

Companies such as Intel and Microsoft, along with the major broadcasters NBC, CNN, PBS, and QVC are working on a process to send Internet to the home via TV. The system, called **Intercast**, requires a Pentium-grade computer and a special TV tuner card that is attached to TV cable wires. Current TV signals transmit up to sixty video images per second. Between each image there are ten blank horizontal lines that the viewer does not see. Internet Web pages will fit in these blank lines. In October of 1997, Microsoft announced that its upcoming Windows 98 operating system will allow computers equipped with television tuners to capture broadcasts of Internet sites through TV cable. However, communications will be only one way—into the home. Because no return signal is currently possible, Intercast will not allow e-mail or online purchase responses. The Intercast computer expansion cards will enable computer owners to watch regular TV shows on their PCs, though. Figure 1.5 shows Intel's Intercast home page.

FIGURE 1.5

Intercast System

Intercast allows computer owners to use cable TV to receive information in the home. The information signals are imbedded in the normal TV signals and appear in a small section of the screen. Currently, communication is only one way—into the home.

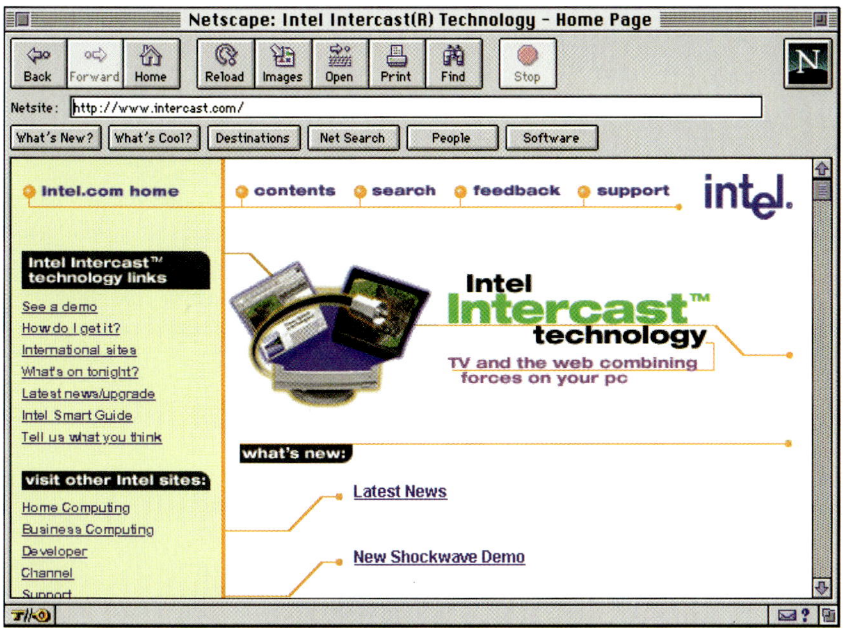

FIGURE 1.6

Wireless Microwave Transmissions

Wireless microwave transmissions are hundreds of times faster than phone lines, but the user must be within a direct line of sight of the transmission tower. Notebook computers, such as the one shown below, will allow users to greatly benefit from this technology.

Another connection is via wireless microwave transmissions to a small antenna outside the home. (See Figure 1.6.) One company recently successfully tested this system. People who want to zoom anywhere they want on the Internet might consider this alternative. Wireless microwave speeds are hundreds of times faster than today's phone modems. It costs about $10 to install wireless cable service in a home, much less than cable companies charge. The big drawback to this

FIGURE 1.7
Satellite Dishes

Satellite dishes are popular today. In some remote areas, this is the only way to receive a TV signal. This may become a major vehicle for Internet communications in the future.

FIGURE 1.8
Net TV Computers

With 60 percent of the U.S. households now connected to cable TV, developers see this link as a major delivery source of Internet services in the future. As inexpensive send/receive devices develop, the TV will act as both an information and entertainment appliance in our homes.

system is that users must live within a line of sight of a local microwave transmitter. There can be no interference or obstructions from buildings or trees. Only about 700,000 households currently have this type of service.

Another two million homes are connected, via eighteen-inch satellite dishes, to satellite signals. Growth projections suggest two to five times this number of subscribers by the year 2000, and Internet capabilities are just a short time away. Figure 1.7 shows a satellite dish installation.

Cable systems have an edge in the race for new Internet connections. They are secure, allow two-way communications and transmit at high speeds. About two-thirds of the homes in the United States subscribe to cable TV. This represents a huge market potential. Can they be attached to Internet? There is an effort to use the normal TV set as a send/receive device so that customers wouldn't even need a PC. Cable companies would install large computers at major cable transmission sites to handle the load, and customers would respond through the cable box on their TV to purchase items or search the Web. These systems are still in the development stage. (See Figure 1.8.) Tomorrow's family rooms might be equipped with keyboards rather than TV remote controls.

Other systems are under review. Electric companies are investigating the possibilities of power customers using electric utility wires to send and receive Internet signals. Even pager companies and phone companies are considering how they can connect their customers to the enormous Internet resources. The box on page 12 discusses a possible new satellite system for Internet connections.

Internet Applications

The Internet offers a variety of services. We discuss the most common ones next. Figure 1.9 lists a sample of Internet content by area. Figure 1.10 highlights the key services available. By far the most popular is electronic mail.

Electronic Mail

Think of electronic mail, or e-mail, as a hybrid combination of U.S. Postal Service, Federal Express, and voice mail. Each user of the Internet has a unique e-mail address. Many users have multiple e-mail addresses for different locations and purposes. Currently your two authors have six active addresses. A person's e-mail address might be found on a Web page, on a business card, in a commercial service provider's directory of users, in a college or university's faculty and student directory, in a newspaper or magazine advertisement, or in a listing of company employees. For example, the Boeing Company in Seattle, Washington, has an internal e-mailing list that contains over 150,000 employee e-mail addresses.

Information Retrieval

Universities, libraries, and government agencies have large databases available to Internet users. By simply logging in, the user can research specialized topics such as geography or genetics. Much of the 1990 federal census data, the world's largest database, is available to be downloaded. It contains extensive national and regional information about housing and population demographics for more than 270 million Americans. Some students find this access to information helpful for doing their course research projects. (See Figure 1.11.)

File Transfer

Literally millions of files are available for download off the Net. These include audio files containing songs, music, and various sounds. Other files contain video clips of famous movies, plays, special events, and so on. Still other files contain photos or animations. Many of these files, if not copyrighted, can be attached or embedded in other documents for dramatic effects.

The Internet in the Future

The Next Step: "Internet in the Sky"

Teledesic is a new, private, communications company co-owned by telecommunications expert Craig McCaw and Microsoft Chairman Bill Gates. Using a constellation of several hundred low-orbit satellites, Teledesic will create the world's first satellite network to provide affordable, worldwide, high-speed access. Services will include broadband Internet access, videoconferencing, and interactive multimedia.

The Boeing Company will be the prime contractor for the company's network. The estimated contract value is $9 billion. On March 14, 1997, the Federal Communications Commission approved Teledesic's license to build and operate this advanced, two-way telecommunications network.

Service partners in worldwide host countries will supply communications to the largest urban centers and the most remote villages. Service is targeted to begin in 2002.

Low-orbiting satellites eliminate the long signal delay in high-orbiting satellite communications. Users simply install small, low-power terminals and antennas, about the size of today's direct broadcast satellite (DBS) dishes. If successful, Teledesic could revolutionize the Internet and world communications.

FIGURE 1.9

Sample Internet Content by Area

The Internet covers every topic you could imagine—from <u>A</u>ardvarks to <u>Z</u>ygotes. This figure shows just a few of these topic areas.

BUSINESS TOPICS

Agricultural Business	Banking
U.S. Economic Development	Economics
Economic Statistics	Entrepreneurship
Finance	Insurance
Real Estate	Management
Marketing	International Sales

ENGINEERING

Careers	Design Guidelines
Engineering Resources	Intellectual Properties

GOVERNMENT

Demographics	Economic Indicators
Education	International Organizations
State Governments	Statistics
Tax Forms: State and Federal	U.S. Government Agencies
U.S. Government Publications	United Nations

HUMANITIES

Architecture Design	Art and Images
Classic Works	Ethnic Cultures
Film and Media	History
Landscaping	Literature
Music	Philosophy
Religion	Theatre
Women's and Gender Studies	

SCIENCE

Agriculture	Astronomy
Biology	Chemistry
Computer Science	Food Science
Geology	Medicine

FIGURE 1.10

Internet Services Available

The Internet offers users a variety of specialized communication and commercial services. It hosts these services as well as the people who come together to use them.

- ✓ **e-mail**—Send and receive electronic mail worldwide
- ✓ **Search engines**—Search Internet sites worldwide
- ✓ **Transfer files**—Once retrieved, can be edited, formatted, saved, and printed
- ✓ **Chat Lines**—Participate with discussion in groups on topics of mutual interest
- ✓ **Play games**—Single and multiple player games available
- ✓ **Shop**—Order products and services

FIGURE 1.11
Student Taps into the Internet

Students use Internet and Web databases to do research for courses and projects. This data can then be loaded into spreadsheet or statistical programs for additional processing.

FIGURE 1.12
Another Way of Getting Connected

Users tap into chat lines and newsgroups for conversations about specialized topics or just for the latest news or gossip. Some chat lines focus on investments, some on employment, and some on world affairs. There are literally thousands of chat lines open to any Internet user.

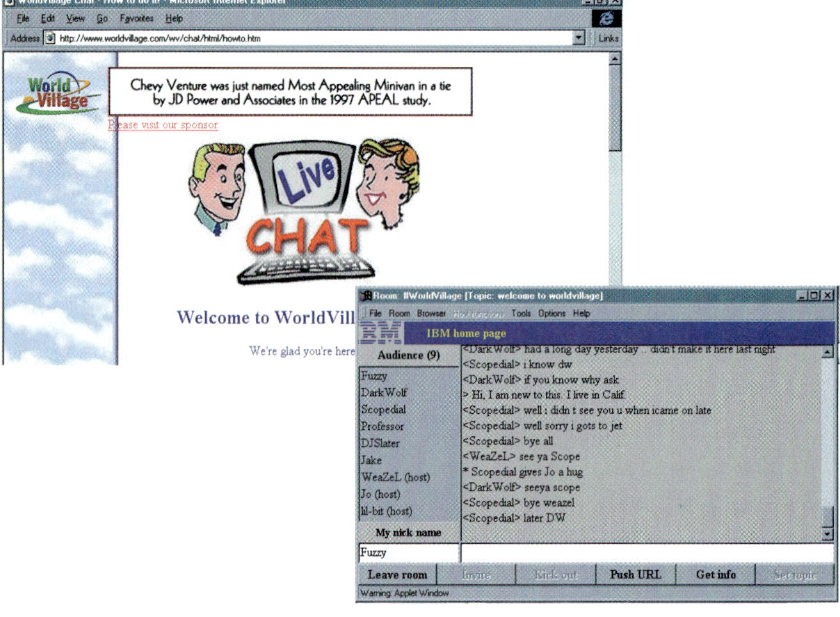

Chat Lines and Newsgroups

Using the Internet as an instantaneous communications vehicle, many people join **chat rooms** or newsgroups to discuss life, current events, or common interests with other people who share those interests. Comments and opinions, often frank and uncensored, are exchanged freely and anonymously with other participants. Figure 1.12 shows students engaged in chat talk.

Entertainment

The Internet also serves to link users in play. Chess, checkers, monopoly, bridge, and even dominos are available on the Net. Some have even tried gambling on the Internet, although this is not widespread for obvious reasons—it's hard to collect your winnings. Intel has a product that allows two parties to communicate over the Internet using videophones. (See Figure 1.13.) Called "Create and Share,™" this new product allows family members or businesses professionals to see each other as they talk and to share documents, photographs, and video clips from anywhere in the world. Because the communication occurs over the Internet, there are no long-distance telephone charges!

Home Shopping

It is now possible to buy products and services via the Internet. Payment is made by supplying the company with a credit card number. Many people are

FIGURE 1.13

Intel's New "Create and Share™" Internet Phone

This new product allows two users to communicate visually over the Internet. The product is directed at couples, families, college students, and businesses. Intel expects this product to revolutionize phone communications in the future.

Wal-Mart's Home-Shopping Page

Wal-Mart is a major U.S. retailer that has found the Web to be an excellent source of new business. Many shoppers are older, handicapped, or simply live in remote locations. Using the Web, these shoppers can order goods through this Web site and have them delivered to their home or place of work.

uncomfortable disclosing their credit card number over the Internet, unsure of the security and privacy of the transaction. Vendors are experimenting with **encryption** systems to improve security on the Internet. Encryption simply scrambles or codes the customer's credit card number at one end of the connection, transmits it in a scrambled format, then unscrambles or decodes it at the receiving end. Wal-Mart, America's largest retailer with 2,500 stores and over 800,000 employees, has initiated an extensive Internet shopping service. Figure 1.14 shows Wal-Mart's home-shopping page.

The World Wide Web

Each year the president of the United States gives a State of the Union address. In it, the president comments on the condition of our economy, the world, and the administration's plans for the future. After hearing the speech, citizens generally have a better understanding of what's going on. This section serves as our state-of-the-Internet address. Before you get involved with the necessary details of how to use the Internet and World Wide Web, we want you to first have a general, overall understanding of the content, users, issues, and trends in the Web world. This chapter supplies this general information. With this background, you will be able to better understand and use the topics that come in subsequent chapters. We are certain you will agree, the Internet is a fascinating and growing industry. Once obscure, the Web is now mainstream. Four years ago, few people knew anything about the Web. Today, it has a major impact on our global society.

The official **World Wide Web (WWW)** definition is "a wide-area hypermedia information retrieval initiative to give universal access to a large number of documents." The Web provides computer network users with a consistent means to access a variety of media in a simplified fashion using popular graphic software interfaces.

How do the Internet and Web work together? Think of the Internet as a complex collection or network of worldwide computers, cables, and signals that carries the computer traffic for its users. View it as a highway for information, much like our national freeways for car traffic or our rail system for freight cars. The Web, then, is the collection of processes and protocols that allow users to find information sites and to transfer that information from one site to another as it travels along the Internet right-of-way. The Internet forms the trail; the Web forms the connections.

The Web was developed in 1989 as a tool that scientists used for collegial communication. It then gained mass appeal in 1994 after a software breakthrough made it simple to use. Today, the mysterious "http://" Web addresses are an integral part of organizations' TV commercials, magazines, and newspaper ads. (See Figure 1.15.) The Web has become a global catalog of products and services, an electronic library, and a communications channel for people from all walks of life.

FIGURE 1.15

Web Addresses in Advertisements

Advertisers use print advertisements to move interested customers to their Web site. Once there, organizations have more time and more space to tell potential customers their story. Web media is more engaging, more complete, and less expensive. Some Web pages even allow customers to place orders and make payments for products and services.

Web
address

www.ask.aep.com

The Internet is also becoming more popular because the cost of Web access is decreasing. Inexpensive connection boxes can be purchased for under $200, and service charges are as low as $6 per month. These falling costs simply increase the number of potential users (and customers) on the Web. Today, about 35 million people in the United States use the Internet or online services.

Once on the Web, where do these people go? **Network Wizards,** a company located in Menlo Park, California, specializes in products related to computers and communications. Every six months, it surveys the total number of Internet host sites. Figure 1.16 shows the results of this survey for the last ten years. Network Wizards estimated there were almost 20 million host sites on the Internet as of July 1, 1997. If we project this trend forward, as in Figure 1.17, that number grows to over 50 million by the middle of the year 2000, a 2.5-fold increase in just three years!

Yet two other statistics are just as amazing. Based on Web site traffic counts, we know that only 50 of those 20 million sites generate more than half of all traffic visits. The top 1,000 sites constitute almost 90 percent of the Internet's total usage. This suggests that there are a large number of sites that are seldom visited. And remember that only about 19 percent of the U.S. households currently use the Internet today. Almost 80 percent of the U.S. households are still not connected to this enormous resource!

FIGURE 1.16
Internet Host Sites

Currently there are almost 20 million Web sites. Yet just a small number of sites account for the bulk of the Web visits.

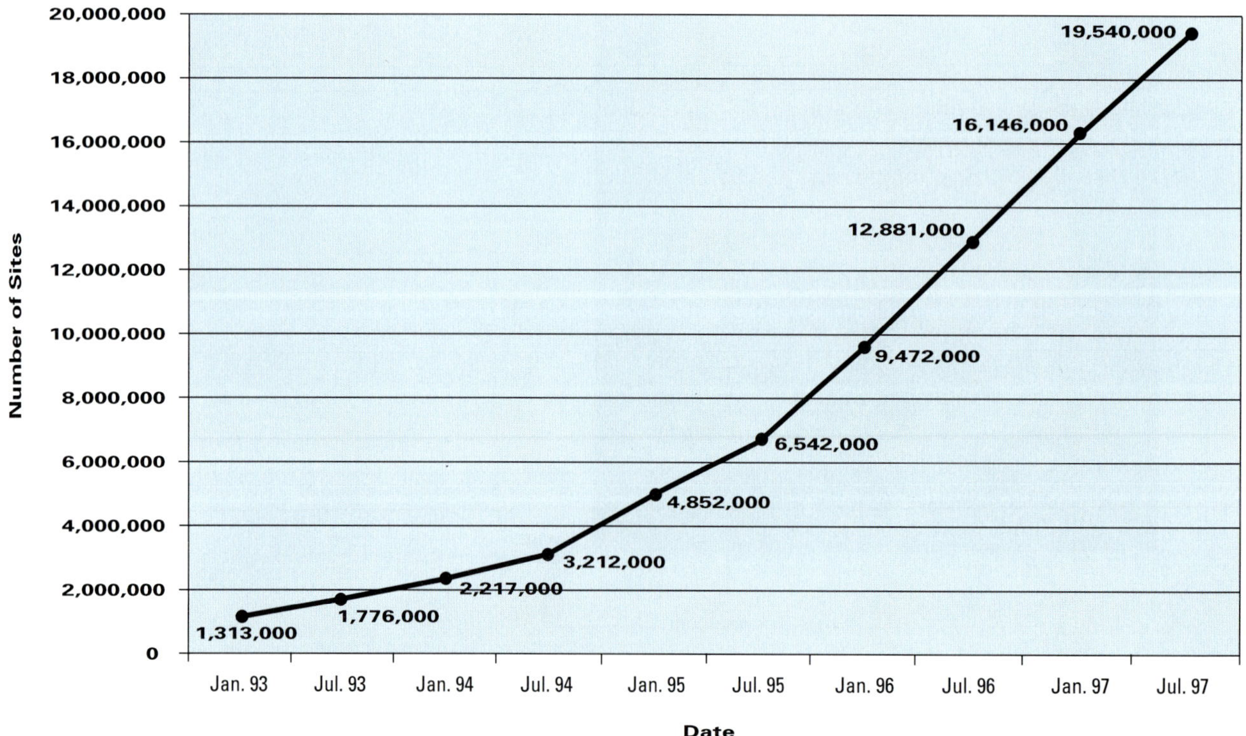

Data from Network Wizards (www.nw.com).

FIGURE 1.17

Projection of Host Web Sites

This figure shows the projected growth in the number of Web sites in the future. It is estimated that the current number of sites will double in just a few years. As more users join the Web and new software makes it easier to create personal sites, it is easy to see why this growth in new sites will be so rapid.

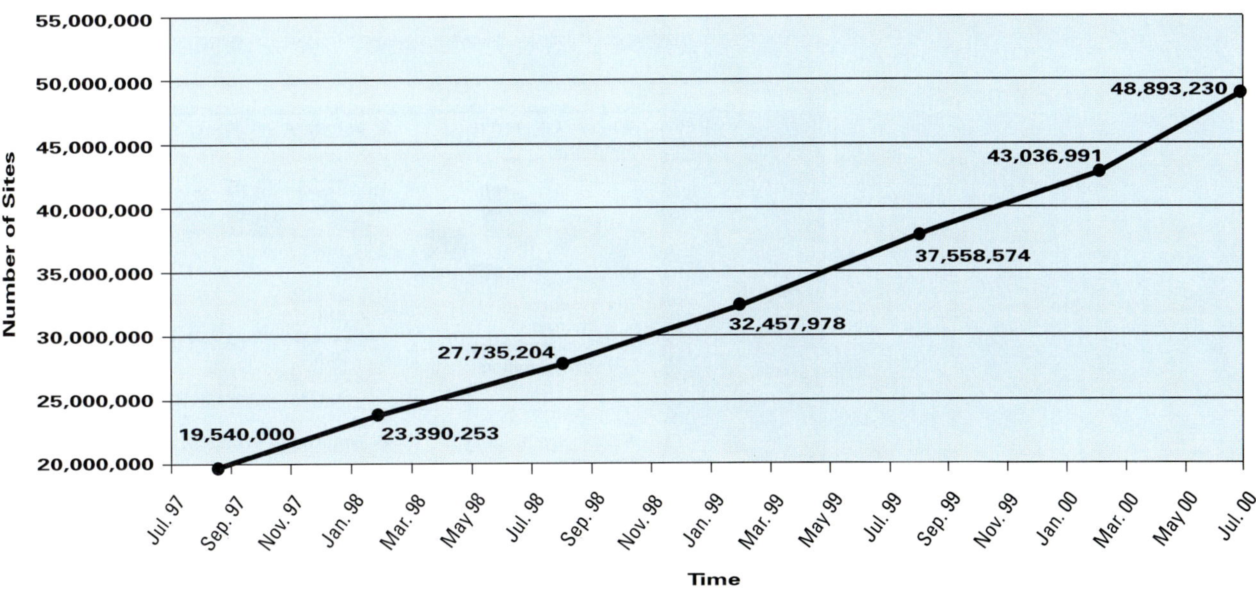

Based on historic data from Network Wizards (www.nw.com).

One major limitation on Web use is the quantity of data it can carry. Most Web connections use telephones and telephone wires to carry their messages. Telephone wires have very limited transmission capabilities. This limits usage to relatively low-volume applications. Large businesses, for example, cannot communicate large volumes of data about production or inventories to customers and suppliers using normal, voice-grade telephones. For them, other, more expensive connections are available. But for many personal or consumer applications—electronic mail, games, shopping, banking, stock purchases, library research, voting, and so on—normal telephone connections are adequate. Many new magazines are now available only on the Web.

Improvements on the Web

Computer networks have been around for years, but they used to be available only to local users. One network could not "talk" to another. Networks began to form connections, or "webs," when a technical standard was created that allowed data in these networks to be linked together. In 1994, a group of University of Illinois students created a program called **Mosaic** that gave the Web environment command icons and a more user-friendly graphic look.

In the beginning, information stored on the Web had to be written in a special programming language, and special commands were needed to create these electronic links. But as the Web grew and software companies such as Microsoft saw the demand and business opportunity, they began to create ordinary word processing, drawing, and spreadsheet programs that could be easily modified, published,

Java Adds Multimedia to Web Pages

The Java language allows Web page developers to add more action to their Web sites. These handy inserts add movement and animation to the sites. They also allow advertisers to place their advertisements on other sites to draw users to their location. Java has had a major impact on the advertising and educational effectiveness of Web sites.

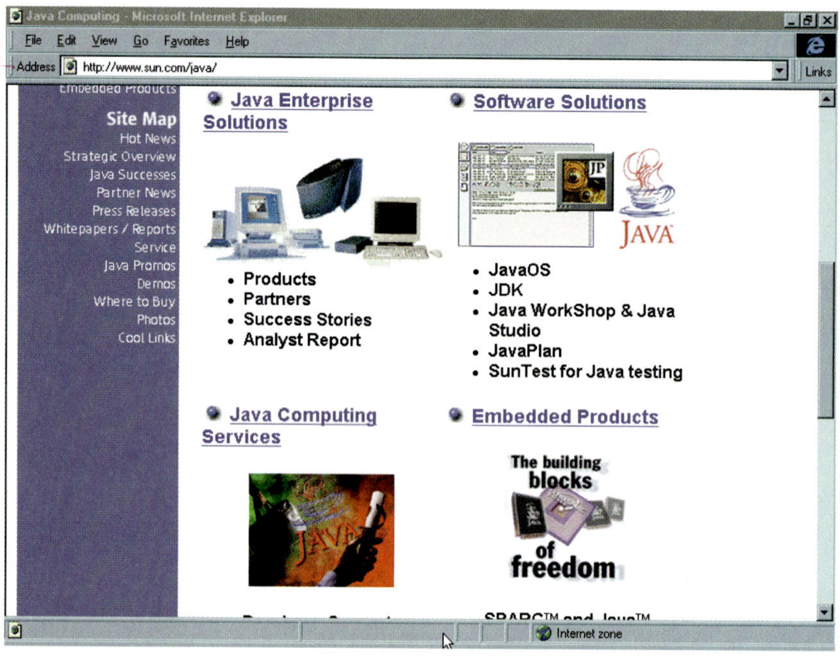

and utilized on the Web. Each of these improvements makes the Web easier to use and thus increases the number of people who can use this new resource.

Today, through a new wave of programming innovation called **Java,** from Sun Microsystems, Web pages can contain new media. Animation, sound, and limited video become feasible, even using ordinary phone lines. Think of the rich information potential this adds to the Web resource. Figure 1.18 shows a recent ad for Java from Sun Microsystems.

Who Uses the Web and Why

As you begin to use the Web, it is helpful to understand whom you will meet there and what they are doing. Remember that the Web is a global resource. Users living in hundreds of different countries all converge there. Think of the educational opportunities available to learn about other countries and cultures as you meet these people.

Twice a year, the Graphic, Visualization, and Usability Center (GVU) at the Georgia Tech Research Corporation in Atlanta, Georgia, conducts an extensive international survey of Web users. In its seventh survey in April/May 1997, it had almost 20,000 respondents. These participants represented seventy-five countries, all fifty U.S. states, and ten Canadian provinces. Survey topics included user demographics, Web uses, and issues and concerns. A complete copy of this report, including over 300 graphs, is available at GVU's Web site. We would like to highlight just a few of the key findings. A more complete report can be obtained from GVU at the Office of Technology Licensing, Georgia Tech Research Corporation, 400 Tenth Street, Atlanta, Georgia 30332-0415. You can also call them at (404) 894-9727 (phone) and (404) 894-9728 (fax).

User Demographics

Thirty-five was the average age of all 20,000 participants in this study. Over the previous six surveys, this value has steadily increased. About one-third of the participants were women. Four out of five lived in the United States.

One-third of the users reported being in a computer-related field; education was second, with one-fourth, and professional and managerial positions were third. There were slightly more Democrats than Republicans, and their favorite late-night TV host was David Letterman. Most users (60 percent) accessed the Web from their home, rather than from school or the office.

Web Uses

What do people do on the Web? The most common activity is gathering information (86.03 percent), followed by searching (63.01), browsing (61.29 percent), work (54.05 percent), education (52.21 percent), communication (47.02 percent), and entertainment (45.48 percent). Shopping was listed at 18.65 percent. This last area shows a steady growth trend that is expected to continue as online transactions become easier, security improves, and more sites and products become available. Figure 1.19 shows this chart and compares Europe with the United States.

Issues and Concerns

Almost one-third of GVU's respondents felt that censorship was the most important issue facing the Internet today. The participants were adamant against any type of censorship of the Internet. One-fourth felt that the largest concern was privacy. Neither culture nor language is perceived as a difficulty in communicating among global participants on the Web.

If we realize that currently, average Web usage time per day equals average TV watching time per day and e-mail usage is equal to phone usage, we begin to see the rapid integration of the Internet and World Wide Web into the fabric of our daily lives. Considering that the Web has been available for only a few short years, this is truly an amazing feat.

There are many other important issues and concerns related to the Internet and Web. Later in this book, we devote an entire chapter to this topic.

Implications

All technologies and improvements must add real value to society, or they are not worth their cost. What are some of the improvements that have been made by Web access, and what value have they added? First, personal and organizational productivity is improved. The world is connected by a new and inexpensive communications channel. Access to data, information, and research is greater. Students learn more in less time, so they can they work more smartly and quickly. The decision-making and problem-solving processes are improved. Processes and products are designed more quickly and brought to market sooner. People can work at home, rather than in an office. Different computers can talk to each other. This allows collaboration and team-based projects where team members are separated by time and space.

FIGURE 1.19
Browser Use Split by Location

Information gathering appears to be the primary use of the Web today. People who need to know something about a specific topic are finding the Web to be the quickest and best source for new information.

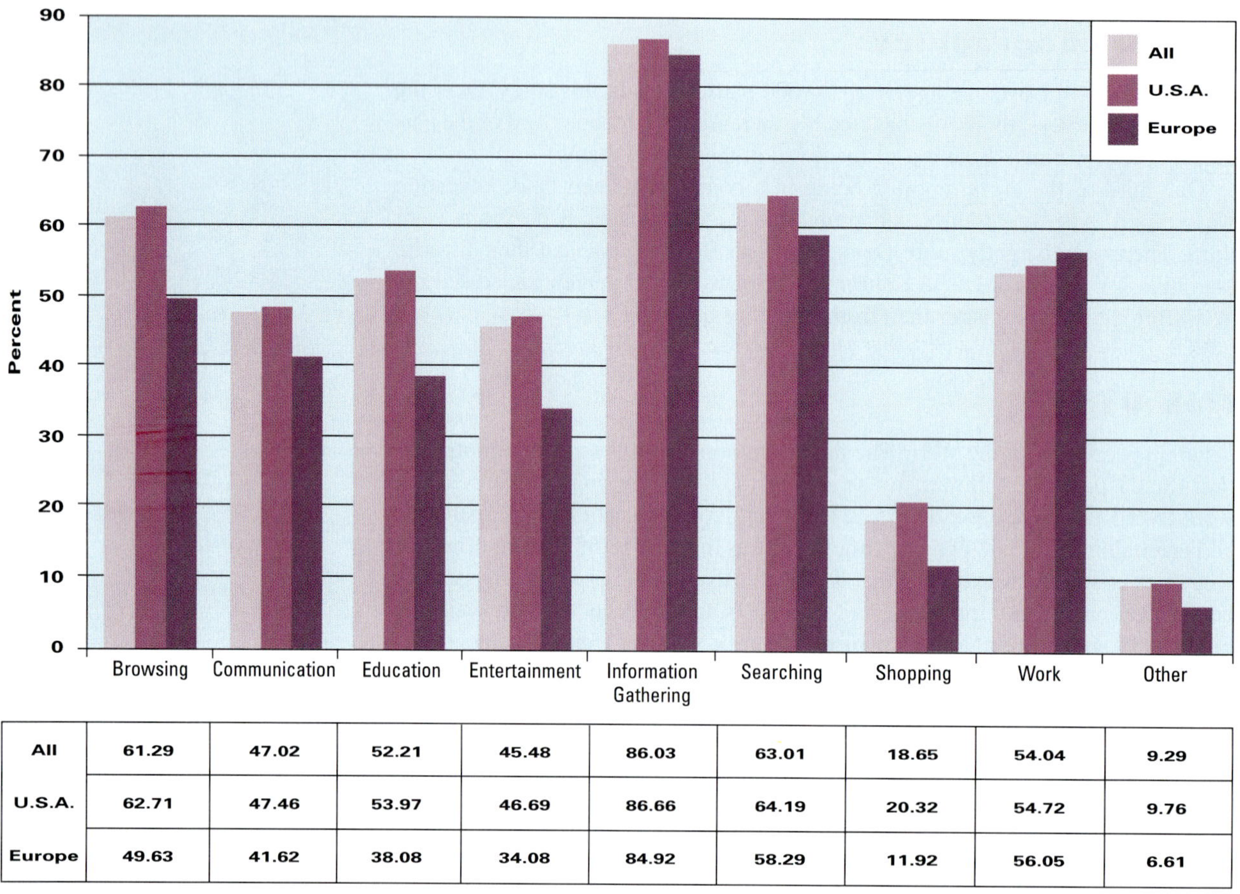

	Browsing	Communication	Education	Entertainment	Information Gathering	Searching	Shopping	Work	Other
All	61.29	47.02	52.21	45.48	86.03	63.01	18.65	54.04	9.29
U.S.A.	62.71	47.46	53.97	46.69	86.66	64.19	20.32	54.72	9.76
Europe	49.63	41.62	38.08	34.08	84.92	58.29	11.92	56.05	6.61

Source: GVU's Seventh WWW User Survey (conducted April 1997).
Copyright 1997 GTRC. All rights reserved. Contact: www-survey@cc.gatech.edu
URL:http://www/gvu/getech/edu/user_surveys/

FIGURE 1.20
Hypertext Example

This is an example of how hypertext appears within a document. The linked word or phrase is color coded to denote that it is the key that allows the user to branch to another section of this particular site or to another Web site.

Here, hypertext link is identified by blue lettering.

The official World Wide Web definition is a wide-area hypermedia information retrieval initiative to give universal access to a large universe of documents. The World Wide Web (WWW) provides users on computer networks with a consistent means to access a variety of media in a simplified fashion using popular, graphic software interfaces.

Another major social benefit of the Web is that it can connect people who live in different parts of the world and have very different cultural and economic backgrounds with others who share common interests. Almost half the participants felt more "connected" to people on the Web who shared their interests worldwide. This suggests that the Web is more than just an information source: It is also a vehicle to link people who share common global causes.

Yet, a paradox exists with the Web. With all the attention, hype, exposure, and value associated with the Web, there are still literally billions of people in our global society for whom the Web is a complete mystery. Even in the United States, there are many who do not know how to use personal computers or do not understand what the Web offers. Others have only limited understanding of this new resource. The goal of this book is to help people fathom the scope of the Web and master its use.

How the World Wide Web Works

Hypertext and Hypermedia

The Web uses hypertext as its means of interacting with users. **Hypertext** is basically the same as regular text—it can be stored, read, searched, or edited. The main difference between hypertext and regular text is that hypertext contains connections to other documents.

Assume you were able to select (with a mouse) the words *World Wide Web* referenced in one of the paragraphs of this text. (See Figure 1.20.) A hypertext system would then have references to other documents related to that hypertext word—a history of the World Wide Web, or a dictionary definition of the World Wide Web. These new references, in turn, would also have links and connections to other documents. These new selections would take you on a somewhat random tour of other information and references related to your original topic. These hypertext relationships, called hyperlinks, literally create a complex virtual web of related information resources. Hypertext words are color coded, usually blue, to separate them from normal text in a document.

Hypermedia adds more media dimensions, such as sounds, images, and movies, to hypertext. These images can also be selected to link to sounds or images in documents. Hypermedia adds additional media richness to the original hyperlink concept.

An Example

The Web uses the popular **client-server model.** A Web server is a special software program running on a computer. Its sole purpose is to find and serve (deliver) documents to other computers when asked. A Web client is the program that interfaces with the user and then requests documents from a server as the user asks for them. The server does a minimal amount of work (it does not perform any calculations) and only operates when a document is requested. It generates a minimal amount of workload on the computer running it. Perhaps an example would help. Figure 1.21 shows how the hypertext word *Network* (in maroon) electronically links to other information sources related to networks. The actual steps in the process are discussed below.

1. Using Web client software (also called a browser), the computer user selects and highlights a hypertext word or phrase. Remember, this word contains

Hypertext Links to Two Other Sites

Hypertext links allow you to instantly move, via a mouse click, to other Web sites that have more information related to the topic. Here, we see two other information sources identified that relate to networks.

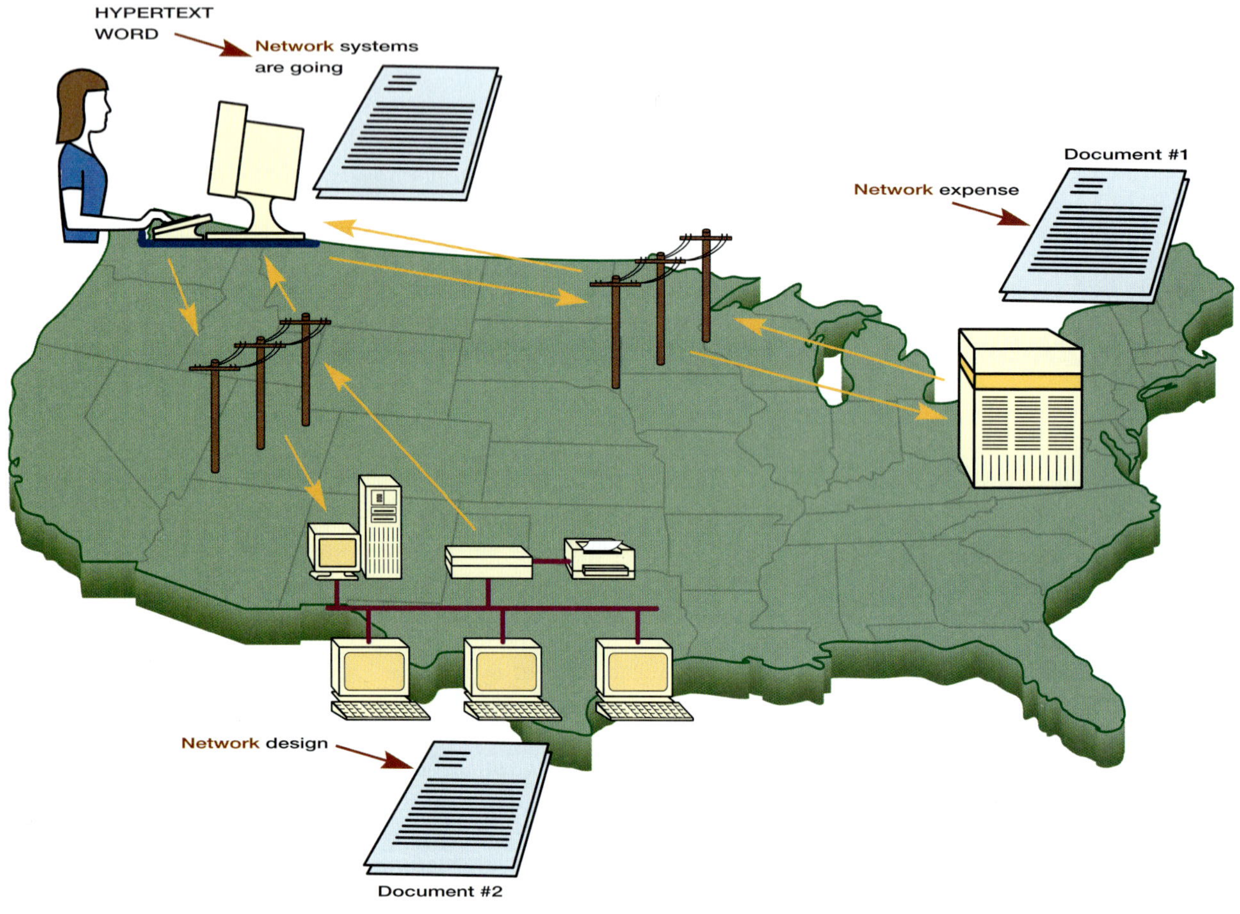

reference locations to associated words housed in other computers on the Web. Assume the highlighted word is *Network*.

2. The Web client, based on the associated address of the word *Network,* connects to the new computer, somewhere else on the Web, specified in the address. This new computer asks that computer's Web server for its associated words related to *Network*.

3. The server finds this material and then sends it, as well as any other media (pictures, sounds, or movies), back to the user's screen.

This whole process operates much like an index in a college textbook. Often there are numerous page references in the book to the same topic. The Web system simply lets you visit each of these different reference points electronically. In later chapters, we will supply more details on how this process actually works, but these three steps explain the basic mechanics of the Web's search and transfer processes.

Web Services and Opportunities

The Web is filled with exciting information and opportunities for you. People who are familiar with the Web and what it can do will be in great demand in the future. The Web offers you both personal and professional growth.

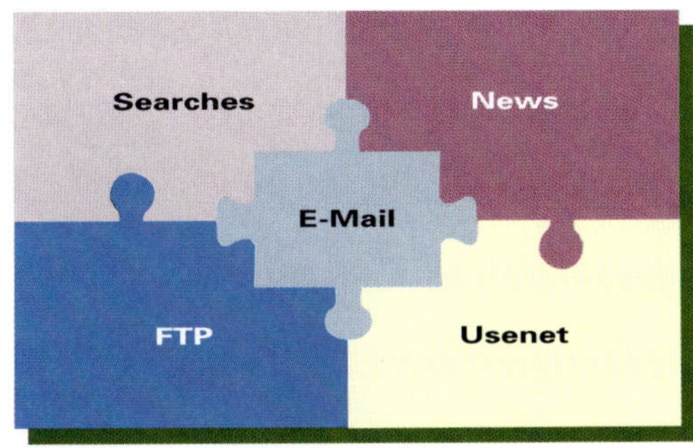

Internet and Web Opportunities for Students

What can the Internet and Web do for students? Your opportunities are almost unlimited. First, you can use these resources to do research for your college courses. Whether you are majoring in engineering, science, business, liberal arts, social sciences, or health and fitness, information is available on topics in all these fields. Figure 1.22 summarizes some current Web services and upcoming opportunities.

Perhaps you are still unsure of your career. The Web is filled with sites that help with career guidance. Some Web sites help you find jobs; write resumes; post your resume so that organizations might see it; and tell you about career options, including starting salaries, educational requirements, and career advancement opportunities. Almost every major employer in the world has a Web site you can visit for insights about the organization and who to contact for more information or employment opportunities.

Are you interested in a career in the Internet or Web field? Web site design, construction, and maintenance in an organization is usually done by a Webmaster. A **Webmaster** builds and maintains the organization's Web presence on the Internet. This is a new career opportunity spawned by the Internet. Today, the average salary for Webmasters in the United States exceeds the average current salary for programmers ($50,000 versus $47,000).

Distance Learning: The Classroom of the Future

Ever wonder what the classroom of the future will be like? Internet and the Web will play major roles. The typical elements in today's educational process are the instructor, the student, fellow students, educational materials, the teaching environment, and the institution. How might the Web offer new educational alternatives in the future?

In the traditional higher education process, students come to the college or university campus classroom at specified times to meet with the professor. There, lectures and educational material are delivered to the students. Periodic testing and assessment lead to each student's final course assessment.

The Internet and Web offer all participants (students, faculty, and the college) new alternatives. The Web can deliver a course anywhere to anyone at any time. A student could live anywhere in the world. Using the Web and normal mail systems, courses are packaged in a variety of format combinations—videotapes, cassette tapes, CD-ROMs, Web sites, printed textbooks, e-mail, and so on. Students take courses at home, at work, during a commute, on vacation, at night, or on weekends based on their schedules and convenience. Different students may progress through the material at different rates and even complete courses at different times. Professors are available to students via e-mail, telephone, chat lines, or through video conferences. Examinations are delivered and taken on the Web. Student teams use mail, e-mail, or conference calls to complete group projects.

Distance learning is still in its infancy, but a number of schools are beginning to offer this option along with their normal, on-site programs. The University of Phoenix, in Phoenix, Arizona, is a major source of distance learning programs. This school offers the convenience and flexibility of attending classes using your personal computer. Small student groups, typically eight to thirteen each, discuss issues, share ideas, and learn—with no commute. With special software, the Internet, and a PC, you can connect to the University twenty-four hours a day, seven days a week, from virtually anywhere.

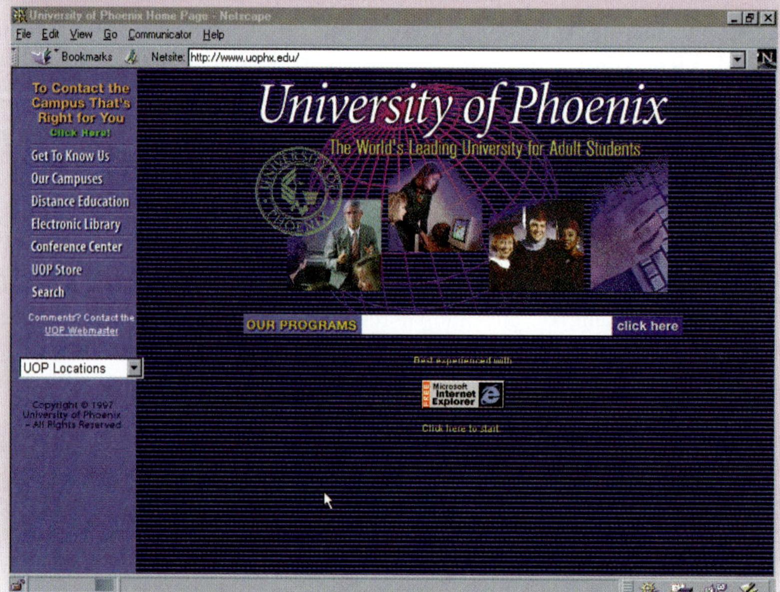

Georgia Tech, in Atlanta, Georgia, is studying future teaching environments. Through the Classroom 2000 research program, students and faculty are investigating how computer technology can best be used to improve education. The goal of Classroom 2000 is to use computer technology to increase the quality of educational engagement both inside and outside the classroom. Professors are using classroom computer technologies—electronic presentations, interactive whiteboards, and electronic note taking—to enhance student learning. Once *(continued)* *(continued from page 26)* perfected, the university hopes to include these improvements in the content of its distance learning program.

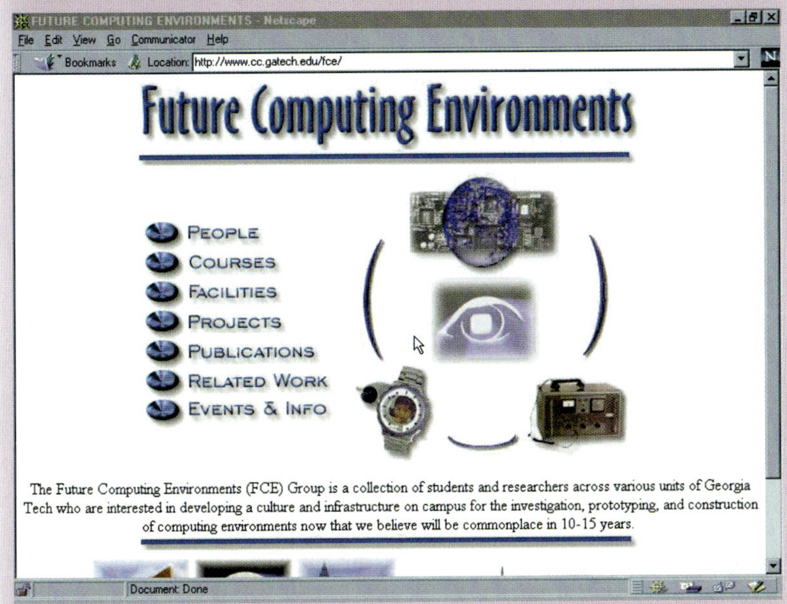

For more information about distance learning and these two programs, visit their Web sites.

The Web also helps with everyday tasks. Need to plan a vacation, buy a car, buy books, buy or sell some stock, shop for a birthday or Christmas present, research a political candidate's past voting record, buy a computer, contact the president of the United States, or get a company's annual report? The Web is filled with sites that will help you in all these areas.

Now that you have a good understanding of what the Internet and Web are and what they can do for you, we move on to the details of how you best learn to navigate through today's new cyberspace environment.

SUMMARY

Computers are increasing personal and organizational productivity. They assist in the decision-making and communications processes. The Internet and the Web play key roles in productivity and communications. The word *Internet* literally means "a collection or network of networks." Today the Internet is everywhere. Creative new Internet sites are springing up daily. The Internet is defined as a worldwide network of computers linked together via various communications channels. The Web refers to the content and processes used on the Internet. The first users of the Internet and Web were four universities and the U.S. government.

Today, the Internet offers the user immediate information search-and-retrieval capabilities. A number of Internet connections are available. They include standard telephone lines, microwave signals, and cable television. Even electric utility companies are experimenting with sending Internet signals along utility wires.

The Internet offers a variety of services. Electronic mail, the most popular, allows users to communicate with each other. Universities, libraries, and government agencies have large databases available to Internet users for information retrieval. The Internet even offers services to link users in play. Home shopping on the Web and Internet is also becoming very popular.

Once obscure, the Web is now mainstream. How do the Internet and the Web work together? Think of the Internet as a complex collection or network of worldwide computers, cables, and signals that carries the computer traffic for its users. The Web, then, is the technology that facilitates information travel along the Internet right-of-way. The Internet forms the trail; the Web transfers the information resources.

Once on the Web, where do people go? Currently, estimates put the total number of Web sites at almost 20 million. Yet the top 1,000 sites constitute almost 90 percent of the Internet's total usage.

Who uses the Web and why? Remember that the Web is a global resource. A research group at Georgia Tech in Atlanta, Georgia, periodically conducts an extensive international survey of Web users. Survey topics include user demographics, Web uses, and issues and concerns. They have found that the average age of Web users is thirty-five. Users work primarily in the computer field, in education, or in management and professional positions. Most users (60 percent) accessed the Web from their home, rather than from school or the office. Web uses include product and company research, collaboration, sports scores, and simple socialization with users from other states, countries, and cultures. The Web also helps with everyday tasks such as travel, investments, sports, or shopping. The bulk of Web users live in the United States.

What can the Internet and Web do for students? Many use it to research course projects and papers. Others study career opportunities and possible employers. Some are interested in a career in an Internet or Web field. A Webmaster builds and maintains an organization's Web presence on the Internet. The future of the Web appears very bright.

KEY TERMS

ARPANET (5)
BITNET (6)
chat rooms (15)
client-server model (23)
communications
   system (3)
e-mail or electronic
   mail (6)

encryption (16)
hypermedia (23)
hypertext (23)
Intercast (8)
Internet (4)
Java (20)
Mosaic (19)
Network Wizards (18)

NSFNET (6)
personalized
   computers (2)
Webmaster (25)
World Wide Web
   (WWW) (17)

END-OF-CHAPTER ACTIVITIES

Matching

Match each term with its description.

a. U.S. Department of
   Defense

b. telegraph

c. cable systems

d. node

e. e-mail or electronic
   mail

f. censorship

g. Internet

h. Webmaster

i. communications
   system

j. hypertext

_________ **1.** This requires a sender, medium, and receiver.

_________ **2.** This communications invention made the Pony Express obsolete.

_________ **3.** A global network of networks.

_________ **4.** The person in charge of maintaining a Web site.

_________ **5.** One connection point to the Internet.

_________ **6.** The government agency that first started the Internet.

_________ **7.** One type of Internet connection that is secure, allows two-way
communications, and transmits at high speeds.

_________ **8.** Allows users to send personal, electronic messages to other specified users on the network.

_________ **9.** This is basically the same as regular text—it can be stored, read,
searched, or edited—but it contains connections to other documents.

_________ **10.** Almost one-third of the respondents in a recent Web survey felt
this was the most important issue facing the Internet today.

Review Questions

1. How do computers increase personal productivity?
2. What constitutes a communications system?
3. Give your definition of the Internet.
4. Name four ways you can connect to the Internet.
5. Explain four applications of the Internet.
6. Describe the World Wide Web.
7. How many people currently use the Web?
8. Describe the demographics of a typical Web user. Where do they live? What type of work do they do?
9. How can students use the Web?
10. What items can you shop for using the Web?

Activities

1. Make a list of all the computing labs at your school. What types of computers does each have? What capabilities do the labs have? What labs have access to the Internet and World Wide Web?
2. Interview one of your parents or older relatives. Ask them what they know about the Internet and Web. Have they ever used it, or do they plan to use it in the future?
3. Check the yellow pages of your local phone company. How many ads do you see for Internet or Web services? Call one and ask about their services. How much do they charge? What are the benefits of their service? How does a customer get connected to their service?
4. Make a list of the possible Internet and Web uses in your home. You should have at least five applications. Which of these would be used most often in your home? Why? By whom?
5. Make an appointment to visit a company in your area that uses Internet and the World Wide Web. Ask to interview their computer director. During the interview, ask the person to describe how the company uses these services and what benefits they receive. What problems have they had? Also ask about any future improvements they have planned. Write up your findings and share them with your professor or class.

Getting Connected

Your Commitment as an Internet User
Getting Started: First Steps
    Establish Your Objectives
    Determine Your Needs
    Gather Information
    Compare Costs and Services
    Make Your Decision
Hardware You Need
    A Basic Computer System
    Modem

RAM and Secondary Storage
Compatibility
    Add-ons and Plug-ins
    Upgrades
Software You Need
    Communications Software
    Navigational Software
    Search Engines
Connecting Your Computer to the
    Internet

Service Providers
    Choosing a Service Provider
Setting Up Your Computer
Summary
Key Terms
End-of-Chapter Activities
    Matching
    Review Questions
    Activities

AFTER COMPLETING THIS CHAPTER, YOU WILL:

1. Complete the first steps for getting started with the Internet.

2. Determine the hardware devices you need to access the Internet.

3. Determine the software you need to access the Internet.

4. Distinguish between communications software, navigational software, and search engines.

5. Explain the procedure for connecting to the Internet.

6. Identify and evaluate some basic browser features.

7. Use basic criteria to evaluate Internet service providers.

8. Distinguish between Internet service providers and online service providers.

Your Commitment as an Internet User

The Internet offers tremendous opportunities for learning, for communicating, for visiting interesting and exciting places, and for establishing your own presence on the Internet and World Wide Web. Using the Internet and Web can be a truly enjoyable experience. You can visit new and different places, view rare art exhibits, and even play hundreds of different and challenging games alone or with others. You can make new friends and participate with groups sharing interests similar to yours. The Internet opens up a world of reality and a world of fantasy for you—a world that was not available to earlier generations.

Approximately 38 percent of homes in the United States have personal computers, and one-half of these households have Internet access. The Internet is used for a variety of popular activities. Figure 2.1 shows the ten most popular activities.

The opportunities made available to you by the Internet are accompanied by responsibilities. No one owns the Internet. Neither the government, businesses, organizations, nor individuals own it. Yet, in a sense, all of us are owners. As owners, we have a responsibility to use good judgment whenever we use the Internet.

FIGURE 2.1

Top Ten Internet Activities

Computers in homes are used for a variety of activities. These are the ten most popular Internet activities.

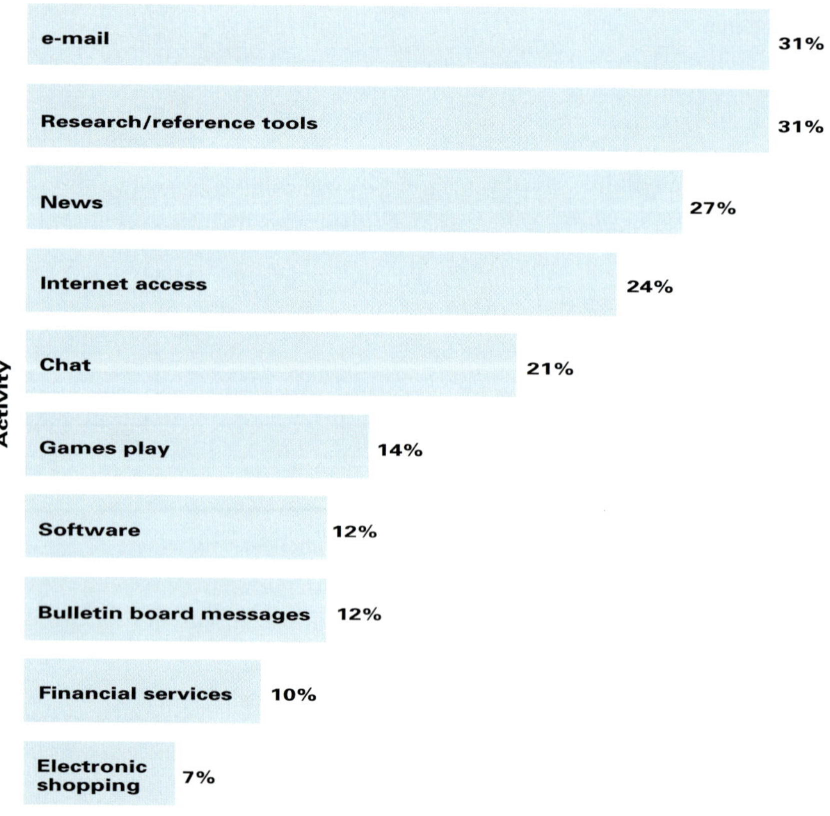

If we abuse our privilege of using the Internet, it might be taken from us. Today, there are several issues and concerns about the Internet and how people are using it. Some members of Congress have recommended censorship of some information traveling over the Internet, but this censorship will not be needed if we exercise care in using the Internet wisely. As a user, you can help keep the Internet available to everyone by using sound judgment whenever you embark on a fascinating journey through cyberspace.

For students, access to the Internet and World Wide Web is often provided by the school. You can usually gain access by using one of the computers located in a computer lab, and some colleges have equipped dormitory rooms with a cable students can use to connect their personal computers to the school's local area network. Many colleges allow students living off campus to access to the school's local area network by using a modem to connect a computer via a telephone line.

Not everyone is fortunate enough to have free and unlimited access to the Internet, though. After you graduate, or if you are not a student, you might still want to have access to the Internet from your home or office. While some employers provide access for employees, others may not. Individuals without Internet access can obtain access from commercial companies. However, purchasing access is similar to purchasing other important goods and services in the market: Knowing what you want and how to go about obtaining it will enable you to make a better decision. In the next section, we examine some things you should know and do before you commit to a company to provide you with access to the Internet.

Getting Started: First Steps

Getting access to the Internet can be frustrating and time consuming. If you will be purchasing access, there are some things you should do before making a commitment.

Establish Your Objectives

To access the Internet and perform other activities, such as word processing, you will have to obtain a computer capable of performing these applications. Prior to purchasing computer hardware and software, you should first decide for what you will use your computer system and how efficient you want to become as a user. You should devote considerable thought to this. In addition to deciding what you will use your computer for presently, you should also give some thought to what you might want to use your computer for in the future. For example, you might have an immediate objective to use your computer for word processing. However, later you might want to become involved in desktop publishing activities. Do these long-range objectives make a difference in your decision? The answer should be *yes*, because desktop publishing programs tend to be much larger and more complex than word processing programs. For desktop publishing applications, you might need a faster computer with more main memory, or RAM. RAM (short for random access memory) consists of small electronic chips located inside a computer that are used to temporarily store programs, data, and information. To permanently store information—including information obtained using the Internet—you need **secondary storage**. Types of secondary storage include floppy disk, hard disk, and CD-ROM. Being a knowledgeable user helps you make a better decision before making a final purchase.

Prepare a list of potential uses for a computer system before making a purchase. The list can be a valuable reference as you determine your specific needs.

Determine Your Needs

After you have compiled a list of objectives, you can proceed to determine your needs. For example, assume an important objective on your list is for you to be able to access the Internet. The computer system you select must contain a modem. Moreover, the modem should be a relatively fast one. Otherwise, you might find yourself waiting several minutes to retrieve information using the Internet. Taking full advantage of a fast modem requires that the computer be fast also. For Internet use, computer professionals recommend using a computer with a minimum microprocessor speed of 133 megahertz (MHz). When shopping for a computer or modem, the seller can provide you with a detailed explanation of computer and modem speeds and their meaning. Because telephone lines are typically used for sending and receiving information, the speed at which the lines can carry information is important. A user needs to be aware that the speed at which information travels from one computer to another is limited to the speed at which telephone lines can carry the information. The better job you do in determining your needs, the more likely you are to make good decisions.

Gather Information

Before making a purchase, gather information for use in making decisions. The process of gathering information includes comparative shopping. If you're considering a specific computer, compare several brands as well as different vendors. Some brands offer more attractive warranties; some companies offer unlimited online technical assistance when you need help. Be sure to ask the companies you are considering what benefits their product or service offers. Ask other people who own computers how they use theirs. If you plan to use the Internet, talk with individuals who already have access. Learn how they obtained access and whether they are satisfied with their arrangement. Remember that the better informed you are, the better decisions you are likely to make.

Compare Costs and Services

Always compare costs and services. The most expensive products or services are not always the best. The best advice is to shop carefully by asking questions, comparing benefits and costs, talking with other customers, talking with vendors, and requesting printed information you can use to become knowledgeable about the obligations, warranties, and services available from potential suppliers. For example, costs and services offered by an Internet service provider often depend on the kind of service you want.

Make Your Decision

Only after you have established your objectives, determined your needs, and compared costs and services can you make good decisions. A good rule is to make your decisions only after becoming well informed. Know what you need and want, whether your purchase satisfies your needs, and whether you can justify your commitment.

If you decide you want to have access to the Internet, you will need some computer hardware and software. In the following sections, we examine the specific hardware and software needed to access the Internet.

Hardware You Need

To have access to the Internet, you need specific computer hardware. You should be mindful that the Internet, like other areas in the computer field, is continuously undergoing change. As changes occur, hardware requirements may also change. Be prepared to modify your system whenever there is a need for you to do so.

A Basic Computer System

Basic computer hardware includes a system unit, a keyboard, a monitor, and a mouse. For relatively easy and simple applications, such as word processing and basic computer games, almost any computer will likely be satisfactory. However, you will be more satisfied with a fast computer with a high-resolution color monitor for Internet use. The speed of your computer is also important. Every computer has an **internal clock** that produces pulses at a fixed rate (like a ticking clock) to synchronize all computer operations. Microprocessor speed, called **clock speed,** is measured in megahertz. One **megahertz (MHz)** represents one million cycles per second. A computer with a maximum speed of 133 MHz executes 133 million cycles per second. A computer requires a fixed number of cycles, so the clock speed determines the number of instructions a microprocessor can execute per second. Computer manufacturers now offer computers with speeds of up to 300 MHz or more. Speeds in the range of 133 MHz to 300 MHz allow you to move around the Internet and World Wide Web and to retrieve information quickly. Using a slower computer will likely result in longer waits while jumping from one location to another or retrieving information from a specific site on the Web.

FIGURE 2.2

A Typical Computer System

For use with the Internet, a personal computer system should include a system unit (computer), high-resolution monitor, keyboard, mouse, and printer. The system unit should contain an adequate amount of primary storage, a graphics board, and a floppy disk drive. A modem is needed for sending and receiving data, and a printer allows you to print copies of information retrieved.

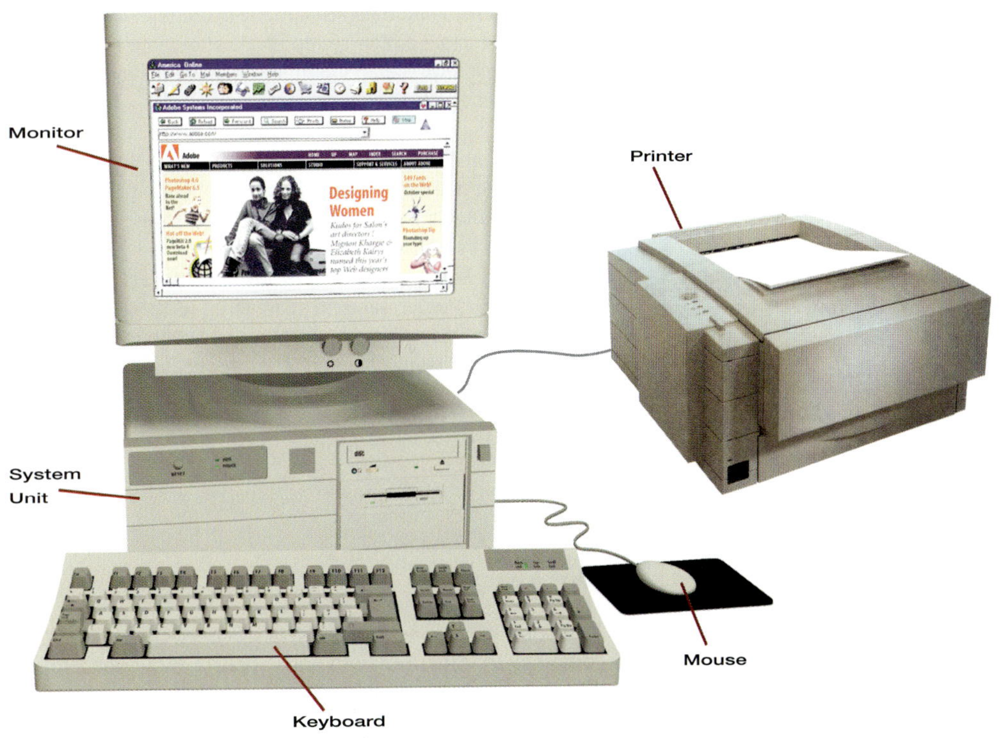

You need a high-resolution color monitor to take advantage of the impressive graphics available at many Web sites. Most Web pages contain graphic images and pictures in vivid color, and you want to be able to capture and display these images on your screen. For the Internet, a minimum resolution of 640 by 480 is barely acceptable, whereas a resolution of 1600 by 1200 offers outstanding color and clarity. If you will use the same monitor for a long period of time (two years or longer), you should consider a more expensive, higher-resolution color monitor.

Modem

A modem is essential for the Internet. A **modem** is an electronic device that enables a computer to transmit (send and receive) data over telephone lines. You can buy either an internal or an external modem. Both types do the same thing, and either type can be used for the Internet. An **external modem** is contained in a small box that is plugged into one of the computer's ports. An **internal modem** is contained on a circuit board installed inside the computer. The main advantage offered by an internal modem is that it does not take up room on the desk or work surface.

As with the computer itself, faster modems are usually better. Modem transmission speeds are measured in terms of bits per second (bps). The fastest modems available are 56 kilobit modems (approximately 56,000 bits per second). However, a modem speed of 33.6 kilobits (33,600 bits per second) is fast and performs well when used for the Internet. Obviously, the faster the transmission rate, the faster you can send and receive data. You should know, however, that you cannot receive data faster than it is being sent. For example, if data is being sent to your computer at 28,800 bits per second, you will receive it at the same speed. Therefore, you might not need the fastest modem available.

RAM and Secondary Storage

Random access memory (RAM), or **primary storage,** refers to temporary storage capacity inside your computer. Any information you retrieve using the Internet is first brought into and stored temporarily in RAM inside your computer and then displayed on your computer screen. Your computer should contain enough RAM to hold your programs and information you receive using the Internet. At present, the RAM capacity of your computer should be a minimum of 16 megabytes (MB). A capacity of 32 megabytes is better. If you are considering buying a computer with 16 megabytes, make certain the computer contains expansion slots that will allow you to add more RAM capacity now or later. Extra RAM means extra cost. However, any experienced computer user will tell you that you can never have too much RAM.

Secondary storage allows for the permanent storage of programs, data, and information. Both floppy disks and hard disks are examples of secondary storage, and most modern PCs come equipped with both. When using the Internet, you can use either to save retrieved information.

Compatibility

The term **compatibility** refers to the ability of one computer hardware or software product to work with another hardware or software product. For example, a computer and printer are said to be compatible if they are connected and work together. Software products are compatible if they use the same data formats.

Compatibility is determined by the standard used to develop hardware and software products. A **standard** is a definition or format that has been approved by a recognized standards organization such as the American National Standards Institute (ANSI), or one that has been accepted as a de facto standard by the industry. A de facto standard is a standard only because a large number of companies have agreed to use it. Standards exist for computer programming languages, operating systems, data formats, and communications protocols. **Communications protocols** allow your computer to communicate with other computers. Without standards, only hardware and software from the same company would likely be compatible.

Compatibility is an important consideration in computing and for the Internet. A user should always make certain that the hardware and software will allow all computer components to work together.

Add-Ons and Plug-Ins

Add-ons, also called **plug-ins,** are hardware and software extras that offer additional capabilities that enhance computer applications, including using the Internet. Add-on boards can be particularly useful when accessing Web sites, viewing Web pages, and retrieving and storing information. All new browsers have plug-ins that are automatically loaded into your computer when the browser is activated.

An **add-on board,** also called an **expansion board** or a **plug-in board,** is an electronic board that can be inserted into a personal computer to provide additional capabilities. An add-on is designed to complement other products. There are several add-on boards available that you can plug (install) into your personal computer to give it additional capabilities. An example of an add-on board is a sound board (also called a sound card). A **sound board** is an electronic board that is installed inside a personal computer to allow you to hear the sounds available at some Web sites and on many CD-ROM disks. The de facto standard for personal computer sound is a board called **Sound Blaster.** Most sound cards are Sound Blaster–compatible, meaning that they can process instructions written for a Sound Blaster board.

Another useful add-on board is a graphics board (also called graphics card). A **graphics board** is an electronic board installed inside a personal computer that enables the user to capture and display vivid pictures and images.

Many newer personal computers are **multimedia computers,** which means they come with add-on boards already installed inside. If your computer does not already have these add-ons, they are available from both hardware and software vendors. Before purchasing an add-on board for your computer, you should request a demonstration.

Upgrades

A new version of a hardware or software product designed to replace an older version of the same product is called an **upgrade.** Software companies frequently sell upgrades at discount prices to prevent customers from switching to other products.

FIGURE 2.3

An Add-On Board

An add-on board for a personal computer "adds" capability to the computer, such as allowing a user to send and receive sounds.

To install an upgrade on your computer, you must have an earlier version already installed.

In recent years, software companies have offered **competitive upgrades,** which means that you can buy a program at a discount if you can prove that you own a competing product. You can sometimes benefit by buying a competitive upgrade of a product better suited to your specific needs.

Upgrades of Internet products are offered at regular intervals. Some software companies allow a user to download a newer version of a particular product. When you **download** a program, you receive the new program via your modem and store the program on your computer. For example, when Netscape Communications Corporation introduces a new version of its popular browser program, a user of an earlier version can simply download the new version. Netscape makes the downloading process easy. Usually, a user can download the new version just by clicking on the name of the new version shown on the Netscape home page and then following the instructions that appear on the screen.

Because the Internet is continually changing, you will sometimes find a need to upgrade your software, and you will occasionally have to upgrade your hardware. Upgrades will enable you to take advantage of new features and applications available on the Internet.

Software You Need

A typical personal computer comes with some software already installed, including an operating system and device drivers. The operating system should include

FIGURE 2.4

A Graphical User Interface

A graphical user interface, available with modern personal computers, makes using a computer easier.

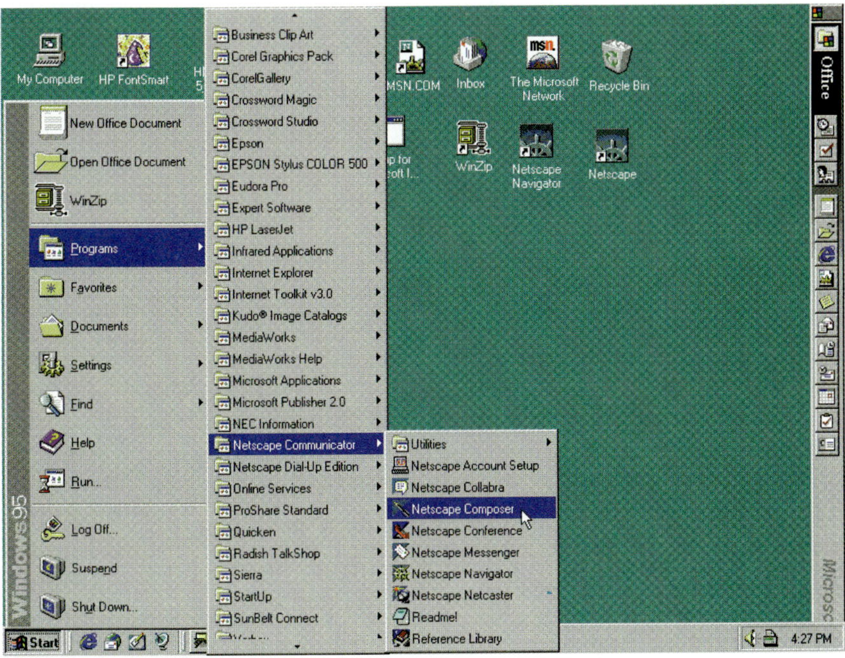

a **graphical user interface**, called **GUI,** that takes advantage of the computer's graphics capabilities. Various graphical user interfaces, including Microsoft's Windows 95 and the OS 8 used by Apple's Macintosh computers, offer special features such as pointers, icons, windows, and menus that make a personal computer easier to use. More recently, some computer manufacturers and sellers have begun selling computers with a modem, modem communications software, and Internet software already installed. Unless this software is already installed on your computer, you will need to install it before you can access the Internet.

Communications Software

Communications software is software that allows you to send and receive information over telephone lines through a modem. Without communications software, you cannot connect your computer to another computer, such as a Web server.

Communications software is produced by several manufacturers and is usually included with your modem. It is also available from Internet service providers and online service companies, both of which are explained later in this chapter. Unless you are an experienced Internet user, you might benefit by obtaining a communications software program from one of these. If you will be using an Internet service provider or subscribing to an online service, either will provide the software you need and assist you in its installation. After making arrangements with the company, the company will send you the software, detailed printed information for installing it on your computer, and a telephone number for technical assistance should you need to reach a company technician. If you are unable to install the software properly, you can call the technician to receive verbal step-by-step instructions.

With some newer operating systems, including Windows 95, you can easily establish a connection to another computer using the **dial-up networking** program. After selecting the dial-up networking program, a dialog box appears on your screen. All you need do is to type the requested information in the dialog box.

A communications software package includes several basic programs. One of the programs contains instructions for data transfer speed. This program should allow for a data transfer speed at least as fast as the maximum speed of the modem you will be using.

Another program allows for automatic queuing and redialing. This can be a useful feature if you use your modem to access a service that is frequently busy, such as an electronic bulletin board service (BBS). By entering the telephone number in a queue, the communications software will continue redialing the number until you are connected to the bulletin board.

Communications software packages also contain other important programs and features. For example, **file transfer protocols** (**FTPs**) enable you to transmit binary files or ASCII files over a telephone line. A **binary file** is a machine-readable-only file in which data is in the form of only two numbers (zeros and ones). Executable files and numeric files are typically in binary format. An **ASCII file** is a human-readable file in which the data is in the form of text. The more protocols the package supports, the better. When discussing communications with a potential supplier, inquire about the features available with the communications software.

Navigational Software

To use the Internet, you need a navigational software package, usually called a browser.

FIGURE 2.5

Windows 95 Dial-Up Connection

One way to connect to the Internet or to another computer is by using the Windows 95 Dial-Up Connection. To use this program, you click on the My Computer icon on your Windows desktop, click Dial-Up Networking, click Make A New Connection, and then enter the information requested in the dialog box. After entering the information, click Next to get the next dialog box. Enter all the requested information in all boxes to make a connection.

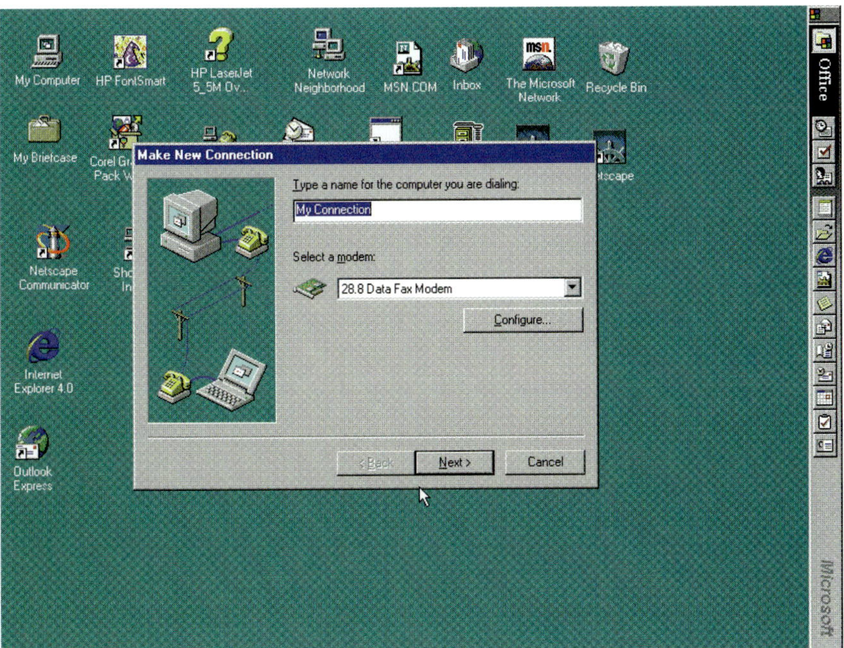

A **browser** is a software tool (program) that makes it easy for the user to find and display Web pages by removing the complexity of having to remember the syntax of computer commands. Browsers are free to educational institutions.

Today, many browsers compete for a share of the browser market. The two most popular Internet browsers are **Netscape Navigator** from Netscape Communications Corporation and **Internet Explorer** from Microsoft Corporation. Netscape Communications' newest browser (Navigator 4.0) was introduced in June 1997 and can be downloaded from the company or purchased from a retailer. The browser is included as part of the software package called Netscape Communicator. Microsoft's newest browser, Internet Explorer 4.0, was introduced in late 1997. It, too, can be downloaded from the company or purchased from a retailer.

Most of the early browsers were stand-alone products. Today, many software products, such as Microsoft's Office 97, allow a user to switch back and forth between a browser and other applications.

If you subscribe to an Internet service provider or to a commercial online service company such as the Microsoft Network or America Online, the company will include at least one browser with the software you receive. Before subscribing to an Internet service provider, inquire about the programs and the features available with the software package the service provides.

Not all browsers offer the same features. Before acquiring a browser for your own use, evaluate the features you want included. Some basic features you should

Electronic Mail

Electronic mail is an important function for most browser users. Unless you have a separate e-mail program, you should consider a browser with this capability.

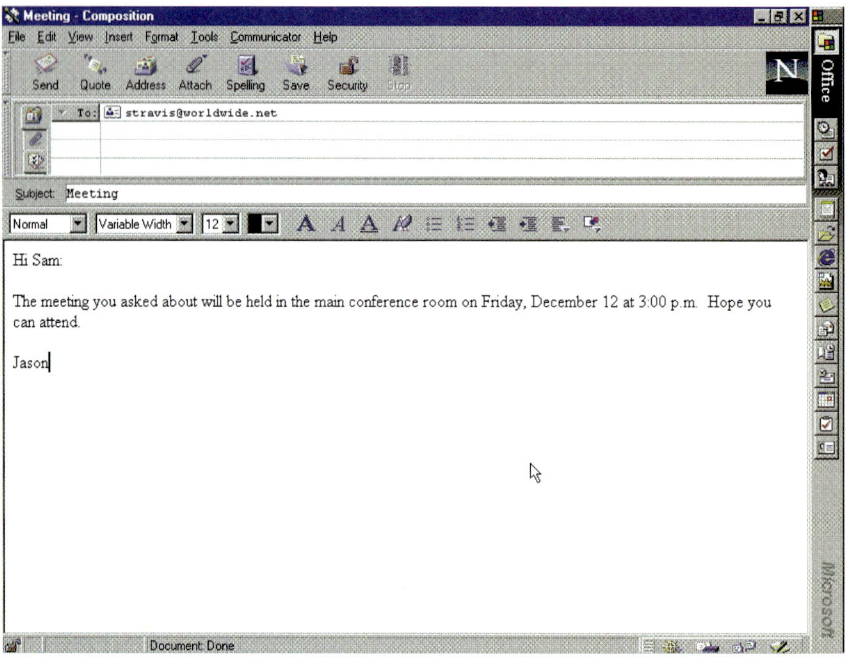

consider include the browser's functions, ease of use, speed, framing capability, multimedia support, publishing capability, and security.

FUNCTIONS

Newer browsers offer users several useful functions, including e-mail, chat, bulletin board access, FTP, and Telnet capability. Some functions may be important, while others may not. For example, e-mail capability is important if you will be sending and receiving messages. On the other hand, Telnet may not be important unless you plan to access a remote host computer such as the main computer on a university campus. **FTP,** short for **File Transfer Protocol,** allows you to upload (transmit) files over telephone lines to another computer and to download (retrieve) files stored on another computer. Although you might not need a particular function now, you might discover a need for it later.

EASE OF USE

Almost all browsers are easy to learn and use. Most offer tools such as a menu bar, toolbars, and special buttons that allow you to locate, retrieve, save, and print Web pages, along with other tasks. Above all, you should request a demonstration and ask to be allowed to test the software yourself to determine if it is easy to use.

SPEED

When moving between Web sites and pages, you will discover that some Web pages take considerable time to retrieve and display. Some browsers are faster than others in the manner in which they handle complex graphic images such as

FIGURE 2.7
A Typical Web Home Page

Most browsers include special tools that make navigating easier. A menu bar, tool bars, and special buttons eliminate the need for a user to remember complex commands in order to access Web pages.

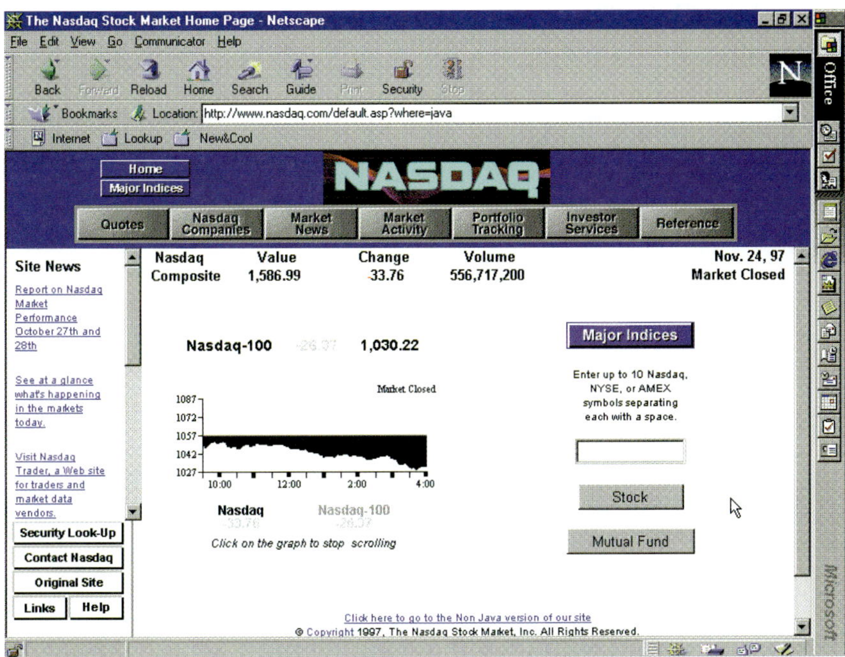

pictures and illustrations. A capability called **progressive graphics capability** allows a low-resolution version of images to be displayed quickly while more data needed to sharpen the images is being downloaded to your computer. This allows you to get an idea of what the final image will look like while you're waiting for the remainder of the data to be downloaded. If you're not impressed with what you are seeing, you can switch to another Web page. Browsers designed to run under a graphical user interface, such as Microsoft's Windows 95, support a feature called **multitasking** that allows you to perform multiple operations in parallel. For example, with multitasking you can be conducting a library search while a file is being downloaded to your computer from an FTP site.

FRAMING CAPABILITY

A **frame** is a rectangular area of your screen in which text or graphics can appear. Many Web pages are segmented into frames so that information can be displayed in a meaningful fashion.

Almost all browsers now contain frame capability that allows for the display of Web pages organized into frames. Because many Web pages are arranged in this manner, you should make certain the browser you will be using has this capability.

MULTIMEDIA SUPPORT

Multimedia capability has become essential for many computer applications, including Internet and Web applications. Multimedia capability allows you to display text and graphics, to hear sounds like voice and music, and to enjoy animation effects on your screen.

FIGURE 2.8

Progressive Graphics Display Capability

Progressive graphics display capability allows you to view a low-resolution rendition of a Web page while more data is being downloaded. After downloading the remaining data, a high-resolution rendition of the page is sharper and more detailed.

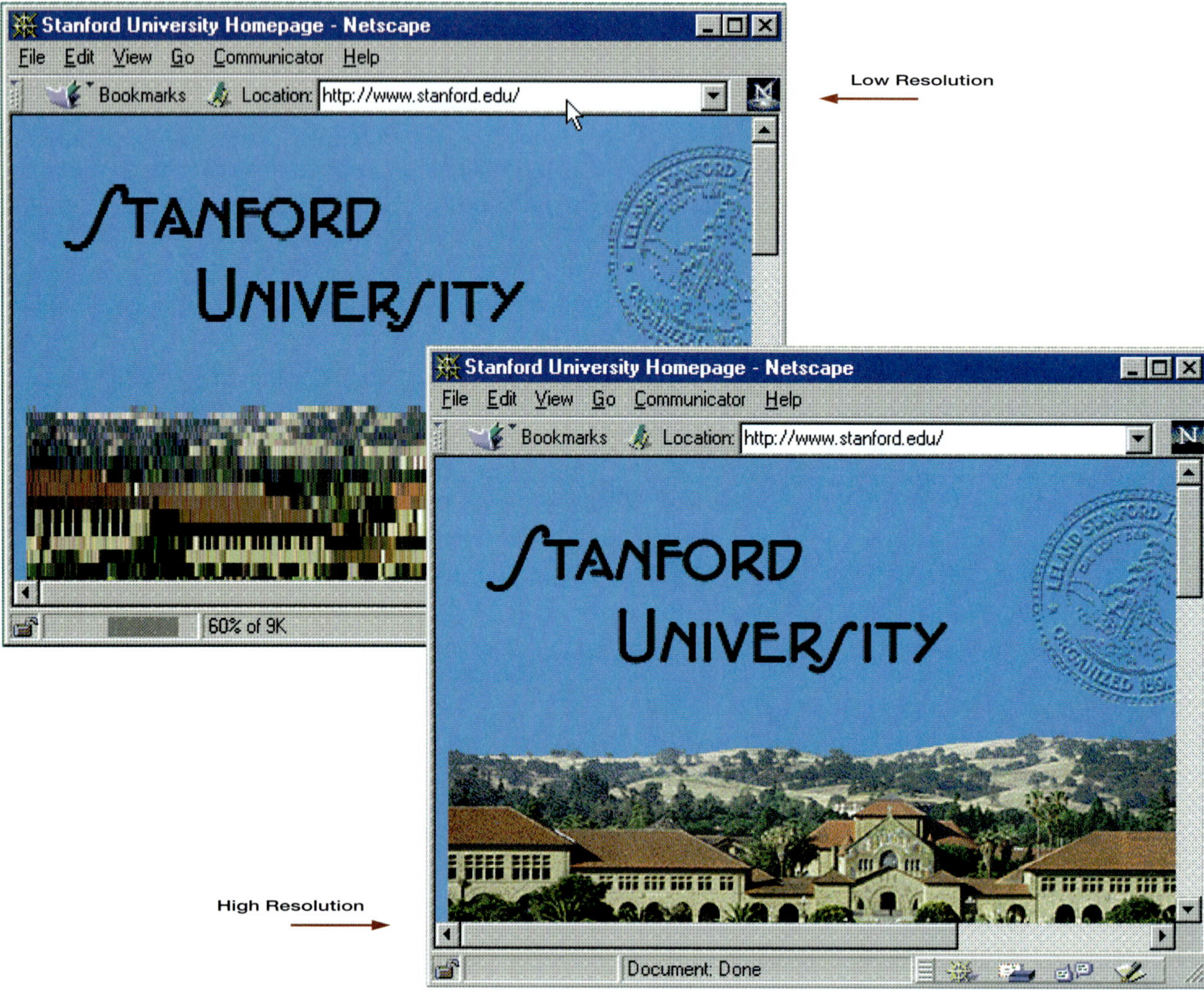

Almost all browsers now have the capability to display multimedia pages, so to enjoy the full benefits of the sounds and graphics these pages offer, your computer must have the same capabilities. Any computer you buy should be equipped with a graphics board, sound board, and high-quality speakers.

PUBLISHING CAPABILITY

Like thousands of other individuals, eventually you might want to publish your own Web page. Many browsers have built-in Web-publishing capabilities. For example, the latest version of Microsoft Word 7.0, a popular word processing program, makes Web publishing simple. You can use the word processor to type the information you want on a page, and it will save what you've typed in HTML format. Chapter Six explains Web publishing, including HTML, in detail.

FIGURE 2.9
Web Page Frames

Newer browsers provide frame capabilities, but some older ones do not. Without this capability, you will be unable to display some Web pages.

SECURITY

The security of information is a serious concern for many users. Personal information is not always as secure as one might prefer. In an age when information travels freely through cyberspace, the information can be intercepted and used in potentially harmful ways. For example, suppose you use your computer to order a product advertised on the Internet and enter your credit card account number to complete the order. There have been cases where the information was intercepted and the account number was used fraudulently by another person.

Newer browsers offer better security. While it may still be possible for information you supply to be intercepted by others, newer browser versions offer greater security by encrypting the information you supply.

If you will be sending important information to another computer, you can safeguard the information by encrypting it. One way to do this is by installing special encryption software on your computer that will allow you to encode the information. Any unauthorized person who might intercept your message will be unable to read it. Several encryption programs are available for purchase.

Another protection method is to refuse to supply important personal information such as your address and credit card numbers over the Internet.

Search Engines

A **search engine** is software that facilitates queries by allowing a user to enter search criteria to locate Web sources. In short, a search engine allows a user to search for, locate, and retrieve information on the World Wide Web. Unlike a browser—in which an address is entered to access a specific Web site—a search engine allows a user to locate specific information and automatically retrieve Web pages by entering search criteria. For example, assume you want to find information about the Battle of Gettysburg for a report you are writing for a history class. You can use a search engine to retrieve a list of articles on this topic simply by typing your search criteria—in this case *Battle of Gettysburg*—into the search box and clicking on the search button. A list of articles will appear on your screen. Then, you can view one of the articles just by clicking on it, as shown in Figure 2.10. Much more information about search engines is included in Chapter Four.

References Retrieved Using a Search Engine

A search engine can be used to locate information by entering search criteria. A user does not have to know the URL address of the specific location of the information.

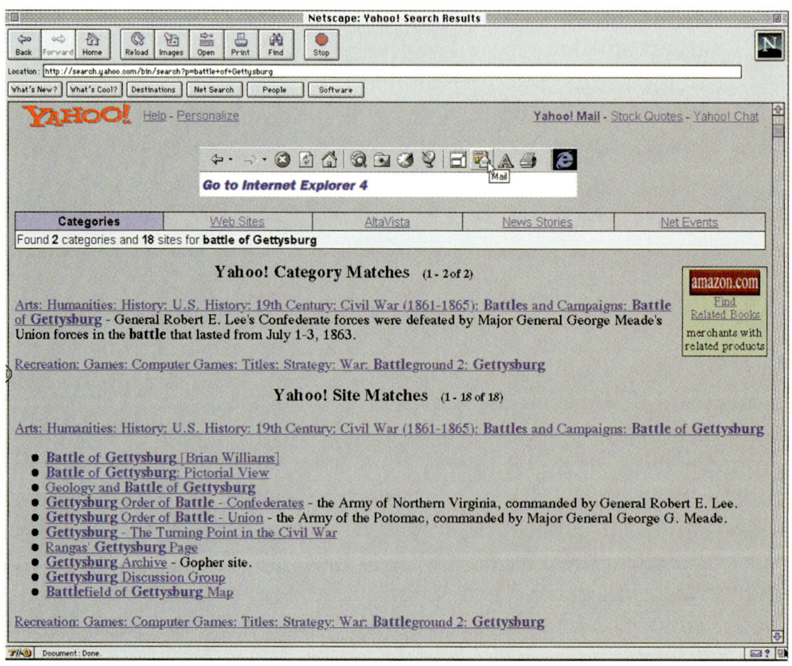

Many excellent search engines are available. Some of the more popular names include Yahoo!, WebCrawler, Excite, Lycos, and AltaVista, to name just a few. Also, some browsers contain a Search button. By clicking on the Search button, a list of search engines appears from which you can make a selection. Microsoft's Internet Explorer contains a feature that allows users to conduct searches from Explorer's address field. A word typed into the address field automatically activates Yahoo!'s search engine.

Some search engines do a better job of searching than do others. AltaVista, for example, searches deeper than most by searching a larger number of databases.

Internet Service Representative

A relatively new career opportunity is that of Internet service representative, sometimes referred to as an ISR. An Internet service representative answers telephone and electronic inquiries from customers who encounter problems while installing communications or related software on their computer or who experience difficulties when trying to access the Internet.

Employment opportunities are available with Internet service providers and online service companies. With the rapidly growing popularity of the Internet and World Wide Web, ISPs and online services are adding millions of new subscribers each year, many of whom are inexperienced computer users. Even many users who are experienced are unfamiliar with the software they will use to access the Internet and Web. Internet service providers and online service companies provide subscribers with phone numbers they can use to speak to Internet service representatives to obtain help in solving any problem they experience.

To qualify for employment, an applicant should possess basic computer skills, should have good verbal communications skills, and should enjoy helping customers solve their problems. The employer trains new employees in the installation and use of software, including browsers and search engines. Before being left alone to respond to customer inquiries and problems, employees are typically required to demonstrate the knowledge and expertise acquired during training.

Some companies offer both full-time and part-time employment. Many part-time employees are high school or college students. Successful employees may advance to higher-level supervisory or management positions within the organization.

Connecting Your Computer to the Internet

Connecting to the Internet normally requires two steps: Selecting a service provider and installing the software supplied by the service provider to get your computer set up and operating properly. Both steps are important because you will want to be able to take full advantage of the many benefits the Internet has to offer.

Service Providers

Although there are several ways to connect to the Internet, the two most common are commercial online services and service providers. When choosing an online service or a service provider, you should inquire about the speed of the modem used by the service or provider. This speed should be at least as fast as the speed of your own modem. If it is slower, you will be unable to take advantage of the speed of your modem. In the following sections, we examine these two methods for making a connection.

COMMERCIAL ONLINE SERVICES

Several commercial online services are available. A **commercial online service** provides a wide range of information and services to subscribers willing to pay a regular subscription fee. In addition to providing access to the Internet, commercial online services typically provide special kinds of information, such as timely news items, information arranged into groupings, newsgroups, e-mail, and business information. By providing online links to information, subscribers can easily locate information they are seeking.

Commercial online services offer the same basic information available to anyone on the Internet. However, the way in which the service organizes and presents the information makes it easier for subscribers to access the information and move from one location to another on the Internet. In addition, these services typically provide subscribers with browsers and with online help when needed.

Commercial services do have the ability to block information deemed inappropriate, such as information and materials considered obscene or pornographic. Most commercial online services offer such features as e-mail attachments, chat groups, Telnet, and FTP. However, some do not. If you plan to subscribe to a commercial online service and one or more of these features are important for you, make sure the features you want are available.

The combined features of commercial online services are attractive to many potential subscribers. If you only need access to the Internet without the extra services available from a commercial online service, though, you might want to consider obtaining access by subscribing to an Internet service provider (ISP) or to an Internet access provider (IAP). Internet service providers typically offer services that Internet access providers do not. For example, ISPs typically offer e-mail, FTP, and Telnet capability whereas IAPs typically provide only access to the Internet.

INTERNET SERVICE PROVIDERS

Private commercial companies that provide basic Internet services are called **Internet service providers** (**ISPs**). Services provided typically include access to the Internet, e-mail, links to browsers and search engines, and the opportunity to communicate with other individuals and groups. Many are local companies listed in the phone book, although some are national companies. Some large telecommunications companies, including AT&T and MCI, have begun offering Internet access to their customers. With their vast resources, these large telecommunications companies may become dominant players in the ISP market within a few years.

INTERNET ACCESS PROVIDERS

Some providers, called **Internet access providers** (**IAPs**), are typically small independent companies that cater only to area residents. IAPs offer only access to the Internet. If you subscribe to an IAP, you will not have access to e-mail or other services.

Some Internet providers have their own network system, called a **backbone,** to handle their Internet operations. Smaller providers are sometimes resellers that purchase or lease connectivity from larger companies and then sell connection service to subscribers.

Earlier it was pointed out that if you are a student your college or university might already provide you with access to the Internet. Many universities offer computers at libraries and other campus facilities to help students, faculty, and staff members take advantage of the access they provide to the Web.

Choosing a Service Provider

Choosing a service provider is a very individual decision because some criteria will be more important to you than will others. Some criteria you might consider prior to making a final decision are explained in the following paragraphs.

COST

Most commercial online services and service providers offer various plans. Each plan offers a different level of service and accompanying fee. For example, a provider might offer fifteen hours per month of online time for a fee of $9.95 per month, with each additional hour at $2.00 per hour. The same provider might allow unlimited online time, called **connect time,** for $19.95 per month. Another provider might offer the first twenty hours for $15.95 with an additional charge of $3.00 per hour.

In choosing a provider, consider telephone cost. Long-distance service can prove expensive. If you subscribe to a commercial online service that does not offer a local telephone access number, you will pay long-distance charges each time you access the Internet.

SPEED

The speed at which the service works should be an important consideration. If you have a modem with a speed of 28.8 kilobits per second (Kbps) but the service moves data to you at a speed of only 14.4 Kbps, you are not being able to utilize the speed of your modem. If the service uses an ISDN line or a T1 line, you will be able to send and receive data much faster, because both are high-speed transmission lines. An **ISDN line** (short for Integrated Services Digital Network) is a special digital telephone line that allows you to connect to the Internet at very high speeds. ISDN speeds range from 64 Kbps to 128 Kbps. To use an ISDN line you need a special ISDN modem and an Internet provider that offers ISDN access. A **T1 line** is a leased telephone line that can carry data at speeds up to 1.544 megabits of data per second. As with ISDN, to be able to use a T1 line you need a special modem and a provider that offers T1 access.

When large volumes of information are to be sent and/or received, an individual, business, or organization might lease one of these lines. Leasing an ISDN or T1 line is expensive. The expense can be justified only when there is a definite need.

SUPPORT AND SERVICE

Most service providers allow you to place a call for assistance when needed. If you're like most users, you will occasionally encounter problems for which you will need technical assistance. Before signing up with a provider, request a telephone number for technical assistance and call the number—perhaps several times—until you contact someone. If you have trouble reaching this department, or if you experience long delays, you might consider a different service.

You should also inquire about the number of users assigned to each of the service's modems or numbers. If the number exceeds fifteen, you are likely to experience delays in getting connected.

Eventually, you might decide you want to be able to develop and display your own Web page at the service's site. Find out whether this service is available and whether there is an extra charge for this service. Some services provide free Web-authoring software and authoring assistance to subscribers.

EASE OF USE

Another criterion to consider is the relative ease with which you can use the software the Internet service provider (ISP) supplies you. Are the interfaces, menus, and buttons easy to identify and use? Are the installation software, the browser, and other features easy to use so you won't find it necessary to spend lots of time obtaining technical assistance? Some, but not all, ISPs offer subscribers updated software, such as the latest browser version. Ask if the software you will receive contains the latest program versions.

Before selecting a service provider, you should talk with companies that provide service in your area. Be sure you get satisfactory answers to any questions you ask, including the important ones listed in Figure 2.11.

FIGURE 2.11

Some Questions to Ask a Service Provider

Before deciding on a particular service provider, you should ask these questions.

1. Can I use a local telephone access number in my local calling area?
2. Do you offer toll-free telephone access in case I am on the road? Will I be charged extra for this service and, if so, how much?
3. Do you offer a fixed monthly price for unlimited use? If so, how much is it?
4. Which browser and e-mail service do you provide?
5. Can I use another browser and e-mail reader of my own choosing?
6. Do you offer more than one e-mail account per subscription? If so, how many?
7. Do you offer 56-Kbps modem access? If so, do you charge extra for this faster access?
8. If you do not offer 56-Kbps access, will the standard that you use work with my 56-Kbps modem?
9. Do you offer free Web-page postings? If so, how many megabytes of server space will I get?
10. Do you offer wizards or other software to help me set up a home page?

Setting Up Your Computer

Whether you will be using an online service company or a service provider, you have to set up your computer before you can access the Internet. The service you select will probably provide you with a **setup package** that contains an instruction manual and a diskette or CD-ROM containing installation software. Typically, all you need to do to install the software is follow the instructions contained on the diskette or CD-ROM. For example, if are using Microsoft's Windows 95 operating system and the setup package includes a CD-ROM, you first insert the CD-ROM in the designated drive. You then click the Start button, then click Run. When the dialog box appears, click OK. Then, just follow the instructions that will be displayed on your screen. Figure 2.12 illustrates some typical steps for setting up your computer if you are subscribing to an online service such as the Microsoft Network or America Online. The installation procedure is similar for most online services. During installation, you will be asked to provide specific information such as your name, the kind of service you want, your method of payment, the telephone number to which your computer is connected, and your modem type and speed.

Setting up your computer for a service provider is usually a little more involved. For example, you may also be required to enter a code number for your modem and specify your maximum modem speed. If you need assistance, you can contact the company's technical assistance department for help.

After completing the setup procedure, an Access icon may be placed on your screen. If so, you can gain immediate access by clicking that icon. By clicking the icon and logging on to the service, you can begin accessing the Internet and using the features available to you, such as e-mail and chat. Then, you will be ready to begin your journey through cyberspace to a universe of information that awaits your visit.

A Typical Setup Screen

Setting up your computer for an online service, such as America Online, is relatively easy. In most cases, you simply provide the requested information. The first screen below is the America Online Welcome screen. If you click on Setup, the Network Setup screen appears for you to enter information in the boxes. After all the required information has been entered in all the dialog boxes, you are ready to access the Internet and to use any of the features available.

(a) America Online Welcome screen

(b) Network Setup screen

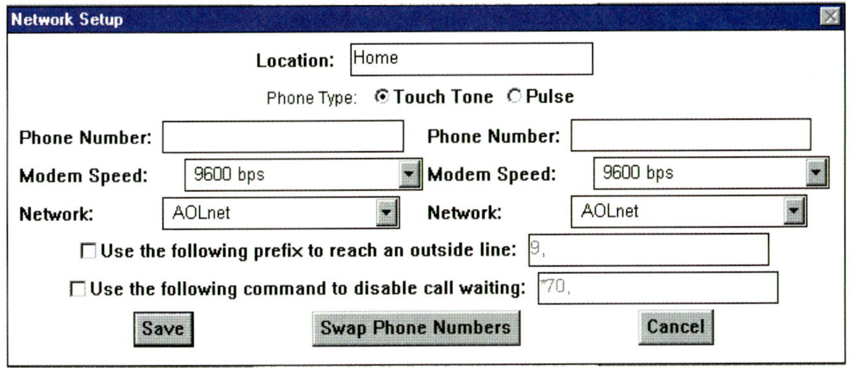

The Internet offers vast opportunities for learning, communicating, visiting interesting and exciting places, and establishing your presence on the Internet. But along with these benefits, you have a responsibility to use the Internet and World Wide Web wisely.

Before connecting to the Internet, you should establish your objectives, determine your needs, gather information, and compare costs and services.

To use the Internet effectively, you need a basic computer system that includes a system unit, a keyboard, a monitor, a mouse, enough RAM to handle your programs and data, and enough secondary storage to permanently hold them.

Add-ons, also called plug-ins, offer additional capabilities that enhance computer applications such as the Internet. A sound board, or sound card, allows you to hear the sounds available at some Web sites. A graphics board, or graphics card, enables you to capture and display vivid pictures and images. Multimedia computers come with add-on boards already installed inside.

A new version of a hardware or software product is called an upgrade. Some software companies offer competitive upgrades to owners of a competing product.

Communications software allows you to send and receive information over telephone lines through a modem. Navigational software allows you to move around, or navigate, the Internet. A browser makes it easy to find and display Web pages. Today, the two most popular browsers are Netscape Navigator and Internet Explorer. Some useful browser features include ease of use, speed, framing capability, multimedia support, publishing capability, and security. A search engine facilitates queries by allowing a user to enter search criteria to locate Web sources.

A user can obtain access to the Internet from a commercial online service that provides a range of information and services for a regular subscription fee. Access can be obtained from an Internet service provider, which will provide e-mail and other basic services, or from an Internet access provider, which will provide only Internet access. In choosing a service provider, you should consider cost, support and service, and ease of use.

KEY TERMS

add-on board (expansion board, plug-in board) (38)	dial-up networking (40)	multimedia computer (38)
add-ons (37)	download (39)	multitasking (43)
ASCII file (40)	external modem (36)	Netscape Navigator (41)
backbone (48)	file transfer protocol (FTP) (40, 42)	plug-ins (add-ons) (37)
binary file (40)	frame (43)	primary storage (37)
browser (41)	graphical user interface (GUI) (40)	progressive graphics capability (43)
clock speed (35)	graphics board (38)	random access memory (RAM) (37)
commercial online service (47)	internal clock (35)	search engine (45)
communications protocols (37)	internal modem (36)	secondary storage (33)
communications software (40)	Internet access provider (IAP) (48)	setup package (50)
compatibility (37)	Internet Explorer (41)	Sound Blaster (38)
competitive upgrade (39)	Internet service provider (ISP) (48)	sound board (sound card) (38)
connect time (49)	ISDN line (49)	standard (37)
	megahertz (MHz) (35)	T1 line (49)
	modem (36)	upgrade (38)

END-OF-CHAPTER ACTIVITIES

Matching

Match each term with its description.

a. megahertz

b. modem

c. secondary storage

d. random access memory (RAM)

e. sound board

f. upgrade

g. communications software

h. add-on board

i. commercial online service

j. graphics board

_______ **1.** An electronic board installed inside a personal computer that enables the user to capture and display vivid pictures and images.

_______ **2.** Software that allows you to send and receive information over telephone lines through a modem.

_______ **3.** Temporary storage capacity inside a computer.

_______ **4.** One million cycles per second.

_______ **5.** Provides a wide range of information and services to subscribers willing to pay a regular subscription fee.

_______ **6.** A new version of a hardware or software product designed to replace an older version of the same product.

_______ **7.** A type of storage that allows for the permanent storage of programs, data, and information

_______ **8.** An electronic board that can be inserted into a personal computer to provide additional capabilities.

_______ **9.** An electronic device that enables a computer to transmit data over telephone lines.

_______ **10.** An electronic board installed inside a personal computer that allows you hear sounds available at some Web sites, as well as sounds available on many CD-ROM disks.

Review Questions

1. Define the following terms:

   a. megahertz

   b. modem

   c.   add-on board

   d.   sound board

   e.   download

   f.   browser

   g.   search engine

   h.   setup package

2. List five things you should do before making a commitment to becoming an Internet subscriber and user.

3. Identify and explain the computer hardware you will need to connect to the Internet.

4. Identify some useful features that should be included in an Internet browser. How do a browser and a search engine differ?

Activities

1. This chapter contains information about your commitment as an Internet user. Using the information provided and information from other sources, prepare a list of obligations that you believe you and other Internet users have.

2. Visit a computer store in your area and talk with a salesperson. Ask the salesperson to explain the basic hardware and software you need to access the Internet. Prepare a written list of the devices and software you need. Find out if the store offers training courses for learning to access and use the Internet.

3. Written procedures are important for computer users. Prepare a written list of the steps you must follow to access the Internet using a computer in the computer lab at your school.

4. Newspapers, including *USA Today,* contain Web sites you can visit to obtain information pertaining to job vacancies. Visit three of the sites advertised, and identify at least three jobs for which you will be qualified after you graduate.

5. This is a group project for three or four team members. Several commercial online services are available today. Each member of the group will select one of the available services and prepare a written report on it. Each report should include the name of the student who prepared it. When all reports are completed, they will be combined into a final report and turned in to the instructor as a group report. Each individual report will include the following minimum information:

   a.   Provide the name and URL address of the commercial online service company investigated.

   b.   List the types of services offered by the company and the cost of each service.

   c.   Indicate the nearest telephone connection line available. If a local phone number is unavailable, indicate the nearest long-distance number.

   d.   Provide the number of connect hours available at the base rate.

e. If access time is limited at the base rate (for example, twenty hours per month), indicate the amount of the surcharge (extra charge) for each additional hour above the twenty-hour limitation.

f. Indicate the fastest modem speed available with the company you are investigating.

CHAPTER THREE

Navigating the Internet and the World Wide Web

The World Wide Web: Growth and Popularity
The Art of Navigating
How the World Wide Web Works: An Overview
Using a Keyboard and Mouse
Protocols: Standards for Communications
Internet Addresses: What They Are and How They Work
  Uniform Resource Locators (URLs)
  Domains
  Examples of Addresses
Navigational Software

Starting Your Browser
Browser Windows
  The Netscape Navigator Window
  The Internet Explorer Window
How a Browser Works
Using a Browser
Web Sites
  Home Pages
  Web Pages
  Hypertext Links
Bookmarks
Structure of Web Sites
  Hypertext Markup Language (HTML)

Virtual Reality Modeling Language (VRML)
Some Popular Web Browsers
Other Internet and Web Activities
  Electronic Mail
  Internet Relay Chat
  Internet Telephone
Summary
Key Terms
End-of-Chapter Activities
  Matching
  Review Questions
  Activities

AFTER COMPLETING THIS CHAPTER, YOU WILL:

1. Explain the growth and popularity of the World Wide Web.

2. Explain how the World Wide Web works.

3. Explain why it is important for an Internet user to be proficient in the use of a keyboard and a mouse.

4. Explain what communications protocols are and why they are important for sending and receiving information across the Internet.

5. Describe the importance of Internet addresses, explain how they work, and give some examples of them.

6. Explain the procedure for starting the browser you are using to access sites on the World Wide Web.

7. Explain how a browser works and identify some of the features of the browser you are using, including menus, buttons, and bookmarks.

8. Describe a typical Web site including the site's home page, Web pages, and links to other Web sites and pages.

9. Tell what bookmarks or favorites are and explain why they can be particularly useful to a user.

10. Identify and discuss other Internet and Web activities, including e-mail, Internet relay chat, and Internet telephone.

The World Wide Web: Growth and Popularity

The World Wide Web, first introduced in 1991, makes it possible for organizations and companies to make certain kinds of information on their networks available to the public. The World Wide Web is a subset of the Internet and is, therefore, smaller than the Internet.

Since its introduction, both interest and usage in the Internet and World Wide Web have grown at a phenomenal rate. In a single day, millions of users access the Internet and visit Web sites. Each destination on the World Wide Web, called a **Web site,** contains useful information that, until recently, was unavailable. The Web allows a user to connect from one place to another. One visit to a Web site is called a **hit.**

The number of Internet and Web users is steadily growing at a rate of about 10 percent per month. The number of hits at a particular Web site ranges from a few to millions. On July 4, 1997, NASA's tiny robot *Sojourner* landed on the planet Mars. The robot and its mother spacecraft, *Pathfinder,* began sending pictures of Mars' surface back to Earth and stored them on servers at NASA, at the Jet Propulsion Laboratory, and at other designated sites, called mirror sites. Within two days, there were more than 100 million hits at these sites by users wanting to see photographs of the planet's surface and environment. Sometimes an organization, such as NASA, wants to make more information (such as photographs) available for public viewing than it can store on its own network. In this type of

FIGURE 3.1

Photograph of Mars

More than 100 million attempts (hits) were made to see photographs of Mars. Pictures like this enable scientists to learn more about the planet Mars, including its origin and history. The popularity of NASA's Web sites increased dramatically during the period of July 4–6, 1997.

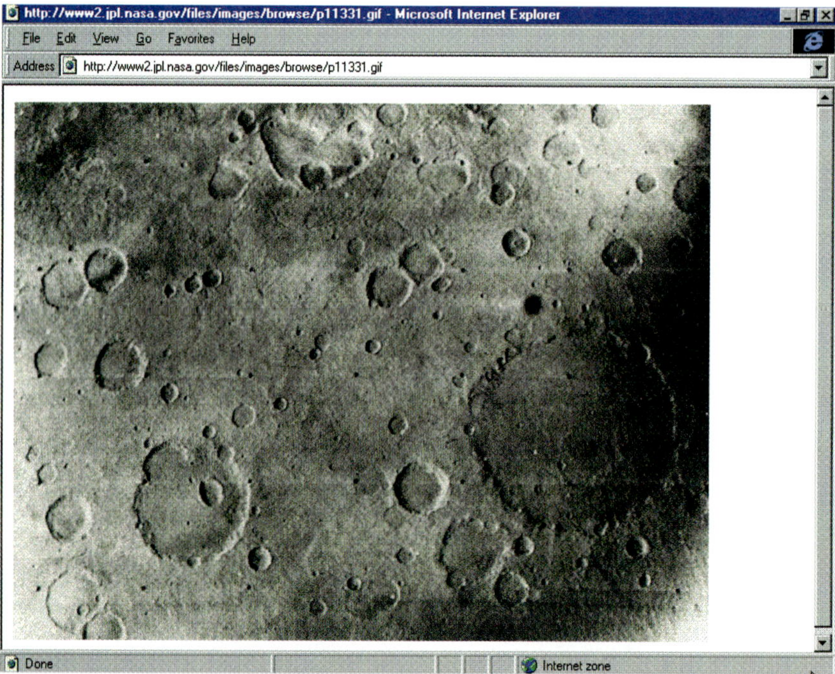

FIGURE 3.2

Selected Web Site Capacities

Sites on the World Wide Web are limited in how many users they can accommodate. However, many sites can handle a large number of hits per day. Some sites, including those in the table, have established sites dedicated to pictures taken on Mars.

Load Capacity of Selected Sites

SITE	SITE ADDRESS	(HITS/DAY)
Silicon Graphics, Inc.	http://mars.sgi.com	20,000,000
Digital Equipment Corporation	http://entertainment. digital.com/mars/JPL	15,000,000
CompuServe	http://mars.compuserve.com	10,000,000
Sun Microsystems	http://www.sun.com/mars	6,000,000
NASA's Jet Propulsion Lab	http://mpfwww.jpl.nasa.gov	5,000,000
National Center for Atmospheric Res.	http://www.mars.ucar.edu	4,000,000
NASA, Ames	http://mpfwww.arc.nasa.gov	3,000,000
Netscape Communications Corporation	http://home.netscape.com	66,000,000

situation, the organization will store some information at its own Web site and the remaining information at other Web sites, called **mirror sites,** that are available for use by the organization. Because NASA wanted to make thousands of photographs available for viewing, some photographs were stored at NASA's Web site and other photographs were stored at the Jet Propulsion Laboratory Web site (mirror site). Figure 3.1 shows one of the photographs sent back to Earth that is available at NASA's Jet Propulsion Laboratory Web site that served as a mirror site.

Although the number of hits a particular Web site can handle each day is limited, many sites have the capacity to handle many users. Figure 3.2 shows the capacity of selected Web sites.

The popularity of individual sites on the Web varies from time to time. Special events such as NASA's landing on Mars in late 1997 create interest that often results in a large number of hits in a relatively short period. However, interest in most sites remains relatively stable.

Where can you find popular Internet addresses? They are available from many sources—newspapers, magazines, television, books, and even the Internet itself. Sites featuring new movies and TV shows are frequently listed in newspapers and on TV. Directories of Internet addresses are available in bookstores. Teachers, classmates, and friends are good sources for addresses.

The Art of Navigating

Once you're connected to the Internet you can begin navigating through cyberspace to thousands of interesting and even fascinating destinations. Navigating the Net is an art that can be mastered quickly after you learn a few basics and gain a little experience. Navigating is not only fun, but also educational.

The Field Museum of Natural History

The World Wide Web offers thousands of interesting places you can visit. Here we see the home page of the Field Museum, a Web site visited each year by thousands of users seeking to learn about its offerings.

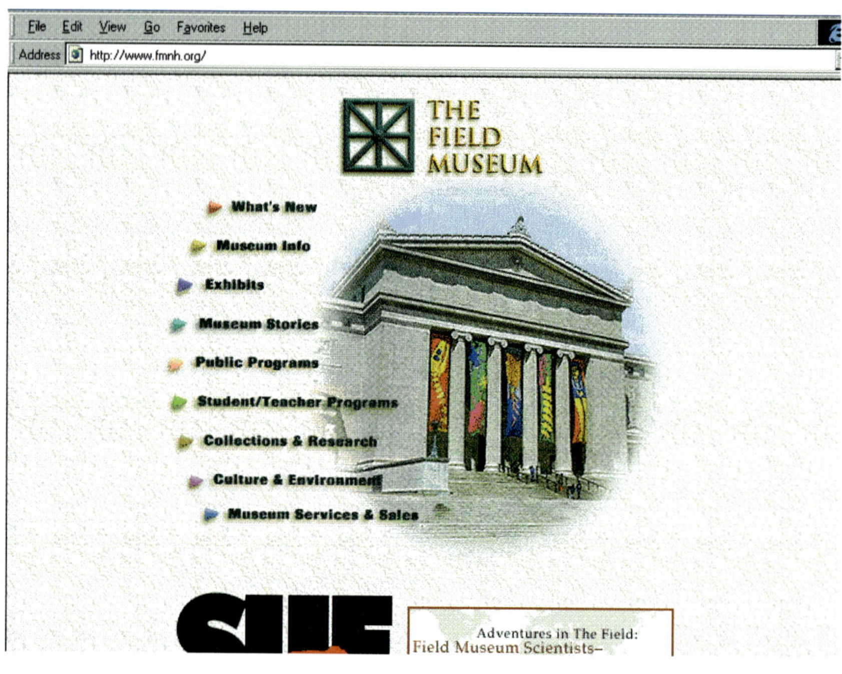

As you navigate the Web, you can visit a variety of different sites. You can tour the White House to see pictures of various rooms, to learn the history of each room, and to get the latest information about activities involving the president, vice president, and first family. You can visit Web sites of government departments and agencies to learn what they are doing to serve public interests.

Many newspapers and magazines offer Web sites where you can retrieve articles on a variety of topics. Commercial organizations have Web sites that allow you to learn about new products and services, such as computers and software products. Museum sites, including the Smithsonian Institute and Chicago's Field Museum of Natural History, allow you to tour the facilities, see pictures of rare objects, and read about their offerings. You can enjoy rare paintings at the Louvre in Paris. Other Web sites are equally interesting and enjoyable.

The Internet offers much more than interesting Web sites. You can use the Internet to send and receive electronic mail messages, chat with other people whose interests are similar to yours, and access large computer networks. In essence, the Internet opens up virtually unlimited opportunities to explore our world. With a PC and an Internet connection, you can travel through **cyberspace,** a term that refers to the invisible realm of the Internet universe. As you navigate through cyberspace, you will be doing what is called **surfing the Net.** As you become an accomplished Internet explorer, or **Internaut,** you will want to use as many of the services and resources as you have available to you.

In this chapter, we will visit several interesting Web sites. The activities at the end of the chapter will allow you to visit others.

The New Netscape Navigator 4.0

Netscape Communications Inc. took the early lead in Web browsers a few years ago when the company introduced its first version of Netscape Navigator—a lead that it has maintained over its nearest rival, Microsoft's Internet Explorer. With each successive version, Netscape has added new and useful features to Navigator and has made the program easy to learn and use.

The newest version of Navigator (4.0) has been updated and improved for greater ease of use. Small programs that add functionality to Navigator, called plug-ins, are now downloaded and installed automatically so that they work immediately without the user having to do anything. New tools make access to favorite sites easy and allow users to perform searches with a single click.

Navigator 4.0 contains many new and improved features. It includes open standards-based security features to protect information such as credit card numbers and personal financial data. The user can customize the toolbar. Bookmarks for identifying and accessing favorite Web pages are easier to use. The Search button provides a direct link to several of the Internet's search engines. The Places button takes the user directly to the Internet's site directory. Navigator 4.0 comes with the most popular multimedia plug-ins. The plug-ins are automatically installed and configured by a program called SmartUpdate. Support automatically allows access to ActiveX applications, such as Microsoft Office, from within a Navigator window.

In short, Navigator 4.0 offers many new and useful features over earlier versions. With this newest version of Navigator, Netscape will likely retain its enviable market position as the most popular browser currently available.

To visit Web sites, you first need to acquire some basic understanding of the Web. In the following sections, we provide information that will help you begin your voyage through cyberspace to new and exciting destinations.

How the World Wide Web Works: An Overview

The World Wide Web, or simply the Web, is the fastest growing part of the Internet. When browsing the Web, you can view home pages consisting of text, graphics, and multimedia that includes video and sound. Hypertext links, or links, used by the Web enable you to jump from place to place on it. The Web uses a language called Hypertext Markup Language (HTML) that allows you to view Web pages.

The World Wide Web works on a **client-server model** in which client software called a browser runs on the user's personal computer and **server software** runs on the host (server) computer. The user first makes a connection to the Internet and then activates the browser.

In the designated area of the browser, the user types the address, called the **URL** (short for **Uniform Resource Locator** and pronounced "earl"), for the location the user wants to visit. The request is sent to the Internet, where **Internet routers** examine it to determine the specific Web server to which it is to be sent. The Web server receives the request and uses HTTP protocol (explained later) to determine which page, file, or object is being requested. On finding the requested home page, file, or object, the server sends it back to the client's computer, where it is displayed on the client's computer screen.

Illustration of How the Web Works

The Web works on a client-server model. Using a Web browser, a request is sent from the user's computer (client) to the Internet. An Internet router forwards the request to the Web server where the document is stored. The Web server then sends the document back to the client's computer, where the browser displays the document on the user's screen.

Using a Keyboard and Mouse

You may already be an experienced personal computer user and know that two common input devices are the keyboard and the mouse. Both devices are used frequently with the Internet and the World Wide Web.

Recall that a **keyboard** is a typewriter-like device used to enter data that is temporarily stored in the computer's primary storage and displayed on the screen. A **mouse** is a pointing device used to select options or other information displayed on the screen. By moving the mouse horizontally about on the desk surface, a small symbol called a **pointer** moves around the screen. The pointer is often the shape of an arrow. The procedure of moving the mouse so that the pointer is touching an object is called pointing. Pointing to and then pressing a button on the mouse—called **clicking**—allows you to select the text or icon at which you are pointing. An **icon** is a picture representing an activity or an object, such as a printer, trashcan, or software program.

Using a mouse requires that you are using a computer with a **graphical user interface (GUI),** which was explained in Chapter Two. Today, most personal computers are equipped with a graphical user interface, a keyboard, and a mouse.

FIGURE 3.5

The NASA Home Page

After the Web server retrieves a request, the server accesses the document or file and sends it back to the client computer, where it is displayed on the client's screen.

The keyboard and mouse are used frequently with the Internet and Web, and you should become proficient in using both of these devices. You will need to use the keyboard to type information, and you have to use the mouse to select objects or information.

Protocols: Standards for Communications

A **protocol** is a set of rules and procedures for exchanging information between computers. Protocols are software programs that define how computers interact, or communicate, with each other and how errors are detected. Fortunately, a user is not required to perform complex tasks to use protocols. Internet service providers or online services provide the necessary protocols for Web use. However, users should be aware of the importance of protocols to the Internet and World Wide Web.

Over the years, numerous protocols have been developed. Efforts are currently under way to simplify protocols by establishing standards that all computer and communications equipment manufacturers will follow. Based in Geneva, Switzerland, the International Standards Organization has defined a set of communications protocols called the **Open Systems Interconnection (OSI)** model.

A Personal Computer System

A keyboard and a mouse are two essential input devices for use with the Internet and World Wide Web. A keyboard allows the user to type information, and a mouse allows the user to select objects and information displayed on the screen.

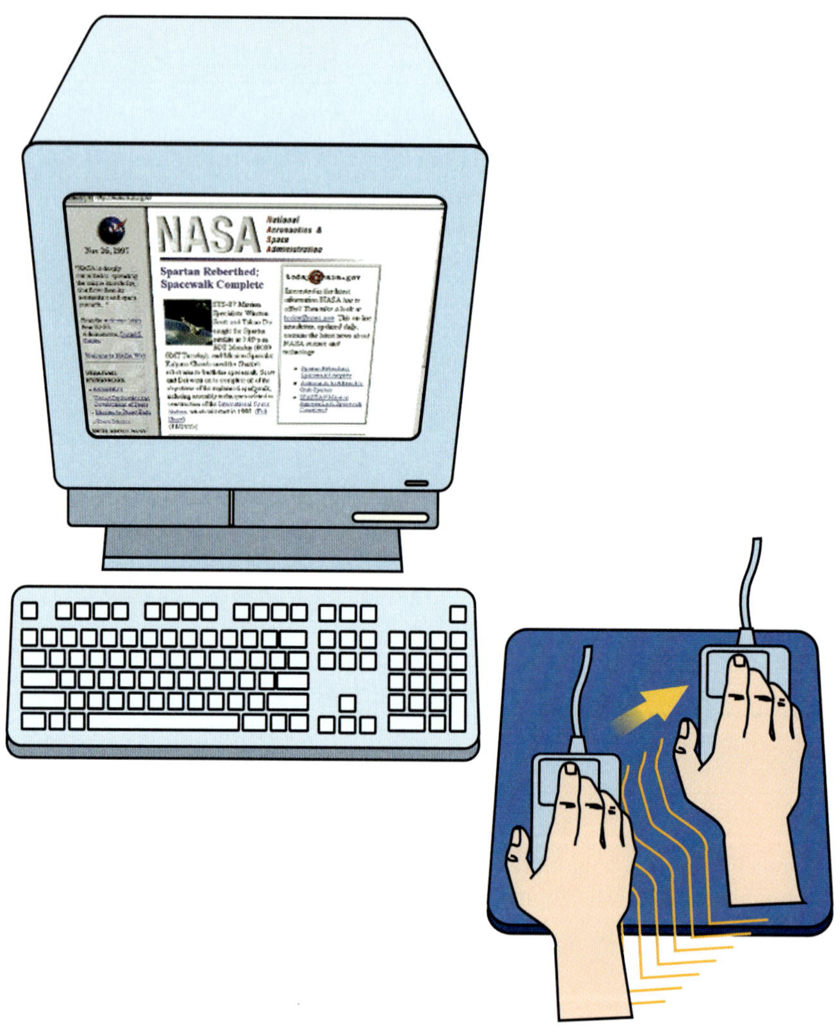

The United Nations has adopted the OSI model. However, unless and until all manufacturers adopt OSI, a variety of protocols will remain in use. Figure 3.7 shows a sample of communications protocols now being used.

Internet Addresses: What They Are and How They Work

An easy way to understand an Internet address is to first think of an address you might place on an envelope containing a letter to another person. A typical address would include the other person's name, address, city, state, and zip code. A hypothetical address is shown in Figure 3.8.

The postal service understands the address and will use it to deliver the letter to the correct address. The letter in the illustration is first sent to a postal distribution

FIGURE 3.7
Some Commonly Used Protocols

A variety of communications protocols are currently being used for exchanging information among computers and networks.

TYPE OF PROTOCOL	DESCRIPTION
ATM	Abbreviation for Asynchronous Transfer Mode. This recently developed protocol allows for the transmission of data, voice, and video over any other type of communication.
Ethernet	A widely used protocol for local area networks.
Token Ring	A local area network protocol that allows only one computer at a time to transmit.
PowerTalk	A protocol that links Apple Macintosh computers.
FDDI	Abbreviation for Fiber Distributed Data Interface. This protocol provides for high-speed transfer of data over fiber-optic cable.
SNA	Abbreviation for System Network Architecture. A protocol for linking large computers.
TCP/IP	Abbreviation for Transmission Control Protocol/ Internet Protocol. This protocol is used with the Internet.
HTTP	Abbreviation for HyperText Transfer Protocol. HTTP is a protocol used by the World Wide Web for transferring pages from the host computer (called the server) to a user's computer (called the client). The protocol is typed in lowercase as http, and followed by a colon, two slashes, and the letters "www," and a period.
PPP	Abbreviation for Point-to-Point Protocol. This is a good protocol that allows a personal computer with a modem to access the Internet.

FIGURE 3.8
Address of Letter to Another Person

An e-mail address and an Internet address achieve the same purpose as a mailing address. To access information located at a specific site, a user types the address in the designated location.

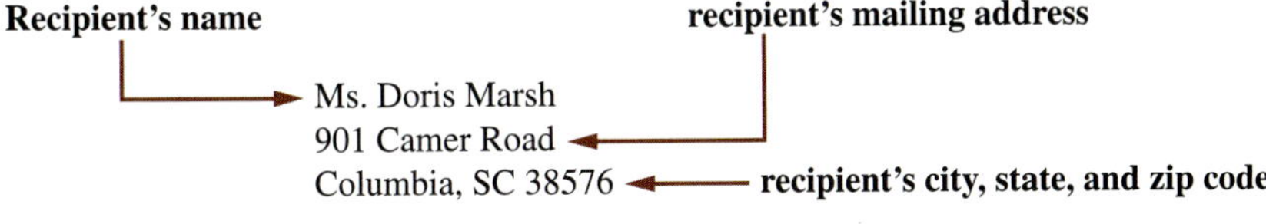

center in Columbia, South Carolina, where all incoming mail is sorted by city location. In this case, Ms. Marsh's letter will be placed into a group of letters for delivery to homes located on Camber Road. A mail carrier will deliver the letter to 901 Camber Road to be retrieved from the mailbox by Ms. Marsh.

Internet addresses achieve the same purpose. On the Internet and World Wide Web, you can specify the exact location of the site you want to visit. To send an electronic message you must specify correctly the address of the person you want to receive your message.

Uniform Resource Locators (URLs)

Internet Web sites and links to Web pages are usually located by entering a Uniform Resource Locator (URL) in the designated box. A Web-site address is somewhat similar to an address placed on an envelope containing a message to another person. (You might want to refer back to Figure 3.8). To access a particular Web site, all you need to do is to type the correct URL in the specified area of your Web browser's screen, as shown in Figure 3.9. Your browser will access the site's home page and display it on your screen.

FIGURE 3.9
An Internet Address (URL)

Typing the correct address, or URL, in the specified location of your browser will enable you to retrieve the Web page you want to view.

Most Web pages use a protocol called **HTTP,** which stands for **Hypertext Transfer Protocol,** for transferring data from the host computer to your computer. Many addresses are typed in lowercase as http and are followed by a colon, two slashes, the letters "www" and a period. However, not all Web addresses require that the letters "www" be typed as a part of the address. For example, the address for Netscape's home page is "http://home.netscape.com." There are also other address formats for Internet addresses and Web sites.

The second part of the address is the **domain** name, which is the Internet address of the computer where the Web page is located. The domain name includes periods and may be followed by a slash, as shown below.

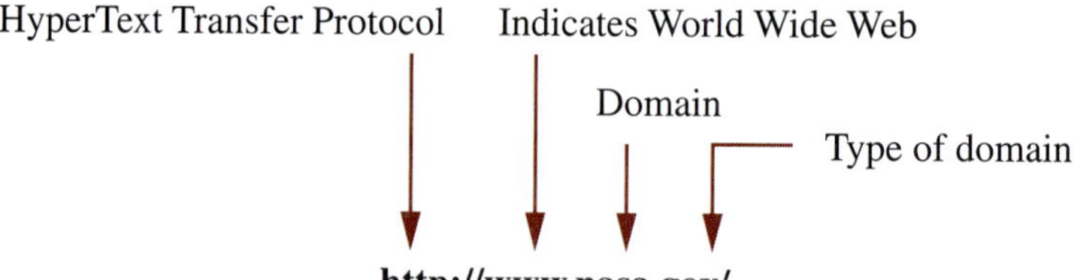

The third part of the address, which is optional, is the file specification. The **file specification** is the name of a particular file or file folder. At some Web sites a vast amount of information is available for retrieval and viewing. At these sites, information is often arranged and stored in folders, just as you might store information in a file cabinet. If you know the name of the particular file you are seeking, or the name of the folder containing the information, accessing the information is easier and faster.

Domain specifications can be fairly lengthy in situations where you want to access specific Web pages. For example, to retrieve a specific photograph of the surface of Mars from the NASA Web site, you can do so by typing the following URL: http://www.jpl.nasa.gov/marsnews.img/80815.gif

In the example, the folder name is "marsnews.img" and the specific photograph is number "80815.gif". Unless you know the file or folder containing the photograph, you would likely have to search through several photographs to find the one you want.

Domains

A **top-level domain** indicates to what the address belongs: a commercial company, a department or agency of the government, or an educational institution. Figure 3.10 shows various top-level domains used on the Internet.

FIGURE 3.10

Examples of Top-Level Domains

Domains are included in Internet addresses to identify the type of site. For example, "edu" typed as part of the domain indicates the site is an educational institution.

DOMAIN	DESCRIPTION	EXAMPLES
gov	Federal, state, and local government entities	the U.S. Department of the Interior, the White House, the FBI
edu	Educational institutions	a college or university
com	Commercial entities	Dryden Press, Microsoft Corporation, Ford Motor Company
net	Network service providers	Bestweb Service Provider
org	Nonprofit organizations	Public Broadcasting Services
mil	Military organizations	U.S. Army, U.S. Navy

All addresses have a location designation, such as "uk" for United Kingdom and "ca" for Canada. However, many addresses in the United States may ignore it. For example, "http://www.duke.edu" is the address for Duke University (a university in the United States), but you are not required to type the letters "us" as part of the address.

Examples of Addresses

Now that we've examined Internet addresses, let's look at some examples. Recall that some addresses consist of the protocol http followed by a colon, two slashes, the letters www, a period, and finally the domain. In the following examples, we will visit different sites. Notice the address typed in the specified area and the page that appears on the screen.

Navigational Software

Earlier you learned that a browser can be used to access Internet resources. Software other than browsers, such as Microsoft's Office 97, can also be used for this purpose.

A **browser** is a navigational software tool (program) that makes it easy to find and display Web pages by interpreting the complex commands used to create the

FIGURE 3.11
Sample Addresses

By typing the specific address in the designated area, the home page appears on your screen.

NASA home page

Duke University home page

United States Navy home page

PBS home page

Major League Baseball home page

pages. Using a browser, you can navigate the Web easily and quickly, just as you might browse through library stacks or stores in a shopping mall.

Today, the two most popular Internet browsers are **Netscape Navigator** from Netscape Communications Corporation and **Internet Explorer** from Microsoft Corporation. Netscape's newest browser, Netscape Navigator (version 4.0), was introduced in June 1997. It is a part of Netscape's Communicator software package. A new version of Internet Explorer was recently introduced as well.

Since Netscape Navigator and Internet Explorer are the two most popular browsers, most of the illustrations in the following sections use them.

Most browsers are designed to work with a graphical user interface such as Microsoft's Windows 95 or Macintosh Windows. Just as a graphical user interface makes using your computer easier by allowing you to just point and click to make your selections, browsers make using the Internet and World Wide Web easier. If a browser icon was placed on your computer desktop when the browser was installed, clicking on the icon can activate it.

Starting Your Browser

Starting your browser is a relatively simple and easy task. Before you can start your browser, the desktop screen must be displayed. On most personal computers,

The Internet and You: Careers & Opportunities

Web Page Designer

One of the fastest-growing and most interesting career opportunities today is that of Web page designer. Many businesses and organizations are recruiting individuals who can design attractive and informative Web pages that contain information and graphics on topics such as company products and services, college and university programs, and organizational services. Many businesses and organizations employ their own Web page designers who create such pages and update existing ones as needed. Others have turned to private companies that employ a staff of Web page designers who can design, construct, and maintain Web pages for their clients.

Many colleges and universities now offer programs and courses in this field. In addition to courses in computer concepts and the Internet, students typically complete courses in word processing, computer graphics, multimedia applications, and Internet programming languages, such as Java and Hypertext Markup Language. There are also other ways to obtain the training needed to become a Web page designer. Training facilities around the country and computer retailers offer intensive training courses that a student can complete in a few days. A Web page designer should possess excellent typing skills, be creative, and should be self-motivated. Professional Web page designers often work independently of others and with a minimum of supervision. Many are self-employed professionals who contract with businesses and other organizations to design Web pages according to the specifications and requirements determined by the customer.

The relative scarcity of well-trained and experienced Web page designers, and the high demand for their services, allows these professionals to earn lucrative salaries and enjoy a variety of employment opportunities.

Netscape Communicator Software Package

Netscape Navigator is a popular browser. After you're connected to the Internet and have installed the software on your computer, you're ready to begin visiting interesting Web sites on the Internet.

Netscape Navigator's Shortcut Icon

After double-clicking on the browser icon, the browser's home page appears on your screen.

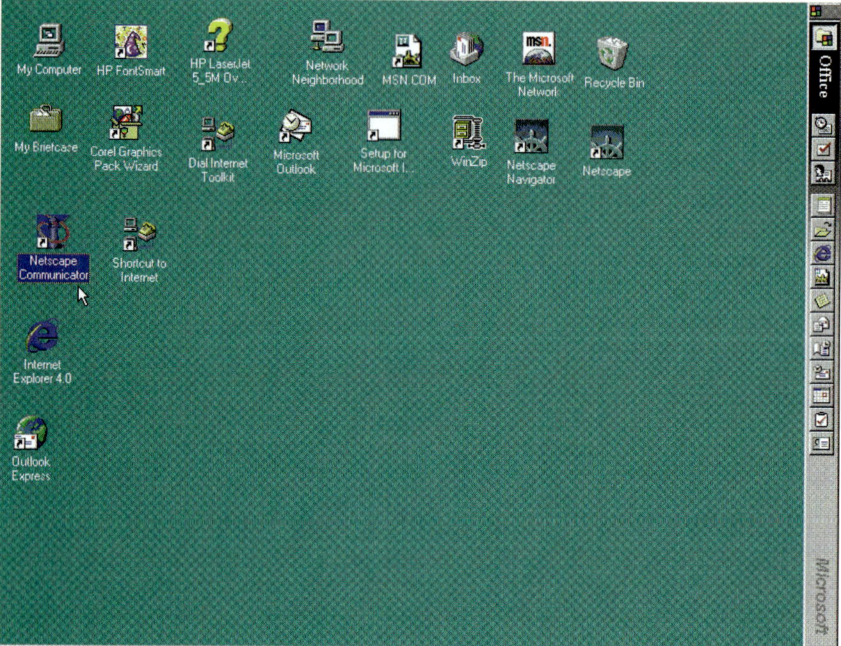

the program you are using, such as Microsoft Windows, is activated when the computer is turned on. Once the desktop screen is displayed, you can start your browser by simply **double-clicking** on the browser icon; that is, by positioning the pointer on the **browser icon** and pressing a mouse button twice. Another icon, perhaps

FIGURE 3.14

Netscape Navigator Home Page

After double-clicking on the browser icon, the browser's home page appears on your screen.

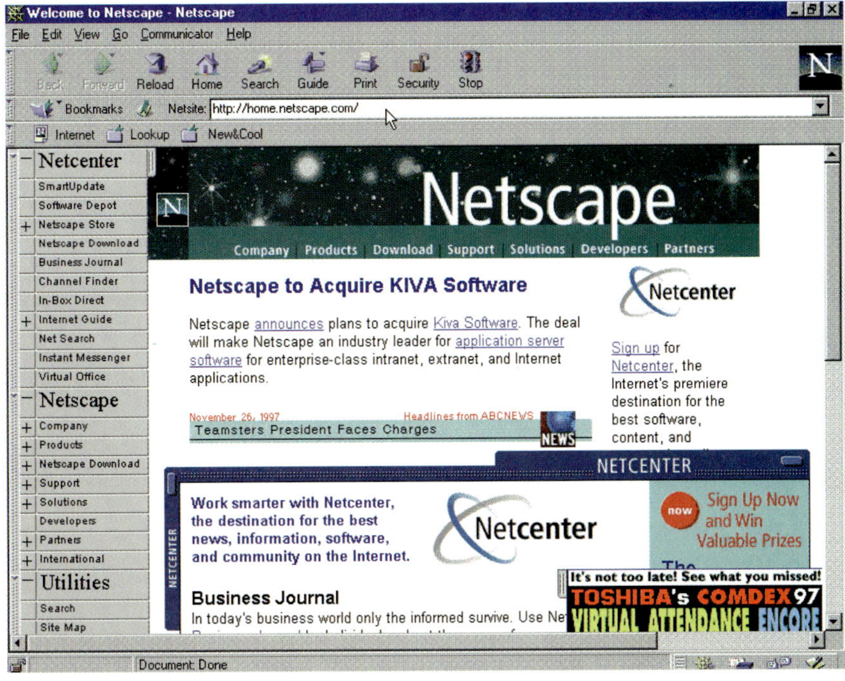

resembling an hourglass, will appear. This indicates that the browser is being loaded into your computer. In a few seconds, the browser's home page will appear on the screen.

Browser Windows

Earlier you learned that Netscape Navigator and Microsoft's Internet Explorer are currently the two most popular Web browsers. For this reason, we will examine the home page of Navigator and Explorer to learn some of the features available with them. First we examine Navigator's home page and then Explorer's. If you will be using a different browser, you can learn about its features from the manual or from your instructor.

Some Web pages may contain links to other pages, files, or resources. For example, a home page may include a link to the company that will allow you to download a new version of the browser to your computer. At this point, we are not concerned with links, but with the title page itself.

The Netscape Navigator Window

The following explanation is based on Netscape Navigator 4.0, the newest version available. If you will be using an earlier version, the Netscape Navigator window you see might appear somewhat different.

The top bar of Navigator displays the title of a Web page. Navigator's home page, for example, displays the message *Welcome to Netscape*.

Immediately below the title of the page is the menu bar. The **menu bar** includes available options, each with pull-down menus, and works like the menu bars in word processing and spreadsheet programs.

Below the menu bar is the **Navigation toolbar,** which allows the user to perform tasks by clicking on one of the **buttons.** This is usually a faster method than using the menu bar**.** For example, selecting the Print button causes the displayed page to be printed. Printed on each button is a word or icon that identifies the button's function, as can be seen in Figure 3.15.

FIGURE 3.15

Netscape Navigator Toolbar

Frequently performed tasks can be performed more quickly by selecting the appropriate button on the toolbar.

The Search button allows you to begin a search for information on the Internet. The Guide button directs you to some interesting places on the Internet. Clicking the Security button displays security data about information being accessed.

Below the Navigation toolbar is the **location text box** for entering the address of the desired location (Figure 3.16). To go to the desired site, you must type the Uniform Resource Locator (URL) in the box labeled "Netsite" and then either press the Enter key or click on the Open button on the tool bar. The URL is updated automatically as the user goes from page to page at a particular site.

FIGURE 3.16

Navigator's Location Text Box

Netscape Navigator's location text box is used for typing the URL of the desired Web site the user wants to visit. An URL is automatically updated as the user moves from page to page at the site.

Below the location text box is the personal toolbar containing a group of directory buttons for the user to access some of the new and interesting pages. Selecting the New&Cool button causes Netscape to display a two-item menu. The What's New item contains links to some of the newer Web pages. Selecting the What's Cool item causes Netscape to display links to some unique and interesting Web pages. Both the What's New and the What's Cool pages are updated frequently by Netscape Communications Corporation as more pages become available. Some pages that are available on a given day might not be available a day or two later.

Navigator's Directory Buttons

The Netscape Navigator browser uses directory buttons for the user to access new and interesting pages. Other browsers have similar buttons.

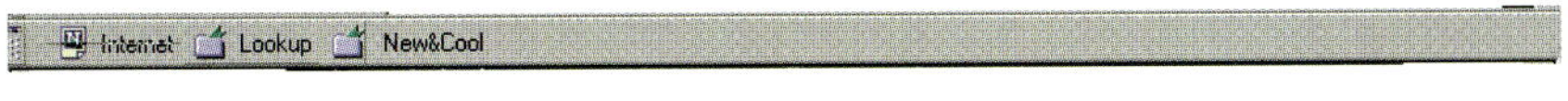

The large area below the directory buttons is the **display area.** When Navigator is first activated, the Netscape home page is displayed in this area. The home page contains current information from Netscape Communications Corporation and links to other pages. As new Netscape products and upgrades become available, they are identified on Netscape's home page and can be downloaded by selecting a designated link and following the instructions displayed on the screen. When other sites are visited, pages from these sites are displayed.

Navigator's Display Area

The current page of a document can be viewed in the display. As the user moves from page to page, or from Web site to Web site, the page(s) displayed will change.

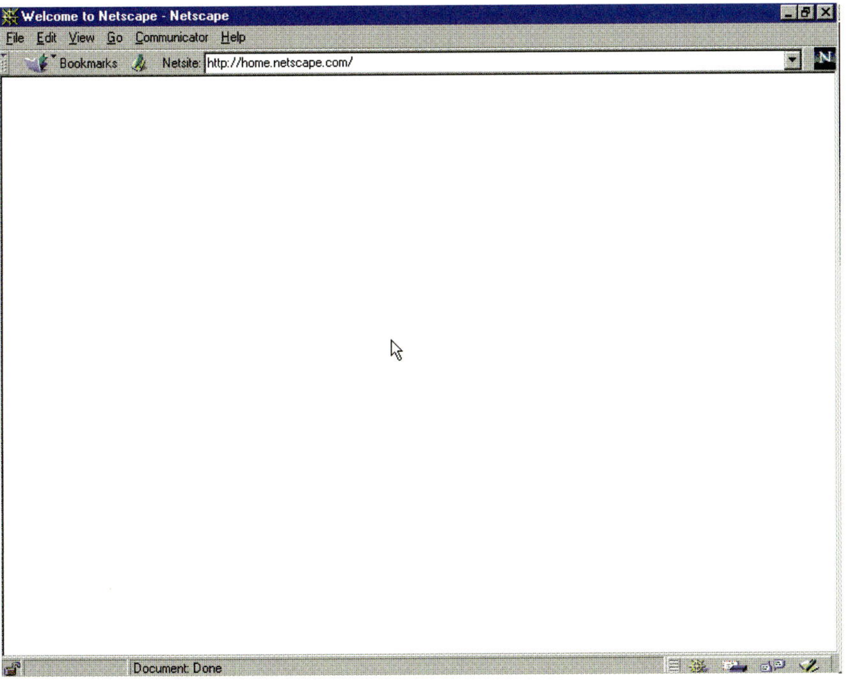

Below the display area at the right is a group of buttons that allow you to quickly access other applications. The first button, which resembles a ship's steering wheel, is the button you can click to access Netscape Navigator. The next button to the right, which resembles a small envelope, allows you easy access to your mailbox so you can read your electronic mail messages. The next button provides access to any discussion groups to which you may belong. The last button in this group allows you to compose a document. In the lower left corner is a button that resembles a lock. An open lock indicates that the information you want to access is unlocked and is therefore available to you. A closed lock indicates that the information is unavailable.

Netscape Navigator is a powerful and full-featured browser. Here, only a few features were explained. Appendix A contains a more detailed explanation of Netscape Navigator and how it can be used to explore the World Wide Web. If you will be using Netscape Navigator, you should study Appendix A carefully.

The Internet Explorer Window

There are similarities and differences between Navigator's home page and Explorer's home page. For example, both home pages often contain links to other pages, files, or resources.

Explorer's top bar displays the title of a Web page currently being displayed on your screen. If you switch to another Web site, the title of the page of that site is displayed.

Immediately below the title of the page is the menu bar. The menu bar includes available options, each with pull-down menus, and works like other program menu bars.

Below the menu bar is the **toolbar,** which allows you to perform tasks quickly by simply clicking on one of the buttons. For example, clicking on the Print button causes the displayed page to be printed. Clicking on the History button displays a list of Web pages previously accessed. Printed on each button are a word and an icon that describe its function, as shown in Figure 3.19.

FIGURE 3.19

Internet Explorer Toolbar Buttons

Explorer's toolbar buttons enable a user to easily perform tasks such as printing a Web document or page.

Below the toolbar is the **Address box** for entering the address of the desired location (Figure 3.20). To go to the desired site, you need to type the Uniform Resource Locator (URL) in the box and then press the Enter key. The URL is updated automatically as the user goes from page to page at a particular site.

FIGURE 3.20

Internet Explorer Address Box

Using Internet Explorer, you can visit a Web site by typing the URL for the site in the address box and then pressing the *Enter* key.

FIGURE 3.21

Internet Explorer Display Area

When a Web document or page is accessed, it is displayed in the display area.

Below the Address box is the Links bar, which includes preselected links to a few Microsoft pages. Included are links to Best of the Web pages, The Microsoft Network, and Product News about Microsoft products. Internet Explorer allows you to add links of your own to the Links bar.

The large area below the Address box is the display area. When Explorer is first activated, the home page of your online service or service provider is displayed in this area. The home page contains current information from the service or provider as well as possible links to other pages. As new products and upgrades become available, they may be identified on the service's or provider's home page and can be downloaded by selecting a designated link and following the instructions displayed on the screen. When other sites are visited, pages from these sites are displayed.

Like Netscape Navigator, Internet Explorer is a powerful and full-featured browser. Here, only a few features were explained. Appendix B contains a more detailed explanation of Explorer and how it can be used to explore the World Wide Web. If you will be using this browser, you should study Appendix B carefully.

How a Browser Works

A **Web browser** is a client software program your computer uses to display Web pages. Browsers are available for IBM-compatible PCs, Apple's Macintosh computers, and for computers using the UNIX operating system. Your browser displays information on your screen by interpreting the Hypertext Markup Language (HTML) that is used to create Web pages. A displayed home page, as well as other pages at a particular Web site, typically contains links to other document pages, other files, and other Internet resources.

Codes in HTML files determine how your browser displays the text, graphics, links, and multimedia files on a home page. The codes contain references to the text, graphics, and files you want to retrieve. Your browser uses the codes to find the files on the Web server, and then displays them on the home page.

If a page contains links to other Web sites, files, or resources, you can click on a link to have your browser retrieve the specified information. If a link specifies a file to be downloaded, clicking on it will instruct your browser to copy it to your computer.

Using a Browser

Web browsers are relatively easy to learn and use. If you purchase a browser software package at a retailer, the package includes a user manual that contains detailed instructions for using the browser. If a browser or an upgraded version is downloaded from the manufacturer, instructions can also be downloaded. If a user manual or instructions are not available, books containing information about the browser and how to use it are available from a variety of sources, including publishing companies and bookstores.

Earlier in the chapter you learned that a browser installed on a computer using a graphical user interface (GUI) sometimes places an icon on the screen. In this situation, you can activate the browser by clicking on the browser icon. Once activated, the first page you may see is the home page of the browser manufacturer. The home page of most browsers contains a location text box, or similar area, for typing the URL of a Web site to which the user wants to go.

Web Sites

Web sites differ in the quality and quantity of information offered. Some provide interesting and informative information displayed on beautifully designed pages with links to other valuable information. Other sites are unattractive and present information of little, if any, use. In short, there is a wide disparity among various Web sites and pages. As you travel across the Internet to various sites, you will likely see some sites to which you will want to return later and other sites that you will probably never visit again.

Home Pages

If you have not specified a certain page within a site that you want to see, the first page that will be displayed when you got to the site is the home page. A **home page** typically contains the basic information the company, organization, or agency wants you to see first. A home page is often the most attractive page available at the site, and sometimes it is the only page available. Some home pages contain only text, while others may contain an impressive combination of text, graphics, and animation to hold the attention of visitors. Private companies such as automobile manufacturers and airlines sometimes spend considerable amounts of money developing and maintaining home pages that will capture the attention of users.

Web Pages

Many Web sites provide several pages containing additional information. The information provided on these other pages may be as important as that on the home page, and most new browsers make moving back and forth among pages simple. Special features such as a Forward button and a Back button allow users to move back and forth between pages. Although additional pages are sometimes less attractive than the home page, they are occasionally more impressive. Links shown on the home page of one automobile manufacturer, for instance, direct viewers to other pages containing high-resolution color photographs of various models of the company's automobiles.

Some pages may contain links to other information, pages, or sites. Such links can be particularly useful to view related information. For example, the page of an individual room in the White House contains a link to another page where a viewer can read about the history and furnishings of the room.

A specific site may contain any number of pages. However, the effort and expense of developing, displaying, and updating pages can limit the number of pages available at a site.

Hypertext Links

Documents at a particular Web site may contain **hypermedia;** that is, a combination of text, graphics, video, sound, and animation. Hypermedia is accessed by means of a **hypertext link** (called simply a **link**), which is a special software pointer that points to the location of the computer at which the hypertext can be accessed. A link can make it possible for an Internet user in St. Louis to click on text or a picture that, by means of special software, accesses and displays a document stored on a computer in San Francisco.

Within any document at a particular Web site, any page may provide links to other document pages, other resources, or other Web sites. When a pointer is positioned on a link, the pointer changes to another form, such as a human hand. Clicking on the link retrieves the information indicated and displays it on the screen.

Bookmarks

You've probably already noticed that the URLs of some Web pages can be long and difficult to remember. Because of their length, typing errors are common. For this reason, some browsers provide users with a way to keep track of favorite or frequently visited Web pages. For example, Netscape's Navigator allows a user to permanently store the URLs of these pages in an area called a **bookmark list.** Microsoft's Internet Explorer offers the same feature. However, Internet Explorer's favorite URLs are stored in an area called the Favorites List, and each entry in the list is called a **favorite.**

A **bookmark** or favorite consists of a Web page's title and its URL. A bookmark or favorites list may be thought of as an electronic address book used to store names and addresses. A user can add or delete a bookmark or favorite as needed. Figure 3.22 shows how a typical bookmark list might appear.

Structure of Web Sites

At this point you may be wondering how Web pages containing text and vivid images are created. Web pages are created using one or more special languages

FIGURE 3.22

A Bookmark List

A bookmark list allows a user to keep track of favorite Web pages. A single entry on the list is called a bookmark. Individual bookmarks can be added or deleted from the list.

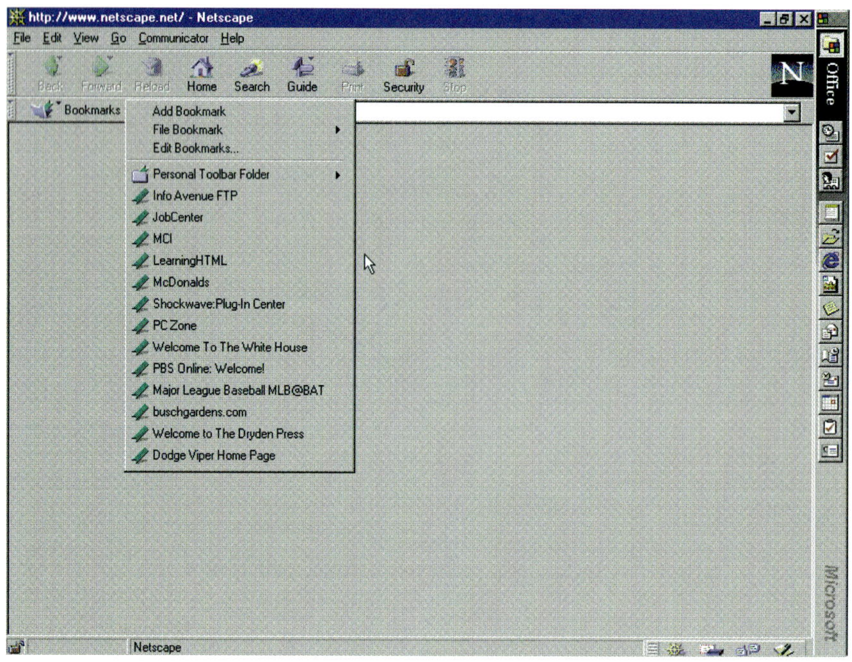

that are briefly described in the following sections. A more thorough description is presented in Chapter Six.

Hypertext Markup Language (HTML)

Web page authors use a language called **HTML** (short for **Hypertext Markup Language**) to create Web pages. The basic information on any page is text. The text on a page is enclosed by special HTML formatting codes and functions that determine the page's features, such as colors and the type and size of fonts. If you want, you can see and read the HTML codes used to create a page by clicking on the View menu and then clicking on Document Source. Figure 3.23 shows a Web page and the HTML used to create the page.

Hypertext Markup Language is similar to the formatting built into a word processor. After learning to use it, you can create your own Web pages and place them on the Web for other users to see.

Virtual Reality Modeling Language (VRML)

A new technology called **virtual reality (VR)** provides for the creation of pages containing lifelike images, graphics, movement, and sound in three-dimensional form.

A special language called **VRML** (**Virtual Reality Modeling Language**) makes it possible to create Web pages in three-dimensional form.

Three-dimensional effects can give you the feeling and sense of being a part of the environment depicted. On the Internet, you can explore many virtual locations

FIGURE 3.23

A Web Page and Its HTML code

(a) Web pages are created using a special language called Hypertext Markup Language (HTML). HTML codes determine exactly how the text and graphics images will look on a page. (b) The HTML codes used to create the Presbyterian College page. Notice the codes surrounding the text.

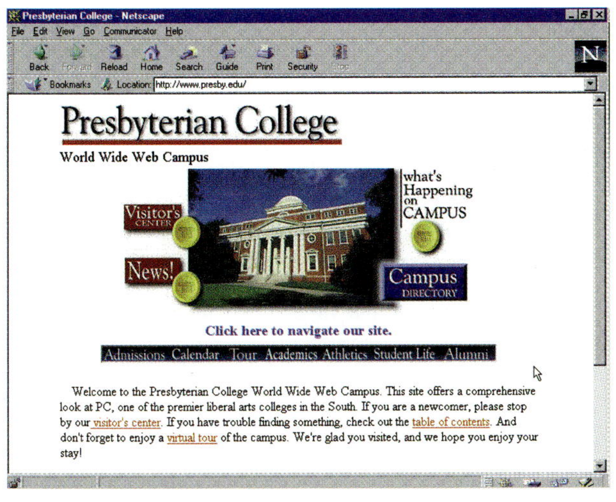

(a)

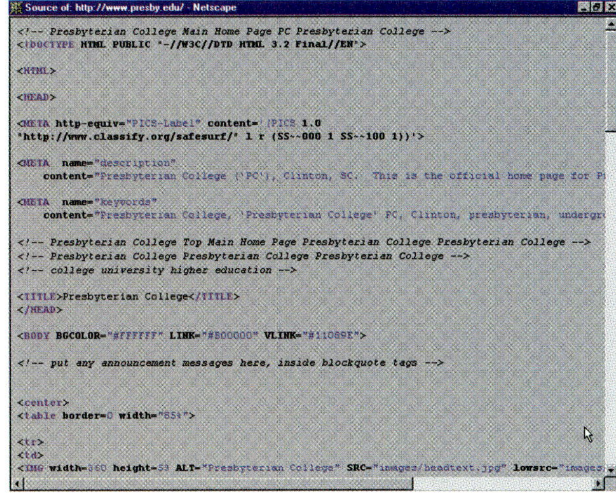

(b)

where you can stroll through buildings, explore the universe, ride in airplanes, or explore the inside of the human body.

To access VR Web sites and view VR pages, you need a virtual reality Web browser. Soon, most new browsers and upgraded versions will likely include this feature. Virtual reality capability is now available as a plug-in to existing browsers. Also, some Web sites offer a limited VR version that is automatically downloaded when you retrieve a virtual reality page.

After a file is downloaded, the VR plug-in creates the virtual world by taking commands in the file and having your computer compute the geometry of the scene. Once the computations are done, the scene will appear on your screen. If a user wants to visit visual worlds on the Web, a VR plug-in will be needed to enjoy the full spectacle of the scenes.

Some Popular Web Browsers

Several popular Web browsers are available that are frequently updated with new features. Not long ago, most browsers were stand-alone software programs with limited features. As the competition among browser manufacturers intensifies, new and useful features and programs are being integrated into what are known as browser suites. A browser suite consists of several programs used with the Internet and Web. For example, individual browsers are available that allow a user to access Web pages, send and receive e-mail, participate in chat groups, use a computer keyboard for making phone calls, and to access newspaper articles— even before the newspaper is printed. One can only imagine the feature-rich and program-rich browser suites that are likely to appear in the near future.

You've learned that the two most popular browsers today are Netscape Communications Corporation's Navigator and Microsoft Corporation's Internet

Explorer. The results of a study by Dataquest reported in the November 24, 1997, issue of *Infoworld* revealed that Netscape Navigator commanded approximately 58 percent of the market, while Internet Explorer's share was approximately 39 percent. The remainder of the market was divided among several lesser-known browsers. Companies with browsing software are in fierce competition to increase the market share of their product.

With their vast financial resources and technological capabilities, Netscape and Microsoft are likely to remain the dominant browser manufacturers in the foreseeable future. Netscape's newest version of Navigator was introduced in June 1997. Microsoft's newest browser version was released in October 1997. Both include new and expanded features that will make browsing even more exciting.

Other Internet and Web Activities

The Internet and World Wide Web offer users a variety of ways to communicate with other individuals and groups. As you become familiar with the Internet and Web, you will likely want to explore these features and opportunities. Using the Internet, you can send and receive messages electronically, participate in chat groups, and even use your computer to make telephone calls to friends and relatives. These are just some of the opportunities available on the Internet.

Electronic Mail

Electronic mail, or **e-mail,** is probably the most popular feature of the Internet. With it, a user can type a message and send it immediately to another person on the Internet who has e-mail capabilities. Most Web browsers can be used to send and receive messages across the Internet. Millions of e-mail messages are sent each day, and they can be saved, printed, and even routed to others.

When an e-mail message is created and sent, it is transmitted across a medium as a stream of small packets (small blocks of data) using the Internet's TCP/IP protocol. The address of the recipient is included in each packet.

Internet routers examine the addresses in each packet and send the packets across the best media. For example, if a particular medium is experiencing heavy traffic, another medium is chosen. Individual packets may take different routes to the destination. When all packets arrive at their destination, they are combined into a message the recipient can read.

E-mail users can communicate with groups of other people by subscribing to a mailing list. A **mailing list** is a database comprised of the addresses of every individual in a group. When a message is sent to the group as a whole, each individual within the group will receive it. You can subscribe to, or withdraw from, a mailing list by sending an e-mail message to the mailing list administrator of the group.

The computer on which the mailing list is stored automatically sends the message to every address on the database. The volume of e-mail messages can be heavy, and subscribers to several groups may receive several messages a day. Because of this, subscribers should check their mail frequently to prevent both their own mail server and the originating ones from becoming bogged down with messages that have not been read.

To send an e-mail message to other individuals, you must know their correct e-mail address. Users of electronic mail typically use abbreviations of their name. However, some use a name that is different than their own. For example, John Smith might prefer to use an alias or nickname, such as "Spike" or "Cosmos." This is perfectly acceptable for e-mail usage. Consider the following hypothetical e-mail address of Richard Jones, a professor of business at Cummings State University. RJONES@CUMMINGSSTATE.EDU

Reading from left to right, a string of characters represents the recipient's user name (a set of unique characters that Cummings State University's mail server assigns to this person's mailbox), followed by the @ symbol, followed by the mail server's domain name. The @ symbol represents the word "at" and separates the user name from the host computer. The domain name is the Internet address of the computer where the mail server is located. In the example, the domain shown identifies the network computer at Cummings State University. The far right portion of the address—the top-level domain—identifies Cummings State University as an educational institution. An e-mail message sent to this person will be received by the computer at Cummings State University; that computer will place the message in Richard Jones' mailbox, and he can access the computer to retrieve the message.

Internet Relay Chat

An interesting way to communicate over the Internet is by using **IRC (Internet Relay Chat),** which allows Internet users all over the world to communicate (chat) with each other by typing messages on their keyboards. The typed words are immediately relayed to people's computers throughout the world and displayed on their screens for them to see and read. Because IRC works in "real time" (meaning immediately) one can read the words as they are being typed.

Like browsers, IRC works on a client-server model. To use IRC the user needs client software on the computer. IRC clients are available for IBM-compatibles, Macintoshes, UNIX, and other kinds of computers. The servers are called IRC servers and use server software.

When you want to use IRC, you first make a connection to the Internet and then start your client software. You will need to log into an **IRC server** on the Internet. IRC servers are located throughout the world connected together in a network so they can send messages to one another.

When a user connects to a server, a specific "channel" is joined, and a username is selected to identify the user at a chat session. A variety of channels cover various topics.

After joining a channel, a user is able to see the conversations as they occur. The user can join the conversation by typing a message on the keyboard. The message is transmitted from the client software on the user's PC to the IRC server to which the user is connected. The message is forwarded from the user's IRC server to other IRC servers where other people on the user's channel are logged in. Each IRC server sends the message to the client software of the people connected to the channel at each server. People at their computers can read the message and respond if they choose to do so.

Internet Telephone

A recent development, called **Internet telephone** or **telephony,** allows a user to make telephone calls using the Internet. The interesting thing is it's free, except for the Internet connection and the software you need for making Internet phone calls. You don't have to pay for the phone call itself, and you can call anywhere in the world and won't have to pay extra for the call.

Various schemes and software packages allow you to make phone calls on the Internet. One drawback is that the other party you call must use a software program identical to yours to receive your call. To make or receive a call, you speak into a microphone attached to your computer and listen through speakers and a sound card installed inside your computer.

A user can only make Internet telephone calls to and receive calls from someone with an Internet address. Because of this limitation, Internet telephony does not replace a standard telephone.

Several software companies offer competing products that allow a user to make and receive electronic telephone calls. WebPhone from the Internet Telephone Company, Internet Phone from VocalTec, and WebTalk from Quarterdeck are just a few of the available products.

Although these products work somewhat differently, they do use similar methods for letting a user make a call. A user must first know the Internet address of the person who is to receive the call, then activate the software, and then select (by clicking) the other person's name.

The number of Internet telephone users is expected to increase significantly. Using the Internet for phone calls is an easy and inexpensive way to communicate with friends and relatives.

We've learned that the Internet and World Wide Web offer users various ways to communicate and to explore our universe. Many Internet and Web users enjoy browsing to see what's available. In cyberspace, an unlimited reservoir of information awaits for Internet enthusiasts to explore. Many users, including students, often search the Internet and Web for information they need. Searching is an important activity that allows users to locate and retrieve information useful in their educational pursuits, research, and work. In the following chapter, you will learn how to search for and find information with the help of your computer and special software.

SUMMARY

In a single day, millions of users access the Internet and visit Web sites. One visit to a Web site is called a hit.

Each destination on the World Wide Web, called a Web site, contains useful information. With a PC and an Internet connection, a user can travel through cyberspace. As you navigate through cyberspace, you will be doing what is called surfing the Net.

Hypertext links, simply called links, enable a user to jump from place to place on the Web. The Web uses a language called Hypertext Markup Language (HTML) that allows the user to view Web pages.

The World Wide Web works on a client-server model in which client software, called a browser, runs on the user's personal computer and server software runs on the host (server) computer. The user first makes a connection to the Internet, and then activates the browser. The user types the address, called the URL (short for Uniform Resource Locator and pronounced "earl"), for the location the user wants to visit.

A protocol is a set of rules and procedures for exchanging information between computers. Protocols are software programs that define how computers interact, or communicate, with each other and how errors are detected.

A Web browser is a client software program your computer uses to display Web pages. A browser displays information on a screen by interpreting the Hypertext Markup Language (HTML) that was used to create home pages containing text, sound, and multimedia files that were placed on the Web. Codes in HTML files determine how your browser displays the text, graphics, links, and multimedia files on a home page.

When you go to a particular Web site, the first page that you will see displayed on your screen is the site's home page. Many Web sites provide several other pages containing additional information.

Documents at a particular Web site may contain hypermedia; that is, a combination of text, graphics, video, sound, and animation. Hypermedia is accessed by means of a link, which is a special software pointer that points to the location of the computer at which the hypertext can be accessed.

Web page authors use the HTML language to create Web pages. The basic information on any page is text. Virtual reality (VR) provides for the creation of pages containing lifelike images, graphics, movement, and sound in three-dimensional form. A special language called VRML (for Virtual Reality Modeling Language) makes it possible to create Web pages in three-dimensional form.

Electronic mail or e-mail is probably the most popular way of communicating on the Internet. IRC (Internet Relay Chat), is another method of communicating that allows Internet users all over the world to "chat" with each other by typing messages on their keyboards. Still another Internet communication tool is Internet telephone, which allows a user to make telephone calls using the Internet.

KEY TERMS

address box (74)
bookmark (77)
bookmark list (77)
browser (67)
browser icon (72)
button (72)
clicking (62)
client-server model (61)
cyberspace (60)
display area (73)
domain (66)
double-clicking (70)
electronic mail
 (e-mail) (80)
favorite (77)
file specification (66)
graphical user interface
 (GUI) (62)
hit (58)
home page (76)
hypermedia (77)

hypertext links
 (links) (77)
Hypertext Markup
 Language
 (HTML) (78)
Hypertext Transfer
 Protocol (HTTP) (66)
icon (62)
Internaut (60)
Internet Explorer (69)
Internet Relay Chat
 (IRC) (81)
Internet router (61)
Internet telephone
 (telephony) (81)
IRC server (81)
keyboard (62)
location text box (72)
mailing list (80)
menu bar (72)
mirror site (59)

mouse (62)
Navigation toolbar (72)
Netscape Navigator (69)
Open Systems
 Interconnection
 (OSI) (63)
pointer (62)
protocol (63)
server software (61)
surfing the Net (60)
toolbar (74)
top-level domain (67)
Uniform Resource
 Locator (URL) (61)
virtual reality (78)
Virtual Reality
 Modeling Language
 (VRML) (78)
Web browser (75)
Web site (58)

END-OF-CHAPTER ACTIVITIES

Matching

Match each term with its description.

a. Internaut

b. location text box

c. hypermedia

d. hypertext link

e. Web browser

f. toolbar

g. home page

h. Uniform Resource
 Locator (URL)

i. Virtual Reality
 Modeling Language
 (VRML)

j. protocol

       1. Allows a user to jump from place to place on the World Wide Web.

       2. Allows a user to perform tasks faster than when using a menu bar.

       3. Set of rules and procedures for exchanging information between computers.

       4. The first page displayed when you visit a particular Web site.

       5. An address for locating a particular Web site.

       6. Makes it possible to create Web pages in three-dimensional form.

       7. An accomplished Internet explorer.

       8. A client software program your computer uses to display Web pages.

       9. Place for typing a Web site address to be visited.

       10. A combination of text, graphics, video, sound, and animation.

Review Questions

1. Two useful input devices for use with the Internet and World Wide Web are a keyboard and a mouse. Why are both of these devices needed? Give an example of when each might be used.

2. What is a Uniform Resource Locator (URL)? Identify each of the parts of a URL.

3. What is a "top-level domain?" What are the six types of top-level domains identified in the chapter?

4. Why is it important to include a domain in an Internet address?

5. What is the purpose of navigational software?

6. Explain the purpose of Hypertext Markup Language (HTML) and Virtual Reality Modeling Language (VRML).

7. What are some of the ways users can communicate using the Internet? Which way do you find the most interesting? Why?

Activities

1. Information about this textbook, *Getting Started with the Internet,* is available at the publisher's (Dryden Press) Web site. The company's Internet address is http://www.dryden.com. Using this address and the Internet, visit the site and find the information provided about the book you are using.

2. Many interesting and informative sites are available on the Internet. Some are listed below:

(a) L.L. Bean	Available at:	http://www.llbean.com
(b) the White House	Available at:	http://www.whitehouse.gov
(c) ABC News	Available at:	http://www.abcnews.com

Visit these sites or other sites suggested by your instructor. Prepare a written summary of each site's contents with a single paragraph about each site.

3. Using the Internet address for your school provided by your instructor, visit your school's site. Explore the site using hyperlinks if they are shown. Prepare a list of the types of information available at the site, such as degrees offered, departments, faculty, and tuition costs.

4. Netscape Communications Corporation and Microsoft Corporation offer the two leading Internet browsers. Netscape recently introduced its newest browser, called Communicator. Microsoft will introduce an updated version of Internet Explorer at a later date. Using the Internet addresses for these companies (shown below) visit each site. Try to obtain information about their new browser products. If you are successful, prepare a brief summary of each product and its main features.

COMPANY	INTERNET ADDRESS
Netscape Communications Corp.	http://home.netscape.com
Microsoft Corporation	http://www.microsoft.com

5. This is a group activity. Your instructor will arrange class members into groups with a small number of students in each group. Below are Internet addresses for some television networks. Each member of a group will be assigned the task of visiting one of the listed television sites. While at the site, prepare a critique of the site, including the site's home page and other pages accessible by using the available links.

TELEVISION SITE	INTERNET ADDRESS
ABC	http://www.abc.com
CBS	http://www.cbs.com
NBC	http://www.nbc.com
CNN	http://www.cnn.com

Searching the Web

The Art of Searching the Web
The Internet and World Wide Web: Storehouses of Information
What You Can Find and Do on the Web
Reasons for Searching
  Curiosity
  Need
  Research
  Work
  Business
Some Popular Search Engines
Searching the Web Using AltaVista
Searching the Web Using Excite
Searching the Web Using Lycos
Searching the Web Using Infoseek
Searching the Web Using WebCrawler
Searching the Web Using NetFind
Searching the Web Using Yahoo!
Using Keywords and Symbols to Search
Search Programs
Accessing Files with File Transfer Protocol (FTP)
Accessing Files with Telnet
Potential Internet and Web Perils
Summary
Key Terms
End-of-Chapter Activities
  Matching
  Review Questions
  Activities

AFTER COMPLETING THIS CHAPTER, YOU WILL:

1. Appreciate the ease with which information can be obtained using the Internet.

2. Explain some reasons for searching the Internet.

3. Identify some popular search engines.

4. Use some keywords and symbols to narrow a search.

5. Explain what a search program is.

6. Explain briefly how files can be accessed using FTP.

7. Explain briefly how files can be accessed using Telnet.

8. Identify potential Internet and Web perils.

The Art of Searching the Web

Not too long ago, searching for information was frequently a tedious, time-consuming, and frustrating experience. A visit to a library in search for needed information often resulted in the information not being found or not being located in the particular library being searched.

People visiting a library usually know what they're looking for, or at least have some idea. They do not always know whether the information they are seeking is located in the stacks, reference section, or reserve stacks. Fortunately, a search for information is simplified by card catalogs. Names, events, words, or terms are typically used to search through the card catalog for the topic of interest. If the topic is not found, other methods may be employed until the topic is found.

In recent years many libraries have modernized by computerizing their card catalogs. A computer or terminal is used to search for the desired information by entering specific search criteria such as a topic, title, name, or event. After initiating a search, the computer accesses and searches a database using the search criteria entered by the user. Often, a list of references and the exact location of each reference will be displayed on the computer or terminal screen. Using this information, the user can go to a location and find the desired information.

Searching for information is an art that can be developed and improved with practice. **Searching** simply means looking for information. By learning how to

FIGURE 4.1

Library Computerized Card Catalog

Most large libraries have computerized card catalogs that enable a user to find information more easily and quickly. By entering specific search criteria, such as a title, name, or event, a search is made of the library's database, and the results are displayed on the screen. The displayed information typically includes sources of the desired information and their location in the library.

search for the information you want and by engaging in searches, you will become more proficient in finding the information you seek.

The Internet and the World Wide Web: Storehouses of Information

The Internet and the World Wide Web may be viewed as huge libraries of information. Like library catalogs, Web page catalogs on the World Wide Web can be searched for information on virtually any topic.

Since its introduction in 1969, the Internet and the Web have grown rapidly each day, and their popularity and usage continue to increase at a phenomenal rate. With the dramatic growth of the Net, it is impossible to estimate the number of users, but there are millions. According to some estimates, the number of users is increasing steadily at about 10 percent per month.

The Internet contains a wealth of information that is readily available to anyone. Unfortunately, the Internet contains so much information that it is difficult for you to find the information you are looking for. While browsing is interesting and enjoyable, it is not an efficient way to locate specific information. Fortunately, there is a much more efficient way to find the information you want. In this chapter, you will learn how to search for, and find, specific information quickly and efficiently.

What You Can Find and Do on the Web

The World Wide Web contains millions of documents with information about thousands of people, places, events, and other topics. You can do research; find people; read your horoscope; get stock quotations; shop for merchandise and services; apply for a loan; make airline and hotel reservations; display weather maps; retrieve and view pictures, movies, and sound clips; and even enjoy visual tours of foreign countries.

The amount and kinds of information available is virtually unlimited, and more information is being added and updated each day. Every day more and more businesses, organizations, agencies, and even individuals join the Web by developing their own Web sites. In Chapter 6, you will learn that you also can add your presence to the Web by developing a Web site of your own.

The Internet consists of hundreds of thousands of computers. It continues to grow as thousands of new users come online every month. The result is an ever-increasing number of Web sites, with each site offering its own information to the public. This information is readily available to anyone having the capability to find it.

Reasons for Searching

There can be many reasons for a user to search the Internet. While the number of reasons can be extensive, some of the more common reasons are identified next.

Curiosity

Curiosity is a valid reason for conducting a search. You might simply want to know if information on a specific topic is available. For example, you might be interested in knowing if information is available about Lake Tahoe, Nevada. Using

Search Results Using Excite

Figure 4.2(a) shows a search for articles about Lake Tahoe using the Excite search engine. Notice the words *Lake Tahoe* typed in the search box of the Excite home page. Figure 4-2(b) shows the results of the search with a list of articles found. The first group of articles is listed. The user can scroll down the list to find a specific article and can click on an article to display it.

(a)

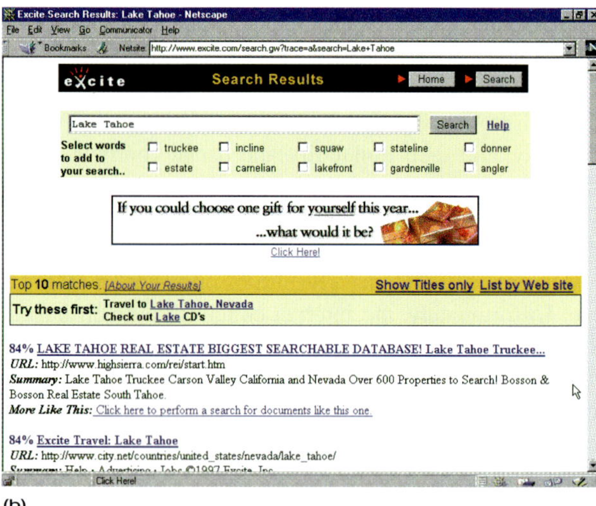

(b)

your Internet connection and a software program that allows you to search the Internet, you can perform a search for information about Lake Tahoe. Figures 4.2(a) and 4.2(b) above show the results of using a search engine called Excite.

As you can see, a search for information can result in several thousands documents being found. In such cases, a user may find it confusing and even impossible to read all the documents. A user can avoid this kind of problem by performing a more restrictive search; for example, to Lake Tahoe hotels. Soon you will learn how to search in a way that will enable you to find more meaningful information.

Need

A user might have a need for specific information. Suppose, for example, that you are interested in a vacation to the Caribbean island of Aruba and that you want to learn about the island. You can find numerous documents on the Web about Aruba just by searching. Figure 4.3 illustrates a typical search for information about Aruba. Notice that 21,214 documents about Aruba were located.

Many users regularly search the Web to find information they need. While needed information may be available from other sources, searching the Web for the information can be more efficient and less expensive than making phone calls or writing letters.

Research

There are occasions when nearly every user engages in research. Students who are assigned research topics may spend several hours searching through library catalogs and stacks. A library may not have sufficient information about the topic being researched. In such situations, a user can search the Web for the information.

Search Results Using Infoseek

A search for information about the Caribbean island of Aruba using the using the Infoseek search engine resulted in the location of 21,214 document titles containing the word *Aruba.* Any document on the list can be viewed by clicking on it.

Lawyers sometimes find the Web to be an indispensable resource, and many lawyers regularly search the Web to find legal precedents. For example, a privately owned database called *WestLaw* contains court transcripts of every case tried in the United States during this century. Using key search words such as *Smith vs Jones,* an attorney can retrieve the transcript of this trial to learn how the case was tried and what the verdict was.

Scientists use the Web for research into their area of interest. For example, a geologist can search the Web for information about rock formations and composition. A chemist can use the Web to find information about a specific chemical element or compound. Using the Web, a physician can search for information about a particular illness and treatment. Even a consumer can find information about a particular product or service.

Conducting research is an important reason for searching the Web. Information on almost any topic is available there, and more information is being added each day.

Work

Many people find the Web useful in their work. Authors often use it to find up-to-date information on topics for a book being written. For example, an author preparing the manuscript for a new book about computers can search the Web for information about new computers, storage devices, printers, and software. In fact, the authors of this book searched the Web for the latest information about the Internet and World Wide Web while preparing the manuscript.

Research on the Web

A search engine allows a user to conduct research of information available on the World Wide Web. Shown is historical information about Grace Hopper, an early pioneer in the computer field.

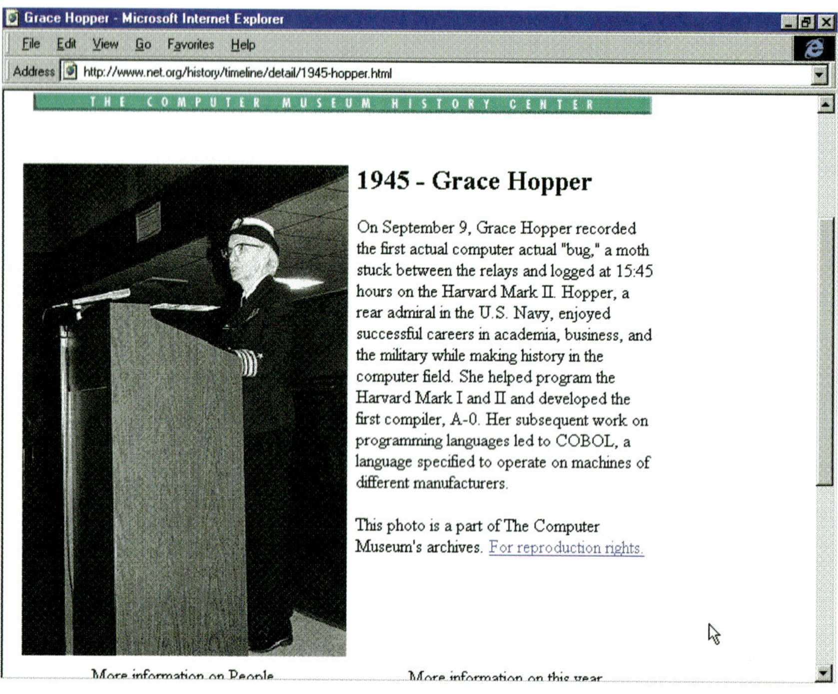

Recently, a real estate developer searched the Web to learn about the availability of land on the Caribbean island of St. Thomas. The developer was able to locate information about specific parcels of available land, prices, and real estate taxes. After finding a suitable parcel, the developer purchased the property on which a new hotel will be constructed.

With a little imagination, almost everyone can use the Web to locate information beneficial to their work. Searching the Web can be a useful activity in any type of work, regardless of whether the search is done by owners, managers, or employees.

Business

Many companies use the Web to conduct normal business activities. Manufacturers use it to locate new raw material sources, to locate suppliers, and to attract potential employees. Retailers are able to find new markets for their products and services and to check on competitors. Mail order businesses can obtain information about shippers and other means for distributing their products and services.

A relatively new development involving the Internet and World Wide Web, called **electronic commerce,** allows companies to conduct business operations on

Data Communications Specialist

You probably already know that data communications systems allow the transfer of data between locations. The responsibility for these systems falls to data communications specialists. Data communications specialists are responsible for developing, implementing, and maintaining the communications networks and the communications software that control the flow of data among devices in the network.

Many colleges are now offering majors with an emphasis in the area of data communications. In addition to basic computer courses, students usually must complete courses in database fundamentals and structures, query languages, and data communications.

Employers typically require new employees to obtain experience in data communications prior to being promoted to the position of data communications specialist. This is usually obtained by working in the area of data communications under the supervision of an experienced senior professional.

The rapid growth and expansion of the Internet and Web have created a high demand for data communications specialists. This high demand has boosted salaries to impressive levels. Employment opportunities are available with businesses, non-profit organizations, and federal, state, and local governments.

FIGURE 4.5

Results of Search Using Excite

A search for information using key search words, such as *Utah Resorts,* can result in interesting findings, such as a Web page for Sundance Resort in Utah, owned by the well-known actor Robert Redford.

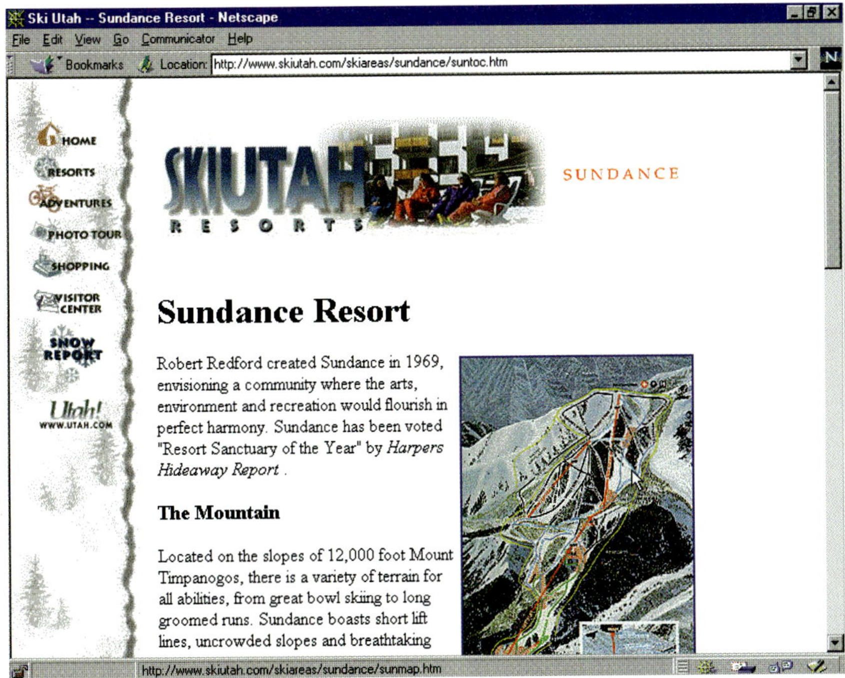

the Web. A company can prepare Web pages and post them on the Web. Typical pages contain information about the company, its products and services, and ordering instructions. Electronic commerce can be a relatively inexpensive way for a new company to get started in business. By searching the Web, you can find new companies offering unique products and services.

A search can result in finding some interesting information. A search using the search words *Utah resorts* can provide you with access to unique business sites such as the Sundance Resort in Utah (Figure 4.5) owned by the well-known actor Robert Redford.

In recent years, several software programs have been developed for searching the World Wide Web. These programs, called **search engines** and search programs, enable you to sift through the Web for the specific information you want. Most search engines are made available in the form of Web pages in which you can execute a search by typing **keywords** (a word or a phrase) that represent topics you want to search for. Search engines are services that allow you to locate information by topic. Figure 4.6 shows a search engine page with the topic being searched typed in the Search box.

When you enter a keyword or phrase—a **query**—a search engine systematically searches the World Wide Web for documents on that specific topic. The search engine scans its database to determine which documents contain the keyword(s) you entered. The titles of documents found (if any), together with a hyperlink to each document, will be listed on your screen.

FIGURE 4.6

Using Keywords to Search

A search engine page allows a user to type one or more keywords representing the topic being searched. After typing the keyword(s) and clicking the Search button, a search is initiated. Notice the keyword *Utah* typed in the Search box.

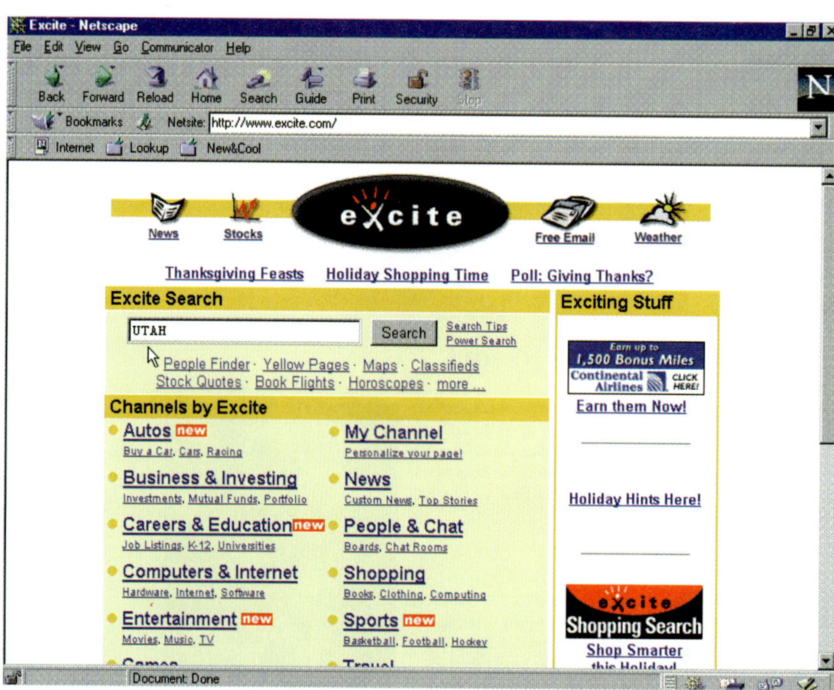

Some Popular Search Engines

Several popular search engines are available that allow you to search the Web for information, but it is not necessary for you to learn all of them. However, you need to be aware that there are differences in the way each searches for information. Just as a library card catalog cannot possibly contain a card for every book or publication in the world, it is impossible for a search engine to catalog every page on the World Wide Web. On the Web, different search engines perform different types of searches. In the following sections, we will look at some of the more popular search engines and the technique each uses to search the World Wide Web.

Searching the Web Using AltaVista

AltaVista, available from Digital Equipment Corporation, is one of the newer search engines with searching capabilities for several different Web resources. AltaVista is one of the largest and most popular search engines on the Web, with more than 30 million entries.

The AltaVista search engine maintains an index of all pages found on the Web. It uses a special program called Scooter to find new and updated pages on the Web. When a new or updated page is found, Scooter copies all the text from the Web page and stores it in the index.

FIGURE 4.7

AltaVista Home Page

AltaVista is one of the newer and most powerful search engines. Notice the rectangular box used to type keyword(s) representing the topic being searched. After typing the keyword(s) and clicking the Search button, a search is executed.

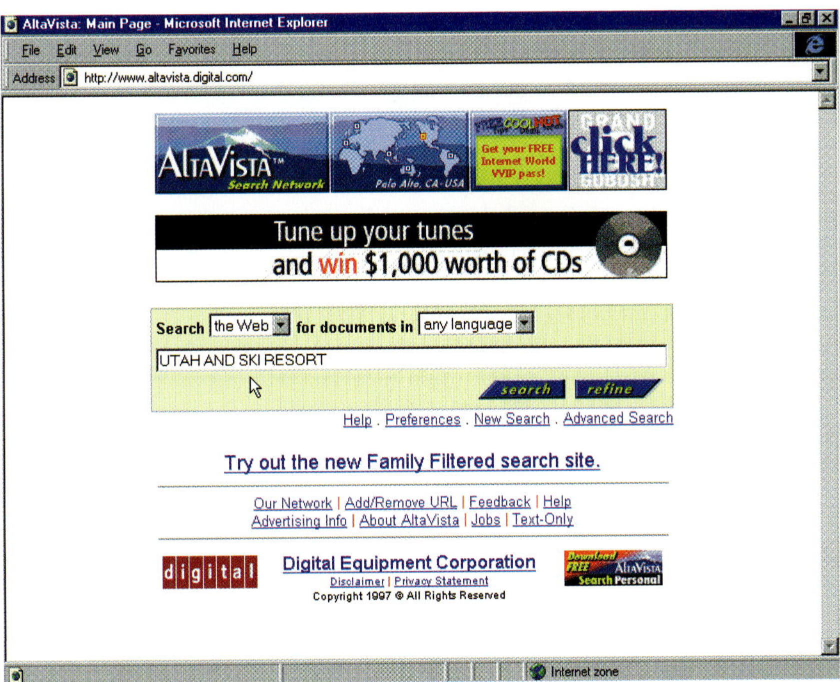

List of Documents Found

When you execute a search using AltaVista, a robot program called Scooter searches AltaVista's index for Web pages containing the keyword or phrase you typed. From the list, you can click on the title of the document you want to see.

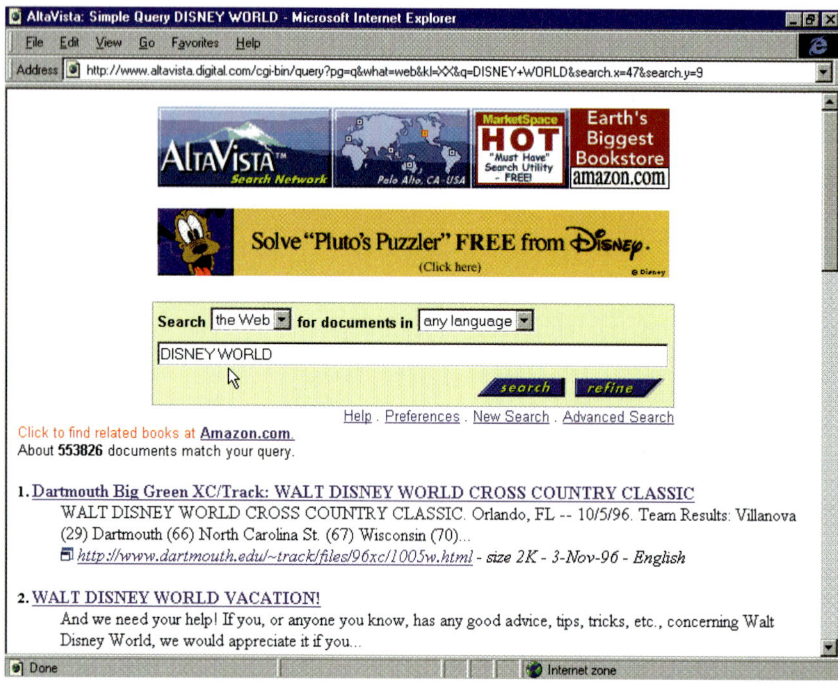

When using AltaVista for a search, you type keywords or phrases to identify the information you want to find. The program searches its index for Web pages containing the word or phrase you typed and displays a list of the pages it found. From the list you can select the pages you want to view, as shown in Figure 4.8.

AltaVista allows you to do a simple search or an advanced search. A **simple search** is executed by typing words separated by a space, or a phrase surrounded by quotation marks. Alta Vista will search for documents and pages that contain the exact combination of words surrounded by the quotation marks. An **advanced search** provides you with more control over your search by displaying only Web pages containing the word or phrase you specify. For example, if you type *bicycles AND NOT motorcycles,* AltaVista will display pages containing the word *bicycles* but will not display pages containing the word *motorcycles.* The following table shows other examples of advanced searches.

KEYWORDS AND PHRASES	WHAT ALTAVISTA DISPLAYS
baseball AND football	Web pages containing the words baseball and football
baseball OR football	Web pages containing the word baseball or the word football
baseball NEAR football	Web pages containing the words baseball and football within ten words of each other.

As you can see, AltaVista is a powerful and versatile search engine. It provides you with a high degree of flexibility concerning how you can execute

FIGURE 4.9

Excite Home Page

The Excite home page contains a list of channels that serve as links to information about a particular topic. For example, if you click on the Business channel, another page containing additional links will be displayed.

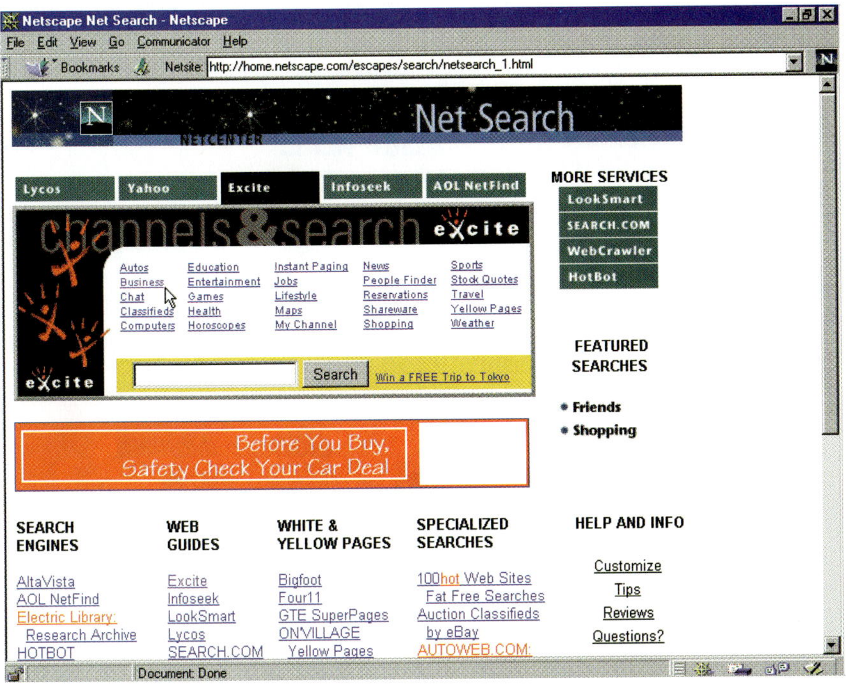

a search of the World Wide Web. You can access the AltaVista Web site at: http://altavista.digital.com

Searching the Web Using Excite

One of the most comprehensive search engines available on the Web is **Excite,** which offers a reference section and online maps for locations across the United States and around the world. The Excite database contains over 50 million Web pages. When you type keywords or phrases representing information you want to find, Excite searches all the Web pages in its database. When pages are located that contain the information you requested, Excite displays a list of those pages.

Like other search engines, the Excite home page includes a **Search box** in which you type keywords or phrases for the information you want to find. It also contains several broad categories from which you can choose. Each category is linked to other Web pages with updated information. Figure 4.9 shows the Excite home page with a list of categories from which you can make a selection.

If you select a channel from the list on Excite's home page, such as Business and Investing, another page will be displayed containing additional lists. One list offers links to other Web sites, another offers links to news items, and a third list provides links to stock market quotations (Figure 4.10).

Linking to Business Page

By clicking on Excite's Business channel, a separate Business page is displayed that contains links to a variety of business and investing information.

Lycos Home Page

Like other search engine home pages, the Lycos home page contains a box in which you type search criteria (keywords or phrases). It also has other options you can choose.

When a search is executed, Excite displays ten results at a time. Beside each item on the list is a rating that indicates the success of the search. A rating of 100 percent means that the Web page definitely contains the keyword or phrase you typed.

Excite allows you to search for a specific group of words. To find a Web page containing the exact keyword(s) you typed, you need to type quotation marks around the word(s) you want to find. Your search can be made more precise by typing a symbol in front of a word without leaving any spaces between the symbol and the word. For example, if you type + *bicycles – motorcycles*, Excite will locate Web pages containing the word *bicycles,* but not the word *motorcycles.*

Excite's main database contains over 60 million Web pages, but not all pages are available to the public. The staff at Excite reviews and makes available more than 65,000 Web pages through which you can search. The reviewed pages are judged on the basis of how well they are organized and developed. The pages the staff deems acceptable are made available for you to access.

When you perform a search, Excite displays a list of pages. Beside each page title is a rating that indicates the success of your search. For example, a rating of 100 percent indicates that the page definitely contains the word or phrase that you entered when you began your search. A rating of 50 percent indicates that there is only a 50–50 chance that the word or phrase that you entered is contained in the page. The rating helps you decide which pages you want to view.

Excite can be accessed by using the Net Search button of Netscape browsers.

Searching the Web Using Lycos

Another search engine, named **Lycos,** searches both titles and Web pages for keywords entered by a user. The Lycos search form contains several options for controlling a search of the Web.

With its database of more than 70 million Web pages, Lycos allows you to find a wealth of interesting information on the Web. In addition, you can use Lycos to search for images and sounds. When Lycos enters Web pages into its database, it also indexes all accompanying images, sounds, and animation files it finds in the pages.

When you enter search criteria (keywords or phrases) for the information you are seeking, Lycos searches its database for Web pages containing the words you entered and displays a list of pages. Each item on the list contains a hyperlink to the corresponding Web page.

Like other search engines, Lycos allows you to restrict your search by entering special symbols with the words you type. Below are some ways to make your search more precise.

WHAT YOU TYPE	WHAT LYCOS FINDS
island	Web pages containing the word *island* only, and not pages containing the words *islands* or *islander.*
show$	Web pages containing the word *show,* even when it is part of larger words such as *shower* or *showboat.*
dolphins – Miami	Web pages containing the word *Dolphins,* but not the word *Miami.*

The Lycos home (search) page contains useful links to other information. You can display road maps, city guides, pictures, sounds, and more. For example, you can access information about a city, such as Charlotte, North Carolina, by selecting City Guide and then following the instructions on your screen (Figure 4.12).

Lycos is a versatile and popular search engine. It can be accessed with Netscape browsers' Net Search button or can be accessed at Lycos' Internet address: http://www.lycos.com.

Lycos City Guide Page

The Lycos search engine allows you to choose from among several options displayed on the Lycos home page. One of these is City Guide, which you can use to get information about a city of your choice, such as Charlotte, North Carolina. After clicking on City Guide on the home page, follow the instructions to obtain information about the city you selected.

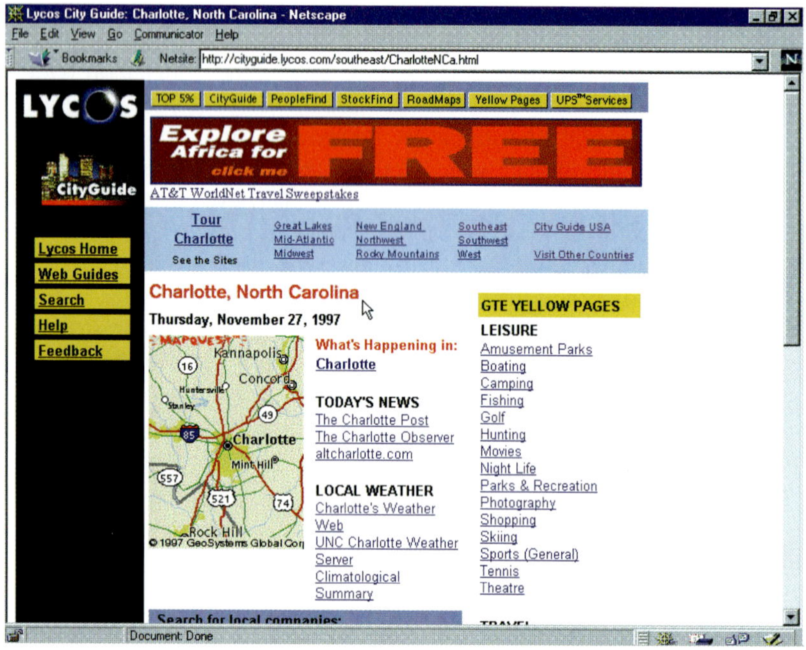

Infoseek Search Page

Infoseek's home page contains a rectangular box, called the Seek box, for you to type in search criteria (keywords or phrases). It also has other options you can choose. The home page lists categories of information you can search through.

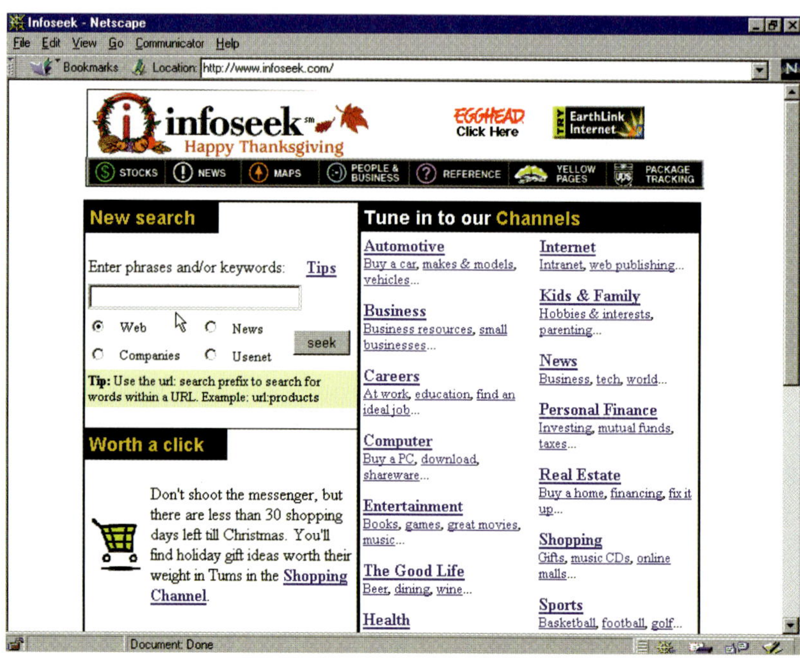

Searching the Web Using Infoseek

Infoseek is a highly rated search engine from Infoseek Corporation. Using Infoseek, you can search a database containing a large number of magazines and more than 19 million Web pages.

When a search is undertaken, Infoseek uses the keyword or phrase you typed in the Seek box on the home page to find titles containing the word(s) you entered. The titles found (if any) are displayed on your screen as a list with hyperlinks to the documents identified in the list. The first ten titles located are listed initially, along with a brief summary of the document's contents. Clicking on the "Next 10" link displays the next ten titles, and so on. By clicking on a title on the list, Infoseek retrieves the document and displays it on your screen.

FIGURE 4.14

Search Results Using Infoseek

Infoseek allows you to perform a search by typing keywords in the Seek box and then clicking the Seek button. If you perform a search using the keyword *Alligators,* a list of titles containing the word *Alligators* is displayed on your screen. Each title is a link to the document. You can view the document represented by a title simply by clicking on the title.

Like some other search engines, Infoseek provides tips for searching the Web. One tip, for example, is that you can undertake a search by typing a specific question, by enclosing a phrase in quotes, or by capitalizing a typed name.

Infoseek is available at the Internet address: http://www.infoseek.com.

Searching the Web Using WebCrawler

WebCrawler, a search engine developed by Brian Pinkerton as a research project at the University of Washington and later bought by America Online, is easy to learn and use. It maintains an index with information on more than 275,000 different documents that its staff has reviewed. The remainder of its database contains data on nearly two million documents.

A useful feature of WebCrawler's search engine is its home (search) page. The page is self-explanatory and easy to use. To begin a search all you need to do is type keyword(s) or a phrase in the Search box and click the Search button. WebCrawler does the rest (Figure 4.15).

FIGURE 4.15
WebCrawler Home Page

WebCrawler's home page is easy to use and self-explanatory. To start a search, all the user needs to do is to type keyword(s) or a phrase, and then click on the Search button.

WebCrawler uses a search program that automatically travels about the Web searching for topics and their links to other documents. When it finds a document, the document title, together with hyperlinks to other documents, are added to WebCrawler's index.

When a search is performed, WebCrawler displays only titles of documents it finds. The titles represent URLs of Web pages containing the keyword(s) you typed for the search.

Like the home page of most other search engines, Webcrawler's page displays information categories, including Arts, Business, Computers, and Science. Selecting a category will result is an extensive listing of titles. Each title represents the URL of another Web page.

WebCrawler is updated regularly. New pages are reviewed and added to the index daily. Webcrawler is available at the following address: http://www.webcrawler.com.

Although WebCrawler is still being used, it is being phased out by America Online in favor of AOL's new search engine, NetFind.

Searching the Web Using NetFind

AOL's new search engine, called **NetFind,** offers a user an easy and comprehensive way to find information on the World Wide Web. With NetFind, you can find people, businesses, organizations, phone numbers, e-mail addresses, a variety of newsgroups, and even Web sites for children. There's almost no limit to the various kinds of information you can retrieve using this powerful search engine.

NetFind searches the Web for names and addresses of people, businesses, and organizations and stores them in a directory. Whether you are an individual, a business, or an organization NetFind contains a form that allows you to add your name and address to the directory. Once added, this information becomes available to anyone to access.

NetFind's capabilities are certainly not limited to finding persons, businesses, and organizations. Using this search engine, you can search for, and probably find, information on virtually any topic. In the search text box, you can type any combination of words, topics, or phrases and then just click the Find button. A list of findings will be displayed on the screen, along with links to the information sources.

FIGURE 4.16

NetFind Home Page

America Online's NetFind is a powerful and versatile search engine. NetFind is available to America Online subscribers and to other users. A user who is not an AOL subscriber can access NetFind by using a browser and typing "www.aol.com/netfind" in the address box. Once NetFind is accessed a search is initiated by entering words or topics in the Search box and clicking on the Find button.

America Online subscribers can access NetFind by clicking on the NetFind button. For other users, NetFind can be accessed by typing http:www.aol.com/netfind in the address box and pressing the Enter key.

Searching the Web Using Yahoo!

The final search engine we will present is **Yahoo!,** one of the most popular and widely used search engines available. Yahoo! was created at Stanford University by two students who wanted to keep a list of Web sites they liked and might want to revisit. Later, they decided to share their list with others in the Internet community. Within a brief time, their list became quite popular, which encouraged them to add more sites and to provide users with the opportunity to submit their sites to the list. Yahoo! is now a public company.

The Yahoo! home page is simple and easy to use. It contains a listing of information categories and a Search box for typing search criteria (words or phrases). The Yahoo! home page is shown in Figure 4.17.

The staff at Yahoo! reviews and catalogs every Web site in the Yahoo! directory. Each category contains Web sites with similar information. Yahoo! allows you to browse through the categories and subcategories until you find pages containing information you want to see.

Among the special features available with Yahoo! are News Headlines, Special Categories, and Personal Information. Clicking on News Headlines allows you to

FIGURE 4.17

Yahoo! Home Page

The Yahoo! home page is easy to use and self-explanatory. To begin a search, all the user needs to do is to type keyword(s) or a phrase, type a number for the number of titles to be displayed, and then click on the Search button. Notice the information categories listed on the page. By selecting a category, Yahoo! will display a list of related titles representing links to documents available on the World Wide Web.

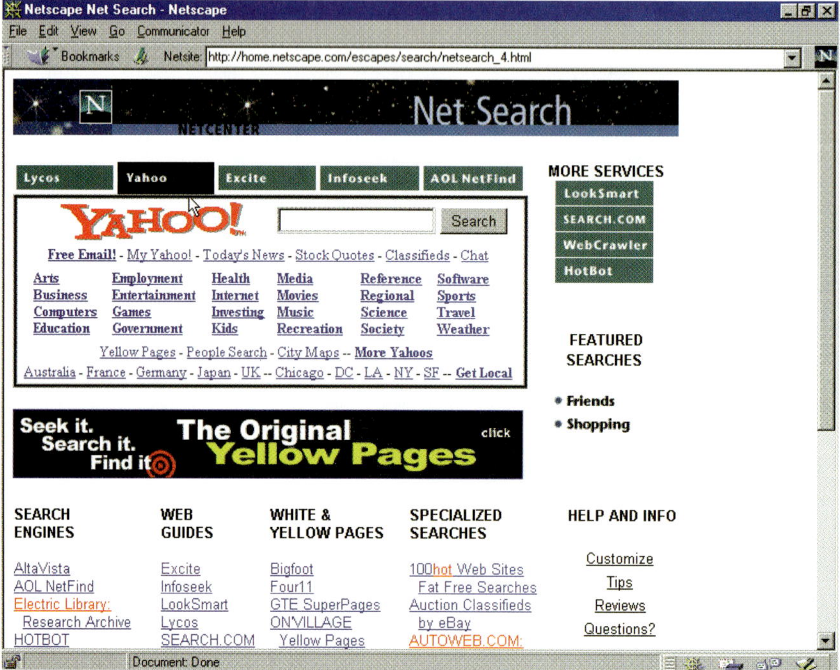

read news stories from around the world. The stories are updated each hour. By clicking on Special Categories, you can view a listing of unique sites. Clicking on Personal Information allows you to choose topics of special interest to you and enables you to have Yahoo! create a custom page for you that causes only the information you request to be displayed.

The search engines presented are just some of the ones available, and you can expect others to be created and made available in the future. Those that have been explained here are among the more popular ones. They are improved and updated periodically and, equally important, they are free. All you need to do to access the one of your choice is to type the URL for the one you want to use. User needs vary. Before deciding which search engine best suits your need, try each one. After trying all of the search engines, you can better determine which one is best for you.

Yahoo! can be accessed with Netscape browsers' Net Search button and other browser programs.

Using Keywords and Symbols to Search

Search engines allow you to type words or phrases to find titles of Web pages that contain the words or phrases you type. Typing a single word will likely result in a long list of titles being found and displayed. In such cases, it may be impossible for you to read all the titles listed, because the list may include several thousand. One way to avoid this dilemma is to narrow your search by typing several words that define it more precisely. For example, if you type the word *apples* in the Search box, the search engine you are using will probably find many more titles than if you type the words *Red Delicious apples.* Remember that you can achieve a more precise search if you type a more detailed query in the search box.

Most search engines allow the use of words and special symbols, called **operators,** to limit a search to specific information. These include a plus sign (+), a minus sign (–), and the words *AND, OR,* and *NOT.* For example, if you type *apples AND oranges* you may expect the list of titles displayed to include titles containing both words. However, if you type *apples NOT oranges,* you may expect a list of titles containing only the word *apples* to be displayed.

Most search engine pages include a Help button or Tips button. Clicking on this button will display helpful tips or hints for searching and will help you perform more effective searches.

Search Programs

Search engines represent the most popular way to search the Internet and World Wide Web, but searches can also be made using search programs. A **search program** runs on your own computer and is similar to other application programs. Search programs are useful for those who perform frequent Web searches and are available for purchase from computer stores and by downloading from the manufacturer.

Search programs are an efficient way to search for information on the Web. Many allow you to perform searches while you are involved with other tasks. You can schedule a search to be performed at any time, even while you are away or during the night.

Some search programs submit your requests for information to several search engines on the Web. Perhaps without your being aware of it, the program will be using several search engines at once to find the information you request.

Several excellent search programs are available. Examples include Teleport Pro, WebFerret, and WebSeeker.

We have learned that files can be retrieved (downloaded) by browsing the Net and by searching for information using search engines and search programs. There are other ways to access and download files, two of which are with FTP and Telnet. These are explained in the following sections.

Accessing Files with File Transfer Protocol (FTP)

You have learned that millions of Web pages are available on the World Wide Web and that these pages can be accessed using search engines. Many more files and programs are available on the Internet that are not part of the World Wide Web. You can access these files and programs using an Internet service called **File Transfer Protocol,** abbreviated **FTP.**

FTP is a popular use of the Internet that allows you to retrieve files from another computer on the Internet to your computer—a process called **downloading.** You can download many types of files, including text files, files that you can run on your computer, graphics files, and audio files. People using FTP download many files daily. FTP can also be used to transfer files from your computer to another computer—a process called **uploading.**

An FTP site is a computer on the Internet where files are stored. Colleges and universities, government agencies, companies, organizations, and individuals maintain FTP sites. Some FTP sites allow for **anonymous access,** which means that you can access files at these sites without entering a userID or a password. Some anonymous FTP sites allow you to view files without having to enter anything at all. Others allow you to access files by entering the word *anonymous* when prompted to your userID or password.

Some FTP sites are private, allowing only users with account numbers and passwords to access files. To access files at these sites, you must use an authorized userID and password.

FTP works on a client-server model. In order to transfer files, you must have **FTP client software** installed on your computer. A program on the FTP server called an **FTP daemon** enables you to transfer (upload or download) files.

FTP has a set of commands used to transfer files. To upload or download files, normally you enter an account number (or username) and password. However, if you are using FTP with some software, including Netscape, you do not have to enter commands. All you need to do is point and click, just as you would to select hyperlinks.

Files and subdirectories at FTP sites are stored in different **directories,** just as some files stored in your computer are stored in directories. Like files stored on your computer, every file has a file name, followed by a period, and then an extension. You can access a file by typing the full file name, or you can simply click on the file name if you are using a program such as Netscape. Many FTP sites maintain a directory called **Pub** (short for Public). Files contained in the Pub directory are available for access by the public.

Some FTP files are quite large and are compressed so that they are stored more easily and can travel across the Internet faster. Before a compressed file can be read, it must be decompressed using a decompression program. Therefore, to access and read compressed files you must have a decompression program installed on your computer. A decompression program is sometimes available from sites where you download a file. A popular decompression program for PCs is PKZip. Another easy to use program is one called WinZip.

FIGURE 4.18

An FTP Site

An FTP site is a computer on the Internet where files are stored. Colleges and universities, government agencies, companies, organizations, and individuals maintain FTP sites. FTP (short for File Transfer Protocol) makes it possible for you to download and upload files. The page in this illustration lists the directories available at this FTP site.

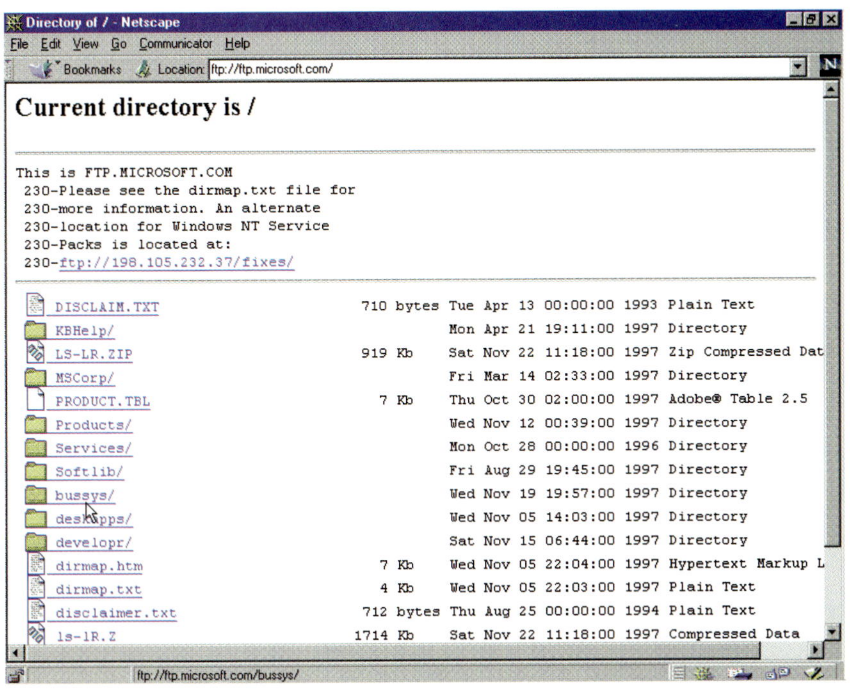

Files containing a combination of text, graphics, and sound are developed using coding schemes. In order to view or use these coded files, you have to download them to your computer and then unencode them using special software. A popular encoding scheme is named UUencode. A **UUencode** program contains instructions for both encoding and decoding these large multimedia files.

A File Transfer Protocol called **WS_FTP** is a client application for use in a Windows environment. It was designed to take full advantage of the point-and-click capabilities of the Windows 3.1 or Windows 95 environment. WS_FTP is easy for a beginner to use and offers a full set of functions for an experienced user. Many Internet providers supply subscribers with a WS_FTP program on an installation disk or CD-ROM together with a manual explaining its use for accessing files stored on other computers. WS_FTP enables a user to access files from computers around the world.

Accessing Files with Telnet

Telnet, based on a client-server model, allows you to use your computer to access programs and information from another computer anyplace in the world. With Telnet software installed on your computer (the client), you can access any of many host computers around the world. The host allows many clients access at the same time.

FTP Main Directory Page

Files at FTP sites are maintained in directories. After choosing a directory, a list of subdirectories and files appears. A user can select a subdirectory or select a file for viewing.

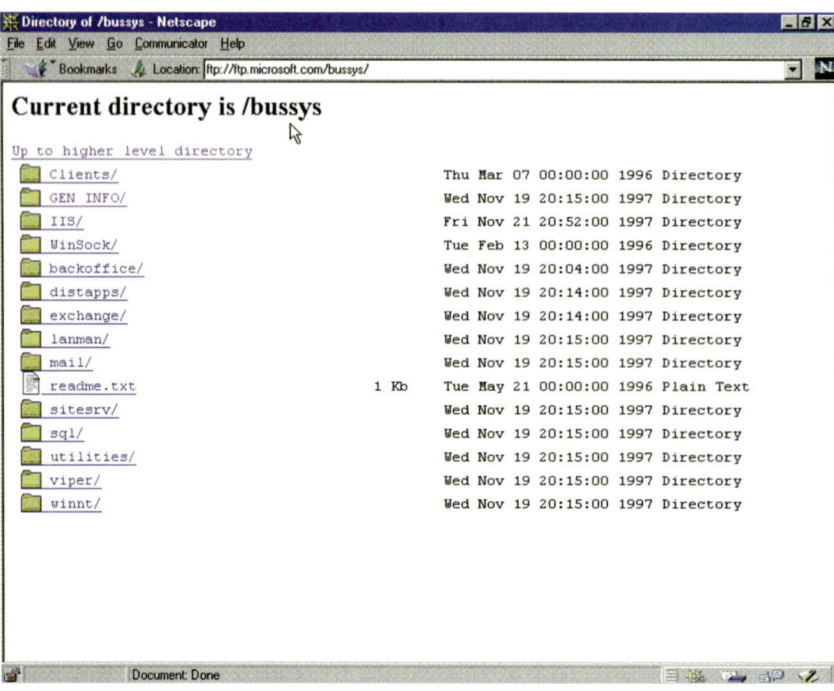

When you use Telnet, you usually have to log on to the host. Sometimes, you can log in using the name "guest" or "visitor." However, many systems require you to provide personal information such as your name, address, and phone number. Some require you to choose a username and a password for you to enter the next time you log in.

To make a connection using Telnet, you must use terminal emulation so that your computer and keyboard acts the same as a terminal. VT-100 is the most common terminal emulation, and it is safe to use.

Client software is available for all computer operating systems, including Windows, Macintosh, and UNIX. Telnet software for Windows and Macintosh operating systems is easier to use because both remember host names. This allows you to maintain an address book of host names you can visit later just by clicking on the name.

There are many companies, organizations, institutions, and agencies that permit you to access and view thousands of files using Telnet. For example, some universities allow you to Telnet to the host computer and view files of library holdings, faculty and staff, and public announcements.

Potential Internet and Web Perils

Not everything about the Internet and World Wide Web is positive. There are some weaknesses.

Although there are millions of worthwhile documents and files available on the Internet and Web, much of the information is relatively useless. Just as some users occasionally send meaningless e-mail messages to everyone in the organization, you can find thousands—probably even millions—of documents on the Internet and Web that are of little, if any, value to most users. As a user, your task is to distinguish between useful information and "garbage."

A user should exercise caution with regard to accessed information. Just because the information was posted to the Internet does not necessarily guarantee the information to be accurate or reliable. It might be wise for you to consult other sources before assuming that the information being viewed is accurate.

Internet users dislike the practice of **spamming,** a term that refers to any advertising in an inappropriate location on the Internet. For example, posting an advertisement to a newsgroup that is not involved in advertising is called a **spam.**

Some software is copied illegally and sent out over the Internet—a practice called **Warez.** Be aware that some software available on the Internet may be illegal and its use subject to copyright laws.

Just as there are people who abuse other forms of communication, there are those who abuse the use of the Internet and World Wide Web. Here, we have identified only a sample of abuses. A more thorough coverage of problems and abuses is presented in Chapter 7. As Internet users, we have a responsibility to use good judgment and to be responsible citizens each and every time we journey into cyberspace.

SUMMARY

Searching for information is an art that can be developed and improved with practice. Searching simply means looking for information.

The Internet and World Wide Web may be viewed as a huge storehouse of information—only larger. Like library catalogs, Web page catalogs exist on the World Wide Web and can be searched for information on virtually any topic. Reasons for searching the Internet include curiosity, need, research, work, and business.

Software programs called search engines and search programs enable you to search the Web by topic. You can execute a search by typing keywords (a word or a combination of words) that represent topics you want to search for. When you enter a keyword or phrase, called a query, a search engine systematically searches the World Wide Web for documents on a specific topic. The search engine scans its database to determine which documents contain the keyword(s) you entered. The titles of documents found (if any), together with a link to each document, will be listed on your screen.

Several popular search engines are available that allow you to search the Web. AltaVista is one of the newer search engines with searching capabilities for several different Web resources. One of the most comprehensive search engines available on the Web is Excite. Lycos searches both titles and Web pages for keywords entered by a user. Its search form contains several options for controlling a search. Infoseek is a highly rated search engine that allows you to search a database containing a large number of magazines and more than 19 million Web pages. WebCrawler, a search engine developed at the University of Washington and later bought by America Online, maintains an index with information on more than 275,000 different documents that its staff has reviewed. Yahoo!, is one of the most popular and widely used search engines available.

A search engine allows you to type a word or phrase to find titles of Web pages that contain the words or phrases you type. Most search engines allow the use of words and special symbols, called operators, to limit a search to specific information.

Search programs run on your own computer. When a search is undertaken, some search programs submit your query to several search engines. There are several search programs that can be purchased at a computer store or downloaded from the manufacturer.

Two other programs that allow a user to find information on the Internet are FTP and Telnet. An FTP site is a computer on the Internet where files are stored. Colleges and universities, agencies, companies, organizations, and individuals maintain FTP sites. Many are anonymous, which means anyone can access files at these sites without entering a username or password.

Some FTP files are quite large and are compressed so that they are stored more easily and can travel across the Internet faster. Before a compressed file can be read, it must be decompressed using a decompression program. Therefore, to access and read compressed files you must have a decompression program installed on your computer.

Files containing a combination of text, graphics, and sound are developed using coding schemes. In order to view or use these coded files, you have to download them to your computer and then unencode them using special software. A popular encoding scheme is named UUencode. A UUencode program contains instructions for both encoding and decoding these large multimedia files.

On the Internet and Web, there are problems. Although there are millions of worthwhile documents and files available on the Internet and Web, much of the information is relatively useless. As a user, your task is to distinguish between useful information and "garbage." Not all information is accurate or reliable. Internet users dislike the practice of spamming, a term that refers to any advertising in an inappropriate location on the Internet. For example, posting an advertisement to a newsgroup that is not involved in advertising is called a spam. Some software is copied illegally and sent out over the Internet—a practice called Warez. Be aware that some software available on the Internet may be illegal and that its use is subject to copyright laws.

KEY TERMS

advanced search (96)	FTP daemon (107)	searching (88)
AltaVista (95)	Infoseek (101)	simple search (96)
anonymous access (107)	keyword (94)	spam (109)
directory (107)	Lycos (99)	spamming (109)
downloading (106)	NetFind (103)	Telnet (109)
electronic commerce (93)	operator (106)	uploading (106)
Excite (97)	Pub (108)	UUencode (108)
File Transfer Protocol (FTP) (106)	query (94)	Warez (109)
	search box (97)	WebCrawler (101)
	search engine (94)	WS_FTP (108)
FTP client software (107)	search program (106)	Yahoo! (104)

END-OF-CHAPTER ACTIVITIES

Matching

Match each term with its description.

a. simple search

b. searching

c. query

d. UUencode

e. electronic commerce

f. Telnet

g. operators

h. search engine

i. anonymous FTP site

j. AltaVista

___________ **1.** Business conducted on the Internet.

___________ **2.** Allows anyone to access files without entering a username or password.

___________ **3.** Allows you to search the Web for information you want.

___________ **4.** Words or special symbols that limit a search to specific information.

___________ **5.** Executed by typing words separated by a space or a phrase enclosed with quotation marks.

___________ **6.** A search made possible by entering a keyword or phrase.

___________ **7.** Looking for information.

___________ **8.** Based on a client-server model, allows you to access programs and information from another computer on the Internet.

___________ **9.** A search engine from Digital Equipment Corporation.

___________ **10.** A program that contains instructions for encoding and decoding files.

Review Questions

1. Explain the main differences between a browser and a search engine.

2. In what ways is a search engine similar to a traditional library card catalog? In what ways are they different?

3. What is meant by the term "query"? Give examples of five queries that can be typed in a Search box to begin a search.

4. Explain how a search for information can be made more precise or restrictive.

5. What are "operators"? Give some examples of how operators can be used to restrict, or limit, a search for information that is more specific.

6. Identify some of the search engines explained in the chapter. Which one do you think would best meet your needs, and why?

7. Explain briefly what FTP and Telnet are.

8. Identify some potential problems you might experience using the Internet and Web.

Activities

1. Using a search engine available to you, find the home page of a college or university. After retrieving the home page, use one of the hyperlinks to locate information pertaining to a degree program you might be interested in learning about. Display the information on your screen. Prepare a brief written summary of the degree program to turn in to your instructor.

2. Choose a single topic of particular interest to you, such as asteroids or planets. Using each of the search engines available to you, search the Internet and Web for information on the topic you select. For each search engine you use, make a note of the number of titles found. Which search engine resulted in the most hits? Which search engine resulted in the fewest?

3. Using a search engine available to you, perform a search for *motorcycles*. See if you can find a picture of a particularly impressive motorcycle. Print a copy of the picture.

4. The Internet and Web contain valuable information about job and career opportunities. Using a search engine available to you, search for employment opportunities for students in your field of study. Make a list of job opportunities found and whether the company or organization allows individuals to submit an employment application using the Internet.

5. Different search engines do not always yield the same search results. Using four search engines explained in the chapter, initiate a search using the keywords *trout fishing*. See if the four search engines yielded the same search results in terms of the number of titles found.

6. This is a team project. For this project, your instructor will divide the class into groups with four to five students in each team. Each student in the group will thoroughly research one search engine. For example, one student will search for information on AltaVista, another on Lycos, and so on. All information found will be combined, and a detailed written report will be prepared on the search engines and turned in to the instructor.

Web Resources and Applications

Decision Making, Problem Solving, and the Web
The Internet, The Web, and the National Information Superhighway
  Computer Power
  Digital Communications and Content
  Information Terminals
Web Applications and Their Impact on Us
  Work
  Life
  Learning
Leisure
Web Applications for Students
  Art and Leisure
  Government
  Home Shopping
  Sports
  Travel
Teams, Collaboration, and the Web
  Collaborative Tools
  Collaboration Opportunities
  Building a Cyberteam: Designing for Success
Improving Web Efficiency
Push/Pull Web Technologies
Spam Mail
Two Sample Internet Case Studies
  Preparing for Your Career While Still in School
  How to Buy a Car Using the Internet
Summary
Key Terms
End-of-Chapter Activities
  Matching
  Review Questions
  Activities

AFTER COMPLETING THIS CHAPTER, YOU WILL:

1. Explain how the Internet and the Web can help improve your decision-making and problem-solving abilities.

2. Discuss the three major components of the National Information Superhighway and their impact on our society.

3. List ten Web applications that students should find helpful.

4. Discuss the role of the Internet and the Web in collaborative, team-based applications.

5. Define the term fiber optics.

6. Explain the difference between pull and push technologies on the Web and when you would use each.

7. Define "spam" mail and the techniques available to reduce its volume.

8. Describe how the Web can be used to find professional employment and help people advance in their careers.

9. List the Web services available to help users purchase a new or used automobile.

10. Discuss how the Internet and the Web have affected our work, lives, education, and leisure.

Decision Making, Problem Solving, and the Web

All of us make decisions (or choices) every day. The quality of these decisions affects the quality of our lives. Some decisions we make might include where we go to school; who we choose to work for; how we spend our money; whom we associate with, date, or marry. Think of **decision making** as the process we use to come to a solution or answer about something. Then, **problem solving** covers the processes and activities we use to implement that decision. If you decide "I am going to increase my income by 25 percent!" problem solving will then add a description of how this will be achieved: by getting a second job, working toward a promotion, or investing in real estate or the stock market. Problem solving will also help you decide what smaller steps are necessary to implement those larger choices. The Internet and Web can play vital support roles in both these processes.

Problem solving begins with collecting the right data. **Data** includes large quantities of random, unorganized, measurements of activities related to your problem. When the problem is defined, the data collection process begins—we collect data relevant to that problem. Once data is collected, we analyze or process that data and convert it to information. Hence the term *information processing*. **Information** is the resulting refined, high-quality, relevant inputs to the ultimate solution of your problem. **Knowledge** defines the processes you use to convert that data into information. Usually, the smarter you are about the topic, the better your processes will be. Think of the knowledge processes used by medical research specialists, genetic chemists, or aviation electronics designers.

Finally, **wisdom** is understanding the value, implications, and other applications of what you've found. It is the highest level of our awareness. The pyramid shown in Figure 5.1 shows the location of each element in this hierarchy. Can you begin to see the contribution that the Internet and the Web might bring to this pyramid?

These new, online resources supply us with an electronic tool kit that supports every level of the wisdom pyramid. They supply relevant data for processing and

FIGURE 5.1

The Pyramid of Wisdom

Data is the raw material for information systems and problem solving. Good data, correctly processed, can lead to wisdom.

information conversion. The Web can even supply tools (statistical programs and other software) to help perform the conversion. After making a decision, we search the Web to see if others have made this decision and what results they had. Finally, if knowledge is the map that guides these processes, we can also review the processes and logic used by others.

If used correctly, we can almost guarantee the Internet and the Web will increase the quality of your decisions and the success of their implementation. This chapter focuses on using these two new tools to improve your problem-solving skills and processes.

The Internet, the Web, and the National Information Superhighway

Today, we are building a digital highway in America. Eventually it will link business, government, education, home, and community. It is called the **National Information Superhighway** or the **National Information Infrastructure (NII).** Small pieces of it are in place today. NII is a high-speed, digital communications system that will deliver information, education, health resources, and government services to all sectors of our society. All groups and users would share in the wealth of information and technologies being developed.

Telephone companies, cable entertainment companies, and the news media are taking the lead in creating the pieces, establishing standards, and implementing the system. Like the two national infrastructures that preceded it—railroads and the automobile highway system—this system will form the national communications backbone for our twenty-first century society. Travel, education, shopping, commerce, sports, and entertainment will all share the same paths. Today, three pieces in the NII puzzle are coming together to lay the foundation for this highway. They are computer power, digital communications and content, and information terminals. Figure 5.2 shows these three components.

FIGURE 5.2

Three Lanes on the Information Superhighway

The Information Superhighway consists of three distinct lanes or channels.

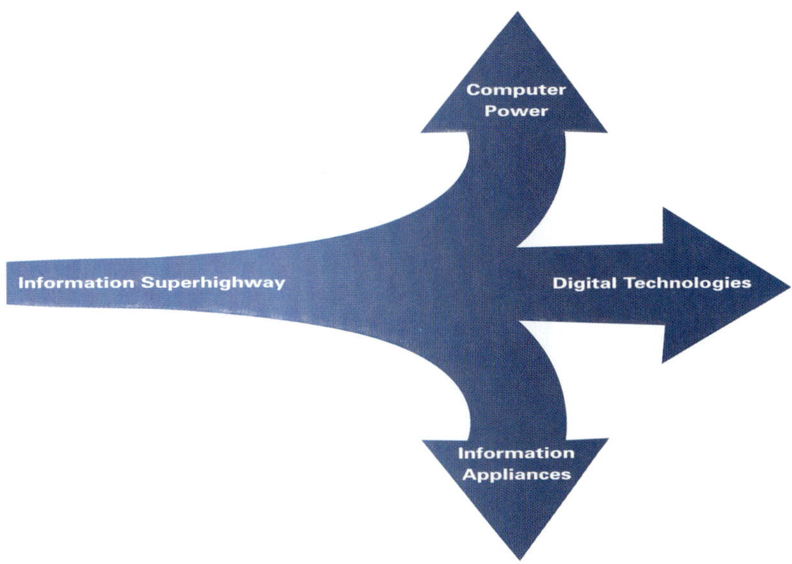

Computer Power

Each day we read about computers becoming faster, cheaper, and smaller. Historically, every eighteen months computers become twice as fast and half as expensive. This is referred to as **Moore's Law,** named after one of the co-founders of Intel, Gordon Moore. As this progression continues, applications that were previously not feasible become possible. And, this trend is expected to continue. The power supply for this highway is inexpensive and growing as more and more users find it financially possible to join. Programs become more user friendly. This broadens the user base.

Digital Communications and Content

Connecting these inexpensive computers is next. The medium must be fast and rich in content. Current home telephone service is the bottleneck in today's delivery service. Normal, voice-grade, phone lines limit the rate of delivery of the message to the home. Voice and text are acceptable, but as we add graphics, video, and multimedia, the display results are too slow and therefore unacceptable. Fiber-optic cable is the answer, but the cost is high to retrofit all U.S. households with this service. Current estimates are $1,000 per household. Many new homes and subdivisions are being connected via fiber optics. Others suggest wireless communications or satellite technology as the global answer. Time will tell.

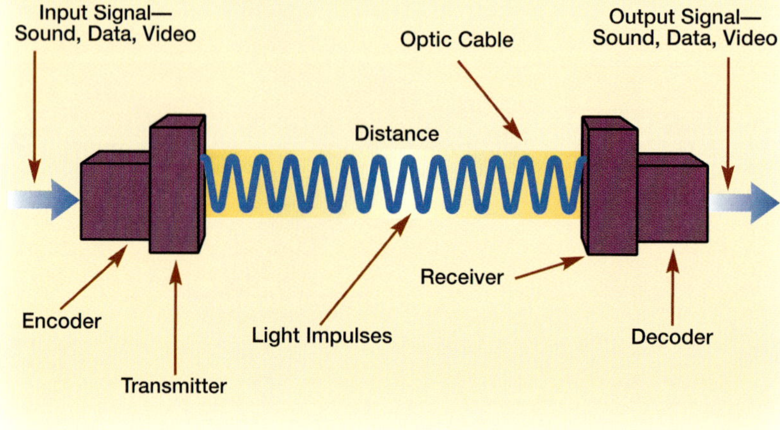

Internet Industry Updates

The Fiber Frenzy

The bottleneck in today's Information Superhighway is the communication's connection or channel between the user and the Web site. Currently, copper telephone connections are the norm, but they are slow. Fiber-optic threads are the medium of the future.

Fiber optics is a new technology for carrying voice, video, sound, and data. A **fiber-optic cable** is simply a bundle of glass strands covered by a protective metallic casing. These strands carry light, flashing at the rate of 10 billion pulses per second.

How Does It Work?

The medium (sound, video, and so on) is first converted to its digital, electronic equivalent. This is done by using an encoder. (See figure below) The digital message is then converted again, into light pulses, and transmitted through glass fibers to the receiving end. At the receiving end, this process is reversed. After decoding, the sound or video is now ready for play.

The Benefits and Costs

The two primary benefits of fiber optics are small size and high transmission rates. A conventional, three-inch-diameter copper cable contains 1,200 pairs of copper wires and can carry about 14,000 telephone conversations. A half-inch thick fiber-optic cable with 72 pairs of fiber-optic strands can carry 14 million telephone conversations. Thus, fiber-optic cable, just $\frac{1}{36}$ the size of copper wire cable, supplies 1,000 times more capacity.

In fiber-optic cable, information travels at the speed of light. A single thread the size of a human hair could carry all the Mother's Day phone calls in the United States made at the peak of demand.

Fiber optics benefit both individuals and businesses. Businesses want to connect electronically to their suppliers, customers, and employees. Today, more people than ever are working at home and communicating with their customers and offices via Internet. This requires the exchange of large volumes of data. Video, a data-intensive medium, can be shown at one hundred frames per second—"movie quality"—using fiber optics. With copper phone lines, it is currently only available at ten frames per second, which results in jerky movements.

But the process is expensive. Costs to lay fiber-optic cable range from $10,000 per mile in rural areas to $60,000 per mile in cities and urban areas. Many large companies such as AT&T, MCI, and Sprint now offer fiber-optic connections to their larger customers. International fiber-optic cable connections exist in the Pacific Ocean that connect the West Coast of the United States with Hawaii, Japan, Alaska, and Australia.

Today, many of the large backbone communications lines are now fiber optic. However, the last connection—the one between the phone company and the household customer—is still copper and still slow. In new residential developments, first-time connections may be fiber optic, but many older residential neighborhoods must first be converted to fiber optics before we all can enjoy the benefits of merging with the Information Superhighway and surfing the Web at the speed of light.

The Internet and the Web now store much of the content for the NII. As these home bottlenecks disappear, we will see a flood of new, rich media being housed on the Web and delivered through the Internet—real audio and video, movies, and even virtual shopping and educational services. Information, commerce, videophones, and entertainment will be at your fingertips, with communications occurring at the speed of light.

Web TV

Web TV is an example of an inexpensive information device. Using an ordinary television set and a specialized computer box, users can attach this system to the Web. Its features are limited.

Information Terminals

The last piece of the NII is the send/process/receive unit at the end of the line, called the **information terminal**. Information terminals are specialized hardware and software devices that collect information coming from the Internet. Once the content is collected, the terminal presents the message to the user, then waits to send the user's response. One common example of an information terminal is the personal computer. Today, a powerful personal computer costs about $2,000. This has been true for the last few years. As capabilities go up and component prices

FIGURE 5.4
Information Devices

Police officers use specialized information devices to send and receive various information they need to do their jobs, such as checking the status of car and driver and maintaining communications with the precinct and other officers in the field.

High-tech cop

Today's street officers use a wide array of advanced technological equipment to fight crime

By PHIL MANZANO
of The Oregonian staff

You think it's tough to get ready for work in the morning?
Hair isn't setting right after that spray of mousse? Tie looking a little crooked?

Can't get your makeup to look quite right?

Well, thank your lucky stars you aren't a street cop.

Because once they're finished getting prepared for a day's work, they've added about 15 pounds of cloth, leather, metal and plastic equipment to their frames.

Today's officers and their cars are walking and rolling mini-police stations, carrying anything from safety kits and report forms, to shotguns and handguns, to "Deputy Crimefighter" badges for the kids.

The whistle and night stick have been replaced by satellite tracking systems, on-board computers and telescoping metal batons • a shift reflecting the technological and social change pushed upon today's police officers.

For instance, the bullet-proof vest, an option in the past, is now required equipment for uniformed Portland police officers. Gresham police carry a nylon pouch on their belts that hold plastic gloves in case they have to come into contact with a suspect's body fluids.

Even the shoes are different. Rather than black, stiff leather boots, most local cops today prefer lightweight athletic walking shoes.

Here's a primer on what's worn by today's high-tech cop:

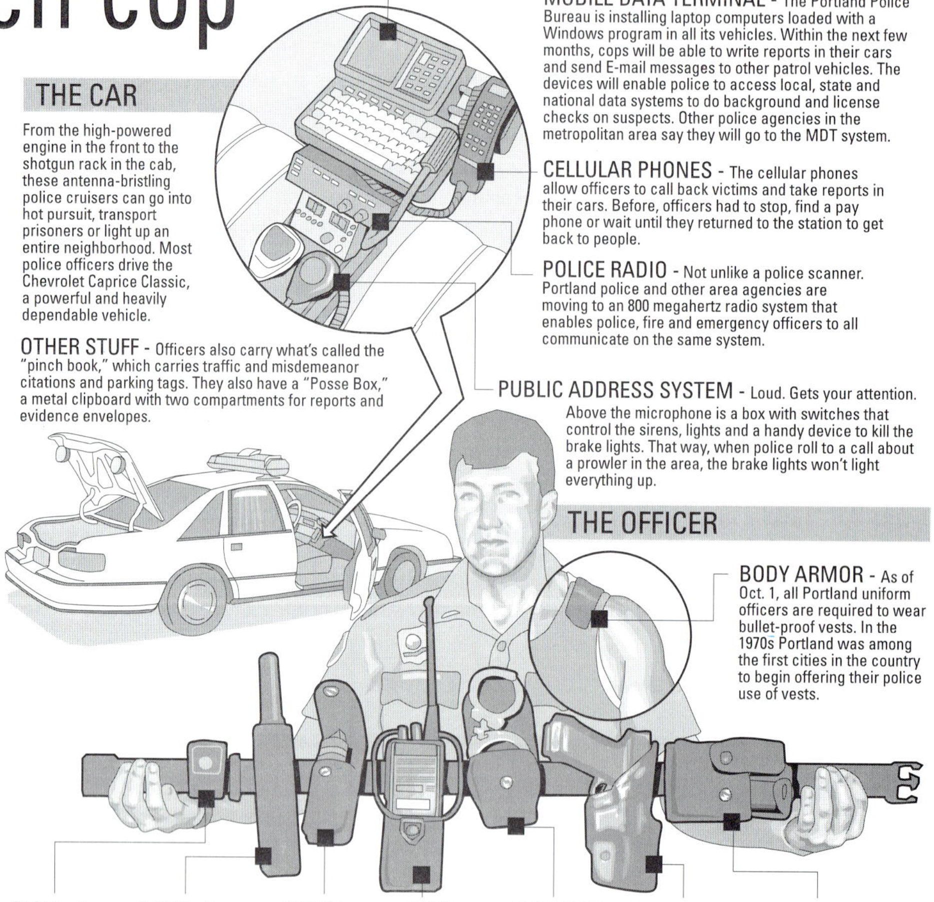

THE CAR

From the high-powered engine in the front to the shotgun rack in the cab, these antenna-bristling police cruisers can go into hot pursuit, transport prisoners or light up an entire neighborhood. Most police officers drive the Chevrolet Caprice Classic, a powerful and heavily dependable vehicle.

OTHER STUFF - Officers also carry what's called the "pinch book," which carries traffic and misdemeanor citations and parking tags. They also have a "Posse Box," a metal clipboard with two compartments for reports and evidence envelopes.

MOBILE DATA TERMINAL - The Portland Police Bureau is installing laptop computers loaded with a Windows program in all its vehicles. Within the next few months, cops will be able to write reports in their cars and send E-mail messages to other patrol vehicles. The devices will enable police to access local, state and national data systems to do background and license checks on suspects. Other police agencies in the metropolitan area say they will go to the MDT system.

CELLULAR PHONES - The cellular phones allow officers to call back victims and take reports in their cars. Before, officers had to stop, find a pay phone or wait until they returned to the station to get back to people.

POLICE RADIO - Not unlike a police scanner. Portland police and other area agencies are moving to an 800 megahertz radio system that enables police, fire and emergency officers to all communicate on the same system.

PUBLIC ADDRESS SYSTEM - Loud. Gets your attention. Above the microphone is a box with switches that control the sirens, lights and a handy device to kill the brake lights. That way, when police roll to a call about a prowler in the area, the brake lights won't light everything up.

THE OFFICER

BODY ARMOR - As of Oct. 1, all Portland uniform officers are required to wear bullet-proof vests. In the 1970s Portland was among the first cities in the country to begin offering their police use of vests.

PAGER - It used to be that only upper-echelon brass had pagers. But now more and more street officers are using them as a way to keep in touch with contacts and people in the community.

BATON - Forget those old-style wooden batons that hung down and banged against the knee as you walked. Portland cops carry the Asp collapsing and telescoping metal baton. It goes from about 9 inches to more than 20 inches with a snap of the wrist.

PEPPER SPRAY - A cayenne pepper-based spray won't kill you, but makes you wish it had. It is especially potent on mucous membranes of the eyes, nose and mouth.

RADIO - The electronic lifeline of the police officer. It gives officers quick contact with colleagues and emergency dispatchers.

HANDCUFFS Lightweight and stainless steel.

GUN - This one is a 9 mm Glock 17 semiautomatic pistol. Other versions include the 9 mm Glock 19 and a .45-caliber Glock 21. Some officers carry either the Smith & Wesson or Sig/Sauer .45-caliber semi-automatic handguns, while others use the age-old .38 Special revolvers.

AMMUNITION- This pouch holds two extra magazines. All the equipment is held on a nylon belt with plastic buckle.

go down, manufacturers have chosen to put more and more capabilities in the equipment but not significantly lower their prices. This price leaves some potential users unable to attach and join the NII. Other suppliers have chosen to produce special-purpose, information terminals information devices that are limited in features, but lower in cost. **Web TV,** a limited-feature, Internet access device is an example (Figure 5.3). It combines with a normal television set to access the Internet and send and receive e-mail. The system is inexpensive ($200 to $400), but cannot store programs or data or do word processing or spreadsheet analysis. Even with these limitations, it has proved moderately popular.

Other professions have specialized information appliance needs (the police officer in Figure 5.4, realtors, bankers, attorneys, salespeople) and may purchase these connection devices rather than a full-featured PC. Regardless, all these appliances simply increase the users and uses of the NII.

Web Applications and Their Impact on Us

Think of the Web and the Internet as **empowering agents.** These new resources allow us to do things that were not possible before. As a result of these new capabilities, we, as a society, change the ways we behave. The capabilities extend to offering us new ways to work, live, learn, and play. Examples are shown in Figure 5.5.

FIGURE 5.5

Web Applications in Life

The Web appears to affect every aspect of life today.

Work

Computers have always affected our work. First came large mainframes, then personal computers, then networks of computers, and now the Web and the Internet. How have these last two affected our work? First, we see collaboration between workers located in different sites. Teams share ideas, resources, and friendships. Collaboration becomes global and not time bound. Businesses easily research competitors' products and processes.

As an example, Hewlett Packard, a major manufacturer of printers, calculators, and computers, uses design teams around the clock and around the globe.

FIGURE 5.6

What is a Cyberteam?

Internet technology allows teams anywhere in the world to join together in solving problems.

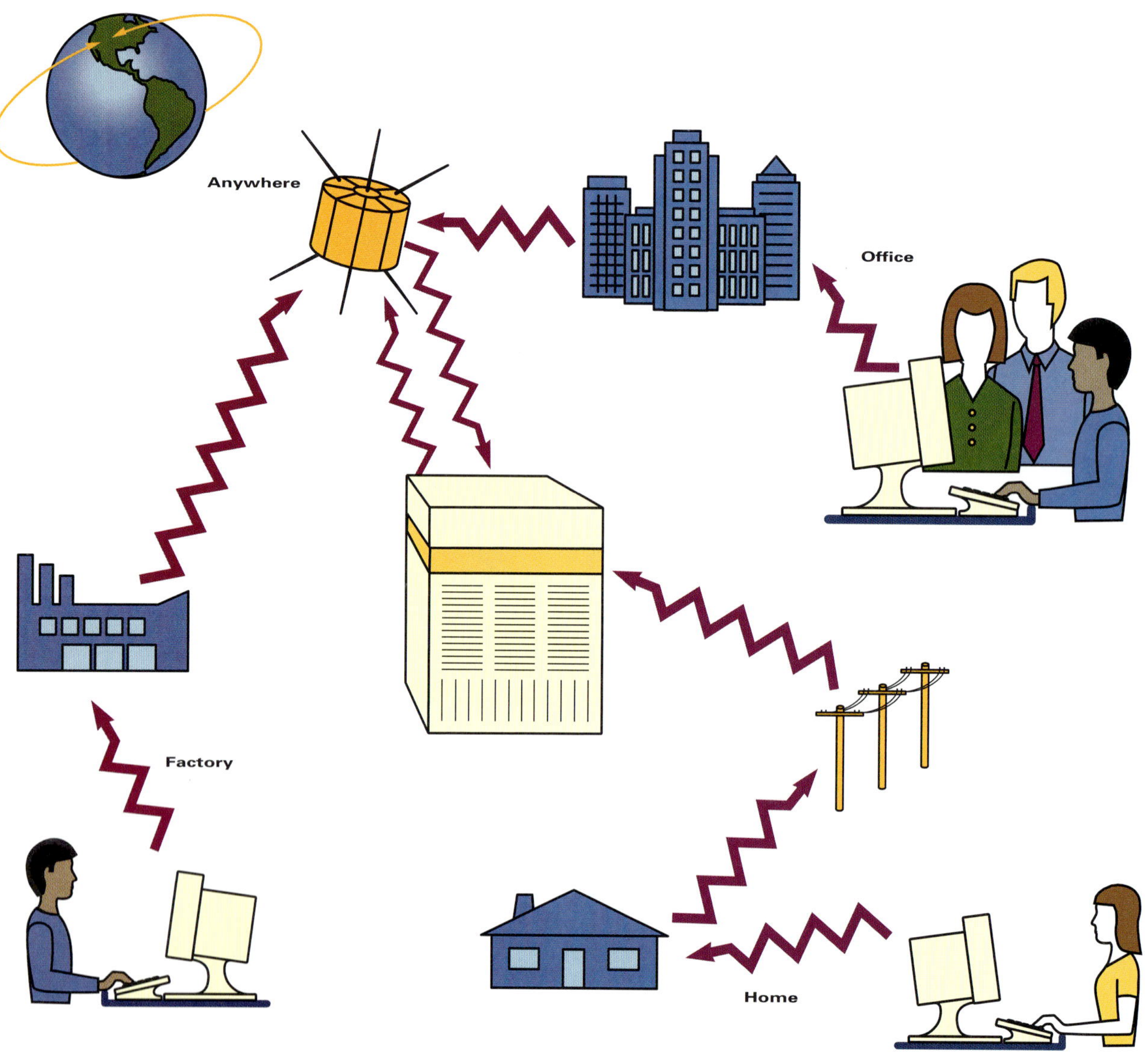

Let's say it's Monday morning and the first shift reports in at 7:30 A.M. in the Vancouver, Washington, plant. This cyberteam works eight hours on the design of a new printer. As they leave for the evening, they transmit their drawings and progress reports to their Japanese counterpart team, who is just arriving for their morning shift. Eight hours later, the Japanese team transmits its work to a third team in France. Finally, the French team wraps up and returns its progress to the Vancouver group, who is just arriving for work on Tuesday morning, twenty-four hours later. Such a process expedites design and reduces the time to market for new HP printers. Think of it as a "5/24" systems team—an international team working five days per week, twenty-four hours per day. Figure 5.6 shows how technology links a cyberteam together.

The Web has also created a new advertising and marketing channel to the customer. With companies being aware that there are 60 million Web users in the United States, note how many national or even local print, television, or radio advertisements mention the Internet address of the advertiser. **Home shopping** is an exploding market. The Web has linked worker to worker, worker to company, company to customer, and company to supplier. Quality is higher, prices are lower, products and services are delivered quicker, and the customer is the beneficiary. Through telecommuting, more and more people are working at home, connected to the office, via Internet. **Telecommuting** is the process of working at home while still communicating electronically with the office and your customers and suppliers. No more commute or traffic jams, no formal suits and ties, and no expensive lunches. These two technologies have substantially changed the business of business. Home businesses have also flourished with the advent of the Internet. Figure 5.7 lists six sample ideas for making money on the Internet, at home.

FIGURE 5.7

Six Money-Making Ideas for Using the Internet at Home

Here is a list of ways that people are currently using the Internet at home to increase their incomes. Can you think of others?

1. **Buying and Selling Stocks and Bonds Online**
   Many Brokerage firms now offer lower commisions and fees for Internet trading

2. **Buying and Selling Real Estate On the Web**
   Today many local real estate companies list their properties on the Web. Shoppers can review home features and compare prices through their computer.

3. **Making Money with U.S. Government Auctions and Surplus Sales**
   Most city, state, and federal agencies post their auction and surplus sales information on the Web. This gives agencies a wider coverage and more bidders for their sales.

4. **Making and Selling Arts & Crafts at Home**
   Turn your hobby into a business by building a Web site and advertising your arts and crafts.

5. **Grants, Awards, and Research Projects**
   Many organizations now post information about their grants and awards on the Web. If qualified, you can submit your project or ideas.

6. **Winning Organizational Sweepstakes and Contests**
   Some Web sites are dedicated simply to informing people about current contests and sweepstake drawings. The more participants, the more effective the resulting product or service advertising.

Web Applications in Bill's House

Even Bill Gates, chairman of Microsoft and the richest person in the United States, finds a variety of uses for the Web in his new home. Miles of communication cable, largely fiber optic, run throughout the house, linking computer servers powered by the Windows NT operating system.

Life

The Internet has changed things at home for children, our parents, our grandparents, our schedules, and our travel patterns. It has changed the way we communicate. (See "The Internet and You," box, below.) Home commerce is automated—automatic bill paying, home shopping, investments, banking, taxes—all through the wonder of electronic communications with the outside world. Even tailored newspaper stories and medical advice can be delivered via the Web to any member of the household.

No home better exemplifies life in the future than that of Microsoft's Bill Gates. (See Figure 5.8.)

Learning

Lifelong learning is the educational theme for future. We will all need to be oriented and educated to new technologies, theories, and practices to stay productive in our work life. How is this possible? The Web will supply the content, and the Internet will be the vehicle. Distance learning is a teaching discipline that allows institutions to deliver credit or noncredit education to your home, at your desired time and pace. Companies are using the Internet to deliver courses to their employees at home or work. Company executives can address their employees live, through video feeds attached to their office computers. Even online questions and answers are possible.

Growing Internet Use: Senior Citizens and Women

We talked earlier in the book about e-mail, which is the primary use of the Internet. The two fastest-growing groups of Web users today are women and those people older than fifty. Once used almost exclusively by young computer jocks, the Internet is now a way of life for us all. Grandmothers are using e-mail to send letters and digital pictures to their grandchildren. Grandchildren think Gramma is cool if she uses the Internet. This technology is forming the Web that binds twenty-first-century families together. It's easy, inexpensive, unobtrusive, and carries a variety of rich media content.

Best estimates are that almost 8 million people over age fifty are now using the Internet, a 100 percent increase from just a year earlier. In America, women account for almost half—27 million—of those users. And there are almost 100 million active e-mail accounts in the United States, as many users have separate ones for work, family, home business, and so on.

Postal officials agree that e-mail, long-distance calls, and faxes are eroding first-class mail as a primary means of personal communication. Today, only about 4 percent of the total mail volume is household-to-household correspondence, less than half the amount of just two years ago.

Now there is a new version of e-mail called instant messaging. Normal e-mail experiences a delay in its delivery. This delay may vary from a few seconds to a few hours. It is not possible to "chat" or talk back and forth with your sender. Chat lines are real time, but they are not private. Everyone reads each message. Instant messaging is a free service offered by a number of service providers such as America Online. It immediately posts the incoming message directly on the receiver's screen. The receiving party then posts a response, and the conversation begins without either party leaving the program currently being run.

Another great Web resource for older Web users is called ThirdAge. The site, founded by Mary Furlong, a University of San Francisco education professor, acts as an electronic front porch where senior citizens gather and share their insights and wisdom. Topics include travel, health, religion, sports, entertainment, and shopping. Chat lines cover a broad selection of general interest topics. There is even an opportunity for members to buy groceries on this Web site and have them delivered to their home.

The site, founded in July of 1997, already has over 30,000 members. While teaching word processing to residents of senior citizen centers, Ms. Furlong recognized loneliness among a number of the people she met there. She sees this site as a friendly, safe environment where older Web users can gather to visit and share their wisdom, experience, and dreams with others. She feels this site adds a new dimension and interest to their lives.

Student **cyberteams** (teams that exist because they are connected via the Web) studying in virtual universities (no walls, no hours, no on-site classes) will form to study specific problems, make recommendations, write group reports, and then move on to new tasks. All testing and evaluations may be done online. Based on student responses, the testing process is altered to strengthen understanding and to improve student performance. Private communication lines will host students, professors, and business managers in roundtable discussions. Libraries will become electronic databases, information resources, and public Web access points to those who have limited choices. Electronic educational opportunities for children in the preschool and primary grades could be the most revolutionary and exciting opportunity of all.

Leisure

Leisure is one of the fastest-growing segments of the Internet. (See Figure 5.9.) If you visit a new-technology entertainment arcade filled with flight simulators, motorcycle racers, and battle stations, you begin to appreciate the many media delivered by these games. By surrounding the participant with stimuli, they are virtually approaching reality.

FIGURE 5.9

Internet Facilitates Leisure

Leisure time is big business. The Internet helps plan leisure activities throughout the world, and its applications are growing rapidly.

Sales of entertainment and travel tickets on the Internet will climb from $475 million this year to over $10 billion by 2001. Forrester Research in Cambridge, Mass., says that Broadway theatres, entertainment companies, and travel agencies have experienced huge successes in selling on the Net.

Exercise, travel, and entertainment are only a few clicks away. You can make an electronic visit to the Louvre in Paris or the Smithsonian in Washington, D.C. If you need a good book, check the 2.5 million available at Amazon.com. (See Figure 5.10.) Finally, who can resist a game of golf against Arnold Palmer or Tiger Woods? Or a basketball game with Michael Jordan? More interested in football? Cyber football leagues are Internet football teams owned and coached by you! They compete weekly, and winners advance to play in the Cyber Bowl championship. The Web brings all these experiences to your house at little expense to you, but it's up to you to take the initiative to join and play.

Web Applications for Students

The combination of the Web and the Internet is the answer to every student's dream. This pair allows you to extend your learning environment beyond the physical confines of the college or university, so you can learn about new ideas and new places without leaving your room. Doing research for student papers becomes almost easy and much more interesting. Local, national, and international perspectives and experts are available on almost every topic. Visit historic sites, hear past presidents speak, e-mail your state or federal congressional representatives. Tell them how *you* feel about a particular issue or bill under study. Buy books, CDs, and concert tickets from the comfort of your room. The process

FIGURE 5.10
Amazon.com Home Page

Amazon.com is the largest seller of books on the Internet. Its home page on the Web is shown below.

is quick, efficient, and fun. It frees time for you to do other, more important or rewarding activities. It gives you the opportunity to take control of your life and your personal development activities.

Next we will highlight only a few examples of how people are using these tools today. As technologies and contents change, more opportunities will be available tomorrow. We challenge you to search for and find your own personal treasure chest of value on the Web. You are limited only by your own imagination.

Art and Leisure

Are you taking an art or history course this term or semester? Would you like to visit some art treasures or historical sites, virtually firsthand? You can "visit" them on the Internet.

In 1996, the Smithsonian celebrated its 150-year anniversary. (See Figure 5.11.) Some communities were fortunate enough to be visited by traveling exhibits from the Smithsonian. If you were not, you can still visit one of its fourteen museums or two art galleries in Washington, D.C., through the Internet. Follow the evolution of man, the development of computers, or our infatuation with the automobile. See the Hope diamond or a space capsule. For most local tourists, the Smithsonian is open only from 10 A.M. to 5:30 P.M. But for you (through Internet), it's open any time, all year round.

Want to visit the Louvre in Paris, France? Find its site and see if you can find the famous painting of Mona Lisa.

The Smithsonian Institute

The Smithsonian is a national treasure for the United States. One of its recent exhibits highlighted the history of computing. Someday the Web and the Internet will become part of its exhibits. Its home page on the Web is shown below.

Government

The Web and the Internet have created a new way to communicate with our government officials at all levels (city, county, state, or federal). Do you know the names and addresses of your U.S. senators and representatives? What do you know about your city or state government? What do you know about the Internal Revenue Service or the FBI? The Web holds the answers. Check it out.

Visit the Whitehouse. See the rooms and note their furnishings. Be sure to sign the electronic guest book! Get the names and addresses of your two U.S. senators. You can even send them each an e-mail.

Home Shopping

From home, using your computer, you can buy almost anything. When you experience the holiday rush (traffic, shoppers, parking, delays, etc,), you begin to see the benefits of home shopping. Figure 5.12 shows how an Internet Mall forms the front door to your online shopping experience. In this figure we see the Internet Shopping site supplies a directory to other online shopping sites (L.L. Bean, FTD Florists, and PC Mall). At each of these sites, you can select items, have them sent directly to you, and charge them to your credit card.

The largest retailer in the world is Wal-Mart. Located in Bentonville, Arkansas, it employs more than 800,000 people in 2,400 stores. Sales are approaching $100 billion per year. It is also the recognized leader in the use of information technology in retailing. It is fitting that we should visit Wal-Mart's Web site to learn more

FIGURE 5.12

Internet Shopping Malls

Internet shopping can be done through an Internet Shopping Mall. The Mall site supplies a directory and link to other sites where specific shopping transactions occur.

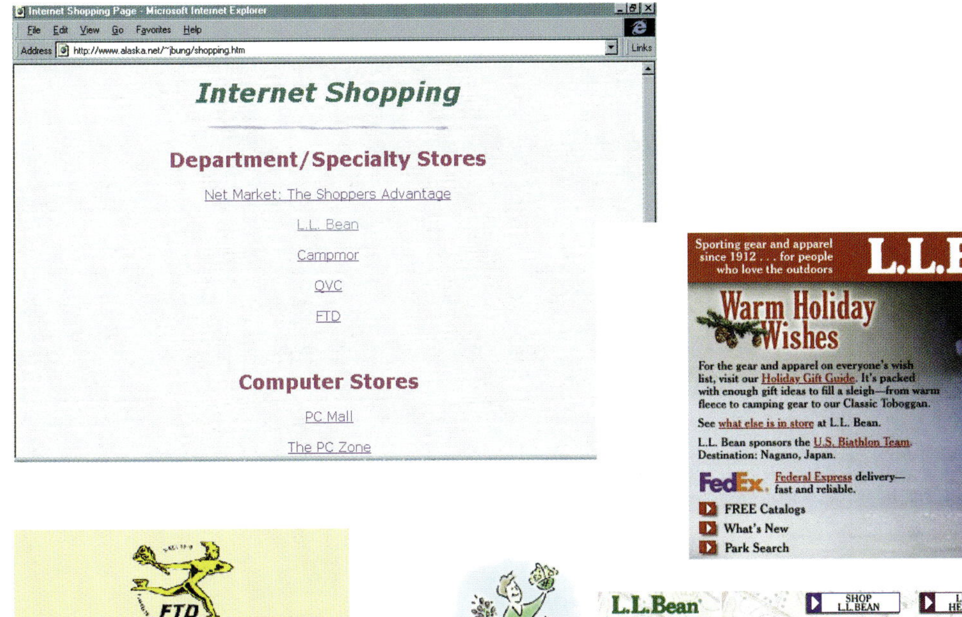

about what they do and what they offer for sale on the Web. Wal-Mart's Web site is shown in Figure 5.13.

On the other end of the spectrum is Surplus Direct. This small company, located in Hood River, a town of 5,000 on the Columbia River in Oregon, sells

Wal-Mart's Home Page

Wal-Mart is the world's largest retailer. Note the items that are sold here. How do they compare to local prices?

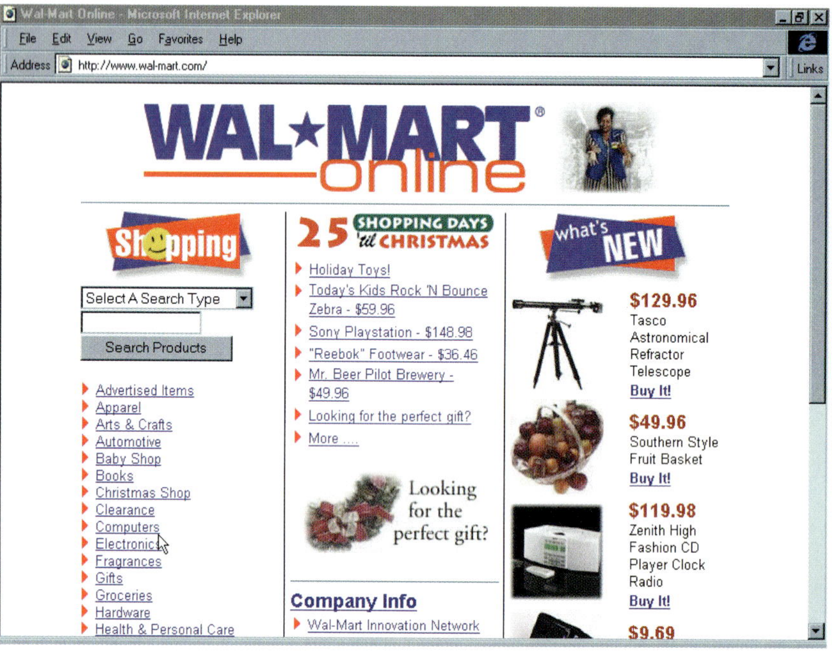

leftover or obsolete computer hardware and software. The company buys large quantities from the manufacturers and then resells them in small quantities to people like us, at great bargains. Visit this interesting company at its Web site.

Sports

Almost every professional team in any sport has a Web page. The pages are usually named after the team if that name was available at the time of registration. The Chicago Bulls professional basketball team is a good example. As the 1997 world champions, you can see the ring each player received as well as photos of all the team members and their statistics. You can even register for free prizes. Who was their best scorer, their best rebounder?

Have you heard of Tiger Woods? He is the newest young golf sensation. A quick search of the Web using his name yields a number of new Web sites. One of them lets you buy his recommended equipment, videos, and books. It is called the Pro Shop. (See Figure 5.14.) The Web has given admirers of Tiger Woods instant access to buy merchandise that he endorses.

Travel

Finally, we look at travel as our last example of Web coverage. Travel is a huge category. It covers everything from backpacking and bicycles to exotic cruises and safaris. This is a category where you can let your mind and imagination run wild as you look at the vast number of ways to spend your money on leisure. We hope it makes you study a little harder!

FIGURE 5.14

Tiger Woods' Home Page for Selling Products

The Web has given the world's admiring public greater access to Tiger Woods. Using this site, Tiger sells products and services he feels will help improve your golf game.

FIGURE 5.15

European Travel Opportunities on the Web

If you are interested in tours of Western Europe, check out this site. Also, watch for Rick Steves' travelogue on a public television station in your area. Rick also has published a number of excellent books on inexpensive travel in Europe. They are available at this site.

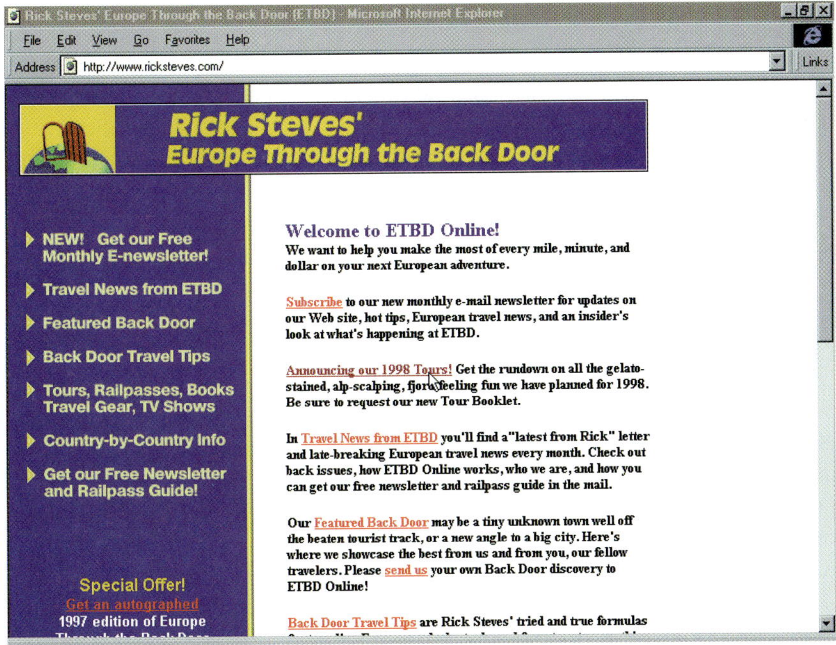

One site we like is "Europe through the Back Door." Rick Steves is a well-known writer and traveler who has a travel show on public television. His preferred method of worldwide travel is to use public transport and carry only a backpack. His travel is affordable and focuses on history, culture, and the unusual nuances of the people and countries he visits. For more information about his travel materials and programs, visit his company site (Figure 5.15).

Do you often get lost in a big city, going from one location to another? A Web site you will surely enjoy is discussed next. Called "Driving Directions," by Lycos, it creates detailed instructions on how to drive from one specified location to another—across town or across the nation! Lycos also offers a mapping service to show you the exact location of a street address within a town or city and a map of the surrounding area. Once the site is identified, it is easy to follow the map to the exact location of the address.

Finally, if you want to go galactic, you can even visit Mars via the Web.

In this section, we showed just a few of the variety of materials available on the Web. With over 20 million Web sites it's hard to imagine a topic or concept that is not covered by some Web home page someplace on the Internet. Now the question is: How do you best prepare to effectively and efficiently use these new electronic resources? How does the Web support team activities and group collaboration projects? What is a cyberteam, and why would we form one?

Teams, Collaboration, and the Web

The Web forms a network that links people together. The term for this is **collaboration.** In this section, we discuss uses of the Web in allowing people to work together.

Collaborative Tools

Collaborative systems focus on people-to-people services. The Hewlett Packard cyberteam discussed earlier in this chapter is just one example of a collaborative system. In today's national or global work environment, the Web offers an ideal resource to facilitate these processes through using team-based problem solving.

A collaborative system provides individuals who are physically separated from each other with the ability to work together using the Web and the Internet. Electronic communication tools that allow this include personal computers, shared whiteboards, conferencing software, and voice and videoconferencing. Figure 5.16 shows the evolution of communications technology that supports collaborative learning.

Shared **whiteboards** (see Figure 5.17) allow remote users to share a common work area on their PCs through a modem or a network. The software tools include electronic pointers, markers, and text that participants use to draw and share information over the Internet. Each participant sees the same board and can react to the drawings and comments of other team members.

Shared spreadsheets and databases are examples of conferencing software. Two or more users work sequentially on the same spreadsheet or database application, inputting data, formulas, or queries to help solve a common problem.

Videoconferencing (see Figure 5.18) allows simultaneous broadcast of audio and video signals to multiple locations. These meeting sites can include desktop computers, classrooms, or specially wired auditoriums. Conferencing tools include a video camera, a microphone, and a sound system. When videoconferencing is combined with computer analysis tools, the teams become virtual. Except for touch and smell, all the senses are active for the cyberteam. The Web and the Internet supply connectivity to link team members together.

Collaboration Opportunities

When we can be electronically joined through technology, our very patterns of living change. Think of the applications in the workplace, in the home, in learning, and in leisure.

FIGURE 5.16

Evolving Communication Technologies That Support Collaborative Learning

The growth in these communications technologies have helped support the use of cyberteams.

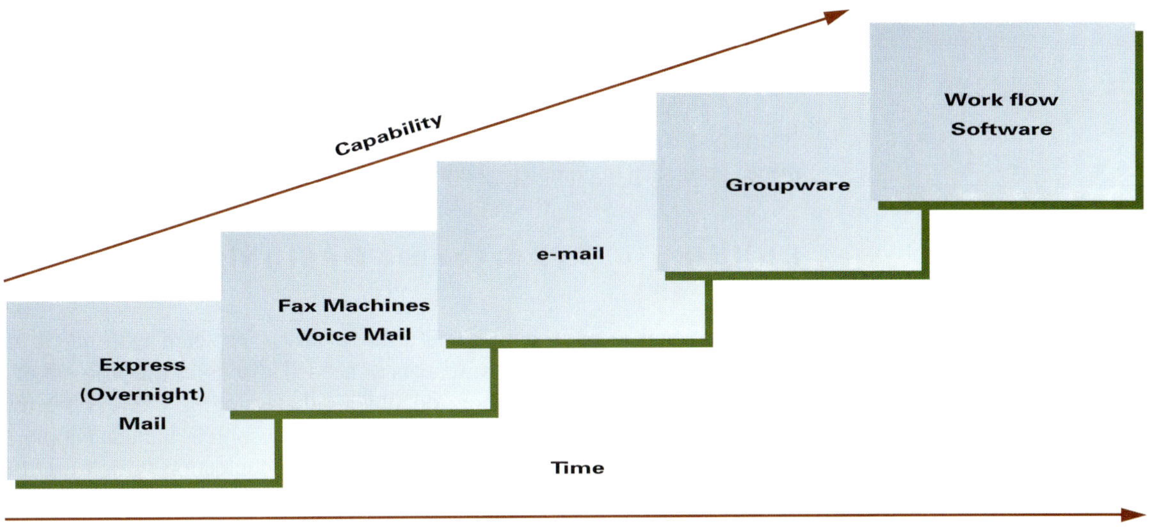

FIGURE 5.17

Shared Whiteboards

Shared electronic whiteboards allow everyone in the group, even if geographically separated, to see what is being presented at the same time.

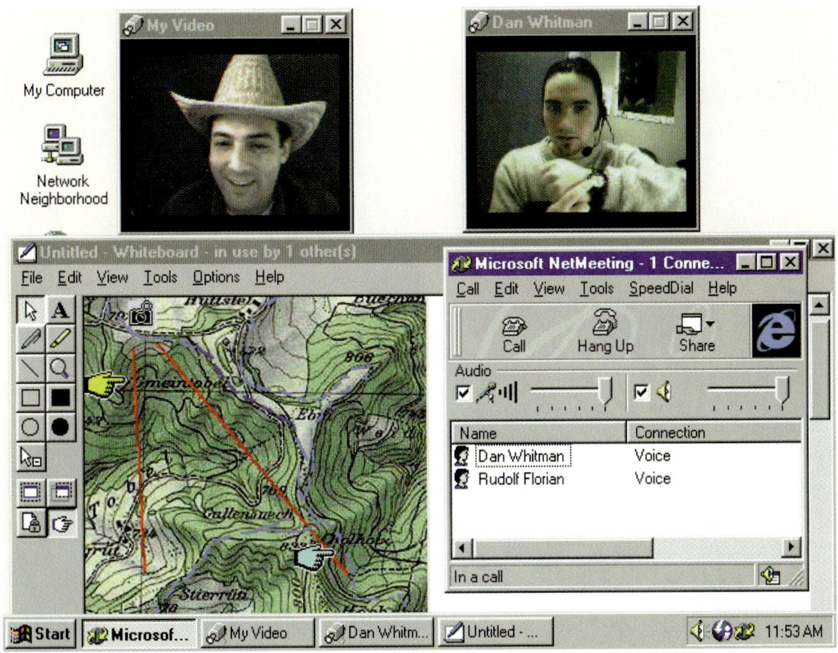

Temporary, as-needed linkages create tremendous opportunities for creative uses. The workplace becomes virtual. Employees can work at home, in a hotel room, on a boat, or at the beach. Work flows out to the people, rather than people coming to work! Think of other impacts: the reductions in commuting time and expense, lower office space requirements, increased home business opportunities, and more time for family relationships.

Organizations form virtual teams to study specific problems. Team members from multiple disciplines and multiple locations can be convened in the problem-solving process. Consultants, academics, and students might join the team.

Education will change. Class members in courses will be able to meet without ever leaving home. The professor, alone in the classroom, or at home, will facilitate class discussion. Virtual education will allow education and other resources to reach physically handicapped students who might not otherwise attend school.

All these new connections and opportunities are facilitated by the Web and the Internet. It is up to us to identify the opportunities and assemble the electronic pieces necessary to complete the job. Now, almost anything is possible.

Building a Cyberteam: Designing for Success

A conventional team is built for a specific task. The team's life cycle might include the following steps: team meets as needed, discusses the problem or task, arrives at a process and solution, documents that solution, delivers the results, periodically reviews progress, and disbands. Team resources include people, technology, data, analytical tools, processes, and communication vehicles. Different

FIGURE 5.18

Videoconferencing

Videoconferencing allows all members of the group to see and hear each other live, even though they may be located in different parts of the world. Video cameras may also show the team exhibits or objects at any one of the participating sites.

team efficiencies are achieved depending on the mix of quantity and quality of these ingredients. Limited resources—time and money—also affect the quality of the process and final results.

With the evolution of the Web, Internet, and cyberteams, the team's resources, processes, and opportunities enlarge. With cyberteams, people can be chosen as team members regardless of their location. The brightest, most talented, most interested people can be drafted for each task. Effective team members should be selected based on their capabilities and interest in the project. While the team is active, these members share their capabilities. Synergy (association and sharing) among members drives group productivity even higher.

The Web, Internet, telecommunication technologies, and PC hardware and software combine to form the communication links and processing tools for the team. Education and training in using these resources improves team productivity. The team's success is also dependent on these technologies working when and where they are needed. Early setup and testing reduces exposure to these technology problems. Figure 5.19 shows some elements of a cyberteam application.

Time is the team's final limiting resource. Completion dates, process activity schedules, and starting dates determine if the project can be done. Also, if a team

FIGURE 5.19

A Cyberteam Application

This diagram shows a three-step process in using cyberteams for group problem solving.

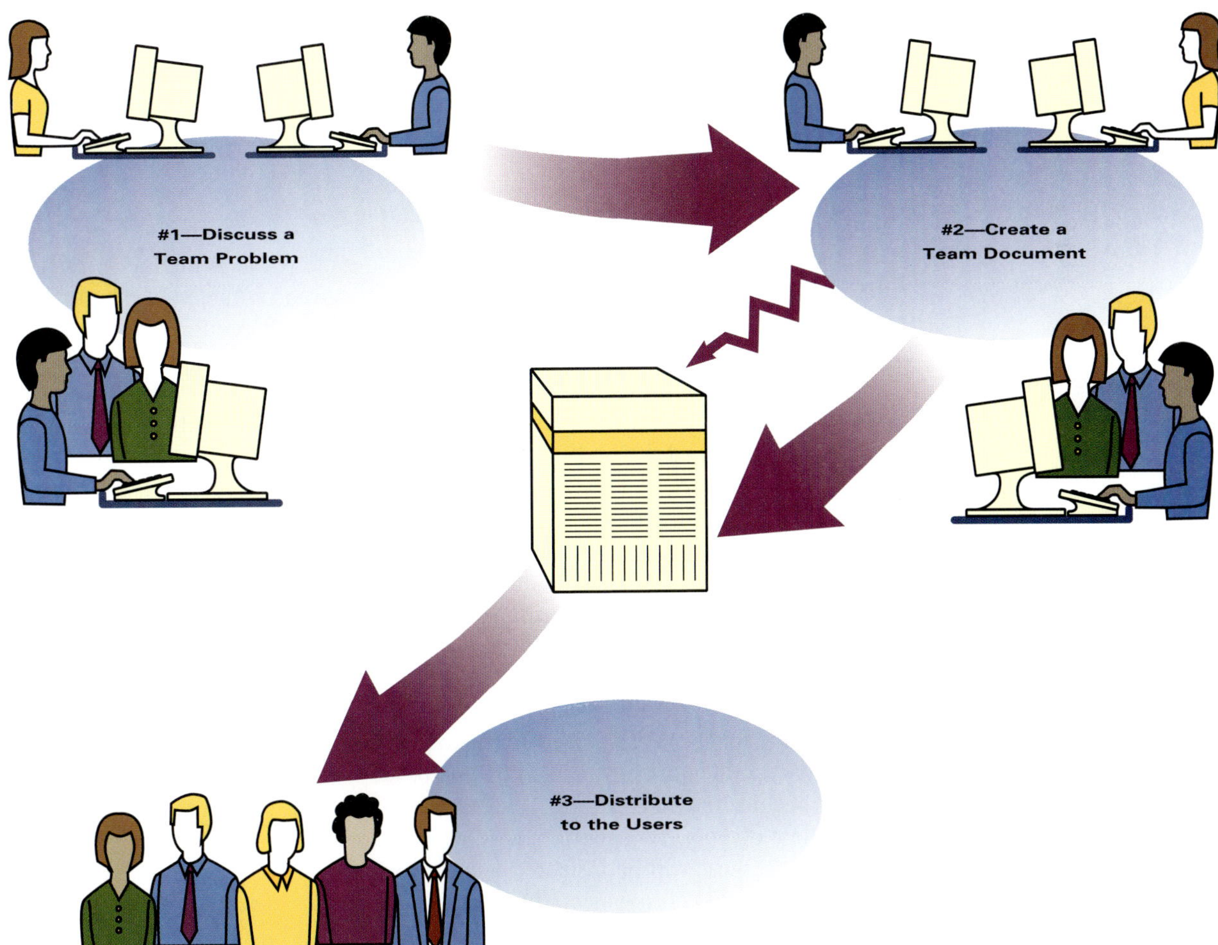

is widely dispersed geographically, time zones and work schedules may interfere. Most cyberteams work in **synchronous communications**. In synchronous communications, there is no time lapse between sending and receiving a message. A telephone conversation is an example of synchronous communications. Synchronous communications allow for simultaneous, real-time, send/receive responses—but it is possible to work in asynchronous mode. In **asynchronous communications** there is a time gap between the time a message is sent and the time it is received. Voice mail and e-mail are examples of asynchronous communications modes. Here members' messages and responses are decoupled. The process may be longer, but it does accommodate differences in time schedules between the sender and receiver.

In the future, we will see more and more use of cyberteams and cyber technologies in organizations, colleges, and universities. At the end of this chapter, we propose two group activities that will let you actually experience some of the benefits and frustrations of this new problem-solving process.

Improving Web Efficiency

With the Web in place, it is only natural to try to improve it. We discuss two improvement technologies below. The first allows you to tailor Web content and what you receive to your personal interests and needs. The second improvement explains how to protect yourself from a deluge of unwanted services and offers.

The normal, most common way to surf the Web is to do selective searches using your favorite Web browser. This often yields a huge volume of references you may want to **"hit,"** or pursue in more detail. Some browsers try to prioritize or rank the references based on the browser's perceived relevance to your interests and search criteria. This helps us find those Web resources that are most relevant to our needs, but it may still leave too many to visit.

Push/Pull Web Technologies

The Web search processes discussed above are referred to in the Internet field as **pull technologies.** Users must *pull* the desired Web resources to the computer they are using. Users of pull technology must identify their information needs, get to a computer to access the service provider, describe their needs to the Web in terms that it understands, and then finally hope that all the Web resources were utilized in their request. This is a lot to ask of users, especially new users. The industry realized this and created push technology sites.

Push services automate Web search and deliver services directly to the user. Rather than waiting for information requests to be pulled by the user, **push technology** services scan the Web for the predefined, specialized needs of their users, then automatically push those information resources to the client's computer. They perform selective surveillance for their users. Now the user is automatically fed only the most current and most relevant information available, often in real time. As new Web content is posted, it is delivered to the client. Webmasters become **Webcasters**, broadcasting their site content to waiting audiences. You don't go to the Web; the Web comes to you. Figure 5.20 shows how this technology works. It's life beyond surfing and browsing.

Imagine the applications—live updates of stock prices via ticker tapes on the bottom of the screen, sports scores, weather forecasts, traffic, breaking news stories. All these can be instantly delivered while you are connected. The service stops when you disconnect, then restarts at the next connection.

Four popular sites for Web push delivery systems are BackWeb, News Ticker, The PointCast Network, and My Yahoo! All are free, but their content

FIGURE 5.20

How Web "Push" Technology Works

Push technology allows Web users to selectively identify their information needs, then have that information automatically delivered to their desktop computers.

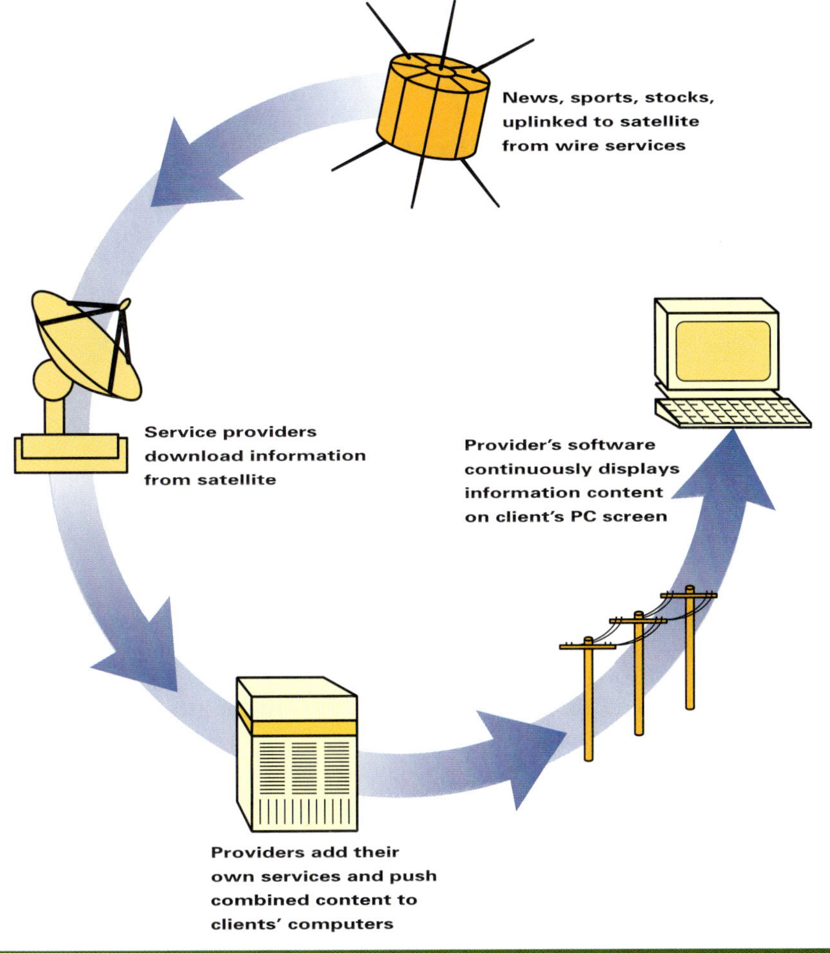

and features vary. For more information, visit any of these sites. PointCast and Intermind homepages are shown in Figure 5.21.

Spam Mail

We all know about junk mail from the post office and have had telephone salespeople call just before dinner. What you might not realize is that these same distractions occur with Internet e-mail. It is jokingly referred to as **spam mail** in the Web world—a collection of unknown ingredients and surprises, all mixed together. This topic was briefly covered in Chapter 4, but it also deserves some attention here.

How big a problem is spam? Cyber Promotions, a company specializing in the distribution of advertising through e-mail, sends up to 20 million e-mail advertisements per day. It is easy to get on junk e-mail lists, but it's hard to get off them.

How do you protect yourself from these unwanted intrusions that fill your e-mail box and block your phone lines? Help is available. Software vendors and the Internet service providers are now supplying users with shields and filters to block these incoming messages. Most of these programs, available on the Web, are free.

Two Web Push Technology Sites

These two sites are examples of how Web users can be proactive. By preselecting information needs (individual stock prices, late-breaking foreign news, etc), users can instantly stay informed in their areas of interest through Web delivery.

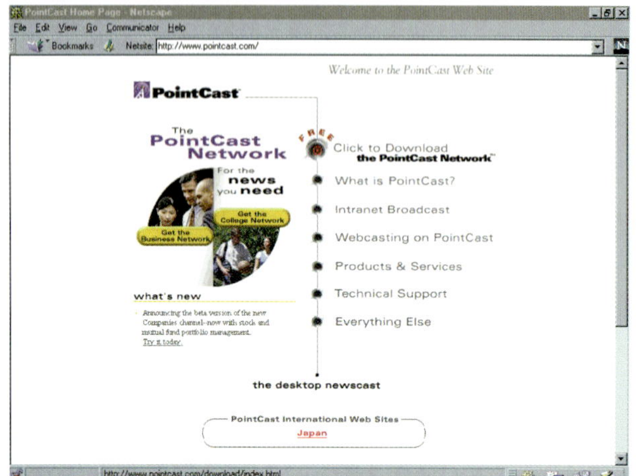
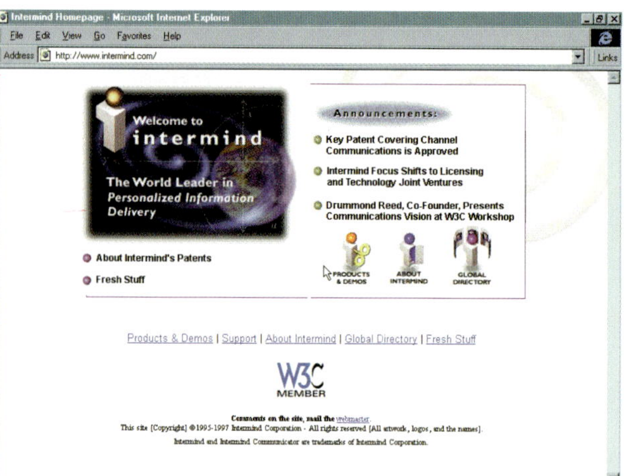

America Online offers its customers a preferred mail option to help filter junk e-mail. Some software companies include e-mail filtering as a feature of their e-mail products. Netscape Navigator offers some relief for its subscription users as well. Spam-filtering program names are creative and colorful—Spaminator, MailJail, Cancel-It, and Junkbuster's SpamOff. Check out these options if spam mail becomes a problem. But, if all else fails, you have the final say. Simply hit the Delete key for the spam message and move on to more pressing issues.

Two Sample Internet Case Studies

To show you the actual value of using the Web and the process of how to use it, we have included two examples of typical student applications. The first deals with researching professional employment opportunities. The second shows how you might use the Web to research a new or used car purchase.

Preparing for Your Career While Still in School

You are unique! You consist of a unique combination of motives, strengths, weaknesses, and experiences. College is an opportunity to learn new theories, practices, processes, and computer skills needed for employment. College builds your academic knowledge, as well as social and political skills. Your search for professional employment requires that you market these new skills and abilities. Figure 5.22 shows the ten skills today's employers say they desire most in their new employees.

The Internet is filled with career-related information. This ranges from career planning to career information sources to companies soliciting new employees through their Web sites. These companies encourage job candidates to submit their resumes via e-mail. Interviews can even be conducted on the Web. The following list details a job search process and the Web sites you will find helpful at each step.

1. Inventory your skills, career interests, job categories, and the industries that interest you. What do you want from your career—compensation, travel, personal growth, advancement? You might want to write a current resume. If you are close to interviewing before graduation, assemble a collection of your highlights and bind them together in a personal portfolio, much like an artist or advertising executive might have. One Web site that talks about work and life issues is Tripod. (See Figure 5.23.)

FIGURE 5.22
Employers' Ten Most Desirable Employee Skills

Here is the list of what employers look for in their employees. Note the heavy emphasis on teams, analytical and decision-making skills, and the use of computers!

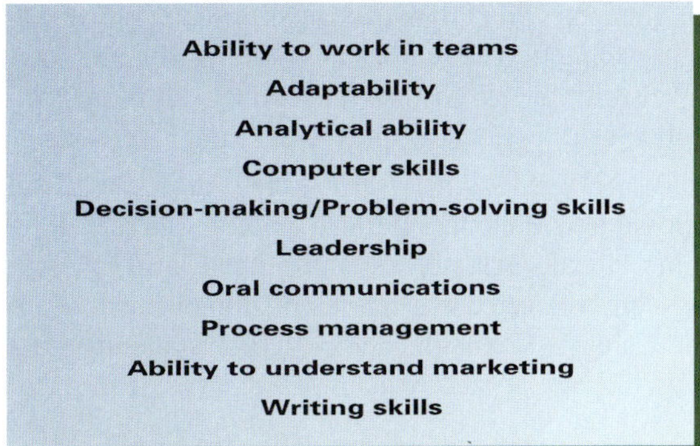

FIGURE 5.23
Tripod Home Page

Tripod offers topics and advice covering all aspects of life, including employment.

2. Now visit career-oriented Web sites. These contain information about careers and companies, employment issues, and how to pursue employment. They all contain links to other career sites and other information sources. Some even contain job postings, free resume development help, tips on how to job hunt, online job fairs, and international opportunities. We refer to the following group of four Web sites as Internet's "Career Central":

- Career Mosaic
- Catapult
- Online Career Center
- Jobs on the Monster Board

Career Mosaic's home page is shown in Figure 5.24.

3. Visit some company Web sites and learn about their career opportunities and how you might apply. You might choose any company you are familiar with, or you might want to look at companies such as Boeing, Caterpillar Tractor, Intel, and Wal-Mart. See if you can find similarities in the abilities and skills requested of new professional employees. A sample of Boeing's employment opportunities, as listed on its Web page, is shown in Figure 5.25.

4. It is even possible to conduct interviews on the Internet. Recently, students attending nine Atlantic Coast Conference and twelve Southeastern Conference universities were connected to a number of employers in the nation's first virtual job fair. Using **VIEWnet** technology, 1000 students interviewed for 300

Career Mosaic Home Page

Career Mosaic, one of the four Career Central Web sites, offers a variety of information and insights about careers and professional employment.

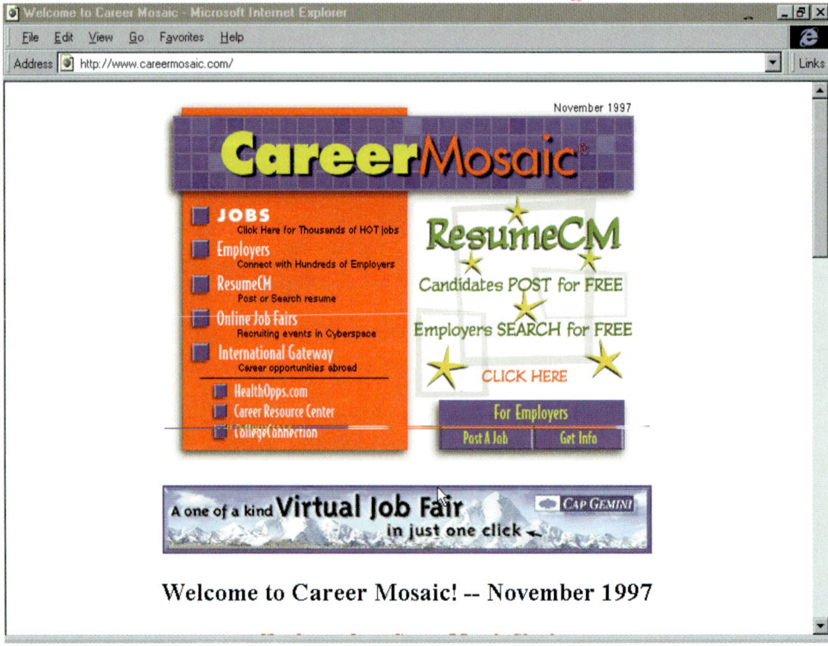

positions. Only head and shoulder images were shown of the candidates and the interviewers. Most agreed that the experiment was a big success!

As you can see, the Internet may not replace the more traditional job search process, but it certainly can complement it.

How to Buy a Car Using the Internet

Buying a car is like having a root canal, only the car purchase takes longer. And, with the root canal, you don't get insulted or waste your time. But computers, electronic communications, and the Internet have come to our rescue. Some feel the recent decline in the number of auto dealerships in the United States is attributed to the changing way people buy their autos today. At the very least, the Web will make you an informed buyer when you arrive at the showroom. You will know a good deal when you see it.

Auto retailing is a $500 billion industry today. Dealers associated with a manufacturer sell almost 30 million new or used cars per year. Private parties sell another 15 million. It appears that technology may offer opportunities for improving this process.

A quick visit to the major Web search engines reveals most have individual search categories related to auto purchases. Microsoft's search site offers a special service called "CarPoint (Figure 5.26). Topics include model features, prices, safety features, financing, comparison with competitors' models, photos, dealer locations, "test" drives, and even "interior surround videos to acquaint you with interior appointments and features.

FIGURE 5.25

Boeing's Employment Opportunities Web Page

Most large companies post their employment opportunities on their Web sites. Here is an example of some employment opportunities at Boeing.

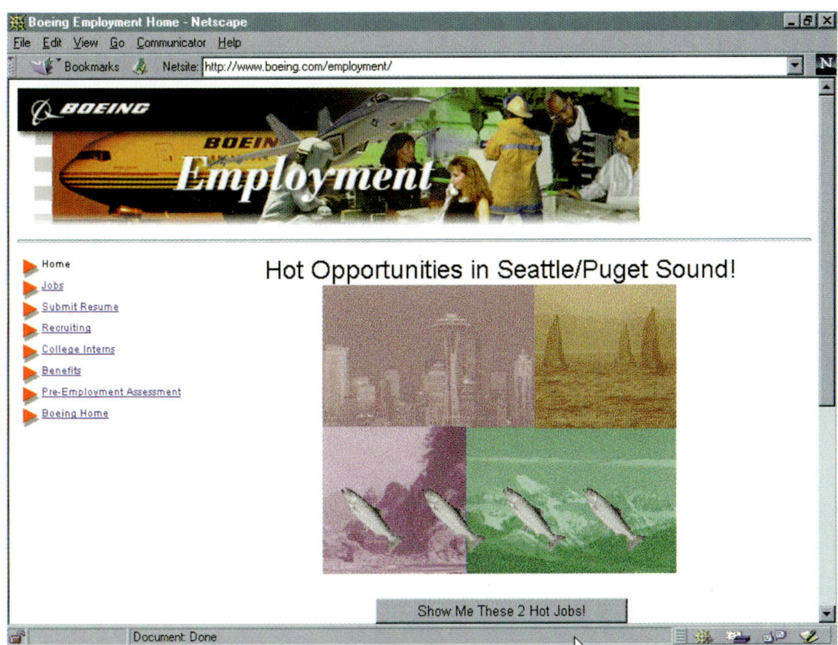

FIGURE 5.26

Buying a Car at CarPoint

Many Web sites deal with auto purchases. CarPoint is one good example. Visit this site and "test drive" your next purchase!

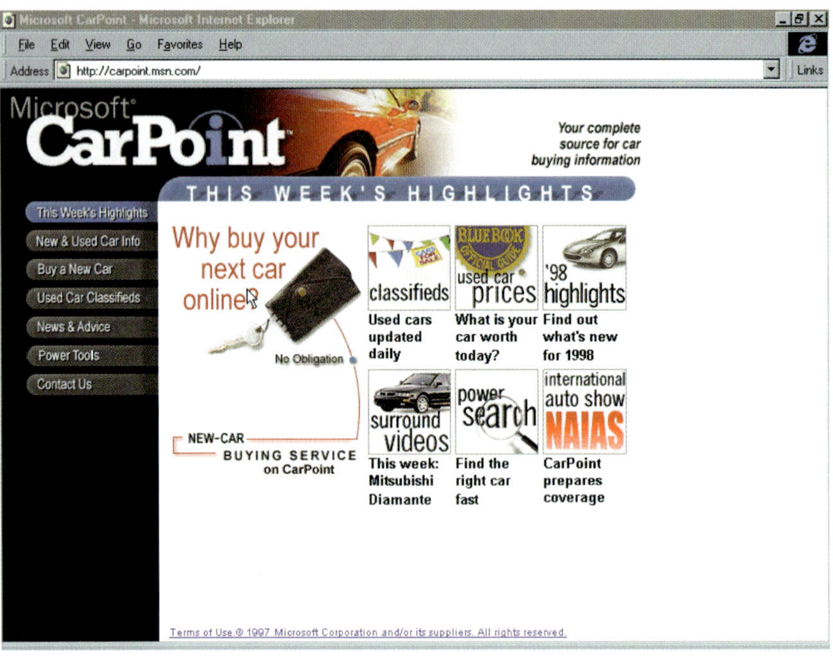

FIGURE 5.27

Visit the CarMax Showroom

CarMax, a subsidiary of Circuit City, is the superstore of auto sales. Both new and used cars with a five-day return policy are available here.

Excite, another Web search engine, also has a special category for autos. There, you will find a number of links to other auto purchase and auto sale sites. Used car sites are also available. There is even a link to the Car and Driver Buyers Guide site.

Perhaps one of the most interesting concepts for auto purchase and sale is that offered by CarMax. This company is a subsidiary of Circuit City, the giant consumer electronics retailer. CarMax locations, the superstore of auto sales, typically inventory eight hundred to one thousand cars at each site.

Because research shows that only about one-fifth of the people like to negotiate an auto price, CarMax offers a one-price policy for each new and used car. There are no negotiations (much like Saturn auto dealers). Each auto comes with a five-day, money-back guarantee. Over 90 percent of the buyers say they are very satisfied with their buying experience at CarMax, an unusually high number by today's standards.

A visit to the CarMax Web site will acquaint you with their offerings and services. It is a unique concept. The Internet and the Web have obviously contributed to the success of this auto sales format. A sample of the CarMax Web page is shown in Figure 5.27.

What's left to buy? How about a personal computer! We address this in the activities section at the end of this chapter.

SUMMARY

Computers have always affected our work—first came large mainframes, then personal computers, then networks of computers, and now the Web and the Internet.

The National Information Superhighway combines computer power, digital communications and content, and information appliances. Users navigate this highway using the Web and the Internet.

Web applications on the Information Superhighway affect how we work, live, learn, and play. Popular Web applications for students include home shopping, travel, research, and entertainment.

Two practical Web applications for students include help with the job search process and help in buying a car.

Information appliances such as Web TV are alternative, limited-feature, Internet access devices.

The Web is also a group collaboration tool. It allows cyberteam members to do group communications and research. Teams share ideas, resources, and friendships.

How does the Web support team activities and group collaboration projects? The Web forms a network that links people together. Collaborative systems focus on people-to-people services. In today's national or global work environment, the Web offers an ideal resource to facilitate these processes using team-based problem solving.

The Web and the Internet supply connectivity to link team members together. Team resources include people, technology, data, analytical tools, processes, and communication vehicles. Collaborative opportunities will continue to grow in the future as the Web grows.

The normal Web search processes are referred to in the Internet field as "pull" technologies. Users must *pull* the desired Web resources to the computer they are using. Now the Web offers *push* technology sites. Push services automate the Web search and deliver specialized services requested by the user.

The Internet is filled with career-related information. This ranges from career planning to career information sources to companies soliciting new employees through their Web sites. Interviews can even be conducted on the Net.

Think of the Web and the Internet as your personal empowering agents.

KEY TERMS

asynchronous communications (134)
collaboration (130)
collaborative systems (130)
cyberteams (123)
data (114)
decision making (114)
empowering agents (119)
fiber-optic cable (116)
hits (134)

homeshopping (121)
information (114)
information terminal (118)
knowledge (114)
Moore's Law (116)
National Information Infrastructure (NII) (115)
National Information Superhighway (115)
problem solving (114)

pull technologies (134)
push technologies (134)
spam mail (135)
synchronous communications (134)
telecommuting (121)
videoconferencing (130)
VIEWnet (138)
Web TV (119)
Webcasters (134)
whiteboards (130)
wisdom (114)

END-OF-CHAPTER ACTIVITIES

Matching

a. Wal-Mart
b. cyberteams
c. hits
d. information device

e. fiber optics
f. National Information Infrastructure (NII)

g. information
h. push technologies
i. spam mail
j. whiteboards

_________ **1.** Electronic chalkboards used in videoconferencing and cyberteam communications.

_________ **2.** Unwanted or unrequested messages received through e-mail.

_________ **3.** Process whereby continuous streams of specialized information are sent directly to the user through the Internet and the Web.

_________ **4.** Processed and refined data.

_________ **5.** An evolving technology and communications system used to connect our society with its information sources and commercial providers.

_________ **6.** Communications technology that uses threadlike glass cables to transmit signals.

_________ **7.** Inexpensive input/output hardware devices used by people in specialized professions.

_________ **8.** Occurs when a Web site is visited by an outside guest or user.

_________ **9.** Groups of people physically separated by distance, but using computers and the Web to work together on a project

________ **10.** Large, national retailer that allows users to shop at home on its Web site.

Review Questions

1. What is the difference between decision making and problem solving?
2. How do the Web and the Internet expand your personal decision-making and problem-solving capabilities?
3. Is the National Information Superhighway really a highway? Explain.
4. What has happened to computing power historically? How does this affect the opportunities in the future for the Web and the Internet?
5. What are information appliances?
6. How can the Web be used in your college education and in your courses?
7. How can the Web help you find a career field and a job?
8. What is a cyberteam? How does it work?
9. What is the difference between Web push technology and pull technology?
10. How could the Web help you buy a car?

Activities

1. Interview two professional people you know. Ask them how the Web or the Internet has changed their job. What do they do differently now? What do they do better? What Web advances do they think will happen next in their field?
2. Find a local newspaper advertisement that references a Web address. Visit that site and assess its effectiveness. What did you like and dislike about the site?
3. Assume you are about to buy a new automobile. Pick a make and model you're familiar with. Go shopping for that car on the Web. Find two different Web sites and get a price for your car. Be sure that the features are comparable. Would you buy a car on the Web? Why or why not?
4. "In the next five years, almost everyone seeking employment will need to know how to use the Web and the Internet." Explain why you agree or disagree with this statement.
5. Visit a local company in your area. Ask the employees how they use the Web in their company. Are the employees provided with Web access and e-mail accounts? What impact has the Web had on employee productivity in this company? Write up your findings and present them to your class.

Student Activities: Two Collaborative Team Projects

PROJECT NO. 1: BUYING A COMPUTER—A CYBERTEAM EXPERIENCE

Background   In this chapter we discussed two sample Internet applications: career searches and how to buy a car. We also discussed how the Internet allows you to join individuals together in a cyberteam to perform a task. We want you to combine both of these topics by participating in a cyberteam, using the Internet. Your primary tools are the Internet, e-mail, a telephone, and a word processor.

Your team task is to research at least four computer suppliers (locally in your community as well as on the Web), then select one to supply the computer you need. You must consider criteria such as features, cost, delivery, warranty, and so on, from each supplier. Your team will create this criteria list. We specify later the minimum characteristics your computer must have.

The Process   If all your team members have access to e-mail, we ask that your team communicate using either e-mail or the telephone. In class, your professor will form the teams (we suggest between three to five members), or you can choose your group. Initially, meet face-to-face to discuss the project and decide how your team will accomplish its goals. Then, do not meet again in person until the end of the project. This will give you a better understanding of how working in a cyberteam would actually feel. If not everyone has e-mail, use the telephone for communications; e-mail correspondence should be used among members who do have access.

Computer Specifications   The minimum specifications your computer must have are listed below. If you significantly exceed these, explain why.

Pentium Pro-II 300 MMX

64 MB EDO RAM

20X CD-ROM drive

6 gig hard drive

4MG video card

sound card

56K voice fax modem

200 watt amp speakers

SVGA card

17" .26 dpi SVGA monitor

Win 98 operating system

mouse

104 key keyboard

one-year warranty

Final Product   Your team will submit a write-up of your project, not to exceed two pages. You must also decide how this final paper will be prepared, and by whom. The write-up should include the following:

the names of all team members

a brief description of the process your team used to complete this project

a recommended supplier, including company address

the price and features of the computer you chose

any features you chose that exceeded the minimum configuration and why chosen

comments on the cyberteam experience:

   benefits of the cyberteam configuration

   problems with cyberteaming

   suggestions for project or process improvement

   other possible applications for the cyberteam concept

   other team thoughts or comments

When completed, discuss this project with your fellow classmates and your professor. Also discuss this project with your family and friends. We believe activities and processes like these will be the methods of the future in every academic discipline.

CYBERTEAM PROJECT NO. 2: RESEARCHING THE STATUS OF FIBER OPTICS IN YOUR AREA

In this chapter we discussed fiber optics as a new, high-speed communications link for the Internet. Yet, throughout the United States, the status of fiber-optics installations varies tremendously. In order for you to better understand your communications options in general and this communications technology in particular, we would like you to form cyberteams and research the status of fiber optics and other communications options in your specific geographic area.

Form teams of five class members. Each member should be responsible for researching a specific geographic area. One member should focus on connections to the home. What communication options—standard telephone lines, ISDN lines, digital lines, fiber-optic lines, and so on—are available to the home? Contact your local telephone company. Introduce yourself and tell them about your class project. Gather information about each home option they provide, including installation charges, monthly service charges, speeds, features, and so on. Also check with your cable TV providers to see if they can supply access to the Internet. A second team member should look at the status of fiber optics at the city and county level. How can businesses and other organizations get connected to each other and to the Internet? Again look at costs and capabilities. A third team member will survey the status of communications at the state level, and the fourth team member will review at it at the national level. The fifth team member will look at the international and global status of communications connections.

Your research should include phone calls, e-mails, and faxes to companies who supply services. It should also include a thorough search of the Internet using browsers and search services to see what additional information is available about communications and fiber optics.

Summarize your findings in a two-page group report. Perhaps your group could also develop a one-page visual aid or graphic to help explain your team's findings. Bring your paper to class and discuss your findings with your professor and other class members.

After completing this project, you will have a much better understanding of how important communication channels are to the Internet and how you and an organization might best connect to the Internet and to other organizations. This should be a very interesting, educational, practical, valuable, and enjoyable project for you, your cyberteam, your classmates, and your professor.

CHAPTER SIX

Building a Web Presence

Why Build a Web Site?
   Personal Sites
   Organizational Sites
Building a Cyber Portfolio: A Student Project
Steps in Web Page Creation: What Makes a Great Web Site
   Step One: Ideate
   Step Two: Formulate
   Step Three: Construct
Designing Sites for Success
   The Customer
   Content
   Site Structure
   Color and Emotion

Web Media Types
   Text
   Graphics
   Clip art
   Schematics
   Sound
   3-D Virtual Reality
Media Considerations
   Bandwidth
   Different PC Capabilities
Specialized Media Hardware Devices
   Digital Cameras
   Scanners
   Video Cameras

Web Site Builders
Web Site Hosts
Registering and Promoting Your Site in Cyberspace
   Registration Process
   Promotion Options
Maintaining the Site
   Timely/Current Information
   Continuous Refinement
Summary
Key Terms
End-of-Chapter Activities
   Matching
   Activities

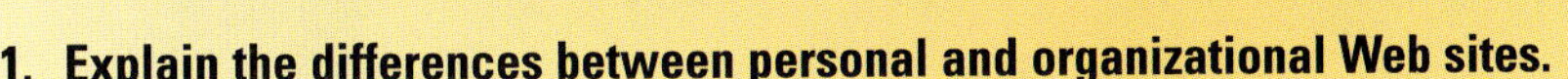

AFTER COMPLETING THIS CHAPTER, YOU WILL:

1. Explain the differences between personal and organizational Web sites.

2. Discuss why and how you would build a cyber portfolio and what it should contain.

3. List and discuss the three steps in Web page construction.

4. Discuss the importance of structure and content in Web site design.

5. List and describe six media types used in Web sites. Discuss two benefits and limitations of each.

6. Discuss the significance and impact of bandwidth on Web designs.

7. Name three types of special media hardware that can help create Web site materials and content.

8. Explain two ways you can register your Web site on the Internet.

9. Describe six ways you can promote your Web site location and content.

10. Explain what is required to maintain and grow a Web site over time.

Why Build a Web Site?

Now that you understand what the Web is about, you need to know how to create a unique Web presence on it. Why build a Web site? What makes a great Web site? How is it done? What media options are available? Constructing a Web site will improve your organizational skills and personal creativity.

Web sites are used by both individuals and organizations. The size and scope of personal and organizational applications may be quite different, but many of the construction processes are the same. The following sections discuss ideas and tools to capture and hold the interest of Web site visitors. Web research suggests that a Net surfer's attention span during the first visit to a site is somewhere between five and ten seconds! If you have not conveyed your site's content or value or why they should stay within that period of time, they simply stop downloading the site and move on. It was a "hit," but not a catch.

In this chapter, we review Web processes—content and features that make a great Web site. We look at the basic Web media building blocks and the steps needed to put them together. When the site is built, it should be registered, advertised, promoted, and maintained. It must be kept fresh. This chapter covers "how to" Web issues related to building and maintaining your site. We ask that you consider building your own personal site and also suggest a possible host and content for that site. Figure 6.1 shows the typical Web site **design cycle.**

Personal Sites

Personal sites exist for a variety of reasons. Some Web authors simply want to master Web site construction. Some want a low-cost, high-technology way of

FIGURE 6.1

The Typical Web Site Design Cycle

The Web site design cycle consists of six steps. Note that the process forms a circle. Once the cycle is completed, it is usually done again.

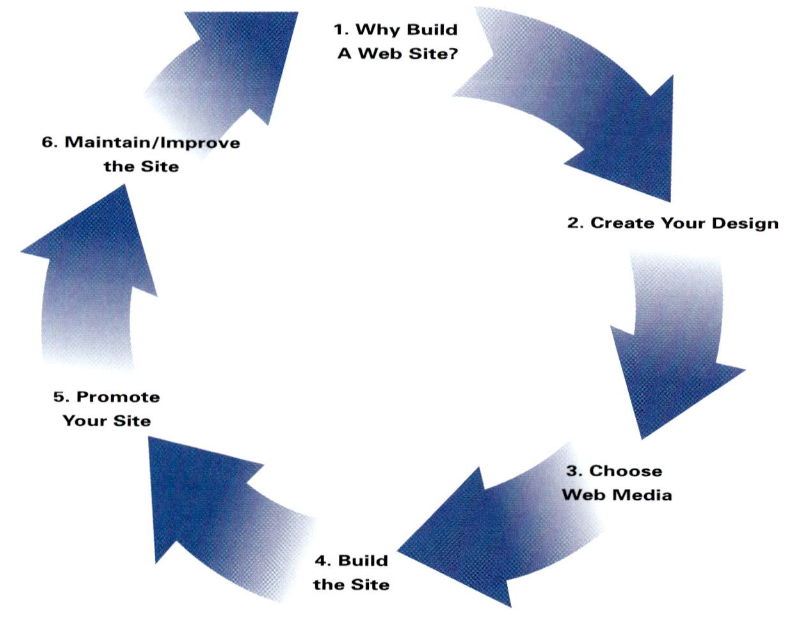

communicating with a larger audience to broadcast personal opinions or special agendas. Some want to meet new people and form cyberspace friendships. Some want to sell something. All want to learn more about this twenty-first century advertising vehicle and communications tool. All see the value and potential of the Web as another communications link to the outside world. Figure 6.2 shows a collage of personal sites on the Web.

FIGURE 6.2

A Collage of Personal Sites on the Web

Here is a variety of Web sites produced and stored on the Web that were created by individuals. Note the variety of content.

This is a small repository of college humor. Yes, I said college humor, which signifies that sometimes it is sophomoric, inane, or just plain stupid (but not *all* of it is). Read at your own discretion...

Matthew and Jake's Adventures

This is surfing. This is Matthew and Jake surfing. It involves water and a surfboard. No computers are involved in surfing.

Organizational Sites

The number of business services listed on the Internet is huge. Figure 6.3 lists just a few. Many businesses are having great success actually selling products over the Internet. The Internet hides the size of the organization from the visitor. Potential customers don't know if the company has one employee or one

FIGURE 6.3

List of Business Services on the Internet

With millions of sites on the Web, almost every business service is represented.

Web Categories

Airlines	Internet/Web Tools
Automobiles, Trucks, and Information	Investments
Business/Computer Publications	Large U.S. Companies
Car Rentals	Librarian's Special
Career Advice and Employment Opportunities	Life and Leisure
Colleges and Universities	Magazines
Computer Games	Miscellaneous
Computers & Technology	Movies
Computer Software Companies	News, Financial Information, and Weather
Entertainment, Music, and Theme Parks	Search Engines
General Business Links	Sports
History	Skiing Information
Hotels and Lodging	Travel Resources
Internet Companies and Services	U.S. Government
Internet Shopping	

thousand. Small companies appear big. This actually equalizes competition and creates an enormous opportunity for the small, entrepreneurial business owner. At the same time, it becomes more of a risk to the customer who is asked to order items and send payments to an unknown entity. Still, today, the fastest-growing sales opportunities for businesses of all types and sizes appear to be on the Internet.

Whether an individual or an organization, these opportunities come with challenges. Individuals and organizations must develop their own Internet business plan and site. The plan identifies the goals and strategies for the Internet site, explaining how it fits into marketing and distribution. Sites should appeal to society's changing needs, time pressures, and lifestyles. Tomorrow's successful organizations will be run by people who recognize these changing needs and have the vision to see how Web-based activities can meet them.

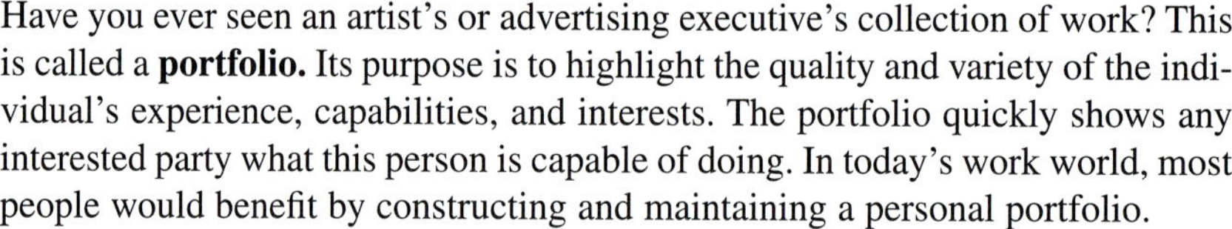

Building a Cyber Portfolio: A Student Project

Have you ever seen an artist's or advertising executive's collection of work? This is called a **portfolio.** Its purpose is to highlight the quality and variety of the individual's experience, capabilities, and interests. The portfolio quickly shows any interested party what this person is capable of doing. In today's work world, most people would benefit by constructing and maintaining a personal portfolio.

Portfolios are used in job interviews, during an annual performance review, or even in career counseling or personnel planning sessions. The content shows what you have achieved and what you can do. It is a very effective personal marketing tool. Preparing a portfolio gives you the opportunity to inventory your accomplishments in a professional manner and then share those accomplishments with others who need to know. Figure 6.4 shows a typical portfolio format.

Historically, portfolios have been published in a printed form, consisting of individual pages in a three-ring binder. Each page might contain a theme or topic

FIGURE 6.4

A Sample Student Portfolio

A portfolio is an excellent way for you to inventory your accomplishments. Because of job uncertainty and career changes, many people today are maintaining their portfolios throughout their careers.

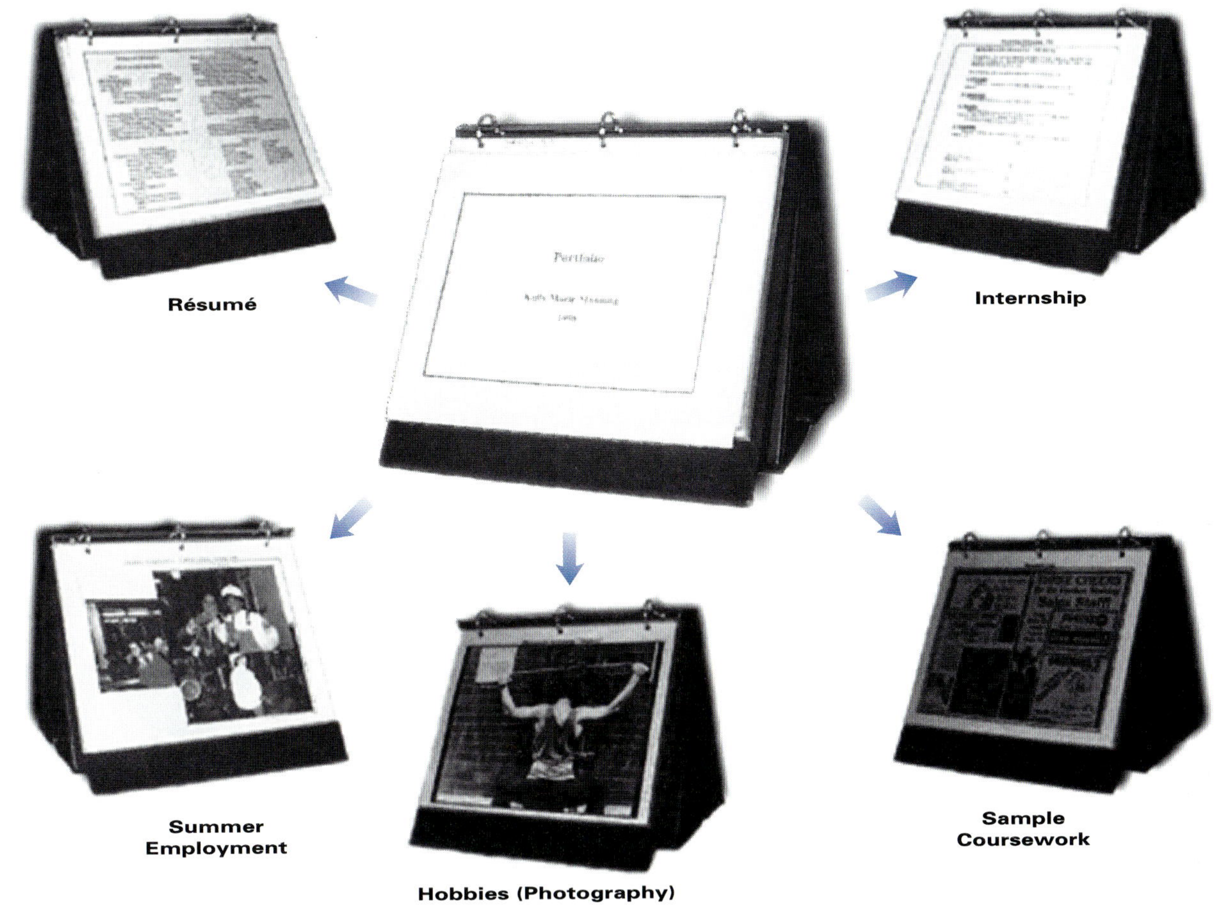

and can include a resume, work activities and accomplishments, hobbies or special skills, honors and awards, samples of school projects and professors' assessments, and letters of recommendation.

This chapter discusses designing and publishing Web sites. If you have an idea of how you might personally create and use a Web site and can then refer to that idea as you read the chapter, the topics become more interesting and useful. If you don't have an idea, think about creating your personal **cyber portfolio** and then publishing it in both printed and Web forms. When you are done, you will have a valuable result. Figure 6.5 shows the portfolio development process. Toward the end of this chapter, we will discuss how you can actually publish your portfolio on your own personal Web site for free!

Steps in Web Page Creation: What Makes a Great Web Site

Think of your Web page as a continuously evolving project. It may never be perfect, but each version is better than the one before, much like writing drafts of a

The Portfolio Development Process

This diagram shows the steps in creating and maintaining a personal portfolio. Once built, the portfolio can be transferred to the Web for distribution and access.

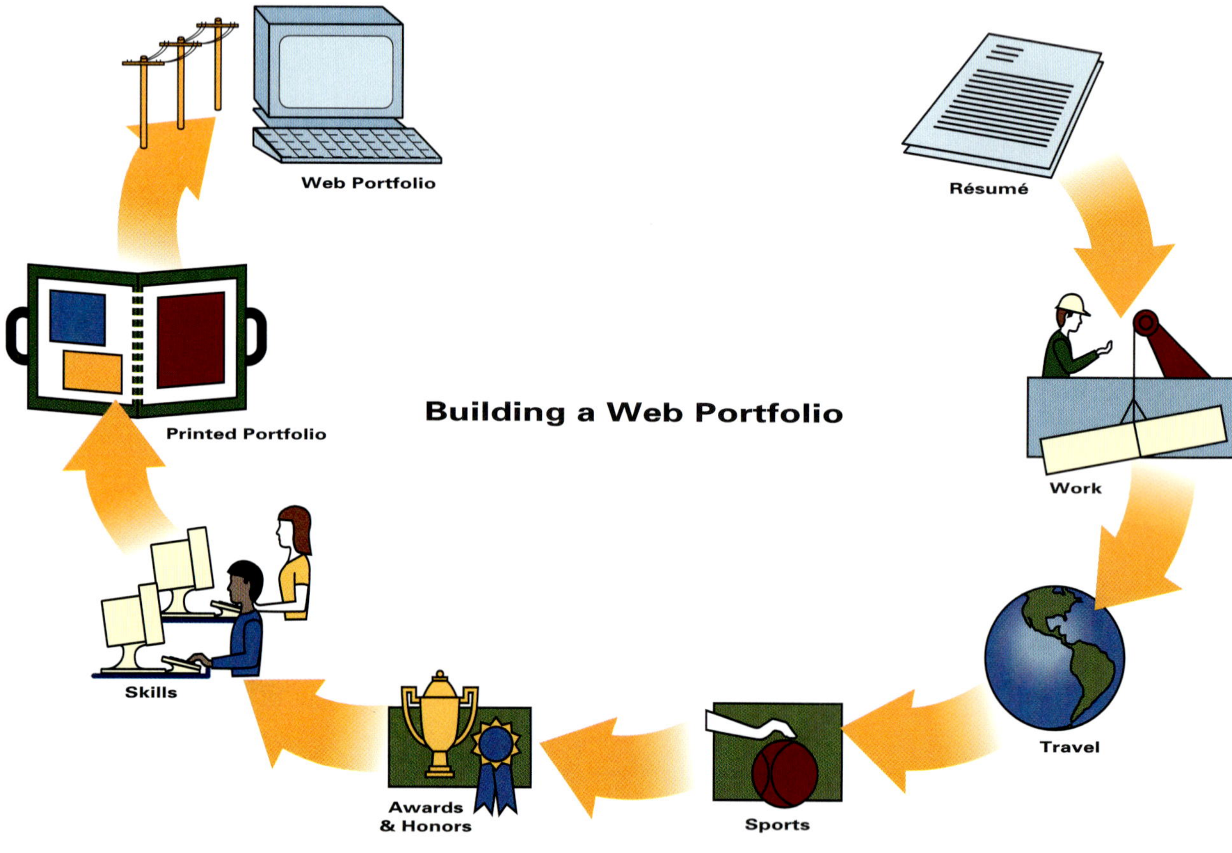

course paper in college or a computer software program. At some point you will stop the design process and move to the implementation of your design. Think of the Web page as an advertisement or a call to action by some predefined audience.

Web pages combine content with images and perceptions to achieve a desired outcome or action. As with any good project, clear thought and quality time spent in the design phase is well worth it. In manufacturing, design engineers say 80 percent of the cost of a product is determined by its design. Design drives quality. This means that quality design leads to quality product that leads to quality results. Spend time thinking about your Web page design. What should you consider including in it?

To help you better understand the process explained below, we need a common example or task to focus on. Let's assume you have been asked by your professor to build a Web page for a college course you are currently taking. Your teacher is not familiar with the Web, but knows it could help promote the course. In the beginning, think of your Web page as a color newspaper ad, explaining this course and its content. Later, you might add sounds, animation, or video clips to the course site—dynamic features and media that are not present in static newspaper ads. Figure 6.6 shows these three steps.

FIGURE 6.6

Three Key Steps in Web Page Development

Time spent in these three steps will improve the quality of your final product. Ask others to review your work and progress along the way.

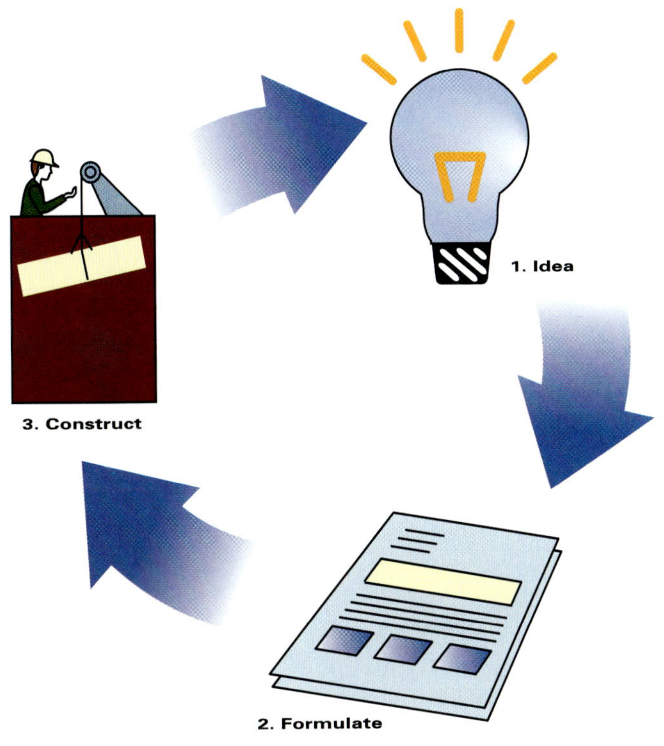

Step One: Ideate

As in any creative process, you brainstorm, or **ideate,** the task without any judgment, preconceptions, or personal evaluation. Think about purpose, content, structure, relationships, expectations, results, quality, visual elements, flow, and connections. What needs to be included for students to understand this course? What are the course objectives? What does your Web page customer need to know? How does the customer (student) make a decision as to what courses to take? What would appeal to you about the course? Could this page be linked to others for even more information—the Registrar's Office, financial aid, the university's home page, or the professor's e-mail address?

Capture your thoughts—write them down. Make sketches. Use graphics. Leave no stone (thought, action, behavior) unturned. Think about different ways this project can be related or viewed. Use strong action verbs to stimulate your relationship thoughts—magnify, invert, turn over, add to, eliminate, combine, grow, rotate.

When you have exhausted this process, stop! Abruptly leave the project for at least four hours. Go for a walk. Work out. Take a nap. Read a book. Take a shower. This lets your subconscious creative process continue to work, even as you do other things.

Then return to the project. Often you will have thought of some new, even more creative solutions. Document these and move to the second step.

Step Two: Formulate

Take the best of the output from step one—text, concepts, visuals, and relationships—that seems to fit and make sense. Begin to design the elements and formulate the relationships that occurred in step one. Try to paste these pieces of the puzzle together in a rough design or layout. Use paper and pencil to create a rough visual of your design.

Don't be too critical of your work. It's hard to make progress when you are evaluating and criticizing each step, impeding your forward progress. Reflect on what you have created, then modify, reflect, and modify again. Slowly, through this iterative process, you evolve toward a rough working draft of what you want.

Step Three: Construct

Now, begin to use computer tools to construct your Web page design. A word processing program will capture the text. A graphics program will allow you to begin to put the text and graphic pieces together. If you are missing an ingredient, simply identify it, locate it, and move on. That piece will come later.

How is the flow? Do the visuals support the flow? Where are you moving the reader and why? Does your design create the path, the story, and the perception? Have you used color? Where? Why?

Will this be a single Web page, or will it be a Web site—a series of pages logically linked together in a natural flow? A good Web site is no accident. Every Webmaster goes through this three-step design process. Practice will make you

FIGURE 6.7

The Customer Is King

Today, successful organizations focus on the needs of their customers. Customers are said to "vote with their wallets" for whom they like best (where they shop). Your Web site should have its visitors' needs in mind.

more efficient at the process. What does your course Web page look like now?
Would your teacher be pleased?

   With this background, we move on.

Designing Sites for Success

This section focuses on specific design and content issues for the Web site. Key
topics include the customer, the content, the site structure, and color. These issues
will collectively determine the success of your site.

FIGURE 6.8

Three Useful Hooks to Capture Your Web Site Visitor

Consider how you will use these resources as you design your Web site.

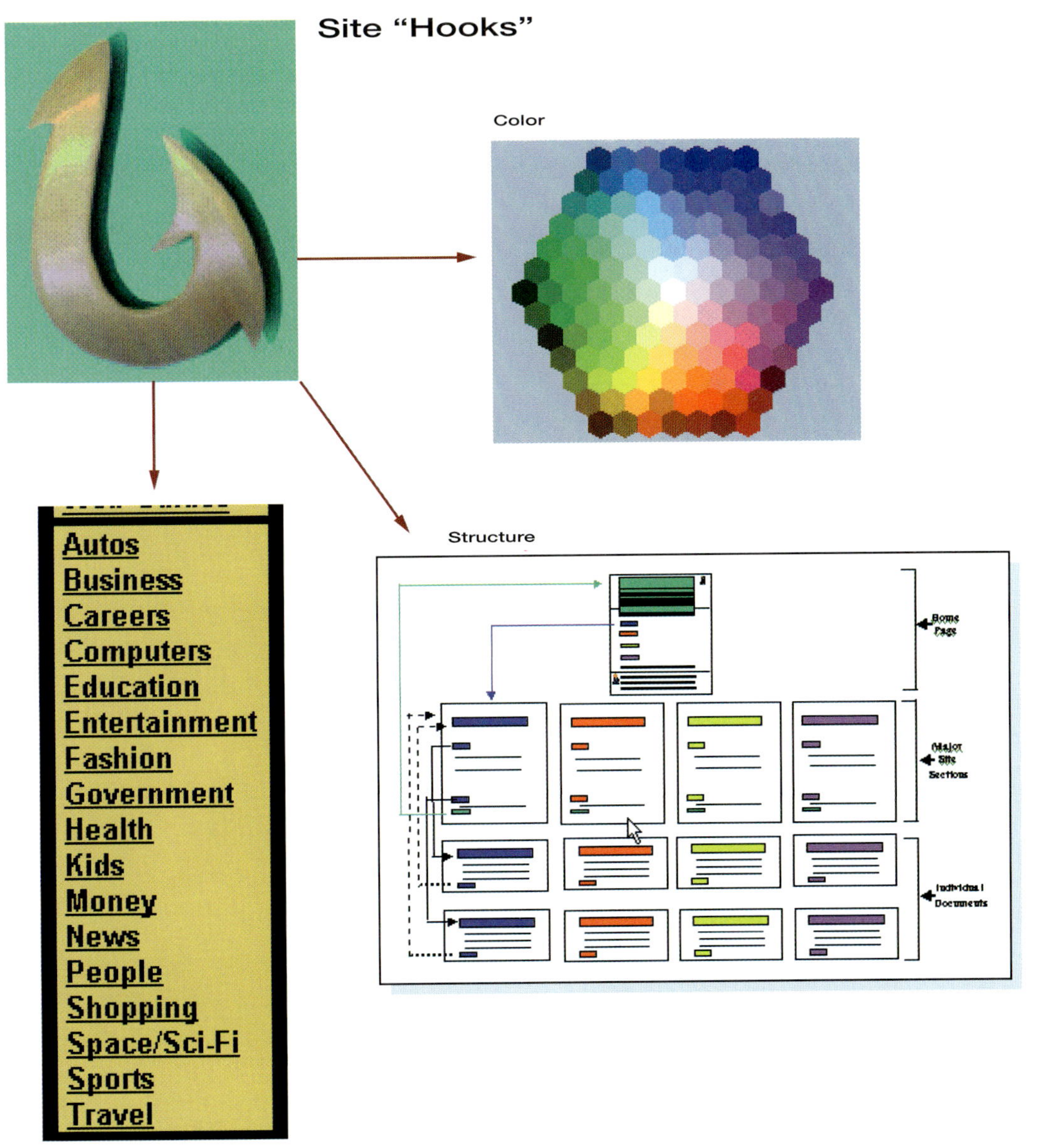

The Customer

Today, among most progressive organizations in our society, the customer is king (see Figure 6.7). Your Web site should be no exception. What is the primary purpose of this site—to educate, to sell, to inform, to persuade, to motivate, or to affect behavior? As you build your site, think of your ideal customers or visitors. Envision what they look like. How old are they? What do they do for a living? Why are they at your site? What do you want them to do while they are there, and after they leave? How long do you want them to stay? What do you want them to know when they leave? Answering these questions gives you more insights into your ideal site design.

First-time visitors form impressions quickly. What's on your opening page? How long does it take to display? Why should a visitor stay? What are your site **"hooks"** or unique features or offerings that get them to stay and move through your site? Figure 6.8 describes three useful site hooks.

Content

Based on your assessment of customer needs, what should the content of your site be? What will draw customers and keep them coming back to your site? What prod-

FIGURE 6.9

Web Content Highlights

Content is the most important aspect of the Web site. Give careful consideration to your message and how it is presented.

Layout 1 (a) is the same as the old Homepage Builder. It offers you five sections, arranged vertically, with a graphical bar separating each of them. This layout offers the most flexibility for what you can place in each section and makes it easy to create an attractive page.

Layout 2 (b) offers a two-column format. The sections in the left column are good for placing small images and link collections. The three sections on the right can be used for personal text, larger images, and a Web counter. This layout requires more tweaking than Layout 1 to build an attractive page. Give it a try if you want something different.

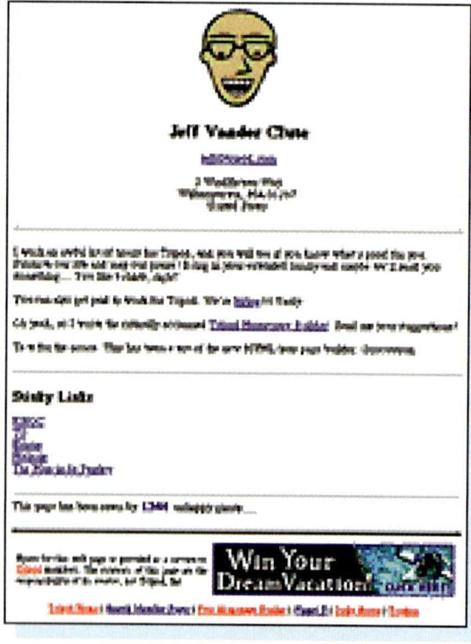

(a)

(b)

uct or service does your site deliver? Content should be relevant, prioritized, easy to use and understand, and easy to navigate. Finally, your customers should leave with some change in emotional state—excitement, mystery, self-improvement, a better feeling about themselves. What emotion do you want your site to trigger? How do you accomplish this?

Content should be your most important concern. All other issues are subordinate to content: They simply support, enhance, facilitate, or convey it. Focus your design on content, then blend the other topics and issues around highlighting content-related issues. Put your most important and valuable content first. Don't hide or bury it. Lesser ideas occur later. Supply high-quality Web site links to other locations that improve or enhance the content of your site. Explain why your content is relevant and helpful to the visitor. Use color, font sizes, and graphics to highlight key issues. Lesser content is assigned smaller fonts. Figure 6.9 highlights Web content.

Site Structure

Keep the site structure simple. Think of the structure as the table of contents for the site. Put the key points first. Then, put title headings for key segments and

Home Page Design Template

This is the first thing your visitors will see. It will determine whether they stay or leave. You need to balance content with speed of delivery. Visitors will evaluate your site in a matter of seconds. To use an old dance saying, "Put your best foot forward."

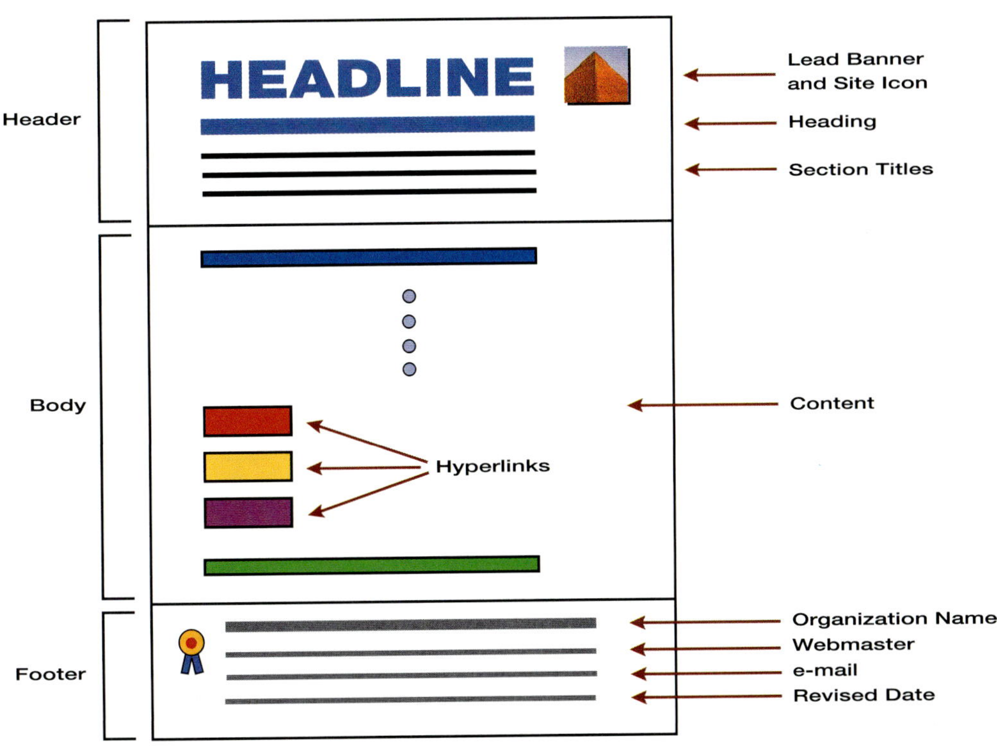

links to each segment. Keep the menu short—five or six choices maximum. Make sure the choices and their content are clear. All of this should be on the first page of the site, and the user should not have to scroll to see it. Figure 6.10 shows a sample home page **design template.**

Once you branch from the home page, be sure to guide your users back to home. (See Figure 6.11.) Notice how each branch from the home page to the major site sections is color coded. All major site sections are reached through links in the home page. Notice in this example that users visit the detail pages in each section but still easily navigate their way back to the home page. Without a way to your home page from each branch, customers might find links to one of your lesser pages through a search but be unable to reach your home page easily once they are there.

Essential items that should be contained in every Web site include the following:

- Name of Webmaster, site author, or contact person
- Links to another home page, if this is only part of a larger site
- Organization name (if applicable)

Sample Web Site Design Template

This design acts as a roadmap to your entire site. Carefully and clearly move your visitor through your site. Let the site unfold before them as they travel.

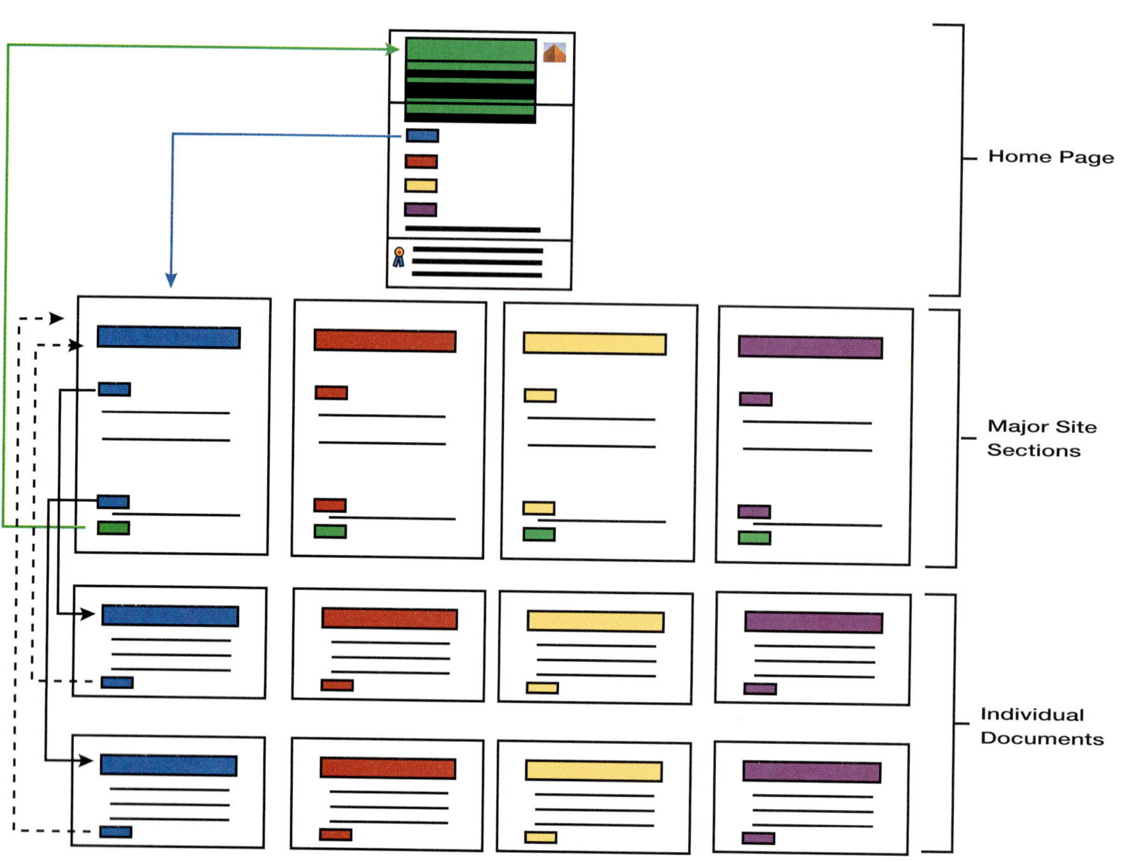

- Logo or seal of the organization
- Date of creation or last revision
- Statement of copyright
- The URL or address of the document
- Links to other related pages in the local Web site
- Contact information (e-mail, FAX, phone)

Figure 6.12 shows examples of some of these items.

Color and Emotion

Color plays a major part in Web site design. Colors elicit emotions. Black signifies terminal, complete, done, death. Blue elicits thoughts of deity, the sky, water, hope. Red is for fear, stop, blood, desire. Green communicates wealth, accom-

FIGURE 6.12

Samples of Recommended Web Site Content

Here are examples of items you will normally find in a Web site. They all help clarify issues for the site user.

Statement of copyright

COPYRIGHT

©1997 Compaq Computer Corporation. All rights reserved.

Date of creation or last revision

COMMENTS

Revised: 26 September 1997

Organization name (if applicable)

Links to another home page

Contact Information (e-mail, FAX, phone)

You may contact Nasdaq in the following ways:

E-mail Nasdaq at isfeedback@nasdaq.com
Feedback on this Web Site.

Links to other related pages in site

Riddle du Jour	
Previous Riddles	Sphinx's Hall of Fame
About Riddle du Jour	Submit a Stumper and Win
Comments	

Logo or seal of the organization

Name of Webmaster or site author

Copyright © 1997 George Schmidt All rights reserved.
Site Content, Design & Development: George Schmidt.
Marketing, Promotions & Advertising: Carolin Benjamin
242985 visitors per day average
129073 visitors to this page today

plishment, good, go. Yellow brings to mind warmth, a new day, the sun. Other color considerations include tints, hues, and intensities. If you place green and red together, with the same intensity, the colors literally vibrate in the viewer's eyes. It is difficult and distracting to look at. Almost 17 percent of U.S. males are color-blind—they can't tell red from green. Safe, conservative color combinations on the Web might include a navy blue or dark green background with yellow print. The "earth-to-sky" theory suggests using darker colors toward the bottom of the screen, with lighter colors on the top. (See Figure 6.13.) If you doubt your own color competencies, get a second opinion.

Not every Web site designer adheres to these guidelines. In fact, some Web sites highlight their favorite bad site designs. It's fun to visit these sites, find their current bad sites, and check them out. See if you can identify their major flaws. It may keep you from making the same mistakes. Search "bad Web site design" to find these sites.

Web Media Types

Different media appeal to different body senses (sight, sound, taste, touch, and smell). Current **Web media** focus primarily on sight and sound. Perhaps, in the future, there will be media that appeal to taste, touch, and scent. Interactive 3-D and virtual reality are attempts to add a third dimension, depth, to the media and literally surround the user in an artificial environment.

Visual systems appeal to the eyes. Eyes read text, view images, see colors, and then combine and interpret those combinations. Web page designers try to create an information synergy, using multimedia tools, to accomplish their Web page goals. One goal is to make this process as simple for the viewer as possible. Confusion detracts from understanding and action. Remember the phrase, "A picture is worth a thousand words." It is easier and more efficient to convey Web site messages using images rather than just text. Text can be enhanced or complemented by images. Most sites combine text and graphic elements to enhance the information transfer between the user and the site.

Text

Text is by far the most common medium in Web site design. Text tells the story. It carries the reader through the site—informing, educating, engaging, advancing. Think of the last paperback novel you read. Usually a novel contains only text, yet, if well written, it can be very satisfying. But, text must be interesting or informative. Think now of the last college textbook you read that was not interesting. Was it hard to read, to understand, to use? How effective would that textbook be as the sole contents of a Web page? Graphics can help.

Graphics

Graphics include tables, charts, illustrations, photos, even animations. New software and Web development tools make these resources inexpensive and easy to use. Many of these same tools are used today in classroom courses or organizational presentations. Most of the design ideas we discuss here are also very

FIGURE 6.13
Sample of Earth-to-Sky Effect (Dark to Light)

Due to our normal orientation, it is common to show visuals that are darker on the bottom and lighter on the top. See if you can find examples of this in magazines, in newspapers, or on the Web.

appropriate for your course papers or classroom presentations. All try to tell a story, educate, or hold the listener's attention. The brain processes words in sequence, but it processes shapes, colors, movement, direction, and image relationships simultaneously.

Images are efficient and effective information- or emotion-carrying vehicles. They aid in decision making and problem solving. Research findings show that visual support in a presentation (or Web page design) can increase the content and understanding of that message by more than 60 percent. Graphics in the form of charts and graphs may be used to show patterns and relationships. **Bar graphs** show relative levels of a key variable. **Pie graphs** visually show the percentage of each part of a whole. **Line graphs** portray trends or the direction of a variable over time. Figure 6.14 shows examples of each type.

Clip Art

Clip art consists of electronically stored figures, cartoons, and images that can be added to a page. Clip art libraries contain thousands of images, including animals, shapes, buildings, people, cartoons, signs, maps, and computers. These visuals are copied from the library and then pasted into the site. They add texture, humor, and insights to your Web design. Figure 6.15 shows some examples.

Schematics

Schematics are illustrations used to show process flow or relationship levels. An order-entry system in a manufacturing company is one example of a schematic.

FIGURE 6.14

Three Types of Graphs

Here is a sample of three different types of common graphs used for different purposes.

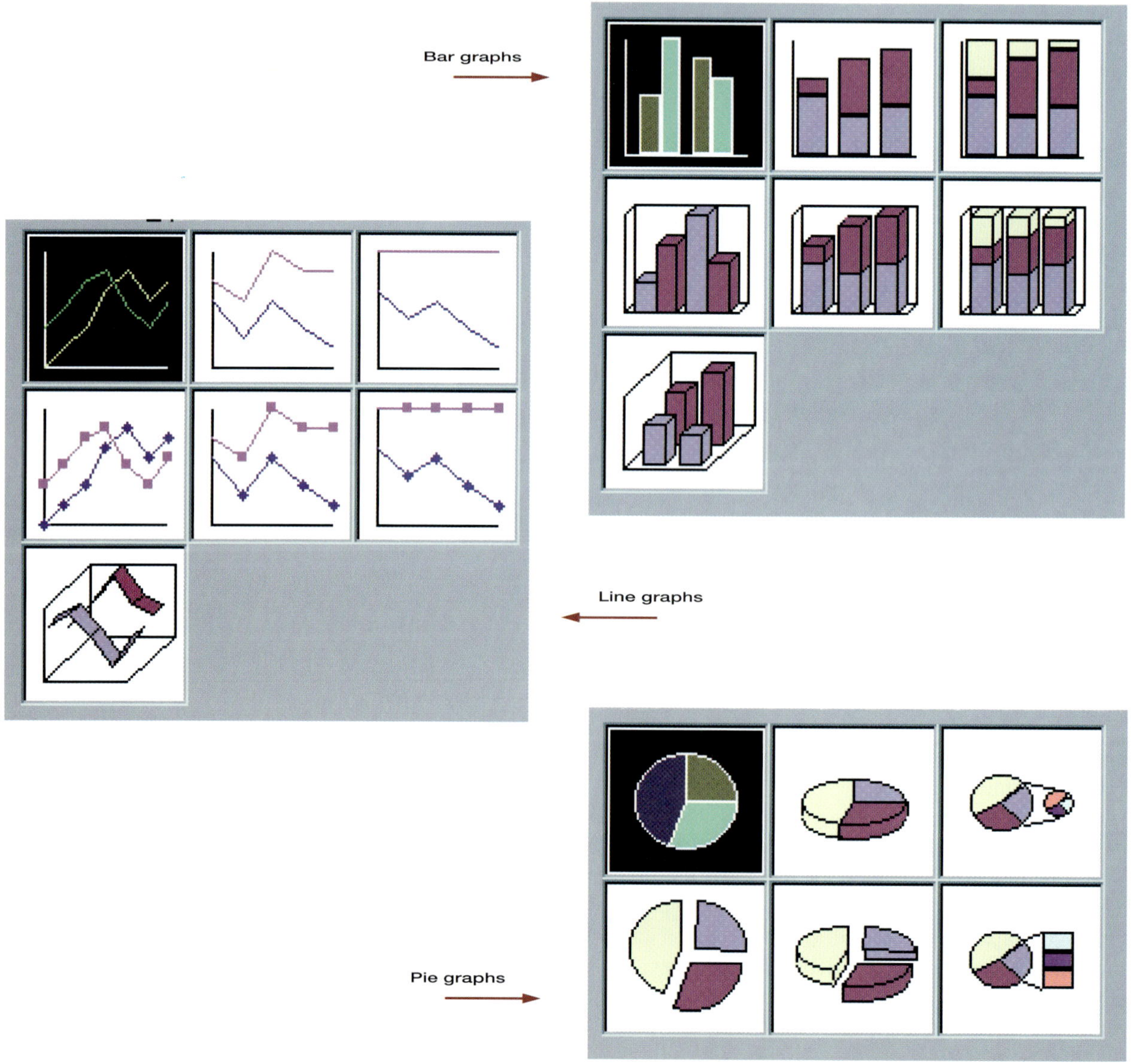

A wiring diagram showing the flow of electricity through a network is another. Organizational charts show levels of authority and responsibility within a group of people. Clip art libraries often have schematic templates for these process charts. Users simply add names or process descriptions to the template, then paste these tailored images into their particular applications. Figure 6.16 shows some schematic samples.

Sound

It is possible to add sound clips to your site. Newer personal computers, equipped with microphones, allow users to record their own voice or background sounds or use sound clips from sound libraries (waterfalls, jet engines, screams, laughter, and so on). These sound tracks or sound bites add interest and informational value to the site if they are well integrated into the overall theme of the design.

FIGURE 6.15

Using Clip Art

Clip art adds humor and informality to a site. Don't overuse this medium. Too many pieces can detract from the quality of your site.

FIGURE 6.16
Schematics

Schematics typically show process flow or direction. They show simple activities, relationships, sequence, and time duration.

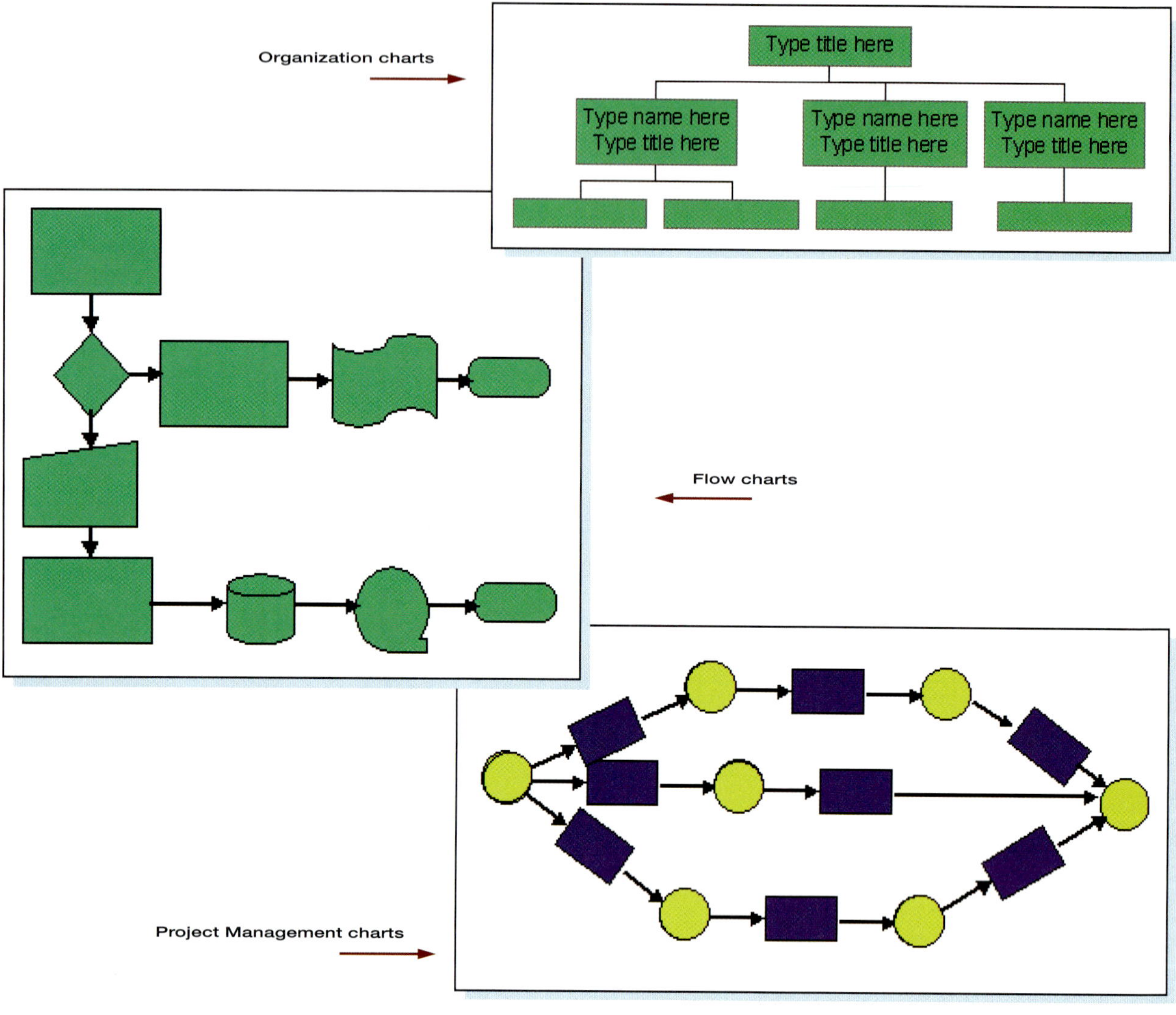

Remember, to hear your sound clips, site visitors must have computers equipped with specialized hardware and software that can recognize and play sound. Most new PCs sold today are equipped with stereo speakers, sound cards, and sound software. Many older computers do not support sound.

3-D Virtual Reality

Virtual essentially means "serving the purpose, but not real." **Virtual reality** (VR) denotes artificial reality. Using technology, we attempt to create the major elements of reality. To replicate reality, applications add a third dimension to the

FIGURE 6.17

Virtual Reality Adds a Third Dimension

Virtual reality surrounds the user with information and sensations. It adds to the reality of the experience.

media—depth. Some applications require the user to don special clothes, gloves, and helmets. The user then experiences a total immersion in the media. (See Figure 6.17.)

Applications for virtual reality are enormous—entertainment, flight and war simulations, education, design. The addition of motion and touch add to the reality of the experience. As technology improves and prices fall, we will see more and more applications of virtual reality. Perhaps some will be delivered on the Web. Imagine virtually "trying on" a suit or dress in your home as it is beamed out of your monitor. Think of applications like virtual shopping, virtual travel, and virtual education. Most experts predict that these applications are just around the corner.

Media Considerations

All the media mentioned are potential ingredients in your site. However, as the designer, you must think about your user's equipment.

Bandwidth

The more information-intensive the media, the wider its **bandwidth** and the slower it will load into your visitor's computer. Think of bandwidth as the size of the fill pipe that the customer's computer uses to download information from your Web site. Large graphic images and video are information intensive. They will load slowly. The longer it takes for the message to display to the users, the greater the probability they will terminate their visit, and move on. You will have lost your opportunity to influence or capture them. Simple, low-intensity designs have high transfer rates and are quickly and easily read by PCs using voice-grade telephone lines, so they may be more effective than other, more information-rich alternatives. Consider the benefits of simple messages and mediums.

Different PC Capabilities

Web sites using text, clipart, schematics, and graphics can be read by almost every computer today. As you add sound, video, animation, and virtual reality, remember that many computers may not be equipped with the hardware and software to utilize those inputs. Those users will not hear the sounds or see the movements at your site. Such features may be exciting to the minority, yet frustrating to the majority. Watch PC configuration sales statistics to determine when it is most appropriate to add these new features to your site. Remember, site development is an ongoing process. New media and improvements can be added later.

Specialized Media Hardware Devices

Additional graphics can be captured and added to your Web page using specialized input hardware. Three popular graphic input technologies include digital cameras, scanners, and video cameras.

FIGURE 6.18
Digital Cameras Use No Film

Digital cameras operate much like a normal camera. They can have zoom lenses, flash capability, and can even play back pictures taken earlier. When done, the user simply downloads the photos into the computer for additional processing. Pictures can even be edited before being placed in a Web page.

Digital Cameras

If you need actual photos of people, places, or items, a **digital camera** might be just what you need. These specialized cameras take pictures and then store them in an electronic format. No film is used. When ready, you simply connect the camera to a specially equipped computer, via a cable, and download the batch of images. Once in the computer, the images can be processed and pasted into your Web site. Today, digital cameras cost between $300 to $1,000. Many colleges and universities have digital cameras available for checkout, or you can also rent them from large copy centers. Photos add reality and personality to your site, but they load slowly. Figure 6.18 shows a digital camera.

Scanners

If you need to convert a chart, logo, photo, or text to its electronic equivalent, a **scanner** is the answer. (See Figure 6.19.) Scanners also connect to a computer. Using a large tabletop bed scanner or the smaller handheld model, you transfer the contents of the item, via the scanner, into the computer. The resulting electronic image can be processed and added to the Web site. Most scanners today read and process both black-and-white and color images as well as text.

Video Cameras

Finally, if you want to add movement to your site, it is possible to add video clips. The original videotape is shot using a **video camera.** Again, the contents are downloaded into a specially equipped computer, processed, and passed to the Web site. Your Web site visitors' computers must be equipped with special hardware and software to view and hear the video portion of your site. Figure 6.20 shows a video camera.

FIGURE 6.19

Scanners Convert Images to Web Page Media

Photos, logos, sketches, and blueprints can be scanned and stored on the Web.

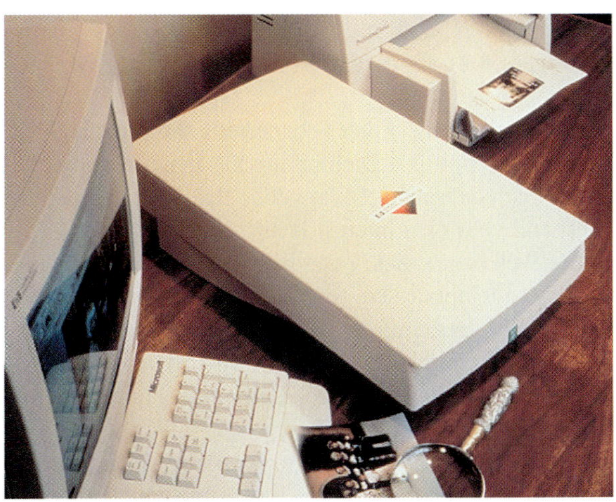
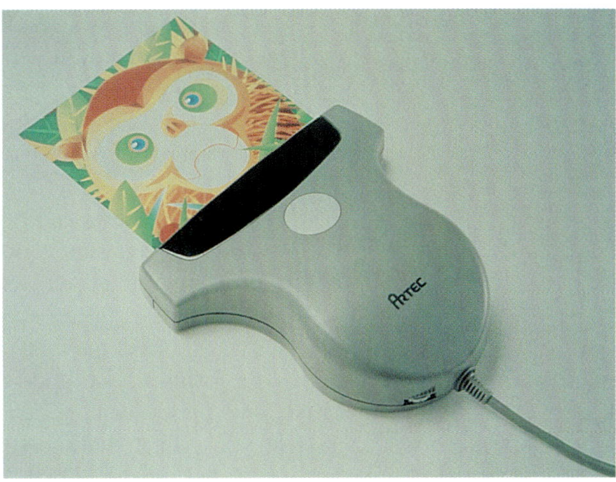

Video Cameras Create Movement on the Web Site

Video clips can add a powerful message to your Web site. You can hear from experts, view historic objects, role-play in groups, or visit faraway places. However, using current technology, video is a relatively slow medium.

Web Site Builders

Once your site is designed, you need to construct it. Your site actually consists of a collection of coded instructions called **Hypertext Markup Language** or **HTML**. These programming codes define the content, layout, and characteristics of your Web site. HTML sets the size and location of your text; the size and location of your graphics; your background colors; and links to other sites, sounds, animations, and even video clips. Figure 6.21 shows a Web page and the HTML code that created it.

As a new site developer, you have many choices concerning the use of HTML code. Below we list just four of your options. Each option has benefits and drawbacks. Criteria for your choice include time, software cost, flexibility, amount of use, features and capabilities, and your own interest level.

If you want to develop your Web page quickly and have little interest in detail, preprogrammed Web software and templates are for you. At the other extreme, if this area interests you, if you want tight controls over what you develop, and if you have the time, then you should combine packaged Web software programs with a good understanding of the HTML language. Remember, however, that these techniques can be combined to create more options.

First, and most difficult, you can write all your own original code. You can become an HTML Web page programmer. This is the most time consuming and difficult option, but it also gives you the greatest understanding and control over the content of your site. Even if you do not choose this option, it is helpful to

FIGURE 6.21

A Sample Web Page and Its HTML Code: The Dryden Press Site

This figure shows the Web site of the Dryden Press (the publisher of this book) and the HTML code that created it. Note the code used to create different size letters in the text.

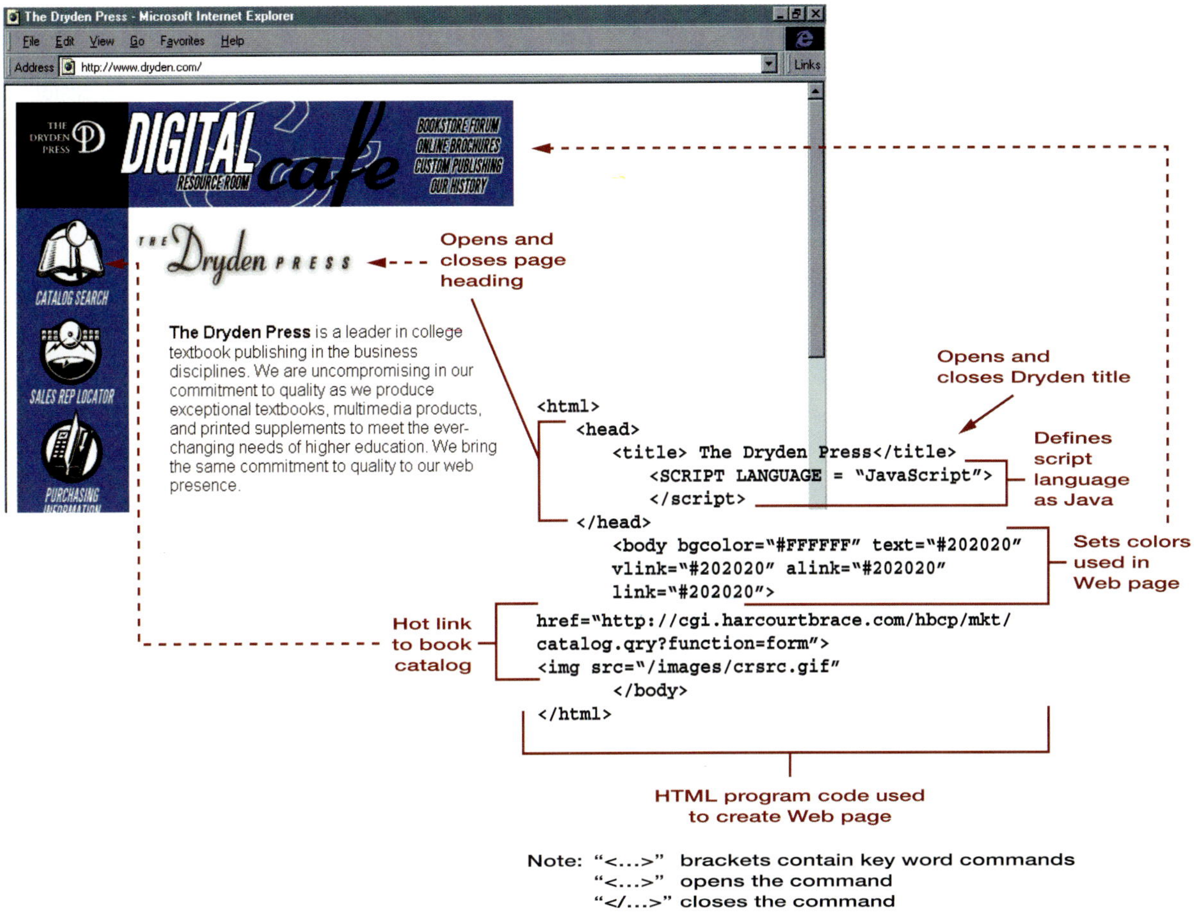

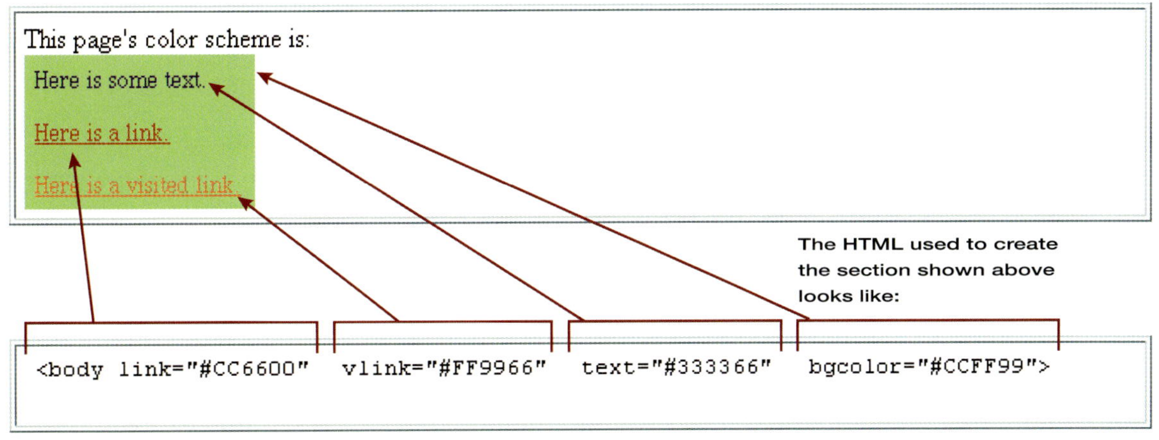

FIGURE 6.22

HTML Codes for Sample Web Fonts and Colors

Note how HTML code determines the content, size, and color of text in this Web site.

understand the basics of how HTML code works. Rather than write the code, it is possible to edit or modify existing HTML code to improve or enhance some feature of a site. Figure 6.22 shows different Web text options (color, size, font) and the HTML code used to create them.

Second, you can buy Web site software editors and packages that guide you through the construction of your pages. These programs supply the HTML instructions that are needed to create your text and graphic designs. They often have libraries and templates that you can modify to make the process even easier. This process reduces your development time, increases your cost (you must buy the software), and lowers your design control over the format. For beginners, this would be a first step for you. Figure 6.23 lists some popular Web page editors.

FIGURE 6.23

Popular Web Page Editor Software

Here are some popular software authoring programs that help you design and create your Web page.

> **AOLpress 1.2.3**
>
> **Claris Home Page**
>
> **Corel Web.Designer**
>
> **HoTMetaL PRO 3.0**
>
> **Microsoft FrontPage 97**
>
> **Microsoft Publisher 97**
>
> **MyInternetBusinessPage**
>
> **Netscape Composer**
>
> **Web Factory Author 3.0**
>
> **WebExpress 2.0**

Third, you can find Web site hosts on the Internet that will both store and serve your site and also help you, in a tutorial format, design your site. This is an easy first step. Typically there is no cost, no programming required, little time invested, and immediate results. However, you have limited choices in how your site will look, and modifications to an existing site are more difficult. Still, this is a great option for the beginner. In the previous chapter, we mentioned one site, Tripod, that allows you to use this process. Currently, Tripod contains over 1,400,000 Web sites built by people of all abilities. It is fun and interesting to visit some of these sites to see what they have accomplished. Figure 6.24 shows some Tripod home page examples.

Fourth and finally, some current application software programs—such as Microsoft's Office 97 package, which is a word processor, spreadsheet, and graphics program—have the ability to create the HTML code necessary to represent any output from these programs. This feature allows you to build a report combining text, graphics, tables, and charts, and then store that report in a form that can be used on a Web site. For example, if you did an in-class presentation using Microsoft's PowerPoint 97 software, you could also store that presentation on your Web site so that anyone in the world could view it! This is a powerful selling feature, one that will grow and improve as more software companies in the future include Web support in their packages. Figure 6.25 shows a PowerPoint 97 graphic and its equivalent representation on the Web.

Sample Personal Web Pages

This collage shows a variety of styles of personal Web sites. These are the results of different needs, different interests, and different levels of skill.

SANTA FE COMMUNITY COLLEGE C.A.S.S. STUDENTS: Sixteen students from Central American countries began studies at Santa Fe Community College August 27, 1996 in a two-year program leading to an Associate of Science degree in Environmental Science technology with a specialization in Aquaculture and Aquatic Food Products Processing. The students, 9

Keith Lehman

klehman@uct.uct.edu

1308 S. Birmingham Ave
Tulsa, OK 74104
United States

Welcome to my world - Tulsa, OK . I live at the University Center assisting students weave their dreams into reality; that earns my food that feeds my wonderfully ecletic family - my wife Betty who helps single parent economically disadvantaged women by providing daycare for their children, Kate, our political environmentalist, vegan photographer and potter , and Abby, our social princess with a heart for friends, a talent for chatter, and a drive to be very good in school and on the soccer fields.

My Favorite Sites

University Center at Tulsa
The Wall Street Journal
Soccernet

From the list above, you can see there are many options. Web development is a powerful skill that is in great demand today by employers. We recommend you build your skills and understanding in this field. It will help you in school, at work, in your hobbies, and in other personal and professional endeavors. We must caution you, though, that the Web industry is large and expected to get even larger. There are many new software products and services announced daily. It is literally impossible to know everything about this area. Our goal is simply to start you along the learning path in this field.

Web Site Hosts

Now that your site is created and designed, it is time to find a place to save or store your site on the Web. Where can you put this masterpiece so that others can access and use it? Your host must be connected to the Internet through a server framework. You would hope that the host offers 168 hours per week of access (24

PowerPoint 97 Graphic and Its Web Page Equivalent

New applications software now has the ability to create images for use on the Web. Now you can publish your work in reports, on slides or overheads, or on the Web, depending upon your audience.

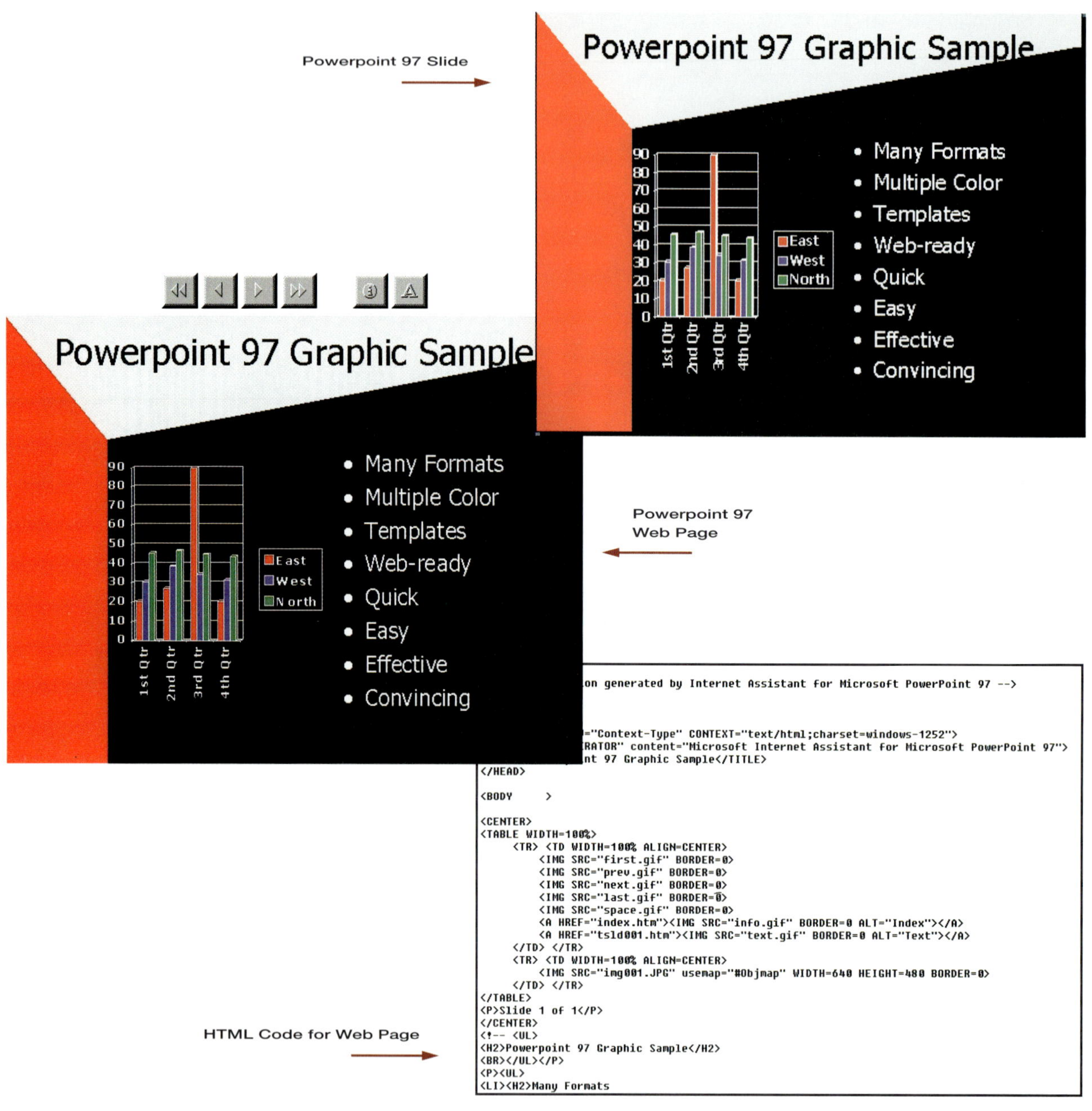


```
on generated by Internet Assistant for Microsoft PowerPoint 97 -->

="Context-Type" CONTEXT="text/html;charset=windows-1252">
RATOR" content="Microsoft Internet Assistant for Microsoft PowerPoint 97">
nt 97 Graphic Sample</TITLE>
</HEAD>

<BODY       >

<CENTER>
<TABLE WIDTH=100%>
    <TR> <TD WIDTH=100% ALIGN=CENTER>
        <IMG SRC="first.gif" BORDER=0>
        <IMG SRC="prev.gif" BORDER=0>
        <IMG SRC="next.gif" BORDER=0>
        <IMG SRC="last.gif" BORDER=0>
        <IMG SRC="space.gif" BORDER=0>
        <A HREF="index.htm"><IMG SRC="info.gif" BORDER=0 ALT="Index"></A>
        <A HREF="tsld001.htm"><IMG SRC="text.gif" BORDER=0 ALT="Text"></A>
    </TD> </TR>
    <TR> <TD WIDTH=100% ALIGN=CENTER>
        <IMG SRC="img001.JPG" usemap="#Objmap" WIDTH=640 HEIGHT=480 BORDER=0>
    </TD> </TR>
</TABLE>
<P>Slide 1 of 1</P>
</CENTER>
<!-- <UL>
<H2>Powerpoint 97 Graphic Sample</H2>
<BR></UL></P>
<P><UL>
<LI><H2>Many Formats
```

hours a day, seven days a week), to accommodate users living in worldwide time zones. Finally, the price should be reasonable.

Most Internet service providers also offer storage for their members' home pages. Small sites, typically under one or two megabytes in size, are stored free. But remember that you are already paying a monthly fee to this provider for your current Internet access.

The most popular providers, such as America Online, Prodigy Internet, and CompuServe offer free Web site storage to their subscribers. Each, however, does it somewhat differently. America Online allows you to upload your site if it is already coded or to download an HTML editor program to create the code for your site. Once completed, it can be uploaded and stored. Prodigy will either download an HTML editor or take you through an online tutorial to build a site. CompuServe's process is much like America Online's. It downloads an editor, you code the site, then it uploads and stores the completed version of your site. If you are not a current subscriber, these options are not available.

If you are interested in creating a Web site of your own or in building a cyberspace portfolio (see student activities at the end of this chapter) and you have no current Internet service provider, consider using the Tripod site. To become a member, however, you must have a current e-mail address. In Figure 6.26 we show a sample of Tripod's personal Web page builder tutorial.

Registering and Promoting Your Site in Cyberspace

Now that you have constructed your site, it is time to store it on the Web and promote it. If you want people to see your work, visit your site, buy your product, or act on the content of your page, you need to tell others about it. You need to advertise or promote your site in cyberspace. You need visitors! You need to register your site.

Registration Process

Ever wonder how the Web search engines find the sites they display when you do a topic search? Sometimes there are just a few references; sometimes there are thousands. Some services even try to prioritize their references based on the keywords in your search phrase. These sites were registered with the search service by the owner or promoter of the Web page through a **site registration process.** This process is discussed in the following paragraphs.

When your page is complete, it must be stored on a computer that is attached or accessible from the Web. For most people, their service provider will do this. If you belong to America Online or CompuServe or the Microsoft Network, they will electronically store your Web page on their computers. Some services charge a monthly storage fee, especially for very large, commercial Web sites. If the site is small, under two megabytes, there often is no charge. The larger the site, the more expensive the storage.

When you store your site, you receive a unique Web address or **Uniform Resource Locator (URL).** The URL defines the exact location of your site on the Web, much like your street address. If others want to access your site, they would first type your location's address in their search engine. If successful, the content of your site immediately appears on their computer monitor. But what if people do not know your exact URL? What if they normally do a search using keywords? How will they find your site?

There are literally hundreds of search services on the Web. The largest and most popular sites include AltaVista, Excite, Infoseek, Lycos, Magellan, Yahoo!, WebCrawler, and so on. For a list of the top 100 search services, visit Multimedia Marketing Group's site. Figure 6.27 shows the Infoseek site.

These services log their inventory of Web page sites typically in two ways. First, individual Web page developers like us can electronically visit each search

FIGURE 6.26

Online Web Page Builder Tutorial

Some Web services carry users through an online Web tutorial to help them create a unique Web page.

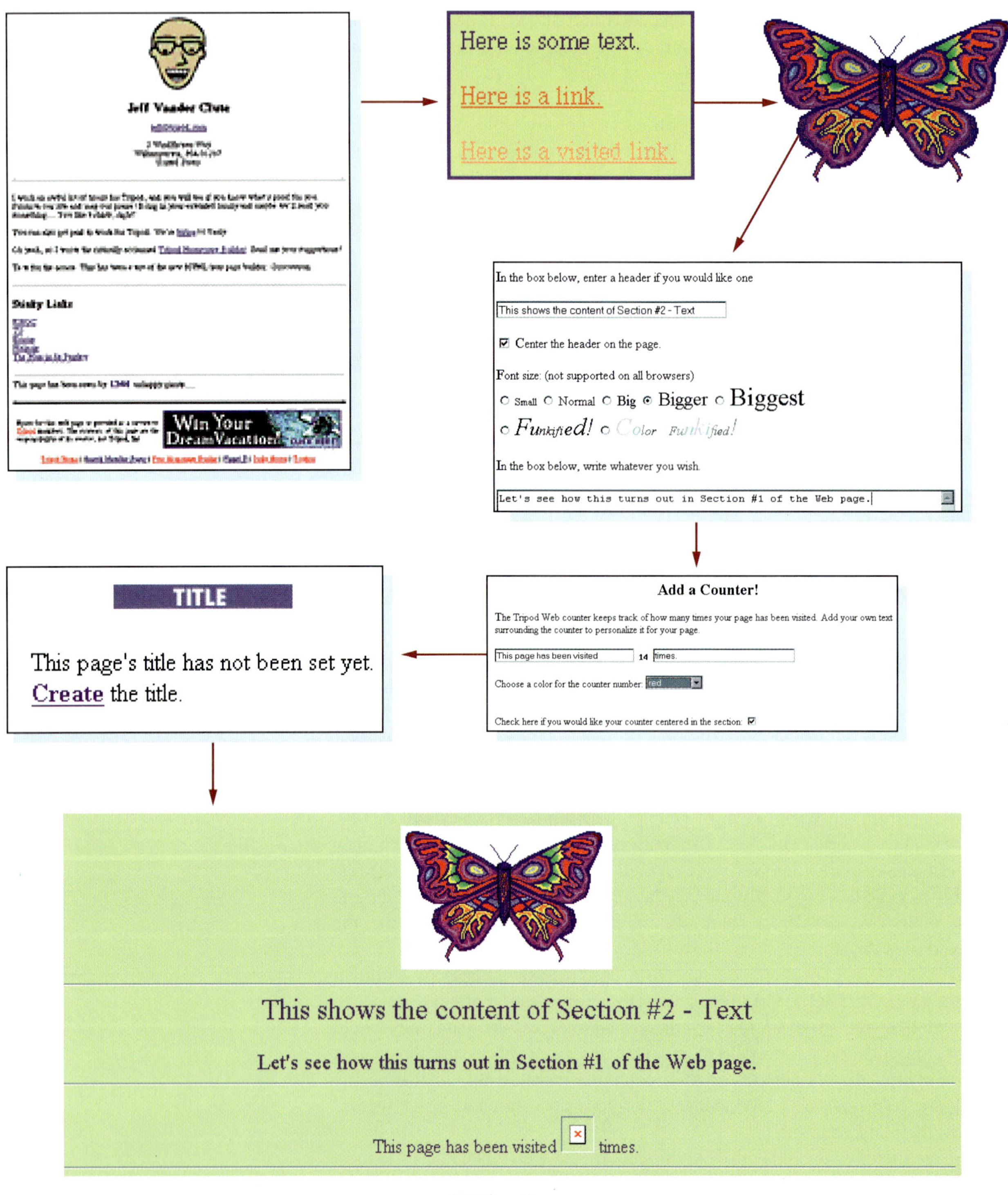

engine's Web home page site and personally register our own URL address. Once notified, the search service visits the site and categorizes its content based on the keywords it finds in the site's content. This may take days or even weeks to complete to bring your site online.

FIGURE 6.27

Infoseek's Site Promotion Page

Once your site is built, you need to register it with the primary search services on the Web. This site identifies the key search services and their registration process.

Second, you can hire Web services or **registration agents** to register your site for you. For complete registration with the top thirty search services, a typical agent fee is about $80. The more registration services you choose, the higher the price but the better the coverage. Typically, this service is quick and saves you the time and effort to visit each site. There are a number of these types of services on the Web. If you visit a site like Infoseek, they will have a search menu option entitled "Internet." If you scroll down that directory to "Web publishing" and then to "Site promotion," you will find hundreds of listing services. Some large Web search engines even recommend the registration services they prefer. Again, once notified, the search engines will visit and categorize your site content. You are now online. Figure 6.28 shows a Web page from a registration agent.

Promotion Options

What can you do to increase awareness of your cyberspace site? There are numerous options. Advertising is the first and most common way. Television is a common vehicle to alert interested parties to Web sites that contain more product or service information. Newspaper and magazine ads are other media where you can cross-list your Web site address. Even radio ads carry Internet addresses. Most organizations include Web addresses in Yellow Page ads in the phonebook. Personal business cards now list e-mail and Web page addresses. Match covers, stationery, billboards, invoices, envelopes, mailers, and flyers can all promote a visit to a new Web site.

Advertising your Web site at another site on the Internet is another option. How many times have you seen an animated banner at one site promoting the content of another site? With a single click of the mouse, you move to this new site. Ad space can be purchased on popular sites that may increase traffic and visits to your site. Visits to chat lines or promotional libraries will give you some

FIGURE 6.28

Web Registration Agent

Web sites like this will help you register your site for a small fee.

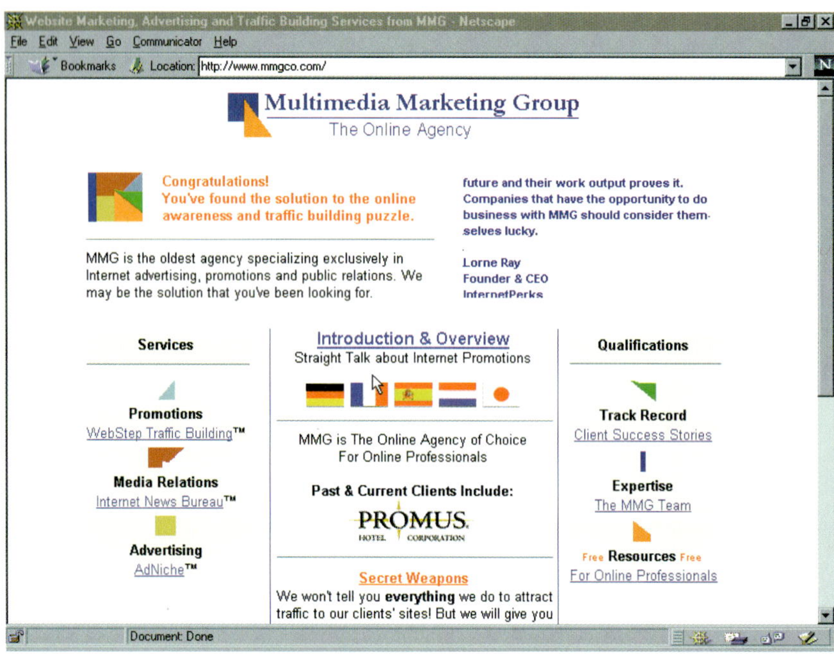

FIGURE 6.29

Microsoft's SiteBuilder Page

Web sites like this will help you with all your Web site needs.

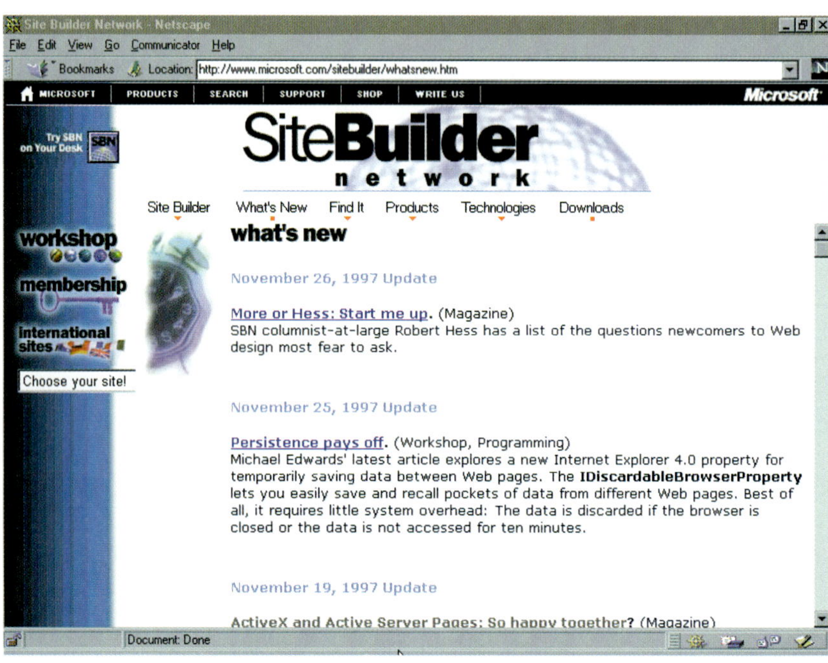

The Internet in the Future

Online Learning on the Internet Blossoms: Customers Range from Individuals to Organizations

With lifelong learning as a basic requirement in today's business world, many employees and organizations are looking to the Web to supply this education. Courses range from diesel mechanics to math to human resource issues to how to use word processing and spreadsheet programs. With rich informational content and convenient delivery times, many content providers and students are enjoying the learning experience.

In the future, organizations themselves may be a major competitor for the traditional school systems. Most large organizations offer in-house educational materials on their own Intranets. Companies can buy prepackaged educational materials or develop their own. A recent survey found that three out of four large companies are turning toward internal, Web-based education. Hundreds of new, online learning products are available.

Online learning includes a variety of topics, from courses and content to development, delivery, and control. Educational systems typically weave a combination of internally focused programs blended with external, third-party educational products and services. Internal programs carry human resource topics such as employment openings, fringe benefit program descriptions, and communications from top management. External courses can include university credit courses and even advanced degree programs in engineering and business.

Only a few organizations are currently delivering internal education programs because of the high startup costs, systems requirements, and course-development overhead to start these services; only about 15 percent of the companies (usually large companies) are currently involved. Intranets, linked to outside suppliers and customers, are natural vehicles to deliver future product announcements, information, and service training to these two groups.

The next wave of online education will focus on external markets. Once courses and content are built and tested internally, it is only natural that organizations will offer modifications of these to outside users. Home health care, homeschooling, and specialized mechanical education are natural growth areas for online education. Even home shoppers have online educational needs for the major products they buy.

Look for online learning to be a major growth area in the future. For more information about this topic, visit the RealAudio and MASIE company Web sites.

new and creative ideas on how to promote your site. Other promotional resources can be found by searching on the Web for promotion topics.

How often have you seen Microsoft's Internet Explorer logo on a site? This is a promotion for their Web browser. If you agree to exhibit their logo on your site, Microsoft allows you to join their SiteBuilder Network. This service helps you stay current with new Web technologies and ideas. You receive tips and ideas to make your site more appealing and effective. Your site also gets highlighted when it is listed as a hit on a search done through the Microsoft search site. Obviously, it has been successful. For more information about this promotional program, visit the **Microsoft SiteBuilder** page. (See Figure 6.29.)

Some words of caution are necessary. **Netiquette** applies, especially to advertising and promotion. Don't try to register one site more than once with each search service. This is called spamming (discussed earlier with regard to junk e-mail) and is not appreciated or acceptable. Some advertisers have been placed on Web blacklists due to illegal, unethical, or unacceptable Web behaviors. Blanket junk e-mail is a sure way to raise your negative exposure in cyberspace.

Maintaining the Site

Often, as you surf the Web, you find links that are nonresponsive. That site has ceased to exist, yet no one has kept the referring site up-to-date. Some people post their sites, then never update them again. Addresses change, and there is no notice to users. There is a natural obsolescence that overtakes a site. Think of your site as a produce stand. How long does it take before produce begins to show its age? Not very long. The older the site, the more obvious it becomes to the user. If the site has a last revision date, this is the best indicator of the site's age. The following sections detail the processes involved in maintaining a site.

Timely/Current Information

Timely information is more useful and reliable than stale information. If you plan to maintain your site, convey this to the user. Using reference dates in the site will show its freshness (like expiration dates stamped on food items).

Oftentimes, graphics and animations date your site. The technology you use to create the site may be an indicator. If you discuss current events or movies, this also dates your site content. Announce what events or content changes you are planning in the future. This shows your interest and willingness in keeping this site on the cutting edge.

Continuous Refinement

College textbooks pass through revisions, and movie producers make sequels. Things change. Not only should your site be current, but it should undergo continuous refinement—evolving, growing, increasing its scope and coverage. As you learn more about the site topic or have more to offer the visitor, grow the site with this new content. Announce these refinements to the users, and direct them to this new content. Take them on a tour of new features.

Promote bookmarking of your site. Keep it high on people's must-visit site list. Ask visitors for input to help you assess your current coverage and possible new features they would like. Update your site on a predefined schedule—monthly, quarterly, starting on the first of the month. Even announce the update schedule in the site.

Finally, you can add new technologies to your site. As sound becomes more common in computers, add sound clips to the site. As video systems improve their performance, add a video clip. Show the user this site incorporates the best and most efficient information vehicles to convey its content. Customers will recognize and appreciate your efforts and will become loyal, repeat visitors.

Grocery Shopping on the Web

Our society is starved for time. No one has enough. Everyone is looking for ways to save time. One solution is grocery shopping on the Web.

Industry research by Andersen Consulting shows the average, round-trip, grocery shopping trip, takes ninety minutes. Home shopping reduces that time to less than ten minutes. This equates to an annual time savings of almost seventy hours!

Today, groceries purchased on the Web account for about 2 percent of $300 billion in annual grocery purchases. By the year 2003, most experts agree this figure will grow to about 12 percent, a 600 percent increase! Forward-thinking retail grocers are looking at ways to capture a share of this market.

Some stores are doing it themselves. But, there are also independent shopping services that connect the shopper to the store. These service brokers supply customers with specialized shopping software and other services. Once the customer places an order on the Web, the shopping service visits a grocery store, picks the order, and then delivers that order to the customer's home.

Two Examples

Two of today's PC shopping leaders are PC Pantry and Streamline.

PC Pantry is a full-service home shopper. But it has some interesting complementary services. Cyber Chef is an integrated recipe notebook, complete with pictures, ingredients, and step-by-step instructions on how to make the meal. You simply pick a recipe and enter the number of servings needed. Cyber Chef then calculates the ingredients required and adds them directly to your electronic shopping cart.

PC Pantry allows its members to donate food items to local food banks or charities. Another service, E-Meals, is an extensive collection of area restaurant menus including prices, directions, and phone numbers. E-Meals periodically contains restaurant reviews and special discounts available only to their members.

Streamline, another shopping service, first visits your home and learns about your product preferences and buying habits. While in your home, it scans the UPC codes on over 250 common products throughout your home to create your initial personal shopping list. You place orders weekly, via phone, Fax, or PC.

Streamline supplies its customers with specially made storage units (including freezer space, cold storage, and dry-goods storage) located in the garage. Outside keypads guarantee the delivery person access to the garage, even if you're not home.

Other Streamline delivery services include:

- Prepared meals
- Health and beauty care
- Dry cleaning
- Videos
- Photo finishing and supplies
- Pet food and supplies
- Postal service
- Can and bottle redemption
- Seasonal items such as firewood and Christmas wrap
- Community clothing and food drives

Currently, home grocery shopping on the Web is limited to just a few of the larger U.S. cities. But expect to see home shopping come to your area (and perhaps your home) in the near future.

SUMMARY

Web sites are constructed by both individuals and organizations. Some Web authors simply want to master Web site construction for future, professional use. Spend quality time thinking about your Web page design.

Key Web page design issues include the following: customer, content, design, site structure, media, construction, registration, and site maintenance.

High-quality Web sites link to other locations to improve or enhance the content of the site. Keep the site structure simple. There are some essential items that should be contained in every Web site, though. Include a contact person for the site.

Web sites using text, clipart, schematics, and graphics can be read by almost every computer today. Remember, site development is an ongoing process.

Photographic images can be processed and pasted into your Web site. Photos add reality and personality to your site. These contents are downloaded through special hardware and software, processed, and posted to the Web site.

You can become an HTML Web page programmer and develop your own site. Or, you can find Web site hosts on the Internet that will store and serve your site and also help you, in a tutorial format, design your site.

You need to store your site. Some services charge a monthly storage fee, especially for very large, commercial Web sites.

You need to register your site. Web agents will, for a fee, register your site for you. Once notified, the search service visits the site and categorizes its content based on the keywords it finds in the site's content.

Promote your site by advertising it at other sites. Ad space can be purchased on popular sites that may increase traffic and visits to your site.

Keep your site current. Old graphics and animations date your site. If you discuss current events or movies, this also dates your site content. Promote bookmarking of your site. Announce your updates and then do them.

KEY TERMS

bandwidth (165)
bar graphs (161)
clip art (162)
cyber portfolio (150)
design cycle (148)
design template (158)
digital cameras (167)
graphics (160)
hooks (156)
Hypertext Markup
  Language (HTML)
  (168)

ideate (153)
line graphs (161)
Microsoft SiteBuilder
  (177)
netiquette (178)
pie graphs (161)
portfolio (150)
registration agents (175)
scanners (167)
schematics (162)
site registration process
  (173)

Uniform Resource
  Locator (URL) (173)
video cameras (167)
virtual reality (164)
Web media (160)

END-OF-CHAPTER ACTIVITIES

Matching

Match each term with its description.

a. cyber portfolio

b. hooks

c. color-blindness

d. graphics

e. bar charts

f. pie charts

g. schematics

h. virtual reality

i. digital cameras

j. HTML

k. registration agents

________ **1.** Visually shows the percentage of each part of a whole.

________ **2.** Features in a Web site that attract visitors to a site and get them to stay.

________ **3.** Affliction that affects almost 17 percent of U.S. males where they can't tell certain colors from others.

________ **4.** Publication of your best work on the Web.

________ **5.** Shows relative levels of a key variable.

________ **6.** You can hire these Web services to enroll your site with search engines.

________ **7.** Illustrations used to show process flow or relationship levels.

________ **8.** Include tables, charts, illustrations, and photos.

________ **9.** An artificial construct with strong elements of reality.

________ **10.** These specialized cameras take pictures and then store them in an electronic format. No film is used.

________ **11.** These programming codes define the content, layout, and characteristics of your Web site.

Activities

1. Check your local yellow page advertisements. How many Web site hosts can you identify? Call two and ask what services they provide. What prices do they charge for hosting a personal Web site? Compare the two alternatives and decide which is better. Write up your findings in a one-page report. Discuss this report in class.

2. Have you ever heard a railroad sound on the Internet? Lycos, one of the popular search engines, allows you to search for sounds. Visit Lycos and search for a train sound. You must have speakers attached to your computer to hear these sounds. Do not download large sound files unless they will fit on your diskette. Were you able to play the sound?

3. Offer to design a one-page Web site for both a friend and a family member. Make sure each person has an active e-mail address. Discuss design and content issues with your "clients." What do they want to achieve with the site? What should the site contain? Sketch out a design and get an approval. Visit the Tripod site and construct the page. Make sure it works, then give your clients a live demonstration. Write up your experience and include a copy of the Web page. Be sure to document your client's reaction to this process and technology. What problems, what successes did you have? Was this a difficult or easy assignment? Why?

4. Visit the "Web pages that suck" site. From the list of bad sites, randomly pick two and visit them. Try not to read the listed problems with the site. Instead, do you your own assessment based on the concepts and principles discussed in this chapter. Write the assessment in two paragraphs. Now, look at the reviewer's comments. How do you compare? Do you agree or disagree with the other assessment? What did you learn from this activity?

5. Optional Assignment: Build a Cyber Portfolio

In this chapter, we discussed a personal portfolio as a vehicle to create a photograph of you as a unique individual. With its various components—resume, interests, work experience, and so on—it becomes a thumbnail sketch of your life.

A portfolio can first be developed as a paper document contained in a three-ring binder. However, once that effort is expended, the next step is to publish it in cyberspace.

If you choose to do this project, share your results and experiences with your professor and your class. Demonstrate your site. Explain how you plan to use it in the future. Good luck. May the "Force" be with you!

6. Optional Assignment: Build a Course Web site

Early in this chapter, we discussed the possibility of building a Web page for one of your classes. Perhaps your professor for *this* course would entertain the possibility of building a Web page.

As a cyberteam exercise, develop a Web site design for the course that is using this textbook. You have all the tools you need to complete the project. Form cyberteams of four to five members. Each team will prepare a different Web site plan. Follow the Web construction cycle explained in this chapter. Review the site development process: site design, content, media, storage hosts, promotion, and maintenance.

To add more reality to the project, visit five different course sites currently on the Web. Try to identify the Webmaster at each of those sites. Through e-mail, contact that person. Ask them questions about their site. How was the site developed? How successful has it been? How do they know? How many hits have they had? What kinds of interesting experiences have they had due to the Web site? What plans do they have for updating the site? Do they have any recommendations for your site or your team? Include the information you receive in your site project.

Write up a short summary of your team's project, process, and results. Include a mock-up of your Web page design. What did you learn by doing this project? Share your team's project and ideas with your professor and classmates. This should be a very interesting and educational experience.

CHAPTER SEVEN

Issues, Problems, and Concerns

Introduction
Control of the Internet
Internet Behavior
   Web Ethics and Etiquette
Mailing Lists
Privacy and Cryptology
Viruses on the Internet
Internet Fraud
Pornography and Obscenity

Security
   Information Theft
   Hackers and Crackers
   Espionage and Sabotage
The Year 2000 Dilemma
Useless Web Sites
Advertising on the Internet
Misinformation
Overburdened Internet

Online Games
Software Piracy
Issues and User Responsibility
Summary
Key Terms
End-of-Chapter Activities
   Review Questions
   Matching
   Activities

AFTER COMPLETING THIS CHAPTER, YOU WILL:

1. Understand who controls the Internet.

2. Explain proper Internet behavior.

3. Explain potential problems associated with the use of mailing lists.

4. Explain the issue of privacy and the importance of cryptology.

5. Explain what a computer virus is and discuss the potential dangers caused by the spread of computer viruses.

6. Define and give examples of Internet fraud.

7. Discuss why the issues of pornography and obscenity are controversial Internet issues.

8. Identify security issues explained in the chapter.

9. Explain how advertising can be an issue or problem for many Internet users.

10. Explain what software piracy is and why it is a serious problem to software publishers.

Introduction

Throughout American history, there has never been a shortage of issues, problems, and concerns, nor is there ever likely to be one. The debates that accompany the issues serve to focus attention on the complexity of them. In some cases, debates continue for many years.

Today our society abounds with a variety of current issues and concerns. Just a sampling of the issues we face today includes equal rights, tobacco, driving under the influence of alcohol, and the role of the military.

The development and introduction of any new technology almost always results in the emergence of issues surrounding it. The more complex the new technology, the more controversial the accompanying issues seem to be. Some individuals still argue the advantages of computers versus the disadvantages, for example.

The emergence of the Internet and World Wide Web is no exception. Today we face a new set of issues regarding the Internet and the Web, some of which may take many years to resolve—if they can be resolved at all. The remainder of this chapter focuses on some of these issues, many of which will be debated again and again in the years ahead.

Control of the Internet

The issue of controlling the Internet and the Web is a controversial one. Should government control the Internet and the Web? Should private business and organizations control the Internet and the Web? Should individuals control the Internet and the Web? Should the Internet and the Web be totally free of any controls? These are among the many questions being asked by people who feel that some controls and regulations are needed.

In confronting this issue, we need to keep in mind that the Internet and the World Wide Web are truly worldwide. They belong to everyone, yet no one individual or country actually controls them. Governments and citizens of countries certainly have a voice in any argument dealing with control of them, but the laws of different countries vary greatly in their application and meaning. Is it possible for every single country to agree to a set of standards that would apply to more than 270 million people worldwide? Even if every country would agree, would all citizens of every country abide by those standards?

The complexity of the issue of control is potentially mind boggling! Few people like being told what they can and cannot do. To reach worldwide agreement on this issue would be remarkable. Perhaps a better solution would be to educate users to act responsibly so that the Internet will remain available to everyone. Doing so will allow users to take advantage of the full opportunities available on the Internet and the Web.

Internet Behavior

Using the Internet and World Wide Web involves communicating with others, whether they are individuals, newsgroups, companies, agencies, or organizations. Users have a responsibility to exercise courtesy and sound judgment in their communications and dealings with others. As cliché as it may sound, a good rule to follow is the one many of us learned as a child: "Do unto others as you would have them do unto you." Perhaps the issue of Internet and Web control would be resolved if all users would practice this simple rule.

Web Ethics and Etiquette

The word **ethics** refers to personal standards involving one's behavior. Basic ethical standards in our daily interactions with other individuals, businesses, and organizations dictate that we will abide by commonly accepted ethical standards in our relationships. For example, everyone should expect us to be fair, honest, and courteous. If we are not, others in our society may regard us as being unwilling to adhere to basic ethical standards and may terminate their interaction with us.

Everyone knows there are acceptable rules of common courtesy in our relationships with other people. These rules are called **etiquette.** For example, there is table etiquette that governs our behavior at the dinner table and classroom etiquette that governs our behavior in school.

Rules for acceptable behavior on the Internet are called **netiquette** (an abbreviation for "Net etiquette"). An important point to remember when using the Internet is that each of us is expected to be ethical and to always practice proper Netiquette any time we use the Internet and the Web. In return, we should expect (and even insist) that others will abide by the same rules and make every effort to be fair, honest, and courteous.

What constitutes acceptable ethics and etiquette on the Internet and the Web? Obviously, there are disagreements. An acceptable action or statement by one person may be considered offensive to someone else. To help clarify some of the confusion on this issue, some users have posted Web pages specifying what constitutes acceptable behavior when using the Internet and the Web. One document that has gained widespread attention was developed and posted by Arlene Rinaldi at Florida Atlantic University. This document offers Ten Commandments for computer ethics and is shown in Figure 7.1. You can view the full document at the Internet address: http://www.fau.edu/rinaldi/net/ten.html.

FIGURE 7.1

Ten Commandments for Computer Ethics

THE NET: USER GUIDELINES AND NETIQUETTE—BY ARLENE RINALDI

FROM THE COMPUTER ETHICS INSTITUTE

1. Thou shalt not use a computer to harm other people.
2. Thou shalt not interfere with other people's work.
3. Thou shalt not snoop around in other people's files.
4. Thou shalt not use a computer to steal.
5. Thou shalt not use a computer to bear false witness.
6. Thou shalt not use or copy software for which you have not paid.
7. Thou shalt not use other people's computer resources without authorization.
8. Thou shalt not appropriate other people's intellectual output.
9. Thou shalt think about the social consequences of the program you write.
10. Thou shalt use a computer in ways that show consideration for others.

These "commandments" apply to computer use in general as well as to the Internet and the Web. The tenth commandment, in particular, addresses the issue of netiquette. Every user should always be aware of how actions, statements, and messages may be interpreted by others. Simply stated, when you are using the Internet, be aware of the potential impact of your actions by being fair, honest, polite, and courteous. Everyone should be a **Netizen,** a term that refers to being a good citizen when using the Internet.

Almost all Internet users send and receive e-mail messages over the Internet and many participate in listserv groups, mailing lists, and Usenet activities. Some guidelines for sending and receiving e-mail messages and participating with others on the Internet are listed in Figure 7.2.

As stated earlier, good judgment and common sense should prevail on the Internet. Common courtesy and respect for other people will help ensure that the Internet remains free from government control and available for everyone to use and enjoy.

Mailing Lists

Companies and other organizations have used mailing lists for many years to send notices, announcements, and advertisements to those whose names and addresses are on the lists. A **mailing list** is a list of entries (often individuals) in which each entry consists of a name or title, mailing address, telephone number, and other information. One example of a potential mailing list is a local telephone directory.

FIGURE 7.2

Guidelines for Electronic Communications

1. Avoid **"spamming"** on the Internet. A **spam** is any advertisement placed in an inappropriate location on the Internet, such as posting an advertisement to a newsgroup that is not involved in advertising. Under U.S. law, spamming is illegal.

2. Do not give your UserID or password to someone else.

3. Keep your e-mail messages brief and to the point.

4. Never assume your e-mail messages are private. Other people, including your boss may be able to intercept and read your messages.

5. An e-mail message should focus on a single point.

6. Do not use your organization's network or institution's network to perform commercial work.

7. Avoid SHOUTING in your messages. Typing messages using all capital letters is considered SHOUTING.

8. Never use the Internet to send chain letters.

9. Be careful and professional in statements you make in a message. An e-mail message can easily be forwarded to another person or group.

10. Be careful when using humor or sarcasm. Your humor or sarcasm may be regarded as criticism.

11. Avoid using a flame in your messages. A **flame** is an inappropriate statement, such as "you jerk," made in response to an offensive statement or message.

12. Be aware of your writing style. Every message should be clear, concise, and free of grammatical errors.

Mailing lists are important to the operations of many companies and organizations, and mailing list use is widespread. In fact, there are thousands of them. Some lists consist of entries that meet specific criteria. For example, one list may contain only names, addresses, and phone numbers of females, whereas another list may be limited to males between the ages of thirty-five and fifty.

Many companies and organizations purchase mailing lists from other sources and may spend considerable amounts for various lists. It is not uncommon for a company or organization to pay $2 or more for each entry on the list. Some companies and organizations specialize in the preparation and sale of mailing lists, which can be a lucrative practice. For example, a mailing list consisting of ten thousand entries at $2 per entry will sell for $20,000.

Some companies and organizations are able to create and store mailing lists free. Consider a local bank, for example. If the bank has 25,000 customers, there will be 25,000 customer records in its database. Customers were paid nothing for providing this information to the bank, and they probably assume the information will remain confidential. What if the bank puts customer names, addresses, and phone numbers into a mailing list and sells the list to another company or organization? Should customers be concerned? No doubt many would be.

Thousands of companies and organizations purchase, sell, and share mailing lists. Even some colleges and churches have begun the practice. Perhaps without your knowledge, information about you may be stored in databases at several companies and organizations. If you order merchandise from a mail order business, you may receive several catalogs from other companies shortly thereafter. Obviously, the company with which you placed an order shared or sold your information.

The use of mailing lists by Internet online service companies and service providers has become a controversial issue. Subscribers to a major online service company with several million subscribers recently learned of the company's intention to sell mailing lists containing information about subscribers. News of the service's plan has drawn widespread criticism and threats to sue the company. As a result, the company has delayed making a final decision.

The central issue concerns the ownership and use of personal information supplied by subscribers. Once a subscriber provides personal information to an online service or Internet provider, who has legal ownership of the information?

This issue is far from being settled. Mailing lists are the lifeblood for many companies and organizations, and they argue that subscribers supplied the information freely and without reservations and that the company should be allowed to use it in any manner chosen. Others, including subscribers and persons who purchase products and services, argue that the information should not be made available to others without their permission.

As with some other issues, the courts may eventually render a decision. Meanwhile, this issue may become even more controversial and may remain with us for quite some time.

Privacy and Cryptology

You need to be aware that it is easy for other people to intercept and read messages sent across the Internet. This is especially true for electronic mail (e-mail) messages and other information, such as that supplied when ordering products and services.

One of the major issues regarding e-mail is centered on the issue of **privacy;** that is, whether an employer has a right to intercept and read messages sent by employees. Some employers regularly monitor employee e-mail.

Some employers argue that they have a legal right to read employee e-mail because the company or organization owns the resources, such as computers and software, used for sending and receiving it. Also, employers argue that employees are being paid for the time they spend using e-mail and are therefore using company time. Employees, on the other hand, argue that they have a right to privacy and that an e-mail message should therefore be considered the private property of the individual. Both are valid arguments.

Legal opinions vary on this issue. Some courts have already ruled in favor of employers, and other cases are pending in the courts. The legal trend appears to be rulings based on the merits of individual situations and evidence.

This issue will likely remain controversial for the foreseeable future. Meanwhile, employees should probably refrain from using company resources for personal communications. If they use company resources, they should remember that messages can be intercepted and read, so they should be careful not to include statements that may jeopardize their position with the organization.

The issue of privacy is not limited to e-mail. The Internet is also used for transmitting other highly confidential information, such as business data and credit card numbers. The Internet will never be a safe place to conduct business unless there is some way to protect confidential data.

Software engineers and programmers have developed a technology that allows data to be secured during transmission. This technology, called **encryption,** allows data to be translated into a secret code. Encryption is the safest way to achieve data security. Once data has been encrypted, it can be transmitted with little concern that it can be intercepted and read by another person. The receiver of encrypted data must have access to a secret key or password to **decrypt** (decode) and thus read the data.

Viruses on the Internet

One of the major concerns on the Internet is the potential for virus attacks. A **virus** is a program that can disrupt or even destroy the normal operations of a computer. A virus can cause a variety of problems, ranging from the appearance of messages on the screen to the actual destruction of files stored on the computer's hard drive, including the computer's operating system.

The nature and structure of the Internet makes it vulnerable to attack. It is free and available to anyone wanting to exchange information, programs, data, and files. The freedom offered on the Internet carries with it a price. One price is the ease with which virus programmers can write virus programs and potentially distribute them to thousands of computers connected to the Internet.

Virus programmers apparently find pleasure in causing damage to computer software and files. Virus programs, like viruses that attack the human body, are numerous and varied in what they do. One virus may simply cause strange images to move about a computer screen, whereas another may result in serious damage to a computer's operating system by erasing important programs. Some do their damage immediately, while others are timed to take effect on a specific date.

A virus can infect your computer if you download software or other files from the Internet to your computer. One type may corrupt a program or data file, causing it to operate strangely. Another type may destroy all the files stored on your computer. Others may cause different problems.

A typical computer virus hides in a program and remains dormant until the user runs the infected program. When the user runs the infected program, the virus becomes activated. When activated, some viruses will attach themselves to other programs by copying themselves onto them. Currently, there are several hundred known viruses. Many are actively traveling the Internet.

Fortunately, programs called **antivirus programs** are available that can detect the presence of viruses and eradicate them. Some effective and popular antivirus programs include Norton Anti-Virus, Virex PC, WebScan, and VirusScan. Antivirus programs are updated often because new viruses appear frequently. You should install an antivirus program on your computer and update it periodically to safeguard against new viruses.

One issue currently being debated is the severity of penalties for distributing a virus over the Internet. Some people feel that harsh penalties should be imposed; others favor milder penalties. However, everyone seems to agree that writing and distributing a virus program is a serious offense and that the author of the virus program deserves to be punished.

Computer viruses themselves are not the only problem. Virus hoaxes (the threat of viruses) can cause serious problems. A **virus hoax** is false information from any source that a computer or computer system has been, or will be, infected by a virus. Try to imagine the resulting panic at your school if an anonymous caller informed the school administration that the school's computer system had been infected by a computer virus. Officials might order an immediate shutdown of the entire computer system as a precaution while computer personnel search for the virus.

Education Going Online

Many people probably recognize the potential impact of the Internet on businesses, but fewer people are likely to appreciate the Internet's potential impact on education. The rapid growth and expansion of Internet technology is already having a profound impact on educational institutions and programs.

One example of this impact involves the Watauga County Schools in western North Carolina. The state of North Carolina and the Watauga County Board of Education have joined together in a proposal to fund the development and implementation of computer instruction at the county's consolidated central high school and at each of the county's six elementary schools.

The plan is comprehensive. In addition to new computers for every classroom, the county will install an all-new computer network with state-of-the-art computers, servers, and software. New computers will be installed in every classroom, administrative office, teacher's office, and library. Every computer will have access to the Internet and World Wide Web. Electronic mail capability will allow students and teachers to communicate with each other and will help administrators submit timely reports. More importantly, students and teachers will have unlimited access to the vast supply of information on the Internet.

When fully implemented, course materials and information can be delivered online that will allow students to access the information in and outside the classroom. For example, a student who is absent from class on a particular day and who has a computer at home with Internet access will be able to catch up at home. Students without Internet access at home can catch up later while at school. The system will provide for online testing and immediate feedback from a teacher.

Other school systems across the country have begun installing and using similar technology. Educators around the country recognize the potential importance and value of this innovative technology that may change the educational landscape for future generations.

New computer users are especially vulnerable to hoaxes, especially new users who have been warned about viruses and the problems they can cause. Virus hoaxes are spread using various names. "Good Times," "Naughty Robot," and "Join the Crew" are some common ones you might see on the Net. The problem is that a computer user may not know whether the threat is real or fake. Whether real or fake, a computer user should be cautious and should follow appropriate procedures to guard against infection when a threat is made.

Users of e-mail need not be overly concerned when opening and reading their e-mail messages because e-mail servers typically contain special virus detection software that can detect and delete viruses. However, attachments to e-mail messages may contain a virus. Therefore, an e-mail user should exercise caution. A user would be wise to avoid opening an e-mail attachment received from an unknown source and should make certain that the e-mail program they are using will not open any attachments automatically.

Internet Fraud

The nature of the Internet lends itself to the real potential for fraud. **Fraud** is defined by Philip B. Bergfield in *Principles of Real Estate Law* as being "a false representation of a material fact, made with knowledge of its falsity and with the intent to mislead or defraud, that is justifiably relied on by the one to whom it is made and which results in injury to him (or her) because of his reliance."

Just as there are persons or groups who defraud others face-to-face, through the mail, and by telephone, there are those who use the Internet to defraud innocent victims.

Internet fraud is on the increase. Victims are being subjected to a variety of scams and cons, ranging from requests for charitable contributions to promises of instant wealth. Fraudulent acts are illegal and punishable under the law. However, it is often difficult to locate and punish those who use the Internet to commit fraud.

The best way for you to protect against fraud is to use extreme caution when contacted by anyone asking for money, credit card numbers, or personal information about you or anyone else. Remember the saying, "If it sounds too good to be true, it probably is!"

The attorney general's office in most states investigates and prosecutes fraudulent Internet activities. If you are contacted by someone on the Internet who makes unrealistic claims or offers, do not allow yourself to be pressured into sending money, giving out your credit card number, or making a commitment of any kind. Instead, you should notify local law enforcement and/or the attorney general of your state immediately.

Pornography and Obscenity

The freedoms provided by the Internet have resulted in a virtual avalanche of bad publicity in recent months. Considerable concern has been expressed concerning the pornographic and obscene information available on the Internet, including text, pictures, and language.

While information of this type constitutes only a tiny fraction of what is available on the Internet, any amount can prove controversial. Some individuals, groups, and organizations have placed pressure on politicians for legislation making it illegal for anyone to put pornographic and/or obscene materials on the

Internet. Therein is the issue. Should laws be enacted to regulate, and perhaps prohibit, pornography and other information considered obscene?

In response to outcries by some individuals and groups, Congress enacted the Communications Decency Act in 1996 to ban the use of these materials from the Internet. Soon after its passage, the United States Supreme Court ruled the act to be unconstitutional on the grounds that it violated free speech. Despite the ruling, some people and organizations continue to press for legislation to ban certain kinds of information from the Internet.

The vastness of the Internet virtually guarantees that any legislation, even if determined to be constitutional, will probably not be enforceable. No foreign government can be forced to abide by laws of the United States. Moreover, material regarded as pornographic by some individuals may be regarded as art by others.

Almost everyone agrees that pornographic and obscene materials should not be made available to children. Congress is taking steps to ensure that certain kinds of materials are banned from viewing by children. Similar actions, such as the development of a special TV chip called the V chip, are being discussed concerning objectionable materials on television. The assumption is that such a chip, if and when developed, would allow parents to screen and block specific programs and materials from being shown on their television sets.

Congress and state legislatures are being pressured to increase penalties for those who put child pornography on the Internet. Almost everyone agrees that such pornography has no rightful place on the Internet, and that offenders should receive severe punishment.

The issues of pornography and obscenity will continue to be discussed and debated in the months and years ahead. Concern surrounding these issues is real and sensitive. The solution may lie in software that will enable parents to make sure their children cannot see material that is objectionable. Some companies already produce this kind of software product. Products including CyberPatrol and SurfWatch analyze the information at Web sites and prohibit children from viewing unsuitable material. Also, some of the larger online services, including Microsoft Network and America Online, have the capability to block access to objectionable Internet material. Other groups are working to develop technologies and methods for barring access to sites and materials considered inappropriate for viewing by children.

Some businesses are concerned with materials that may be viewed by employees during company time, as they fear that the display and viewing of sexually explicit pornographic materials by some employees may be viewed as a form of sexual harassment. To eliminate this problem, some businesses have installed software on their network servers to block the reception of these materials.

Software is available that makes it possible to tell what users view while using the Internet. For example, some software keeps keeps track of the addresses of all Web sites and pages viewed by users of a network. This allows a supervisor or manager, for example, to visit those sites and see the same pages other users have visited.

Security

Security is a major concern of businesses, organizations, and agencies, many of which have invested millions of dollars to develop programs, files, and data. General Motors Corporation, for example, spends millions of dollars designing future automobile models that are stored on their computer systems. Having access to the designs would give competitors an important advantage. General

Motors is but one of hundreds of companies that could suffer severe damage if unauthorized users were to gain access to confidential files. Even authors sometimes go to great length to protect the confidentiality of manuscript files.

The adage "If there is a system, someone will figure out a way to beat the system" may be true. Evidence suggests that there are computer users lurking in cyberspace trying to gain access to other computers and files.

Many companies have intranets connected to the Internet, and almost all take extra precautions when any of their computers is connected to the Internet. One of these precautions is the building of firewalls around their systems. The term *firewall* originally referred to a wall built of brick, stone, or other fireproof material that was set between structures to prevent fire from spreading. On the Internet, a **firewall** is hardware and/or software that restricts information that passes between a private intranet and the Internet. Other measures often taken to ensure security include requiring the use of user IDs and passwords and restricting access to certain parts of the Internet, such as FTP sites and chat groups. Other measures may also be taken to safeguard information.

Information Theft

Information theft is a very serious problem today in our society. Thieves are using the Internet to steal all kinds of information, ranging from corporate secrets to individuals' credit card numbers. Thieves can use the Internet and illegally obtained credit card numbers to purchase products and services and charge them to the card owners. Each year, thousands of unsuspecting card owners are billed for millions of dollars in merchandise and services.

America Online recently notified its 8 million subscribers about a growing number of e-mail messages being received by its members that enable unauthorized persons to use the subscribers' accounts. The messages offer such things as free software or a free pornographic picture. To obtain the gift, the recipient must open a file that is attached to the message. This kind of scheme, in which a secret or concealed file is attached to another message or file, is known as a **Trojan horse**—a term taken from the Greek story about a large wooden horse filled with marauding soldiers. When the file is opened, a concealed program within the file collects the subscriber's account name and password and returns them to the thief. With access to a subscriber's account, the thief can impersonate the subscriber and purchase products and services online that will be charged to the subscriber. Trojan horse programs have plagued the Internet for many years, and many go undetected by most antivirus programs. The point to remember is to beware of messages offering free gifts.

Hackers and Crackers

The Internet offers exciting challenges to many computer enthusiasts who are willing to devote endless hours to searching for unique ways of doing things on the Internet. In recent years, two new groups of users have gained widespread attention and caused concern.

One of these groups has been labeled **computer crackers.** These are people who try to gain unauthorized access to computer systems for the purpose of altering, damaging, or stealing information by guessing user IDs and passwords. Sometimes they succeed. Evidence suggests that typical crackers are malicious teenagers who enjoy the thrill of altering or destroying information on a computer system. The FBI has reported that an average of more than five thousand attempts are made by crackers each day to gain unauthorized access to federal government computer systems.

The other group consists of **computer hackers.** These are individuals who generally have expert knowledge about many computer systems and may test their skills by breaking into computer systems. While computer hackers do not necessarily cause damage or steal information, they may view information stored in computer systems. Hackers tend to be very knowledgeable about computer systems, programming languages, and communications software protocols. After gaining access into a computer system and looking at stored files, a hacker's curiousity is usually satisfied and he or she will move on to the challenge of gaining access to another computer system without altering or destroying computer files.

Both hackers and crackers can cause problems—whether intended or innocent. Even if no damage is intended, large computer systems monitor attempts to gain access. Information system managers will know if an attempt was made to gain access, but they may not know whether programs, files, and data were damaged, destroyed, or stolen.

Espionage and Sabotage

On the Internet, **espionage** refers to the act of spying. There are many well-documented cases in which unauthorized persons used the Internet to gain access to government and private computer systems for the purpose of viewing confidential information. Recently, the U.S. government learned that attempts were made by spies of former Soviet Union countries to gain illegal access to U.S. government computer systems and files. Just as there are spies depicted in novels and in the movies, there are spies seeking to penetrate confidential computer files.

Sabotage refers to the willful destruction of property. On the Internet, saboteurs try to gain entry into computer systems to destroy information. The work of saboteurs can be devastating. Imagine the potential consequences if a saboteur broke into the computer system of the Social Security Administration and destroyed the records of millions of citizens. Because of the potential seriousness of acts of sabotage, penalties for these offenses are often severe.

The Year 2000 Dilemma

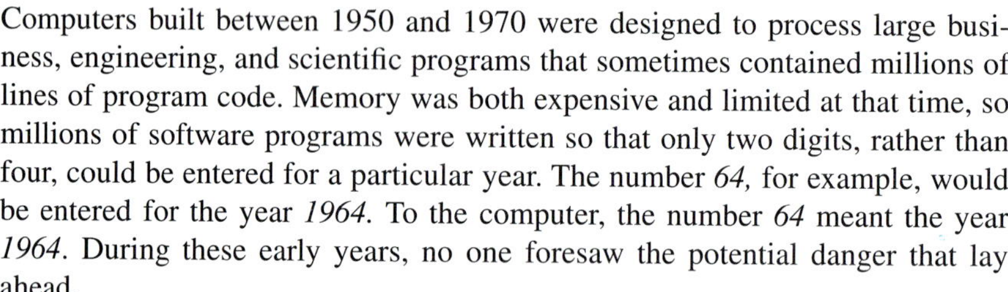

Computers built between 1950 and 1970 were designed to process large business, engineering, and scientific programs that sometimes contained millions of lines of program code. Memory was both expensive and limited at that time, so millions of software programs were written so that only two digits, rather than four, could be entered for a particular year. The number *64,* for example, would be entered for the year *1964.* To the computer, the number *64* meant the year *1964.* During these early years, no one foresaw the potential danger that lay ahead.

As the year 2000 approaches, we are facing a problem of immense proportions: Immediately after midnight on January 1, 2000, computers will read the year 2000 as the year 1900. The year 2001 will be read as 1901, and so on.

The worldwide dependence on computers means that the potential effects of this problem may be devastating. Suppose, for example, that you own a bank certificate of deposit that matures on January 1, 2000. On that day, the bank's computer will show the date as being January 1, 1900, and you may be unable to collect your money.

Programmers changing the millions of lines of code everywhere the problem exists can solve the problem, but the task will not be easy. Many large companies, organizations, and government agencies use thousands of computer programs containing millions of lines of code. The cost of making the necessary changes is expected to reach $600 million or more, but the process has already begun.

Time will tell whether the problem will be successfully solved. A solution to the problem will benefit everyone.

Much has been written and posted on the Internet about the year 2000 problem. One source of information on the Internet where you can learn more is at the address: http://www.year2000.com. You can find other sources by searching the Web.

Useless Web Sites

The quality of information available at various Web sites differs significantly. You probably know already that some sites are interesting and informative while others offer little, if anything, of value to the user.

Because anyone can put up a site on the Web, some people believe the Web is rapidly becoming cluttered with useless sites. Conversely, others feel that everyone has a right to have their own Web page regardless of how others feel about its value or usefulness.

As long as the Internet and the Web are free to all users, the views expressed by users are merely academic. No efforts are presently under way to prohibit anyone from placing pages on the Web—nor should there be. The authors of this book believe—like many other people—that to deny this privilege to anyone would be like denying a reader an opportunity to write, and have printed, a letter to the editor of a newspaper.

Web Site for Year 2000 Information

The concern and potential seriousness of the year 2000 problem has resulted in volumes of information being posted on the Web to inform the public. Shown is the home page of one site that contains useful information about the problem.

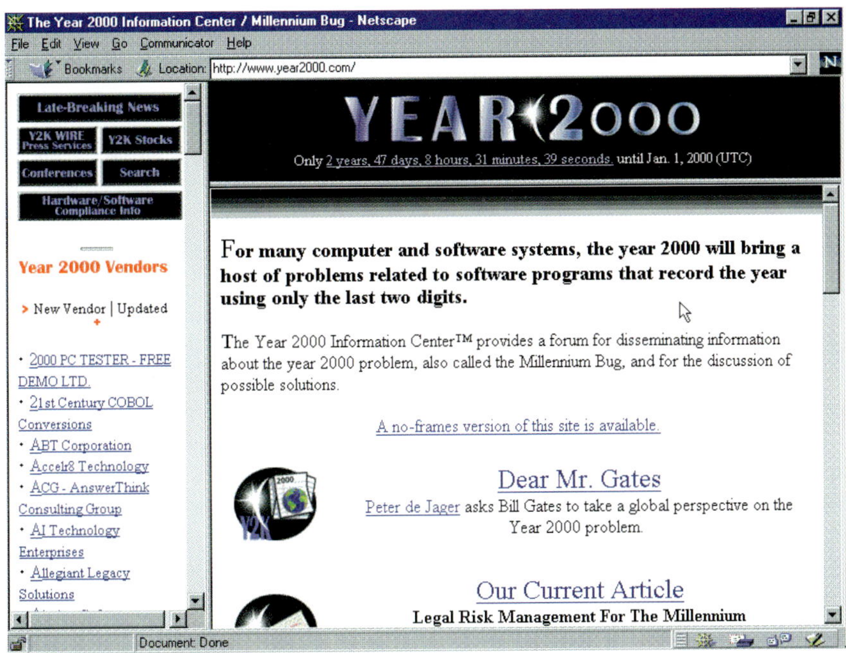

Advertising on the Internet

Using the Internet and World Wide Web for advertising is becoming big business. Most online services and Internet service providers sell advertising space and time to anyone wanting to advertise products and services. Moreover, business sites contain ads describing a variety of products, services, and special promotions.

How extensive is the practice of advertising on the Internet? According to one source, spending for advertising on the Internet is expected to reach $166 million during 1998. The rapid surge in the popularity of the Internet and the Web may result in even greater advertising expenditures in the future.

Some people believe advertisers are taking advantage of users by saturating the Internet with advertising. Some believe that much of the advertising on the Internet is misleading or inaccurate. Others disagree. Many who disagree believe that advertising serves to inform the public about new products and services and that most ads placed on the Internet are accurate and helpful.

This issue, like that of potentially useless Web sites, is at best academic. With a freely accessible Internet, the amount of advertising will probably increase dramatically.

Misinformation

Misinformation may be defined as information that is inaccurate, incomplete, misleading, deceptive, or confusing. Unfortunately, there is nothing to prevent misinformation from being placed on the Internet and inserted into Web pages.

Misinformation can occur for several reasons. It can appear on the Internet as a result of Web site and Web page developers' failure to verify information prior to posting the information on the Internet. It can occur simply because those posting the information just assumed it to be accurate. In an effort to conserve space, time, and expense, developers sometimes post a condensed version of the information, thereby rendering the information vague or misleading. However, misinformation can be deliberately posted. Large amounts of misinformation may result in Internet and Web users questioning or perhaps doubting the validity of other accurate information they see.

Anyone posting information on the Internet should be careful to verify that the information is factual. Preparing information for posting on the Internet in such a way as to sensationalize the information to make it more appealing to viewers is called **puffing.** Puffing should always be avoided. Information should be presented factually and in an unbiased manner so that viewers can accurately determine its value.

The accuracy of information on the Web is an important concern to Net users. Obviously, inaccurate information is useless.

A related concern involves the fact that the amount of information currently available on the Internet and the Web is growing at a phenomenal pace. Some users believe there is already too much information available on the Internet, yet in the months and years ahead, the amount of information will continue to increase—not decrease.

At present there are more than 100 million pages available on the Web. Many of these pages contain the same or similar information. Some users consider the redundancy of so much of the information to be a problem. For example, some teachers believe that student assignments could be completed faster if some of the redundant information was removed.

Obviously, all users should make certain that any information they post is accurate and useful.

Overburdened Internet

Despite the enormous size and scope of the Internet and the Web, some users express concern that the Net and the Web are already overburdened and unable to handle the millions of users who regularly travel through cyberspace.

Evidence suggests that the Internet and the Web are not overburdened as a whole, but that some parts of them are. Consider the problems encountered in 1997 by America Online and its subscribers. Problems began to occur when America Online changed its fee structure. For a fixed monthly fee, subscribers were allowed unlimited access to AOL's services. Thousands of AOL's 8 million subscribers immediately began taking advantage of their new unlimited access. In fact, many would remain online for hours at a time, thereby tying up AOL servers and preventing others from gaining access. Some users admitted to remaining online twenty-four hours a day. The problem was that the America Online servers were unable to accommodate all users wanting access. To keep from losing subscribers, America Online began frantically to install a larger number of more powerful servers. Within a short time, the problem was solved. However, many AOL subscribers filed a class-action suit against the company. Recently, the company announced an out-of-court settlement with subscribers. Other online services and intranets have experienced similar overload problems and have dealt with their problems effectively, as did AOL.

Successful online services and Internet service providers will likely experience overburdens from time to time as more people begin using the Internet. Adjustments will be made to accommodate the increase. Moreover, some popular Web sites periodically experience heavy usage. An example occurred when NASA's *Pathfinder* began sending pictures of the planet Mars back to earth. The demand for access to NASA's Web site by people wanting to view pictures of Mars far exceeded the abilities of NASA's servers. To accommodate public interest, NASA established mirror sites at which viewers were able to see the pictures. Mirror sites were explained earlier in Chapter Two.

Improvements, changes, and adjustments are continually being made to the Internet and the World Wide Web. As users, we will probably encounter access problems in the future. While these delays may be inconvenient, they will probably be minor problems that, in time, will be corrected.

Online Games

Several Web sites offer computer games that users can play and enjoy. Some games have some measure of educational value. For example, one game available on the Internet requires a player to enter the capital city of other countries. A correct answer results in a smiling face being displayed on the screen. A wrong answer causes a frowning face to appear. Another game requires a player to enter answers to historical questions such as "What were the names of Columbus' three ships?" The player hears the words "Your answer is correct" when the right answer is entered, and "Your answer is incorrect" when a wrong answer is entered. Many other games are similarly educational and challenging.

While many games are challenging and fun, some are of little, if any, educational value. Some even contain violent materials. Some educators and parents object to games of this kind on the Internet. In addition to violence, they argue that playing some games cause users to experience stress, anxiety, and tension.

Some educators and parents feel that computer games have no legitimate place on the Internet and should be banned altogether. Some educators argue that games capture students' interests and that unsupervised students in a computer lab spend too much time playing games and too little time completing assignments.

Many businesses and organizations prohibit employees from using the Internet to access and play computer games during working hours. A nurse employed by a local hospital in North Carolina was fired when it was discovered that she was spending more than half of her eight-hour shift playing Solitaire on her computer.

It would probably be impossible to eliminate or prohibit games from the Internet. Educators, parents, and employers, however, can closely monitor students' and employees' activities and establish rules, practices, and standards on an individual basis. A company can establish specific rules regarding games in the workplace, for example, and can closely monitor employees to enforce the rules.

Software Piracy

The nature of the Internet and World Wide Web is such that anyone having a connection and publishing software can create and publish Web pages. Such freedom often results in abuses that can occur innocently or deliberately.

One abuse that is illegal is software piracy. **Software piracy** refers to the distribution of software by copying, loaning, or renting it to people who have not legally purchased it. A legal copyright may be granted by the U.S. Copyright Office to cover a person's or business' original work, such as computer software, a book, an article, a poem, or music. The copyright grants the holder exclusive rights to the material. For example, the publisher of the book you are now using has a copyright to all information contained in the book. Therefore, permission to reproduce, transmit, or store in a retrieval system any portion of this book must be obtained from the publisher.

Much of the information and many of the pictures contained on Web pages are not copyrighted, but some are. Anyone wanting to use materials from any source to create a Web page should check to see if the materials are copyrighted before using them. Unauthorized use of copyrighted materials may result in embarrassment and litigation in the courts. In the past, many violators of copyright law have been sued and fined.

Some people believe they should be able to use, and even copy, any materials found on the Web in their own Web pages. Others argue the opposite—that the creators of Web pages should be able to have their pages copyrighted to protect their material from being copied by others.

This issue has been settled for the time being. Copyright laws do protect one's own creative work and the U.S. Supreme Court has ruled that the same copyright laws that apply to printed materials, such as books, also apply to computer software and other creative works, including creative material placed on the Web. Unless copyright laws are changed, the creator of Web pages should be careful not to violate the laws by copying information and materials from other Web pages without first obtaining written permission.

Software piracy is a serious problem that costs software publishers millions of dollars each year in lost revenue. As a result, they have taken measures to prevent the practice. With support from publishers, the Software Publishers Association (SPA) was formed to monitor the problem and to educate the public. You can

FIGURE 7.4

Software Publishers Association Home Page

The Software Publishers Association was formed to educate the public about the problem of software piracy and to monitor the problem. The association is supported by software publishing companies and can bring legal action against people who engage in the illegal practice of pirating copyrighted computer software.

learn more about SPA and the problems associated with software piracy by visiting the SPA Web site at http://www.spa.org.

Issues and User Responsibility

Because the Internet and the World Wide Web are relatively new and are growing at a phenomenal pace, many new and controversial issues and concerns have emerged. Over time, some issues and concerns will be resolved, and new ones will emerge. Some will likely be ignored while the courts will decide others.

Some issues will remain controversial due to a consensus of worldwide opinion. Social standards and customs vary among the nations of the world. Individual opinions among citizens are influenced by many factors, including religion, social and political persuasions, and personal and family values. These and many other factors influence human attitudes and beliefs.

As Net users, we are all responsible for our opinions, actions, and attitudes. In order to preserve a free and worldwide Internet, we all have a responsibility to respect the opinions of other users. Only then will we be able to enjoy the full benefits of the Internet and World Wide Web.

SUMMARY

The emergence of the Internet and the World Wide Web has brought new and controversial issues into public awareness. The issue of *who,* if anyone, should control the Internet and the Web is extremely controversial.

Etiquette on the Internet is referred to as netiquette (an abbreviation for Net etiquette). On the Internet, everyone should be a Netizen, a term that refers to being a good citizen when using the Internet.

The use of mailing lists by Internet online service companies and service providers is one currently controversial issue. A mailing list is a list of entries (often of individuals) in which each entry consists of a name or title, mailing address, telephone number, and other information.

One of the major issues regarding electronic mail is centered on privacy; that is, whether an employer has a right to intercept and read messages sent by employees. The issue of privacy is not limited to e-mail messages. The Internet is also used for transmitting other highly confidential information, such as business data and credit card numbers. A technology called encryption allows data to be translated into a secret code. The receiver of encrypted data must have access to a secret key or password to decrypt (decode) and thus read the data.

A virus is a program that can disrupt or even destroy the normal operations of a computer. Antivirus programs are available that can detect the presence of many viruses and eradicate them.

Fraud may be defined as "a false representation of a material fact, made with knowledge of its falsity and with the intent to mislead or defraud, that is justifiably relied on by the one to whom it is made and which results in injury to him (or her) because of his reliance."

The presence of pornographic and obscene materials available on the Internet, including text, pictures, and language is another issue that concerns many people. To combat this problem, some businesses have installed software on their network servers to block the reception of these materials.

Security is a major concern of businesses, organizations, and agencies, many of which have invested millions of dollars to develop programs, files, and data. One method of maintaining security is to build firewalls. On the Internet, a firewall is hardware and/or software that restricts information from passing between a private intranet and the Internet.

Information theft is a very serious problem today in our society. Thieves use the Internet to steal all kinds of information, ranging from corporate secrets to individuals' credit card numbers.

A computer cracker is a derogatory term that most often refers to a person who tries to gain (and sometimes succeeds in gaining) unauthorized access to computer systems for the purpose of altering, damaging, or stealing information. Computer hackers are individuals who may test their computer skills by breaking into computer systems.

On the Internet, espionage refers to the act of spying. Sabotage refers to the willful destruction of property. On the Internet, saboteurs try to gain entry into computer systems to destroy information.

While the Internet and World Wide Web is free to anyone wanting to put a site on the Web, some people believe the Web is rapidly becoming cluttered with useless Web sites and information.

Using the Internet and World Wide Web for advertising is becoming big business. Some believe that much of the advertising on the Internet is misleading or inaccurate. Others believe that advertising serves to inform the public about new products and services and that most ads placed on the Internet are generally accurate and helpful.

Misinformation may be defined as information that is inaccurate, incomplete, misleading, deceptive, or confusing. Unfortunately, there is nothing to prevent misinformation from being placed on the Internet and inserted into Web pages.

Despite the enormous size and scope of the Net and the Web, some users express concern that the Net and the Web are already overburdened and unable to handle the millions of users who regularly travel through cyberspace. Evidence suggests that the Internet and the Web as a whole are not overburdened, but that some parts of them are.

Several Web sites offer computer games users can play and enjoy. Some games have some measure of educational value. Some provide little, if any, educational value, and some contain violent materials.

Software piracy refers to the distribution of software by copying, loaning, or renting it to persons who have not legally purchased it. Copyright laws do protect one's own creative work. Unless copyright laws are changed, the creators of Web pages should be careful not to violate the laws by copying information and materials from other Web pages without first obtaining written permission.

KEY TERMS

antivirus program (189)	firewall (192)	puffing (196)
computer cracker (193)	fraud (190)	sabotage (194)
computer hacker (193)	information theft (192)	software piracy (197)
decrypt (188)	mailing list (186)	Trojan horse (193)
encryption (188)	misinformation (195)	virus (188)
espionage (193)	netiquette (185)	virus hoax (189)
ethics (185)	Netizen (186)	
etiquette (185)	privacy (187)	

END-OF-CHAPTER ACTIVITIES

Review Questions

1. In the chapter, a list of ten commandments for computer ethics was presented. Without referring to the list, write down as many of the commandments as you can remember.

2. Some guidelines for electronic communications were presented. Without referring to the chapter, note as many guidelines as you can remember.

3. Many companies and organizations use mailing lists to contact prospective customers and inform them about products and services. Should online service companies and Internet service providers be allowed to sell subscriber information to others? Explain and give reasons for your answer or opinion.

4. Internet fraud has become a serious problem. What does the word *fraud* mean? Are there ways in which fraud can be minimized or eliminated from the Internet?

5. One of the most controversial issues today is the presence of pornography on the Internet. In your opinion, is it possible for pornography to be banned from the Internet? Why or why not?

6. Two groups of Internet users are called computer hackers and computer crackers. What is the main difference between the actions of these groups of users?

7. More and more computer games are being made available to Internet users. Identify some potential problems of online computer games.

8. Define each of the following terms that were explained in the chapter.
   a. ethics
   b. netiquette
   c. Netizen
   d. flame
   e. cryptology
   f. virus
   g. Trojan horse
   h. espionage
   i. misinformation

Matching

Match each term with its description.

a. netiquette
b. misinformation
c. copyright infringement
d. mailing list
e. computer cracker
f. encryption
g. firewall
h. sabotage
i. privacy
j. virus

________ **1.** Allows data to be translated into a secret code.

________ **2.** An issue concerning whether or not an employer has a right to intercept and read employee messages.

________ **3.** A program that can disrupt or destroy the normal operations of a computer.

________ **4.** Rules for acceptable behavior on the Internet.

________ **5.** The willful destruction of another's property.

________ **6.** The unauthorized use of material on which someone has been granted a copyright by the U.S. Copyright Office.

________ **7.** Hardware and/or software that restricts information that passes between a private intranet and the Internet.

________ **8.** Information that is inaccurate, incomplete, misleading, deceptive, or confusing.

________ **9.** Usually refers to a person who tries to gain unauthorized access to computer systems for the purpose of altering, damaging, or stealing information.

________ **10.** A list of entries (often of individuals) in which each entry consists of a name, mailing address, telephone number, and other information.

Activities

1. Using your browser, go to the following Web site: http://www.fau.edu/rinaldi. A list of articles will be displayed. Click on the article "The Net: User Guidelines and Netiquette" by Arlene Rinaldi and read the article. This informative site contains pages explaining proper Internet ethics and behavior. If you are unable to access this site, do a search using the word "Netiquette" to find other information about user Netiquette and read the information available.

2. Using a search engine, locate five documents containing information about the issue of privacy. Select and print the article you believe best explains this issue.

3. Using a search engine, locate several documents containing information about different viruses. For each virus, prepare a brief written summary describing the harm to a computer system that may be caused by the virus.

4. Using a browser, visit ten different Web sites. Compare the information available at each site. In your opinion, is the information at any of the sites useless?

5. Several issues, concerns, and problems were explained in the chapter. Choose one specific issue, such as "hackers" or "the year 2000 dilemma," and do a thorough search for more information about the issue you select. After studying the information you find, prepare a written summary of the information you located and studied.

6. The Web contains information about virus hoaxes. Using your browser, visit each of the two Web sites listed below. Read and prepare a brief summary of the information you find.

(a) http://ciac.llnl.gov/ciac/CIACHoaxes.html

(b) http://www.kumite.com/myths/home.html

7. For this activity, your Instructor will divide the class into groups made up of four or five students. Each student in a group will use the Internet to locate information concerning a specific Internet issue, such as privacy, fraud, or pornography. After accessing the information, members of each group will prepare a written report summarizing the group's findings.

Internet Commerce: Doing Business on the Internet

What Is Internet Commerce?
Foundations of Internet Commerce
    Information and Competitive
        Advantage
    A Growth Projection
    Internet Commerce and the
        Organizational Value Chain
    Building Blocks and Connectivity
Internet Commerce System
    Configurations
    People-to-People Systems (PPSs)
    People-to-System-to-People
        Systems (PSPSs)
    System-to-System Systems (SSSs)

Internets within an Organization:
    Intranets
    Definition
    Applications
    Intranet Benefits
Internet Commerce between
    Organizations: Extranets
    Definition
    Combining Internets and Intranets
        to Form Extranets
    Two Extranet Examples
    Extranet Pitfalls and Security
        Issues
Internet Commerce between an

Organization and Consumers
    The Customer Is King
    Electronic Marketplaces
    Intelligent Shopping Agents
    Web Financial Systems and
        Electronic Payments
    Local Web Shopping
In Closing
Summary
Key Terms
End-of-Chapter Activities
    Matching
    Review Questions
    Activities

AFTER COMPLETING THIS CHAPTER, YOU WILL:

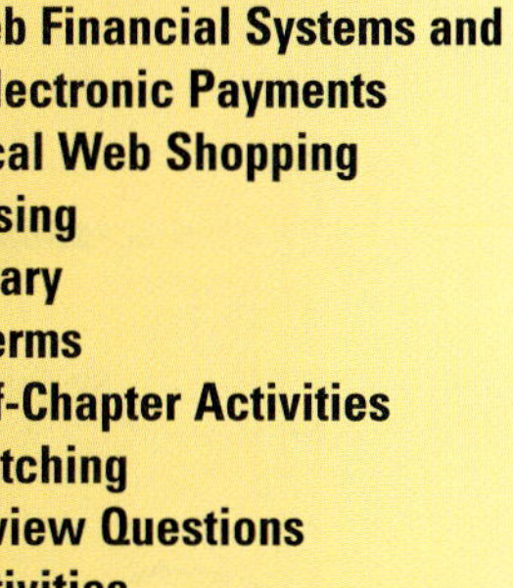

1. Define Internet Commerce (IC).

2. Explain the benefits of IC to the buyer and the seller.

3. List and discuss three IC system configurations.

4. Define intranets, including possible applications and benefits.

5. Define extranets, and list their benefits and limitations.

6. Describe how Internet Commerce operates between consumers and organizations.

7. Describe an electronic marketplace and how it operates.

8. Explain what an intelligent shopping agent is and how it works.

9. Describe the various payment options in Internet Commerce applications.

10. Discuss the impact of IC on our society and how this will affect our future.

What Is Internet Commerce?

There is a technology transformation occurring in today's society in which individuals and organizations are getting together—electronically. **Internet commerce (IC),** sometimes referred to as **electronic commerce (EC),** is the use of computer networks to conduct business—the buying and selling of goods and services electronically—with one's suppliers, customers, and competitors.

Internet commerce uses technologies that automate business transactions. It focuses on highly structured transactions among large commercial and governmental organizations. Now it has expanded to include applications among individuals using less rigidly structured transactions. It even facilitates communication processes within an organization. Figure 8.1 states the impact of connectivity on a society.

Foundations of Internet Commerce

Over time, the United States has changed from an agrarian society to an industrial society to today's information society. Now we are moving to a global communications society. Global business requires continuous surveillance and rapid response by organizations to their sophisticated buying public.

Information and Competitive Advantage

Andrew Grove, the CEO of Intel, in his book *Only the Paranoid Survive,* refers to **"critical inflection points"**—opportunity points in the life of an organization or industry where its growth either ramps up to achieve even greater successes or turns down to eventual difficulties. Internet commerce is the technology on-ramp

FIGURE 8.1
Connectivity

This is a recent ad from the Sprint Communications Company that shows the importance of connectivity to the cultures of both the United States and the world.

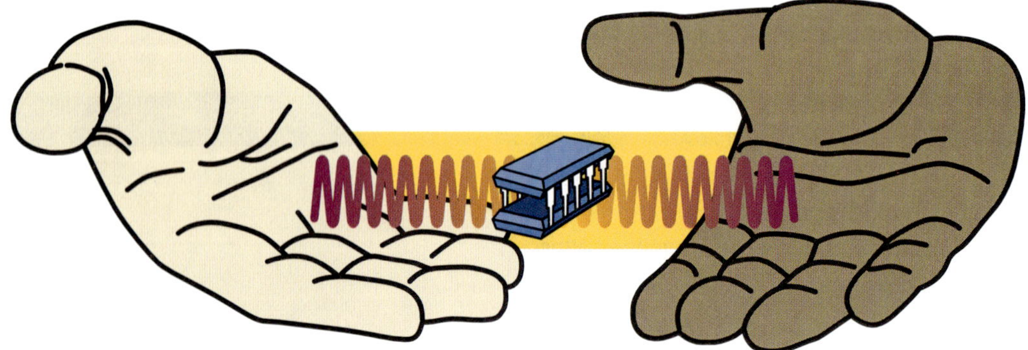

Copy from a recent Sprint Communications Company advertisement.

to the modern Information Superhighway. It may well be many organizations' critical inflection point during the next decade.

Industries are made up of **business chains,** or **value chains.** The chain includes a flow of products, services, and information linked through suppliers, distributors, channels, retailers, markets, and consumers. IC supplies the connectivity and communications in that chain. Telecommunications and computer industries are joining with each other and with the financial industry to facilitate electronic trading among these partners.

Emerging Internet and World Wide Web technologies offer IC users new business connections, marketing opportunities, and communication channels directly to consumers—with no cumbersome interface of mail, time, and buildings. IC will have a major impact on retail, financial, and consumer-based industries. It redefines connection points between organizations and consumers. Supplier and consumer information will be more complete—buying patterns, timing of purchases, new product innovations, and future expected needs. Companies that successfully capture and use this information for consumer insights and behavior patterns will achieve a new competitive advantage through their technology systems.

A Growth Projection

A mid-1997 business report issued by Forrester Research Inc., an international research company, estimated that the value of goods and services traded electronically between companies will explode in the next few years. Forrester Research estimated that today's $8 billion IC business could grow to over $300 billion in just five years! (See Figure 8.2.)

Business over the Internet reduces costs, speeds up order processing and delivery times, and improves the quality of information exchange between trading partners. In traditional paper systems, one company's paper output becomes another company's paper input. In IC systems, once a transaction is entered, it stays "electronic," allowing the same data to be used for billing, accounts receivable, banking,

FIGURE 8.2

Projected Growth of Internet Commerce in the Next Five Years

Internet Commerce growth is expected to explode in the future. This growth will contribute to continued improvements in Web features and content.

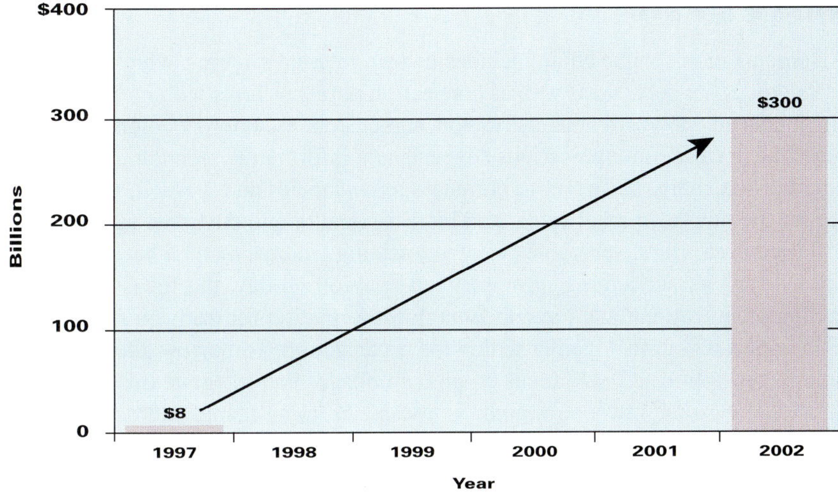

FIGURE 8.3

Electronic Commerce Growth in the Future: A Sample of Recent Article Headlines

Electronic commerce has received international attention recently. As new development occurs, we will see more stories about it in newspapers, magazines, and on the Web.

4,000 Companies Recruit via Internet by 1998

Online Retailing to Reach $7 billion by 2000

15.5 Million New Jobs Created in Last Five Years: More Projected for the Future

Home Shopping to be $5 Billion Market by 2003

Home Offices Projected to Grow at Exponential Rate

Moore's Law: Number of Transistors on a Chip Double Every Year

Microsoft Promotes New Electronic Commerce Solution for All Merchants

Electronic Commerce Worth $98 Billion by 2000

---

and account analysis. Figure 8.3 shows a sample of recent electronic commerce article headlines.

In today's global business environment, productivity and competitiveness are keys to organizational success. The organization decides how to allocate its scarce labor, capital, and technology to create an advantage in the market. Over time, as cost and efficiency of these resources change, substitutions occur in the organization's business processes.

Internet Commerce and the Organizational Value Chain

An organization's value chain includes its own internal systems, which add value to its product or service, as well as connection points or links with its "upstream" suppliers and "downstream" distributors and customers. Internet commerce combines the newest communications concepts and information technologies used to upgrade this chain. IC strives to eliminate redundancies and waste in the system, reduce the time-to-market cycle, and increase quality and customer satisfaction.

Fifteen years ago, companies were automating tedious, manual business transactions such as accounting, inventory, and payroll. Today, the focus is on converting organizational data into meaningful information for decision making and linking business units together within the organization. Tomorrow, the next technology generation, IC, will focus on global linkages that integrate different organizational systems into one seamless process. IC joins manufacturers, distributors, retailers, and customers in a system that eliminates idle resources and improves responsiveness to changing consumer needs and expectations.

Organizations will no longer be defined by the four walls that surround them. Computer technologies complement bricks and mortar (buildings). Emphasis is now on inter- (between)—and intra- (within) company communication systems. New outreach technologies will integrate with older, in-house systems. New marketing data will help business planners focus messages, services, and marketing media on customers with pinpoint accuracy. Wireless technologies, in the form of laptop computers, now allow sales and service functions to operate more efficiently. Figure 8.4 shows how Wal-Mart, the world's largest retailer with $100 billion in sales and 800,000 employees, uses Internet commerce to track and react to its consumers' purchases.

Building Blocks and Connectivity

This final chapter supplies an introduction for students who want to know how Internet technologies will improve organizational and individual performance. How are individual technologies woven into integrated systems?

FIGURE 8.4

Wal-Mart Installs World's Largest Internal Electronic Commerce System: Five Trillion Bytes of Data

Wal-Mart captures data at the point of purchase, then sends it to their company headquarters. There it is analyzed and redistributed to all parts of the organization. Wal-Mart places new orders with suppliers when inventories run low. Payments for those orders are made electronically.

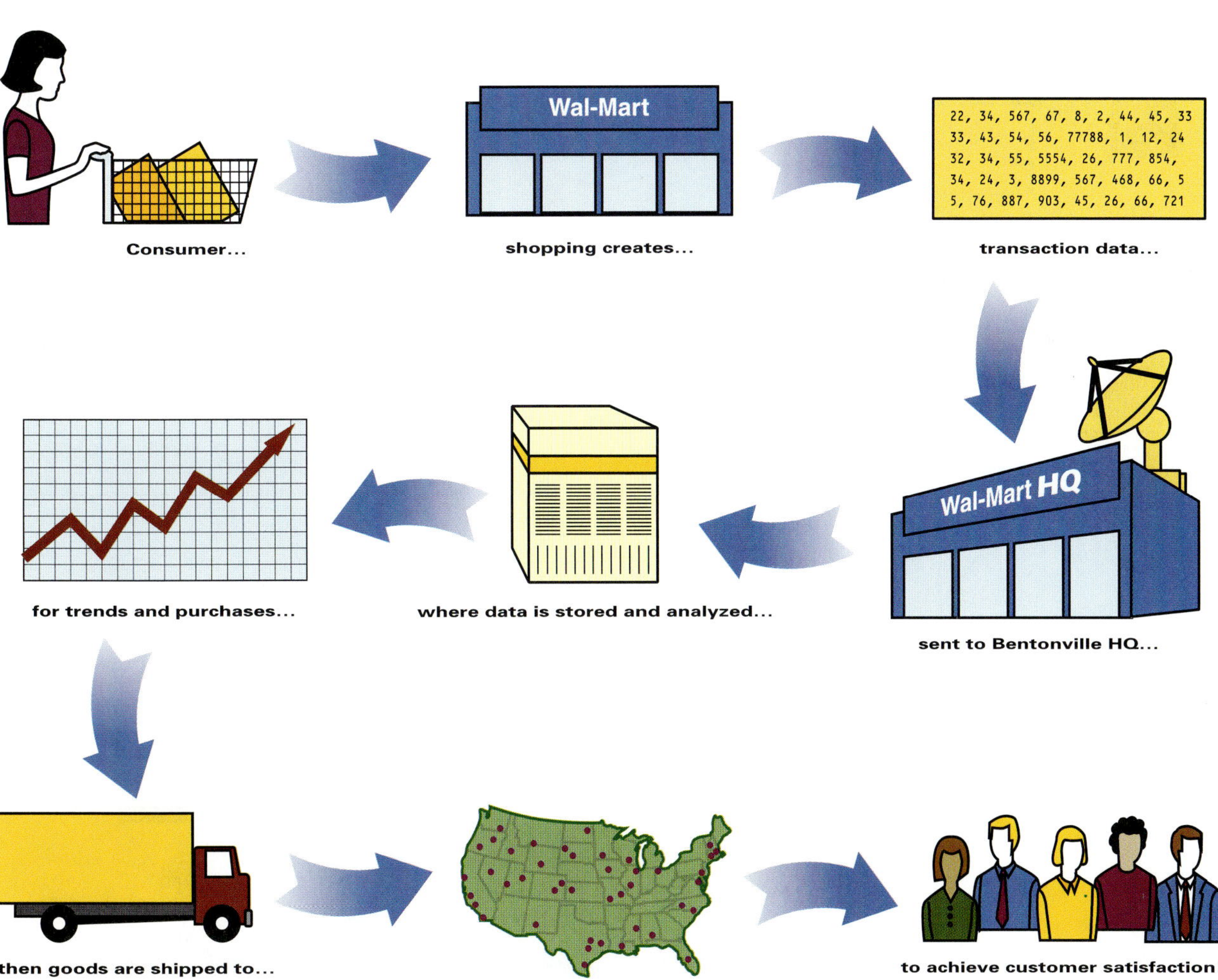

A better understanding of Internet commerce shows students the future needs and expectations of employers. It helps you plan college courses, majors, and academic programs. Students can build skills and insights that will add to their marketability and employability. Entrepreneurial students can dream about home-based businesses with a global presence. Perhaps another Bill Gates (the CEO of Microsoft and the richest man in the U.S.) lurks among our readers!

The first part of this chapter examines Internet commerce concepts and suggests a framework for IC. It marries the foundations of IC with telecommunications systems.

FIGURE 8.5
Internet Commerce and the Value Chain

The Web is applied in three different ways in this figure. Intranet use is restricted to use only within the organization itself. The extranet allows the organization to link with its suppliers and distributors. Finally, the Internet allows customers and noncustomers to reach all parts of the value chain. The organization also can use the Internet to communicate with all those parties not connected to either its intranet or extranet.

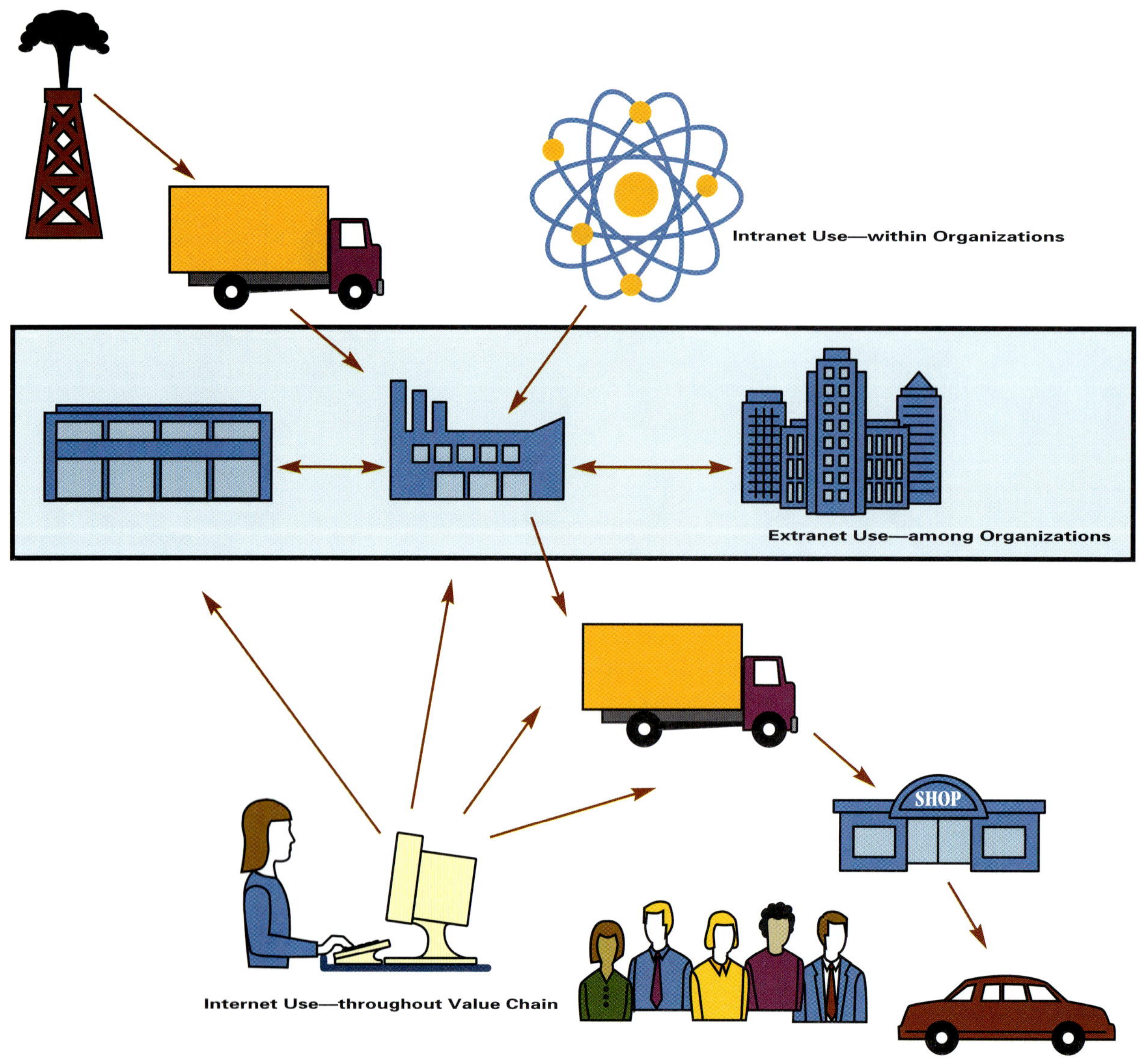

Online World Goes AOL (America Online, That Is)

Internet commerce between consumers and enterprises is conducted through an extensive network of third-party communications providers called Internet service providers (ISPs). These providers supply the electronic pathway over which IC travels. But there is also an Internet commerce aspect related to these providers. They are profit-centered companies that charge for their products and services. Here, we highlight the world's largest ISP, America Online (AOL). AOL currently has approximately 50 percent of the ISP market.

AOL has survived computer meltdowns, system failures, and irate customers to become today's largest and most successful Internet service provider. As can be seen from the following graph, the company has grown from its meager beginnings to serve over 11 million users with 5,500 employees. Its stock price on the New York Stock Exchange has risen from less than $2 in 1992 to over $75 in 1997.

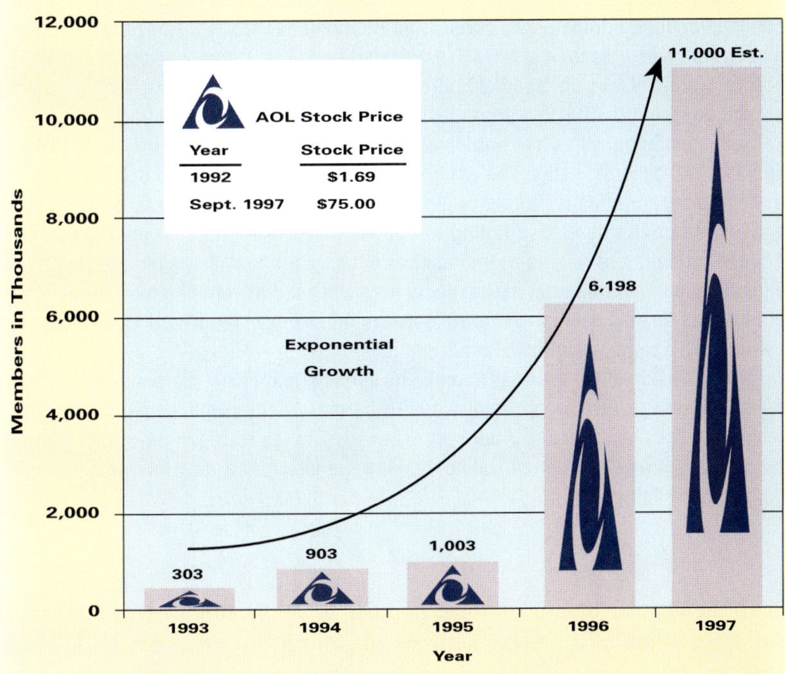

Internet users are a demanding bunch. They are typically well-educated, upper-income family units, as can be seen in the following AOL user demographics table. Many use their Internet service for both personal and business applications. All the major ISPs have suffered at the hands of irate customers. As volume increases on the Web, providers must supply more and more computing power and communications capabilities, or user delays grow quickly. Typical billing schemes now offer unlimited access time to users for a flat monthly fee, usually between $15 and $25.

TABLE 8-1

AOL User Demographics: Well-Educated Family Units

1. Female AOL users: 41 percent; male: 59 percent

2. AOL users who report other AOL user(s)in household: 56 percent

3. AOL users who report spouses who use the service: 42 percent

4. AOL households that have children: 46 percent
   (U.S. Census reports 35 percent households have children.)

5. AOL users with children ages 6 to 17 in household: 54 percent

6. AOL user college graduates: 63 percent
   (U.S. Census reports 23 percent of population are college graduates.)

7. AOL users who use service for both personal and business use: 41 percent

Source: 1996 AOL Annual Report

In 1997, AOL users averaged 40 minutes per day using its services versus just 13.5 minutes per day in 1996. Not all 11 million users are online at the same time. In the spring of 1997, the company spent $350 million for new computers, modems, and communications equipment to support its phenomenal growth. After the improvements, AOL was able to host 400,000 users simultaneously, compared to just 120,000 before. Before these changes, 80 percent of AOL's subscribers first-attempt calls did not go through. After the upgrade, the figure dropped to 34 percent.

Still, the company has had hard financial times. In 1996, AOL lost almost $500 million on $1.68 billion in sales. The company's new sales strategy is much like that of the newspaper industry. In newspapers, reader subscription fees pay for the expense of printing and distributing the paper. Advertising fees create the profits. Advertising fees are related to the number of people who will see the ads. With its exploding membership size, AOL expects the increased advertising fees paid by the enterprises on its system to generate substantial profits in the future. User fees will help pay basic operating expenses.

AOL's mission in the future is to make its service usable by "mere mortals." They want to package their Internet services to be more accessible, user-friendly, and technologically transparent. Their corporate mission, as stated in their 1996 annual report, says it best. "America Online: making the vision of a new interactive medium a global reality."

Next, the chapter highlights three popular IC applications—those within the organization (intranets), those between organizations (extranets), and those between organizations and their customers (Internets). Figure 8.5 shows how these three applications fit together in the value chain. Finally, we view IC through the eyes of the typical customer.

To help you understand these areas, we include actual examples of how America Online, Boeing, Wal-Mart, and Charles Schwab use Internet commerce. Also, see what banks and retailers have in mind for your home-banking and home-shopping choices in the future.

Internet Commerce System Configurations

Web commerce systems are categorized into three major groups or service types. These categories, graphically illustrated in Figure 8.6, are described in

FIGURE 8.6

Computer System Classifications

Computer users are currently connected in one of three ways. This figure identifies the elements and relationships used in each of these connections. In some systems, the connection is immediate. In others, the connections allow for delays in the communications process.

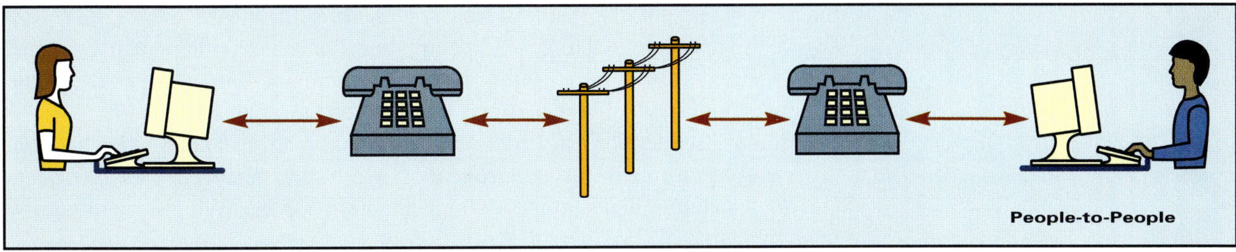

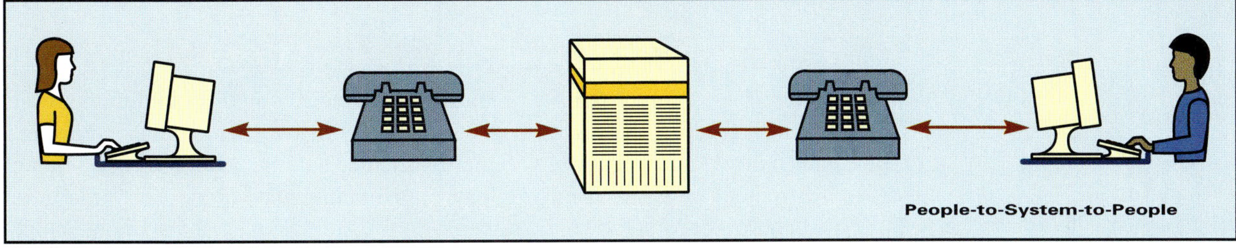

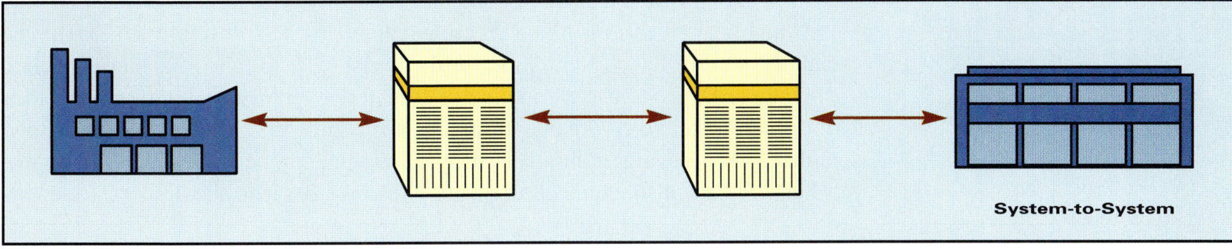

the following sections. Each category has unique functions and support software. Note the roles of user, personal computer, mainframe computer, and communications technology in each category.

People-to-People Systems (PPSs)

People-to-people systems (PPSs) directly connect individuals or groups together to collaborate on common problems or to communicate specific issues. Two or more users share a common application over the network, even if the application is not on one user's computer. The connections, made when needed, allow simultaneous discussions and exist long enough to complete the task. There is tremendous flexibility in how the connections are made and who will be involved.

Software support for a PPS ranges from applications such as word processing, spreadsheets, and graphics to shared whiteboards, databases, and videoconferencing. This configuration is much like a conference telephone call, with the added feature that each participant also has powerful computing capabilities available to process, analyze, and share common information.

People-to-System-to-People Systems (PSPSs)

People-to-system-to-people systems (PSPSs) are an extension of the people-to-people configuration. In this process, a computer is added to the network to supply support, storage, or coordination for all users. The central computer allows all participants to connect and process with each other, but at different times. Communications do not have to occur at exactly the same time—another example of asynchronous communications, as discussed in Chapter 5. The best example of this system type is e-mail: If the recipient is not available when the message is sent, the mediating computer stores the message until the receiver is ready to accept it. Think of the computer as an answering machine for each participant that inventories all forms of communication between the group members and then delivers them on demand, when requested.

Principal applications of PSPSs are electronic mail, calendar and scheduling programs, electronic forms, data collection, work-flow management systems, and electronic catalogs and shopping. Home shopping via the Web is a rapidly growing application of PSPSs today.

System-to-System Systems (SSSs)

System-to-system systems (SSSs) directly connect computers in different organizations together. The systems operate autonomously with little or no direct human involvement. They replace paper-oriented communications processes such as inventory ordering, invoicing, payroll, shipping, and so on. Electronic information flows up and down the organization's external value chain among suppliers, the organization, and its customers.

Principal applications of a SSS are **electronic data interchange (EDI),** payments systems such as **electronic funds transfer (EFT),** and transfer of technical data. EDI systems automatically transfer inventory, delivery, and billing information between organizations, using computers. Electronic data flows replace paper document flows. EFT systems send payments between buyers and sellers. Banks also connect to these systems to clear the traders' financial

Boeing Connections, Access, and Firewall

Notice how both the intranet and Internet can operate at the same time. The intranet carries personal and proprietary information about the organization and its employees. Its content and access must be protected from the outside Internet users through the use of passwords and specialized connections. The firewall provides this protection.

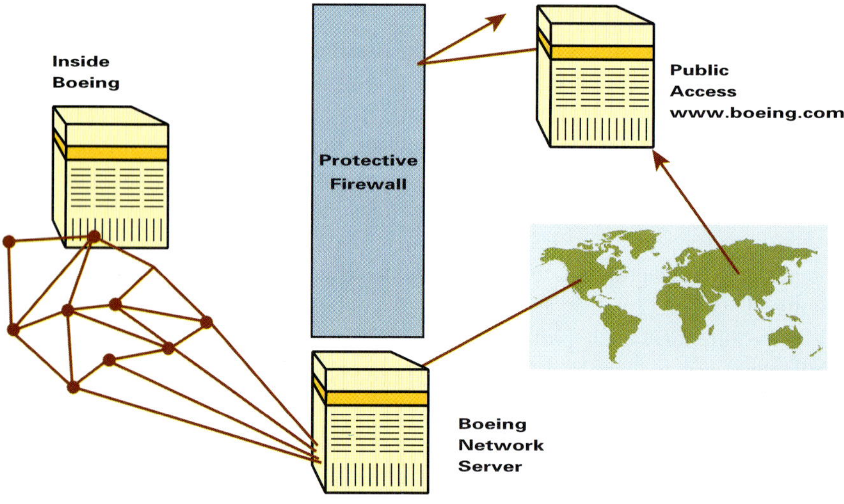

accounts. Both these systems reduce paper flow and reduce the "float" or delays of money transfers in banking and credit transactions.

Internets within an Organization: Intranets

Until now, this book focused on the Internet and how it connects people to the outside world. Now an organization can use this same resource to connect its internal communications together. This quickly developing communication channel is called an intranet. These people-to-system-to-people Web networks keep employees informed and up-to-date regarding company plans, opportunities, and issues.

Definition

Intranets are internal networks much like the Internet, but they are separated from the Internet by a protective shield or firewall. The **firewall** supplies protection and security for the intranet, ensuring that only those qualified and authorized can access its content. Intranets are constructed primarily for the use of employees and managers. Users gain access through assigned passwords. Figure 8.7 shows how a security firewall at Boeing separates internal applications from the company's public Internet.

Applications

Internal nets act as another communications channel within the organization, delivering and receiving communications messages from employees separated by

FIGURE 8.8

15 Common Intranet Applications

This list shows the variety and diversity of how intranets can be used. These applications often reduce paper use, answer employee questions quickly and efficiently, contribute to employee development, and improve internal communications and understanding. Intranets are very popular in today's organizations.

Company Phone Books
Company Vision, Mission, and Objectives
Current Financial Statements
Document Storage and Retrieval
Education and Training Opportunities
House Publications
Internal Company Communications
Internal e-mail
Internal Job Openings
News Releases
Organizational Charts
Process and Product Improvement Teams
Product Documentation and Designs
Retirement Planning
Technical Libraries and Internal Research Reports

time or space. They connect employees in an information medium where they can learn, exchange ideas, and conduct business together. Figure 8.8 lists fifteen common uses for today's organizational intranets.

Volume on these communications systems is enormous. It's not uncommon to experience 4 to 5 million visits per month on a large, active, corporate Internet site. For most medium-to-large organizations, the number of visits to the organization's intranet site will be about one-half the total number of visits to its Internet site. An internal web site can contain hundreds of thousands of pages of information for employee use, much of it personal and confidential.

Some companies are now adding employee schedules, telephones, and audio and video features to their intranet sites. These systems allow employees to "tune into" live, video-based, management press conferences and announcements via their personal computer monitors, without ever leaving their office or desk.

Intranet Benefits

Intranets keep employees current with late-breaking company events without the time and inconvenience of attending group meetings. Think of the time and paper these systems save and the speed at which they communicate information to those employees who need to know. A company president can open communications with 100,000 employees with a single keystroke!

Many of these systems allow employees to check the status and level of their retirement accounts, stock investment plans, medical and dental benefits, and even vacation days. The systems become a personal information resource for the workers. Figure 8.9 shows a cartoon of an overwhelmed employee reviewing all the information choices contained in a powerful intranet system.

FIGURE 8.9
Intranet Applications

Sometimes intranets offer so much information that, at first, it is overwhelming to the employees. This feeling quickly disappears as the employee navigates through the uses.

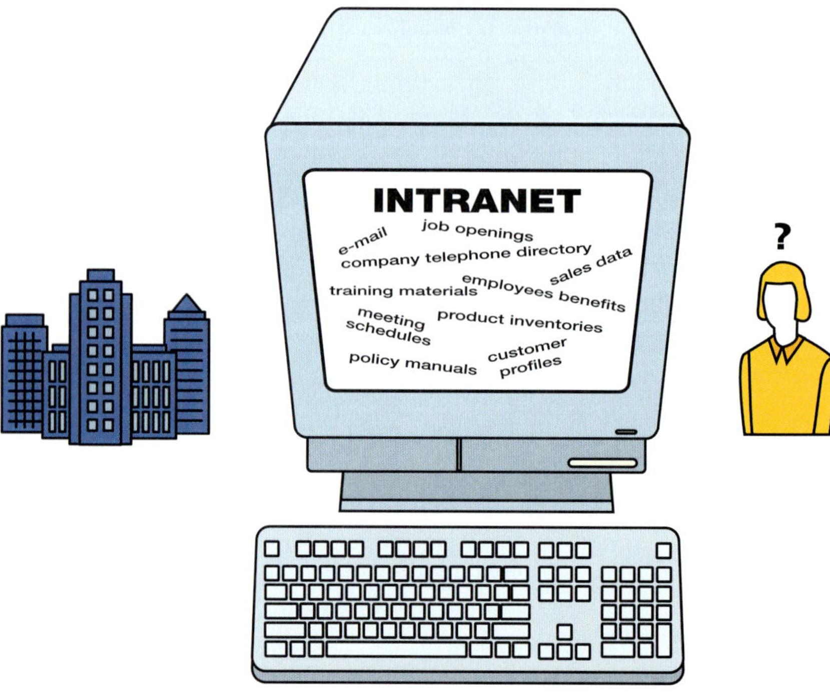

The Internet Creates a Shortage of Qualified People

Today, there is a dramatic shortage of qualified people in the Internet field. In response to this, Microsoft, in May of 1997, launched its "Skills 2000" program. This multimillion-dollar program, to be implemented over the next two years, focuses on supplying education and training to help fill the current job openings worldwide in this field. The Information Technology Association of America reports that over 200,000 Information Technology (IT) jobs are vacant today in the United States because companies can't find people with the requisite skills. There are currently 2.5 million people employed in IT, and this number is forecasted to grow by 7 to 10 percent annually. The Bureau of Labor Statistics forecasts that employment in the IT service segment alone will nearly double by the year 2005. At the same time, the number of computer science and computer engineering graduates is falling.

Future Opportunities

What does this mean for you? In means opportunity! The Internet is changing the way the world behaves. It affects how we live, learn, work, and play. Every profession will change. Three professions that will benefit directly from these changes are business, education, and law.

Businesses need qualified graduates that understand this new technology and how it helps the customer. These employees will find new products, new markets, and new media to reach the convenience-conscious, time-poor customer of the future.

Grade school, high school, college, and corporate education will utilize the Internet to deliver new educational material. People are needed to design, construct, and administer these new Web-centered programs.

The Web also presents new legal and security issues. Privacy, export, free speech, taxation, control, and content are just a few. Our society will create laws and policies to guide the evolution of this new communication technology. The legal profession will play a key role in that process.

As you plan your courses and college education, think about ways you can make yourself a more knowledgeable, more valuable, and more effective individual for life in the twenty-first century. Quality time spent planning in school today will reap large rewards for you in the future.

Internet Commerce between Organizations: Extranets

As far as inter-company communication is concerned, there's never been a better time to be in business. As discussed before, companies are building intranets to reduce the problems they face with internal communications. The same technologies that work inside the company are just as effective between different companies. Whether it's computer-aided engineering drawings, purchase orders, design specifications, or payment instructions, extranets can handle it. Extranets have indeed arrived and may well change the way we view business relationships.

Definition

An **extranet** is a business-to-business network based on Internet network technology. This is a relatively new application of Internet technology. It will revolutionize how business is done in the future, affecting Internet service providers, consumers, and security processes.

An extranet is a part of a company's intranet made accessible to other companies. Often, it includes components that enable the company to collaborate with other companies.

Combining Internets and Intranets to Form Extranets

The most commonly used definition of extranets involves building bridges between the public Internet and private corporate intranets.

A current example of an extranet application is Federal Express' tracking system. (See Figure 8.10.) Through the Web, you gain access to FedEx's public site, enter a tracking number assigned to your particular package, and then find the location of your package in their system. Other successful uses of extranets include:

- Specialized groupware software used by cross-industry work teams to collaborate in developing new products and services.

- Shared inventory databases accessible only to wholesalers or selected customers.

- Project management and work-flow control tools for cross-industry companies that are part of a common work project.

FIGURE 8.10

Federal Express Tracking System

In this application, Federal Express, through its Web site, has created a porthole to its extranet. You, as a customer, can track your own package through the FedEx distribution network. The tracking number becomes your entry permit to the extranet. Imagine the customer goodwill this process generates! Here, its Web technology has given FedEx a competitive advantage.

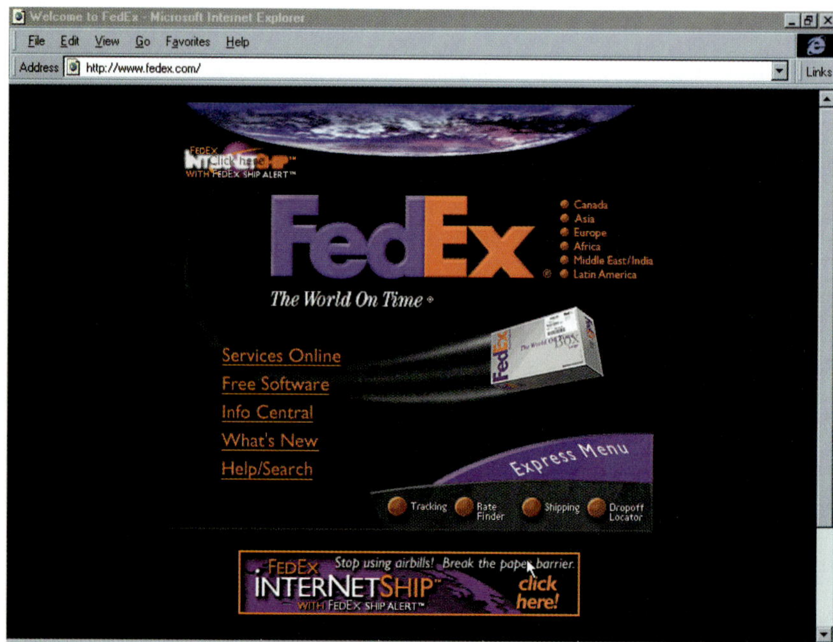

Two Extranet Examples

Extranets pay for themselves by removing time and cost in the organization's value chain. Inventories move through the system more quickly and efficiently when the entire delivery chain is electronically connected, coordinated, and scheduled. The common term for this effort is called **Just-in-Time (JIT) inventory systems.** Inventory arrives at each location just in time to be used in the manufacturing or assembly process.

THE AUTOMOTIVE NETWORK EXCHANGE (ANX)

Today, Chrysler, General Motors, and Ford have joined together to build an extranet that links them with their suppliers through a virtual private network called the **Automotive Network eXchange (ANX).** Its goal is to save billions of dollars in inventory costs. Deliveries are coordinated and scheduled to the assembly plants only as they are needed. The system also routes deliveries and even helps coordinate design and manufacturing efforts. Quality information replaces inventory in this system.

BOEING'S CUSTOMER INVENTORY SYSTEM

The Boeing Company, located in Seattle, Washington, is the world's largest producer of commercial airplanes. (See Figure 8.11.) Annual company sales exceed $35 billion. Internet commerce helped Boeing establish closer relationships with a larger group of potential partners, suppliers, and customers.

Boeing Company has implemented an extranet application that allows its customers to order airplane parts directly from the company's inventory stock. Idle planes are a big expense, and the bigger the plane, the bigger the expense. It costs

FIGURE 8.11

Boeing Home Page

Boeing has implemented both intranet and extranet applications. Sales exceed $1 billion annually through transactions on their extranet.

about $1,000 a minute to have a plane like the large model 747, with a purchase price of $175 million, on the ground when it is scheduled to be flying! To minimize this expense, Boeing has implemented a new online system that will enable the company's five hundred customers to quickly locate, order, and track shipments of aircraft spare parts, using Web technology and the Internet.

Using the Boeing Web site, a customer interactively queries Boeing's spare parts database. By typing in the part number, a customer can then order that part and locate the closest stocking warehouse. Once shipped, Boeing's Web site includes hot links to both Federal Express and United Parcel Service so that a customer can track a part even after it's been shipped.

Boeing sells over $1 billion of aircraft spare parts annually from an inventory of over 2 million different aircraft parts through its extranet. This extranet application has been a huge success.

Extranet Pitfalls and Security Issues

Extranets offer extraordinary benefits, but at potentially high risks. Imagine how critical security and reliability are for an extranet.

Common pitfalls for extranets include the following:

- As more systems are connected, cost and complexity (and potential for error) increase.
- The use of certain technologies may exclude some businesses and customers from connecting to the extranet. The extranet must be accessible to as many users as possible.
- Extranet operators may incur a legal liability for losses of another business if a system is unavailable or crashes.
- Education and training at all levels is expensive and continuous.
- Extranets require a high degree of security and privacy from competitors. Think of extranets as intersections of several different company intranets. Each net can contain sensitive material, valuable to outside sources. Theft and sabotage are always possible, especially with outsiders accessing these files. IDs and passwords are assigned to track access and user behaviors.

Currently, extranet benefits far outweigh their risks. In the future, more and more organizations will extend the reach of their Webs to include trading partners up and down their value chain.

Internet Commerce between an Organization and Consumers

The Customer Is King

Today, the consumer is king. We earlier referenced this topic in regard to Web page design. Organizations are quick to respond to consumer needs and expectations. In our busy society, time is often more valuable than money. Many experts say time will be the currency of the next decade. Thus, activities and processes that reduce time requirements will be in greater demand. Shopping, banking, investing, and communicating are examples of time-consuming activities we all participate in. How can these processes be made more efficient (faster and cheaper)? Consumers want convenient, inexpensive, simple, thorough, hassle-free, time-independent business transactions; the answer is Internet commerce

EC Exchange Model between Enterprise and Individuals

This model shows the steps in the typical exchange process between enterprise and individuals. A detailed process map like this helps all parties see what activities might be done on the Web and what parties would be involved in that activity.

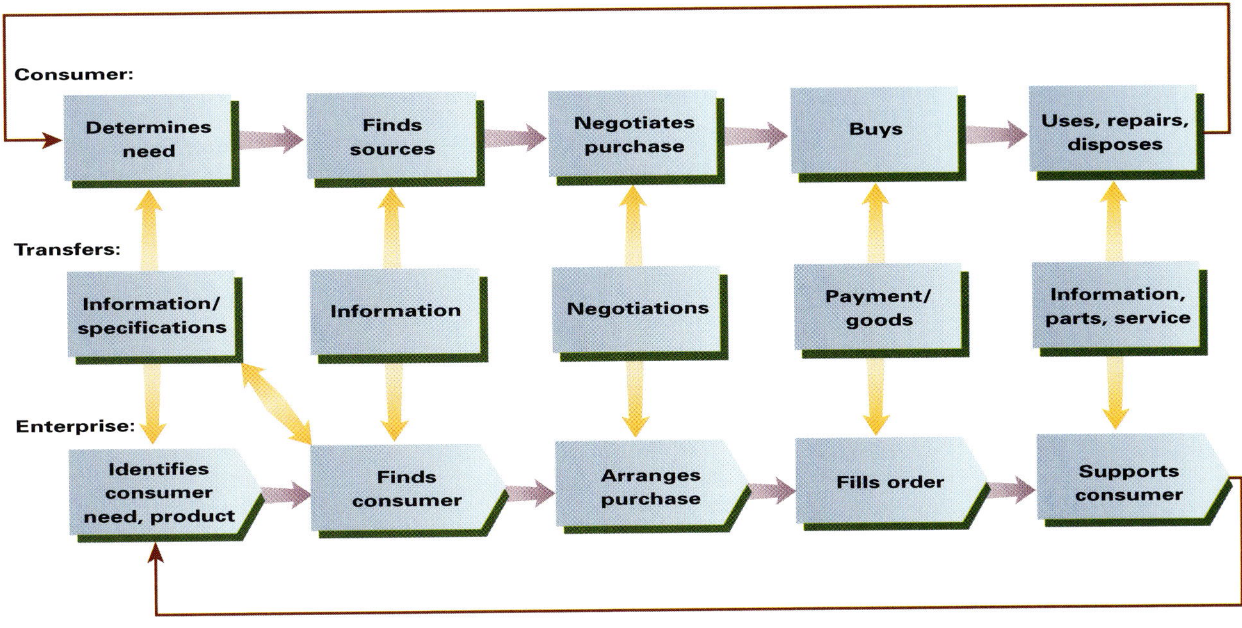

applications between organizations and consumers. Figure 8.12 diagrams key steps in the exchange model between an enterprise and the individual.

Electronic Marketplaces

Electronic marketplaces are virtual shopping malls. Computer services allow customers to use Internet-based, interactive, online system to browse catalogs of products and services. Once an item is selected, the shopper places an order, makes payment, and receives the products or services, either immediately over the same communications network or later through a physical shipment.

To date, electronic marketplaces have been primarily housed on the online services such as America Online or CompuServe. We are now seeing a general movement of these services to the Internet. **Electronic malls (e-malls)** are forming to combine a variety of products and suppliers into one convenient shopping location. One site, for example, the Internet Mall, shown in Figure 8.13, hosts over 27,000 stores, and markets itself as the largest virtual shopping mall in the world.

Television home-shopping networks are now building a second presence on the Web. As the Internet continues to grow, more sites will appear. Many will offer specialized products and services—sports, leisure, health care, automobiles, and so on. Other sites will focus on the needs of commercial and industrial customers.

Electronic marketplaces meet customer needs. They provide worldwide market access, comparison shopping, and twenty-four-hour, 365 days-per-year access. Because of lower supplier costs and better logistics, customers should benefit

Schwab Discount Brokers Increase Online Presence: A Business-to-Consumer Internet Commerce Application

Charles Schwab is a national discount stock, bond, mutual fund, and commodities company. This company has led the way in using the Internet and the Web as major transaction and communications channels for their customers. The results have been phenomenal.

Based on their June 30, 1997, quarterly financial report, the company reached a major milestone during June 1997, as customer assets exceeded $300 billion just fifteen months after reaching the $200 billion level in March 1996.

The company continues to invest in new services, distribution channels, and technology. Their customer accounts held a total of $142 billion in mutual fund assets at the end of the quarter, up 40 percent from last year. They also announced an alliance with CheckFree Corporation to develop a system that will enable their customers to pay bills through their SchwabNOW!™ Web system.

By the end of June the company had 865,000 active online accounts containing $60 billion in assets. Trades through various online channels equaled 36 percent of total trades during the quarter, up from 23 percent last year. This company has been rated as number one in *Smart Money* magazine's annual survey of discount brokers in breadth of products, responsiveness, and online services.

Who is Charles Schwab and what are they doing? Schwab is the world's largest discount stock brokerage company. They communicate with their customers by phone, in one of 235 branch locations, or using online, twenty-four-hour services. Over three-fourths of their customers have a computer.

The Schwab Approach: "Online" is our business

A stock brokerage performs customer transactions (buy/sell investment securities) and supplies information. The PC is their delivery unit, or information appliance. Online services complement their other communication channels. Information via PC gives investors breaking news, online.

Branches, service centers, and telephones are all complementary communication channels for the PC. Different customers want to connect in different ways. Two years ago, online services accounted for 7 percent of all transactions; one year ago the figure was 28 percent; today it is 36 percent. Schwab projects that online accounts will grow to 10 million in five years. Below are some questions and answers from Charles Schwab about Internet commerce.

In a recent presentation at COMDEX in Las Vegas, a Charles Schwab representative shared some lessons the company has learned about Internet commerce.

1. *"What have you done wrong along the way? What have you learned from your mistakes?"*

   "In 1986, Schwab offered customers, for a fee, specialized hardware and software systems to get online stock information and quotes at home. It was a failure. No one wanted to pay for this specialized computer and application. People want general-purpose information devices."

2. *"Should you develop Internet commerce applications using outside or inside help?"*

   "Schwab chose in-house. They thought, rather than give learning to someone else, they would build the expertise and learning in-house. It gave them quicker response, control, and access to industry partnerships. We moved fast, but with smaller releases. Each new release was focused at even bigger user groups. The customers and the company learned as they went."

3. *"How do you provide customers with real value?"*

"Many Web sites today are simply electronic 'brochure ware.' They are electronic catalogs. They do not offer real value to the customer. This approach will not grow the business. Schwab used the Web to create a "financial information center" for their customers. The system allows trades of all types, quotes, balances, and a full line of information sources. The customer can get stock charts, articles, financial statements, constant market updates—live, and current."

4. *"Did you segment your Internet commerce market and customers? How?"*

"Online customer segmentation is just as important as offline.

"Our PC desktop computer users are offered different Web financial products. There are certain core offerings for accesses and services by our main customers. For those customers who require very little maintenance (few phone calls), E-Schwab' is a product that offers a cheaper, channel price per thousand-share trade. Schwab also offers a preferred service for the highly sophisticated, private investor. There are offerings for those just starting through those investors needing help planning their retirement. 'Online is our business, our future,' states a Schwab executive.

"Schwab's goal is to collect, analyze, and channel information for their customers—true, value-added tasks that are more difficult for their customers to do. In return for this value, customers will transact their financial business with Schwab."

from lower prices and quicker deliveries. And, all these activities can be done in the comfort of the consumers' homes or offices. Today, we see many organizations (LL Bean, Wal-Mart, Microsoft) offering products and services on the Internet as well as through their traditional outlet channels. Many companies list their Web site addresses in print and media advertising to move customers into this new shopping environment.

Intelligent Shopping Agents

But even these systems can be improved. Why must the shopper search out the best products at the lowest cost? Why not enlist the services of a "personal shopper"—an **intelligent shopping agent.** Electronic marketplace intelligent agents are unique software entities that can be programmed to perform a variety of search and analysis functions for the purchaser.

Intelligent agents can do continuous comparison shopping across several electronic marketplaces, presenting only the best of the best. They also do periodic scans for new products or close-out items. As shopping increases on the Web, we will see intelligent-agent technology routinely available to the electronic shopper.

Internet Mall: World's Largest Virtual Shopping Mall

This is an example of how one site creates a directory or doorway to thousands of other sites. E-Malls are shopping alternatives to large physical malls in your area or to home shopping on TV. Because these sites have lower overhead than actual stores in your area (less land, smaller buildings, and so on), they might be able to sell for lower prices.

Again, note how these agents save the customer time and effort—valuable resources in the next decade.

Web Financial Systems and Electronic Payments

Financial institutions play a major role in Web commerce. We can view banks in two different ways. First, they are actually electronic shopping malls themselves, offering different financial products and services at different prices. You can shop banks for rates and services much like you shop grocery stores. Figure 8.14 highlights several ways people today interact with consumer banks.

But banks also facilitate collections and transfers among all the trading partners in the shopping cycle. Once an item is purchased, how is it paid for? How are funds collected, distributed, and reported? What is the process, and what are the risks involved?

Currently there is a general concern about privacy, security, and theft of financial data on the Web. Different sites offer different degrees of security and protection during the financial transaction. Data encryption, or scrambling of electronic signals, is one method of security that is used today.

Electronic funds transfer (EFT) is the name of the process used to facilitate electronic exchange of payments, payment-related information, and financial documents between an organization, its customers, suppliers, and financial insti-

Multiple-Access Internet Commerce System in Consumer Banking

Today there are a large variety of ways we can do banking. Many of these alternatives rely on electronic connections between the customer and the bank. Our lifestyle helps determine our personal choice.

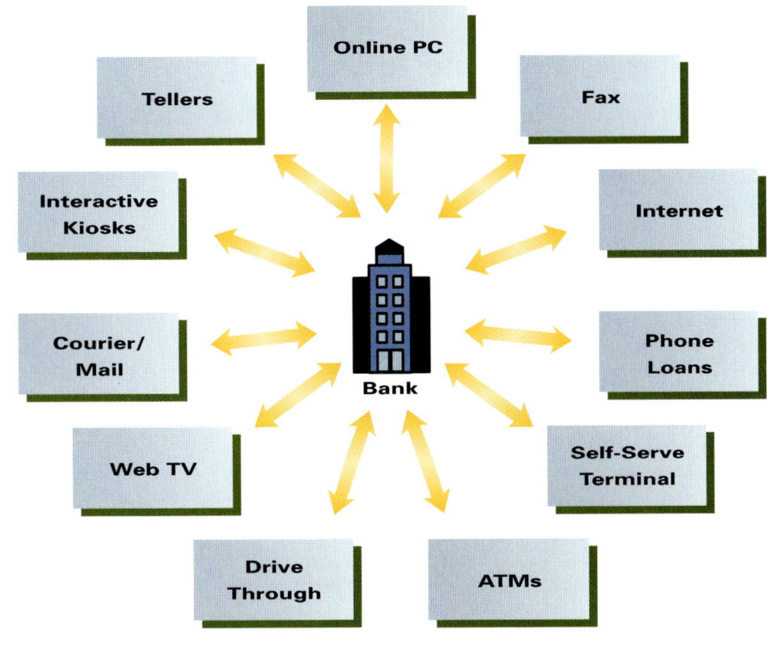

tutions. Current payment systems include cash, check, credit, debit, and prepayment systems.

We all understand cash payments. With checks and credit cards, the seller is accepting our promise to pay. Debit cards ensure that the buyer presently has sufficient funds available, so the purchase amount is immediately transferred from the buyer's account to someone else's (the seller's) account. Think of these prepayment systems as stored-value cards. Phone cards purchased from a vending machine are another example: A specified amount of cash value is preloaded into the card and then deducted as it is used. Some stored-value cards can be recharged; others are disposable.

Local Web Shopping

Internet commerce can also be local. Busy families with two working parents find little time to shop for essentials. Thus, grocery shopping has gone online. Many specialty food stores offer a Web shopping option and home deliveries for little or no extra charge.

Other organizations are offering grocery shopping services to Web customers. Peapod, shown in Figure 8.15, is an example. For a one-time software and setup fee, plus delivery charges, Peapod will accept your shopping order, actually go to a local grocery store, buy the items, and deliver them to your home. You receive

Peapod's Home Grocery Shopping Page

Home grocery shopping via computer is projected to grow rapidly in the next five years. Here is an example of one service available in some parts of the United States.

a monthly bill on your credit card. Other shopping services were discussed earlier, in Chapter 6. Flowers can also be purchased and delivered this way.

As more and more consumers flock to the Internet as time and convenience become more important, Internet commerce between organizations and consumers will continue to grow at an accelerated rate. Companies that combine Web marketing strategies with traditional approaches are sure to see improvements in sales and performance. Figure 8.16 suggests a propensity grid for consumers to help explain what consumers consider before they choose a shopping channel.

In Closing

What's the motivation for the customer to use the Internet and Internet commerce? Commercial customers lower procurement costs, ease the tracking of

FIGURE 8.16

Consumer's Commerce Propensity Grid: Which Alternative Will They Choose?

This grid shows the primary ways people shop today. Along the top, the grid lists the criteria used in making the shopping vehicle selection. Inside the table, we see the relative ratings for each alternative of each criterion. Note that each shopping alternative has its benefits and drawbacks.

Choice Criteria

Commerce Technology Alternative	Time access flexibility	Information-gathering efficiency	% connected	Ease of use	Security	Degree of support	Quality of service	Transaction cycle time	Cost of entry time, money, resources	Cost of error
Computer	High*	Average	Low	Low	Average	High	Low	High	High	High
Telephone	Average	Average	High	High	Average	High	Low	Average	Low	High
Mail	Low	Low	High	High	Average	High	Low	Low	Low	High
In Person	Low	High	Low	High	High	High	Average	High	Average	Average

* Note: Ratings are the authors' and are relative and constantly changing due to time and technology.

orders, and reduce product cycle times. This results in lower inventories and financing costs. Commercial customers are in better control of their production and delivery schedules, and that makes their consumers happy. Personal users save time and money, shop smarter, and shop at their own convenience.

What's the motivation for a business to enter the IC field? The answer is lower costs, better service, new markets, and new customers. Paper and handling costs are reduced, and customers know immediately if items are in stock and when and how they can expect delivery. Internet commerce allows businesses to sell more and to sell more efficiently. Internet commerce complements the traditional selling process—it doesn't replace it.

Neither Internet commerce nor traditional sales methods alone can carry the burden in the future. The best results appear to blend the two. The old Internet as we know it, the Information Superhighway, is giving way to a new Internet in our world society—a "Commercial Superhighway."

Commerce and trade normally lead to an improved quality of life for all trading partners. In the tenth century, spice routes through Turkey joined Asia and Europe. In the evenings, traveling merchants and caravans, spending the night at wayside encampments, shared songs, stories, cultures, and beliefs as well as silks and spices. Perhaps Internet commerce will play a similar role today to help improve the prospects for world peace and prosperity in the twenty-first century.

This book suggests that the Internet and Internet commerce are here to stay. Growth projections for these two areas are almost unbelievable. Clever students and smart businesses will learn more about this field and apply what they learn to benefit their companies, their customers, and themselves.

The future will be filled with new and marvelous technological changes. We hope this book has helped prepare you for some of them.

In closing, we leave you with a quote from a report delivered in 1954 to the U.S. Senate by its special subcommittee on computing: "After growing wildly for years, the computer industry now appears to be approaching its infancy."

It is as relevant and appropriate today as it was almost forty-five years ago.

SUMMARY

Internet commerce (IC) uses technologies that automate business transactions between entities. IC offers connectivity and communications between an organization and its business chain—suppliers, competitors, distributors, channels, markets, and consumers.

Business over the Internet reduces company costs, speeds up order processing and delivery times, and improves the quality of the information exchanged between companies. In a paper system, one company's paper input becomes another company's paper output. With IC, the sender and receiver share information electronically.

Internet commerce includes the newest communications concepts and information technologies used to strengthen this chain. Emphasis is on inter- and intra-company communication systems. This chapter highlighted IC applications within the organization (intranets), between organizations (extranets), and between organizations and their customers (Internets).

Web commerce systems are categorized into three major groups or service types: people-to-people systems (PPSs), people-to-system-to-people systems (PSPSs), and system-to-system systems (SSSs).

Electronic marketplaces are virtual shopping malls. These computer services allow customers to use Internet-based, interactive, online systems to browse catalogs of products and services. Intelligent shopping agents automate the shopping search process. Current payment systems include cash, check, credit, debit, and prepayment systems.

Internet commerce can also be local. Many organizations are offering grocery shopping and financial services to Web customers. What's the motivation for the customer to use the Internet and Internet commerce? Personal users save time and money, shop smarter, and shop at their own convenience. What motivates the seller? Internet commerce allows businesses to sell more and sell more efficiently.

KEY TERMS

Automotive Network eXchange (ANX) (219)

business chain (value chain) (207)

critical inflection points (206)

electronic commerce (EC) (206)

electronic data interchange (EDI) (214)

electronic funds transfer (EFT) (214)

electronic malls (e-malls) (221)

electronic marketplaces (221)

extranet (217)

firewall (215)

intelligent shopping agent (224)

Internet commerce (IC) (206)

intranets (215)

Just-in-Time (JIT) inventory systems (219)

people-to-people systems (PPSs) (213)

people-to-system-to-people systems (PSPSs) (213)

system-to-system systems (SSSs) (214)

END-OF-CHAPTER ACTIVITIES

Matching

Match each term with its description.

a. value chain

b. intelligent shopping agents

c. local Web shopping

d. people-to-people system

e. e-malls

f. critical inflection point

g. Commercial Superhighway

h. electronic funds transfers

i. Internet commerce

j. extranet

________ **1.** The use of computer networks to conduct business—buying and selling of goods and services—electronically with one's suppliers, customers, and/or competitors.

________ **2.** A point in the life of an organization or industry where its growth either ramps up to greater successes or ramps down to eventual difficulties.

________ **3.** Includes a company's suppliers, competitors, distributors, channels, markets, and consumers.

________ **4.** Systems that directly connect individuals or groups together to collaborate on common problems or to communicate on specific issues.

________ **5.** A business-to-business network based on Internet network technology. This relatively new application will revolutionize how business is done in the future.

________ **6.** Virtual shopping malls that allow customers to use Internet-based, interactive, online system to browse catalogs and purchase products and services.

________ **7.** Unique software entities that can be programmed to perform a variety of search and analysis functions on behalf of the purchaser.

________ **8.** Allows customers to shop for groceries, flowers, and services in their immediate community.

________ **9.** Process whereby financial institutions facilitate electronic payments between buyers and sellers.

________ **10.** The old Internet as we know it, the Information Superhighway, is giving way to this new Internet in our world society.

Review Questions

1. What is your definition of Internet commerce?

2. How do people-to-people Internet commerce systems work?

3. How do system-to-system Internet commerce systems work?

4. Explain the benefits of an intranet system for a company.

5. What is an extranet and what is it used for? Give some examples.

6. How has Boeing used extranets?

7. What is an electronic marketplace?

8. What are intelligent shopping agents? Why would you want to use one?

9. What are the future projections for the use of Internet commerce? Why?

10. Compare today's Internet commerce on the Information Superhighway with older methods of trade. How are they similar and different? What impact do you think IC will have on the future of our global society? Why?

Activities

1. Go to the Internet and visit an electronic shopping mall (e-mall). How did you find the site? What products or services did they have? Were the prices higher or lower than you expected? What types of payments would they accept? Would you buy something from an e-mall? Why or why not? Write-up your e-mall experience and discuss it in class.

2. Using your school library or the Internet, find an organization that has installed an extranet. Research the application. What products or services are being traded? What have the results been to date? What plans does the organization have for the extranet or for new Internet commerce applications in the future?

3. Find a company in your community that is using the Internet to sell its products or services. Visit the site and become familiar with the company and its products or services. Contact the company and see if you can get more information about their experiences with their Web site. Has it been successful? Who created and maintains the site? How did they decide to go on the Web? Do they have plans to change or improve the site in the near future? Write up your research and discuss it in class.

4. Where will Internet commerce be in the next five years? Do research on this subject. Try to get some growth figures in dollars or in number of sites. What companies are the current industry leaders in IC? What is your personal assessment of the growth projections in IC? Do you see yourself taking an active role in IC in any way? How? In this chapter, we compared IC to the old spice routes in Turkey. What impact do you see IC having on our society? Are they good or bad? Explain.

5. In one section of this chapter, we talked about three IC system configurations—PPS, PSPS, and SSS. On your college campus, try to find some examples of each of these system configurations. You might want to visit your school registration and business offices. See if they use systems that fit this framework. You might also visit with the athletic department and the school bookstore. Make a list of your findings.

6. This is an optional group activity.

   Throughout this book we have discussed a variety of concepts, technologies, and actual business case studies related to the Internet. We have also discussed trends and possible directions the Internet and the Web will take in the future. For the last activity in this book, it is most fitting that you add your own personal insights and do your own research on this topic.

   Form teams of four to five members. Each team will meet and discuss key issues, do its own research, and form its own opinions about where the Internet and the Web will take us and our global society by January 1, 2000. Use personal interviews, your school library, and the Internet to do your research. Perhaps some members of your team could join a Web chat group and ask its members for their ideas and comments. Check with local government leaders and company executives in your area.

   Prepare a short team paper (three pages) and a short presentation (five minutes) for your class. Include a visual aid for presentation. Share your research activities, findings, and group conclusions with the entire class. Finally, include some discussion about the impact these changes may have on your class members personally and how they might best prepare for these changes.

   We hope this project will help personalize the content of this book and identify unique Web opportunities for you.

Getting Started with Netscape Navigator 4.0

Introduction
Starting Netscape Communicator
The Netscape Home Page
Browsing the Web
Using a History List
Using Bookmarks
   Bookmarks
   Adding a Bookmark
   Deleting a Bookmark
   Retrieving a Web Page with a
     Bookmark

Saving Information with Navigator
   Saving a Web Page
   Saving an Image
   Inserting a Picture
Printing a Web Page or Document
Using Navigator's Electronic Mail
   Accessing Netscape's Electronic
     Mail
   Preparing and Sending Mail
     Messages
   Reading Mail Messages

Saving a Mail Message
Printing a Mail Message
Deleting a Mail Message
Using Netscape's Address Book
Exiting Electronic Mail
Exiting Netscape
Conclusion

Introduction

Today there are many Web browsers from which to choose. The most popular is **Netscape Navigator,** sometimes referred to as simply Navigator. Approximately 58 percent of Internet users use Navigator to browse the Internet.

The newest version of Netscape's Navigator browser is part of a powerful and versatile product from Netscape Communications Corporation called **Netscape Communicator.** Communicator includes several useful applications in addition to Navigator.

In this appendix, you are introduced to the newest version of Netscape's **Navigator** browser and to Netscape's electronic mail (e-mail) application, called **Messenger.** Space will not permit coverage of the other applications or a complete coverage of all Navigator features. However, Navigator's basic features are explained sufficiently to help you get started using Navigator to browse the Internet and the World Wide Web. For convenience, some of Navigator's features that were explained in Chapter Three are repeated here along with additional features. After carefully studying this appendix, you should be able to use Navigator's main features to browse the Internet and visit interesting locations on the Internet and the World Wide Web.

Like other newer browsers, Navigator uses a graphical user interface (GUI). Recall that a **graphical user interface** allows you to select a specific application, such as a word processor or Navigator, by using your mouse to point to the icon representing the application and then clicking on the icon. Also, using a GUI

FIGURE A.1

Windows 95 Desktop Screen

The Windows 95 Desktop screen contains icons representing applications or groups of applications. The user can select an application by moving the mouse to point to and click on an application (icon). Once a selection is made, the desktop screen disappears and is replaced by the selected application.

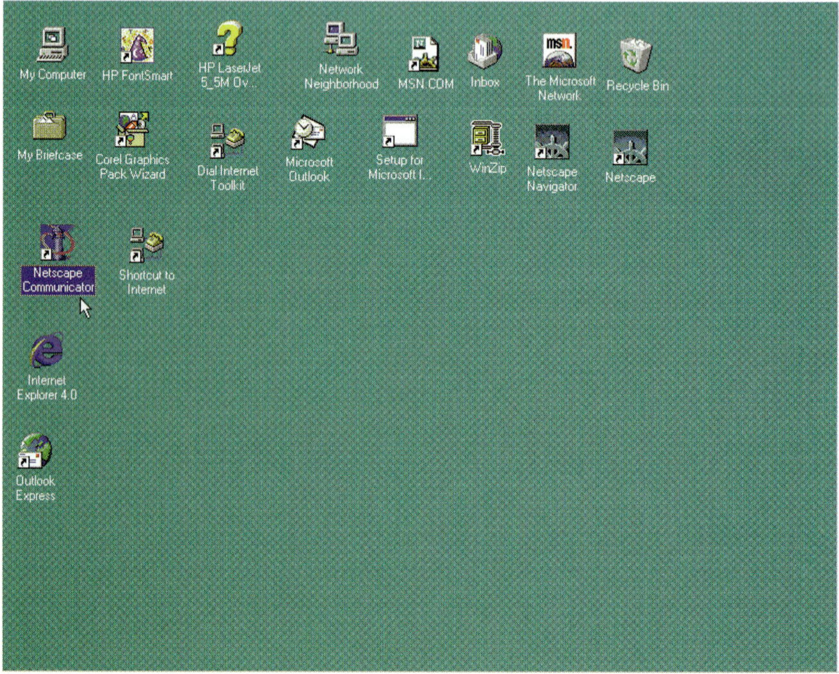

allows you to select an action from a menu by pointing to and clicking on a specific menu item.

Windows 95 is a graphical user interface available with most IBM and compatible computers. If your computer uses Windows 95, the Windows 95 logo screen will automatically appear and then quickly disappear when you start your computer. Within a few seconds, a screen called the desktop will appear. The **desktop** appears as a screen on which icons representing various applications, or groups of applications, are displayed. When Netscape Navigator was installed on your computer, an icon representing Netscape Communicator may have been placed on the desktop (Figure A.1).

Starting Netscape Communicator

If the Communicator icon is displayed on the desktop screen, you can start it by simply double clicking on the icon—a small picture of a lighthouse with the words *Netscape Communicator* underneath. Icons of earlier versions show a small picture of a ship's steering wheel with the words *Netscape Navigator* or the single word *Navigator* underneath the wheel (Figure A.1). If the icon representing the version you will be using is not displayed on the desktop, you will need to start it using the Start button, explained next.

FIGURE A.2

Windows 95 Desktop Screen Start Button and Menus

In the lower left corner of the Windows 95 desktop screen is the Start button. Clicking on the Start button displays a menu of commands. By clicking on the Programs command, a menu of program applications appears that includes the Netscape Communicator program. The submenus may be different on your computer because your computer may have different programs installed than the ones shown in this illustration. Clicking on Netscape Navigator starts Navigator on your computer.

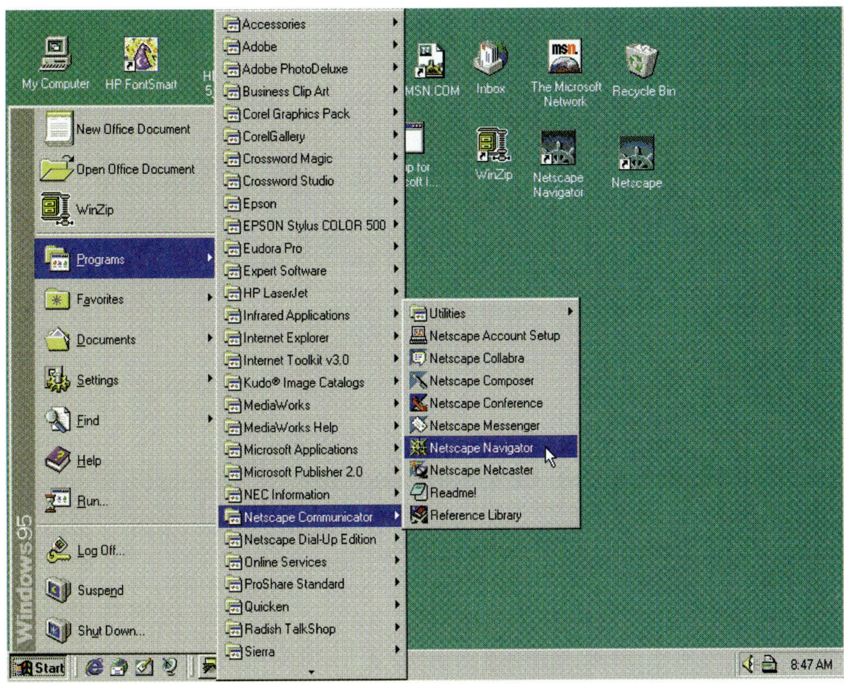

In the lower left corner of the desktop screen is the **Start button.** Clicking on the Start button displays a menu of commands. One of the commands is the **Programs command,** with a small arrowhead pointing to the right (Figure A.2).

If the icon is not available on your desktop screen, you can start the program easily and quickly. Click on the Start button. Click on the Programs command. Finally, double click on Communicator.

After completing the above steps, the Netscape Communicator program is activated and loaded into your computer. The first Netscape page is Netscape's home page, shown in Figure A.3. Examine this figure carefully, as the following information is based on it.

The Netscape Home Page

The Netscape home page consists of features that make browsing easy. When Netscape is first started, Netscape's home page appears. This page contains information Netscape wants you to see. However, this information will be replaced by a Web site's home page when you begin browsing the Internet.

Like the home page at many other Web sites, Netscape's home page contains **links** to other pages, files, resources, and even other Web sites on the Internet. For example, a home page may include a link to the company that will allow you to download a new version of the browser. Because home pages and other pages at various Web sites are continually being updated, links also change frequently. At this point, we are not concerned with links, but with the title page itself.

FIGURE A.3

The Netscape Home Page

Netscape's home contains menus, tools, and buttons useful for browsing the Internet and the Web. An understanding of the home page helps a user to become efficient.

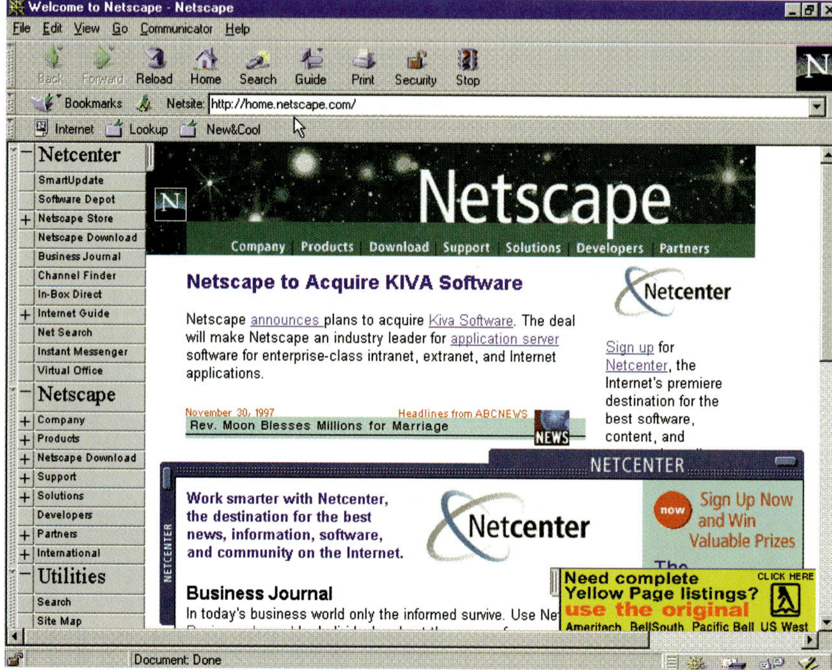

The top bar of Navigator is the **title bar** that identifies the title of the Web page. Navigator's home page, for example, displays the message *Welcome to Netscape—Netscape.*

Immediately below the title of the page is the menu bar. The **menu bar** includes available options, each with pull-down menus, and works like other program menu bars, such as word processing and spreadsheets. For example, clicking **File** on the menu bar results in a drop-down menu containing several options. One option is **Print.** By clicking on Print and supplying appropriate information in the dialog box, the user can print an entire Web document or selected pages.

Below the menu bar is the **Navigation toolbar,** which allows you to perform tasks faster than when using the menu bar by clicking on one of the buttons. For example, selecting the Print button causes the displayed page to be printed. Printed on each button is an icon and a word that describes the button's function.

Other toolbar buttons can be particularly useful. Clicking on the **Search button** displays a search screen containing several search engines you can select to search for information on the Internet. Clicking on the **Home button** returns you to Netscape's home page. Clicking the **Back button** returns you to the previous page you viewed, and the **Forward button** displays the next page of a document.

Below the Navigation toolbar is the **Location toolbar.** The first button at the left is the Bookmarks button (explained later). At the right is a rectangular **Location text box** in which you enter the Internet address (URL) of the Web site you want to visit. To switch to a particular site, you simply type the Uniform Resource Locator (URL) in the box and then press the Enter key. The URL is updated automatically as you move from page to page at a particular site, and the new URL appears in the Location box. The name of the Location box changes automatically to **Netsite** when a specific site is visited.

FIGURE A.4

The Netscape Menu Bar

The menu bar contains several items you can choose—including Communicator—to access Navigator or another application.

FIGURE A.5

Navigation Toolbar

The Navigation toolbar includes several buttons that allow you to perform actions faster and more easily than may be possible by using menus.

FIGURE A.6

Location Toolbar

The Location toolbar contains a Bookmarks button and a Location box for entering an Internet address for the Web site you want to visit.

Below the Location toolbar is the **Personal toolbar.** The **Internet** button at the left activates Navigator if it is currently idle. One interesting button you will see is the New&Cool button. When clicked, you can select What's New or What's Cool from the displayed sidebar. Selecting the What's New button causes Netscape to display the What's New page containing links to some of the newer web pages. Selecting the What's Cool button causes Netscape to display links to some unique and interesting Web pages. Both the What's New and the What's Cool pages are updated frequently by Netscape Communications Corporation as new and interesting pages are made available. Pages that were available on the buttons on one day might not be available a day or two later.

The large area below the Directory buttons is the **display area.** When Navigator is first activated, Netscape's home page is displayed in this area. The home page contains current information from Netscape Communications Corporation and links to other pages. As new Netscape products and upgrades become available, they are identified on Netscape's home page and can be downloaded by selecting a designated link and following the instructions displayed on the screen. When other sites are visited, pages from these sites are displayed.

At the lower left beneath the display area is the status line. The **status line** shows the current status of a Web page being retrieved. When a Web page has been retrieved and displayed, the message "Document: Done" or a similar message is displayed. At the bottom of the screen and at the right of the Start button is the **active link indicator.** When the pointer is positioned over an object linked to a Web page, the URL that will be used to retrieve the page is displayed in the active link indicator. At the lower right is a small icon that looks like an envelope. Clicking on this icon activates Netscape's e-mail program. When a Web page is being retrieved, the progress of the transfer is displayed in the rectangular box to the left of the mail icon, called the **progress indicator.**

In the following sections, you will use the menu bar, Navigation toolbar, Location toolbar, and buttons to browse the Internet and the Web. The more you browse the Internet and the Web, the more proficient you will become.

FIGURE A.7

Display Area

The Home page of a visited site appears in the display area. The display area is also used for displaying Web documents and pages.

Browsing the Web

When you browse the World Wide Web, you move from one Web site (location) to another. The purpose of browsing is to visit various Web sites to learn what is available there. Recall from Chapter Three that you can go to a Web site by typing the Internet address, or URL, for the site in Netscape's Location box. Also, recall that an URL uses the format explained earlier in Chapter Three.

Suppose you are planning a vacation to Williamsburg, Virginia, and want to find information about a nearby Busch Gardens theme park. You can obtain the information with Navigator by typing the Internet address (URL) for Busch Gardens and pressing the Enter key, as shown in Figure A.8.

After you've typed the Internet address (URL) for the Busch Gardens Web site and pressed the Enter key, soon the Busch Gardens home page will appear on your screen, as shown in Figure A.9. Notice on the home page that there are two

FIGURE A.8

Typing an URL in the Location box

You can go directly to a Web site by typing the Internet address (URL) of the site that you want to visit in the Location box. After you've typed the address correctly, press the Enter key to go to the site.

FIGURE A.9

Busch Gardens Home Page

The Busch Gardens home page contains links to other pages that provide you with information about various theme parks. You can retrieve a page by clicking on the link for the page you want.

Busch Gardens theme parks, one that is located at Williamsburg, Virginia. By clicking the link for the Williamsburg page, information about the theme park at Williamsburg will be displayed on your screen.

Remember that Navigator allows you to move from one Web site to another and that many pages contain links to other pages and sites. Practice moving around the Web and using available links to view other pages and sites. You will discover many interesting sites containing useful information.

Using a History List

As you move around the Web from site to site and page to page, Navigator keeps track of the sites and pages you've visited in the current session in a special place called a **history list.** When you first start Netscape, the history list is empty because you have not yet visited any sites. As you visit pages, Netscape stores the page titles and the URLs of the pages in the order they are visited since you began the current session. You can return to a previous page by clicking on the Back button on the Navigation toolbar. If you have returned to one or more previous pages, you can move forward to the next page by clicking on the Forward button on the Navigation toolbar.

Another way to move quickly to a page already visited is to display the history list and select a page to which you want to return. To display the history list, click on the Communicator menu. The bottom of the menu contains a list of page titles. To switch to a specific page, click on its title from the list, as shown in Figure A.10. A history list is permanent.

FIGURE A.10
History List

A history list is a list of Web pages previously viewed. To view a page on the history list, click on the Communicator menu, click on History, and then click on the page you want to see.

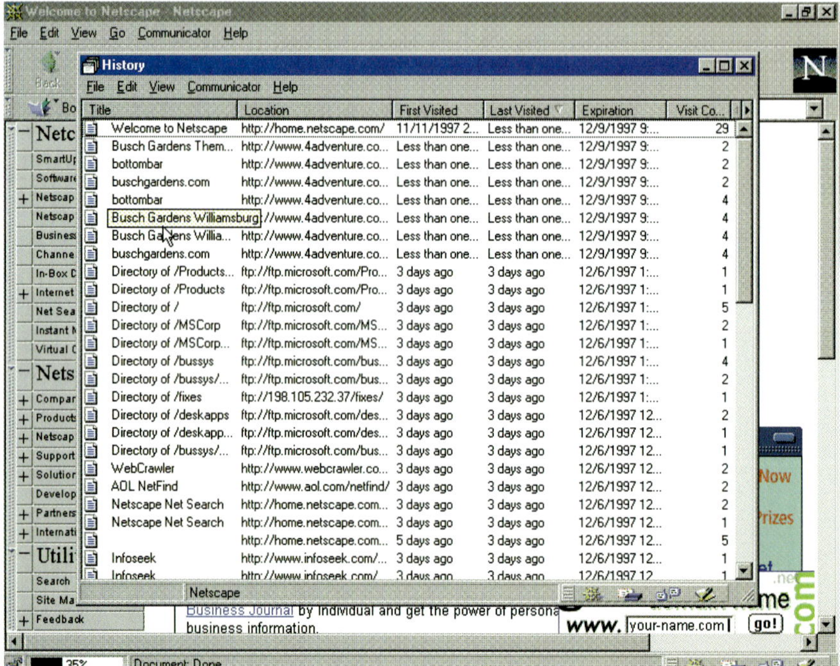

Using Bookmarks

As a student you've probably used bookmarks to keep track of book pages containing important information. Perhaps you inserted a piece of paper or turned down the corner of pages to which you wanted to return.

Bookmarks

Typing a long URL for a Web page can sometimes be tedious, and typing errors can occur. Fortunately, Navigator contains a **bookmark feature** that allows you to permanently save the URLs of pages to which you may want to return. A **bookmark** consists of the title of the Web page and the URL of that page. Navigator can use a bookmark to quickly identify and find a Web page.

With Navigator, you can add new bookmarks and delete bookmarks you no longer need. Bookmarks are stored in a **bookmark list,** which is a permanent list of Web sites you want to save, illustrated in Figure A.11.

Adding a Bookmark

Adding a bookmark to a bookmark list is easy. With the Web page you want to add to the list displayed on your screen, click on Bookmarks on the Location toolbar. When the Bookmarks' drop-down menu will appears, click on Add Bookmark. After you've added a bookmark you can check to verify that it was added by clicking on Bookmarks on the Location toolbar, and then clicking on Go to Bookmarks to see if the bookmark was added correctly.

FIGURE A.11

Bookmark List

A bookmark list contains a list of titles of Web pages and the URLs of those pages. New bookmarks can be added to the list, and those you no longer need can be removed.

Deleting a Bookmark

Deleting a bookmark is also easy. With the Web page you want to delete displayed on your screen, click on Bookmarks on the Location toolbar to display the Bookmarks window that contains the bookmark list. On the list, move the pointer to highlight the page you want to delete. Press Delete to remove the bookmark.

Retrieving a Web Page with a Bookmark

Typing URLs that are long and sometimes difficult to remember can be a cumbersome and time-consuming activity. However, you can use bookmarks to retrieve Web pages quickly and easily. To retrieve a Web page using bookmarks, click on Bookmarks on the Location toolbar. When the bookmark list appears, click on the bookmark representing the page you want to retrieve. Point to and click on the bookmark you want to retrieve. Within a few seconds, the page you selected will appear on your screen.

Saving Information with Navigator

As you travel the Internet and World Wide Web, you may find information you want to save for use later. Navigator allows you to save documents, pages, and pictures you find at various Web sites on a floppy disk or hard disk. In the following sections, you will learn how to save important information, including pictures you can insert into a word processing document such as a letter or report.

FIGURE A.12

Retrieving a Page Using a Bookmark List

Any Web page can easily be retrieved using a bookmark list. A user can click on a page on the list to display the page on the screen.

Saving a Web Page

On the World Wide Web there are millions of Web pages containing useful information. You may find pages you want to save for use later, such as those containing valuable information for use in preparing a report for a class you are taking. With Netscape you can save pages and retrieve them later when needed.

Saving a Web page to a floppy disk is easy. With the page you want to save displayed on your screen, insert a floppy disk in your floppy disk drive (for example, drive A if drive A is your floppy disk drive). Click on File on the menu bar to display the File drop-down menu. Click on the Save As command. The Save As dialog box will appear. In the dialog box is the File name box. In the File name box, type the letter designation for your floppy disk drive followed by a colon and the file name you want to use. For example, if your floppy disk drive is drive A, and you want to name the file "apples," you should type *A:apples* and then press the Enter key or click on the Save button to save the page. The page or document is now saved as a normal disk file, or as the type of file you specify, and can be opened by any Windows word processor, such as Microsoft Word.

Saving an Image

As you view various Web documents and pages, occasionally you may see an image (for example, a picture) you want to save and perhaps insert into a word processing or other application. Navigator allows you to save images you can use later.

FIGURE A.13

Save Image As Dialog Box

By pointing to the image and clicking the right mouse button, a menu appears. Clicking on Save Image As on the menu causes the Save As dialog box to appear. There you can specify your floppy disk drive and a file name for the picture. Clicking on the Save button will save the picture on a disk. The picture can then be inserted into other applications.

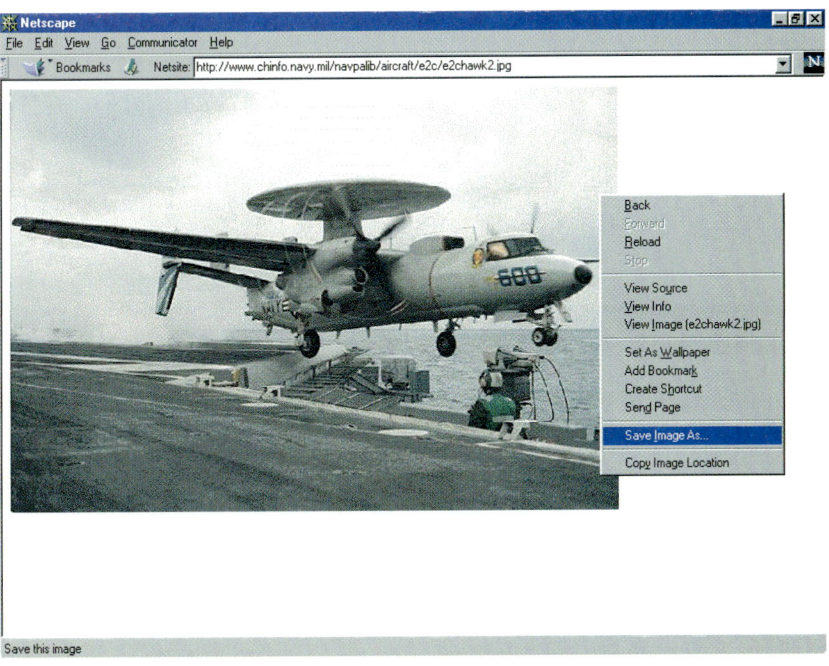

Suppose you want to save a picture of the U.S. Navy's E-2C *Hawkeye* aircraft contained on a page. With the page containing the picture you want to save displayed on your screen, point to the picture and press the *right* mouse button. (Do not press the left button because a picture may be a link to another document or page.) A menu will appear on your screen (Figure A.13). On the menu, click on Save Image As… to display the Save As dialog box. In the lower portion of the dialog box, type the letter for your floppy disk drive followed by a colon and the file name you choose (for example, A:viper) and click on the Save button. The image is saved on your disk.

Inserting a Picture

A saved image can be inserted into other applications, such as a Microsoft Word document or a Microsoft PowerPoint slide. The following steps are for inserting a saved image in a Microsoft Word document. If you are using another program, the steps may be somewhat different. You will need to consult with your instructor or refer to the user's manual for instructions if that is the case.

With a Microsoft Word document page displayed on your screen, click Insert on the menu bar to see the Insert drop-down menu. Click on Picture. Click on From File. In the Look in box, type the letter for your floppy disk drive and press the Enter key. Click on the file name of the picture saved on your floppy disk. Click on Insert to insert the picture into the document. In a few seconds the picture will appear in the document.

Printing a Web Page or Document

Navigator contains a feature that allows you to print Web documents and pages you can keep and refer to when needed. Printing a Web page is easy. First, make sure your printer is ready. You are now ready to print a page.

With the document you want to print displayed on your screen, click on the **Print** button on the Navigation toolbar. The Print dialog box will appear on your screen. In the dialog box, enter your print specifications, such as the number of copies or the range of pages to be printed. Then, click OK.

Another printing method is to click on File on the menu bar to get the File drop-down menu. Click on Print to display the Print dialog box. In the dialog box, enter your print specifications, such as the number of copies or the range of pages to be printed. Then, click OK. Either method will result in the document or page being printed.

Using Navigator's Electronic Mail

Electronic mail, or **e-mail**, is the single most popular service on the Internet. With e-mail you can send and receive messages to and from anyone in the world having an Internet connection. E-mail represents the fastest and cheapest way to converse with other people. Using e-mail you can prepare and send messages, receive and read messages sent to you, save your messages, print messages, and delete messages you no longer want to keep.

There are some preliminary steps you must take before using e-mail. In order to send an e-mail message, you need to know the recipient's e-mail address. A person's e-mail address consists of an account name followed by the @ symbol and the Internet address (domain name) of the computer where the person's account is located. Also, to send and receive messages you must supply your

Internet account name to Netscape so that Netscape can deliver the messages. Then, you can begin sending and recieving e-mail messages.

Accessing Netscape's Electronic Mail

Netscape's e-mail is an application within Netscape Communicator called **Messenger.** To activate Messenger, click on the **Communicator** icon and then choose Messenger Mailbox. Another easy way to activate Messenger is to first start Navigator and then click on the mail icon (the small envelope) located at the bottom of the screen. Within a few seconds, the Message Inbox window will appear on your screen. The toolbar at the top of the screen contains buttons you use to send a message, read a message, reply to a message, and complete other actions for messages (Figure A.14).

Preparing and Sending Mail Messages

With the Inbox window displayed on your screen, you can send a message easily and quickly by following these steps. Click on the **New Msg** (for New Message) button. Soon Messenger's Composition window will appear (Figure A.15).

To send an e-mail message, first you enter (type) the Internet address for the recipient. Press the Tab key to move to the Subject box and type a subject for the message. After you've typed a subject, press the Tab key to move to the text message window and begin typing the message. After you've finished typing the message, click the **Send button** on the toolbar. Your message will be sent over the Internet to the recipient.

FIGURE A.14

The Inbox Window

Pointing to and clicking on the mail icon (the small envelope in the lower right of your screen) displays Netscape Messenger's Inbox window. The window contains a list of messages received. A message on the list can be read by clicking on the message subject.

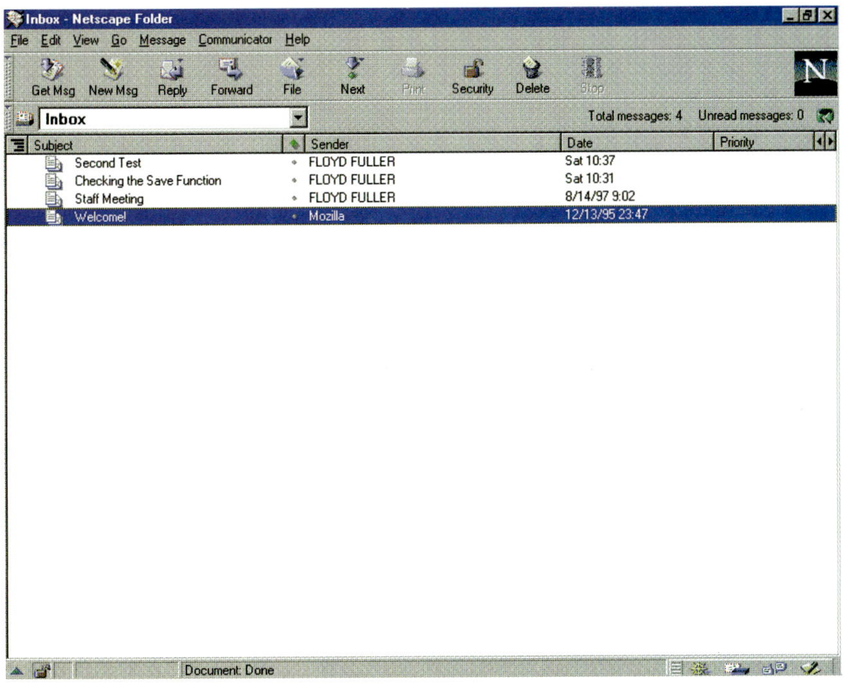

FIGURE A.15
Composition Window

The Composition window is used for composing and sending electronic mail messages. The window contains a menu bar, a toolbar, a box for entering the address of the recipient, a text box for entering a subject for the message, and a text box for typing the message to be sent.

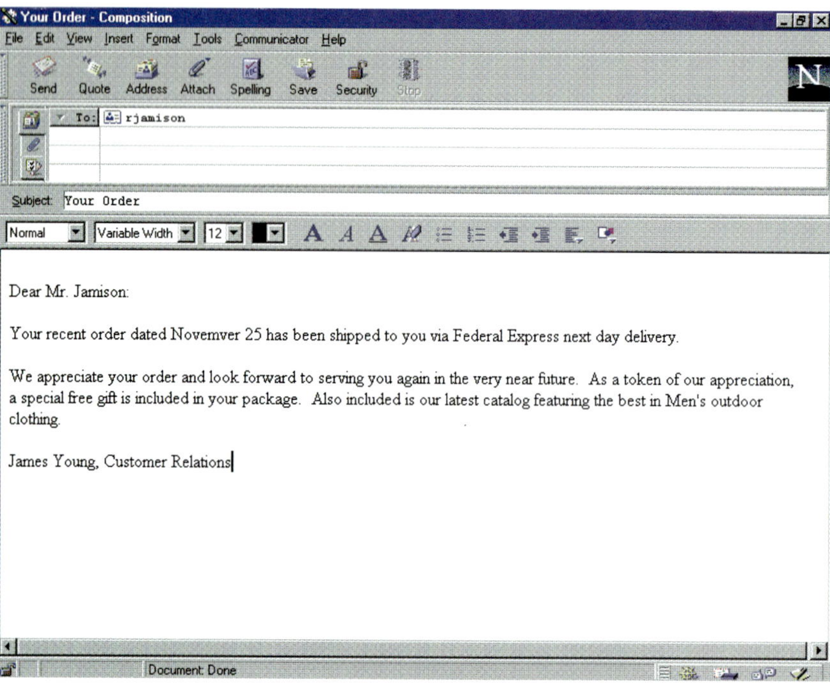

You can practice by sending an e-mail to yourself. Just type your Internet address in the To box, then enter a subject and the message. When you click on the Send button, your message will be sent to you.

Reading Mail Messages

Look again at Figure A.14. The toolbar on the Inbox window contains a button with the words **Get Msg** (for Get Message). Clicking the Get Msg button displays a list of messages that have been sent to you. To read a message, click on the message to display it in the window. To read a lengthy message, use the scroll bar to scroll as you read. You can read any message on the list by clicking on it.

Saving a Mail Message

With the message displayed on your screen, you can save it on a formatted floppy disk inserted in your floppy disk drive. To save the message, click File on the Menu bar to display the File drop-down menu. On the menu, click on Save As to display the Save As dialog box. In the File name box, type the letter for your floppy drive followed by a colon and a filename (for example, *A:Meeting*). Finally, click on the Save button. The message will be saved on your floppy disk.

Printing a Mail Message

There may be an occasion when you want to have a printed copy of a mail message.

With Netscape you can print a message on your printer. Before attempting to print a message, make sure your printer is turned on and ready to print.

To print a mail message, select the message to be printed in the same way you select a message to be saved—by clicking on the message. The message you select will appear in the window. Click on the Print button on the toolbar to display the Print dialog box. In the box, enter the print specifications you want (number of copies, pages to be printed, and so on) and click on the OK button. Soon the message will be printed.

Deleting a Mail Message

Over a long period of time, many e-mail messages may accumulate in your Inbox. Some you may want to delete. You can delete any unwanted mail messages easily and quickly.

To delete a message you no longer want to keep, click on the title of message from the list. The text of the message will appear in the message window. Click on the Delete button on the toolbar.

Using Netscape's Address Book

Over a long period you are likely to send e-mail messages to many people, each having a different Internet address. Netscape's address book feature makes it easier to keep track of Internet addresses, and you can use it anytime you send a message. An **address book** is a file containing the names and Internet addresses of persons to whom you frequently send messages. You can create as many address

FIGURE A.16

Netscape's Address Book

Netscape's address book allows you to create and store a list of e-mail addresses of those individuals with whom you communicate frequently. When sending a message, you need only to access the address book and click on the name of the recipient of your message.

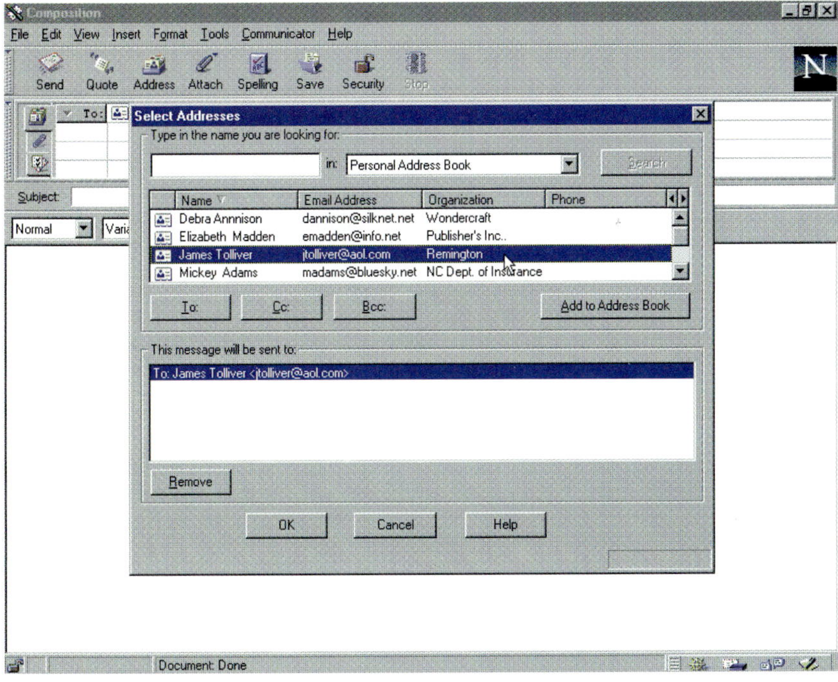

books as you want and save them on a hard disk or floppy disk. For example, you can create and store one address book for family members and another for your friends. You can add and remove addresses at any time.

To access the address book, click on Communicator on the menu bar. Click on Address Book. The address book will appear. Click on the New Card button to display the New Card dialog box. Type in the information requested in the appropriate boxes, using the Tab key to move between boxes. After entering the information, click the OK button.

Placing an address from the address book into a message is easy. Just click Address on the toolbar to display a list of stored addresses. Click on the name of the person to receive the message. Then click on the New Msg button. When the composition window appears, the individual's name is automatically inserted in the To box.

Removing an address you no longer need is equally easy. With the address book displayed on your screen, highlight the name and press the Delete key.

Exiting Electronic Mail

After using the address book to send a message, you can leave Netscape mail by completing two steps. Click the close button (marked X and located in the upper right corner of the title bar) to close the Composition window. Then, click the close button to close the Messenger window.

Exiting Netscape

When you have finished using Netscape, you should close Netscape before turning your computer off or using a different application. To close Netscape, point to and click on the close button (marked X) located in the upper right corner of the title bar.

Conclusion

In this appendix we examined several useful features available with Navigator and Messenger—two of the more popular applications available with Netscape Communicator. This information will help you get started using these two popular applications. Communicator is a powerful and versatile software package that contains several other applications. You are encouraged to learn the others. Doing so will expand your computing horizons and enable you to become a more productive user of this software program.

Getting Started with Internet Explorer 4.0 and MSN Mail

Introduction
Starting Internet Explorer
The Internet Explorer Start Page
Browsing the Web
Using a History List
Saving and Using Favorite Web
  Pages
    Adding a Favorite Web Page
    Deleting a Favorite
    Retrieving a Favorite Web Page

Saving Information with Explorer
    Saving a Web Page
    Saving a Picture
Inserting a Picture
Printing a Web Page or Document
Using Internet Explorer for Searches
Getting Started with MSN Mail
    Accessing MSN Mail
    Preparing and Sending Mail
      Messages

Personalized Address Book
Reading Mail Messages
Saving a Mail Message on a
  Floppy Disk
Deleting a Mail Message
Printing a Mail Message
Exiting Electronic Mail
Exiting the Microsoft Network

Introduction

In an earlier chapter you learned that an online service allows subscribers to perform some useful operations, such as sending and receiving electronic mail, browsing the Internet, and participating in chat groups. You've probably heard of services such as America Online, CompuServe, and Prodigy. **The Microsoft Network,** commonly referred to as **MSN,** is one of the newest online services.

The Microsoft Network is packaged with Windows 95, an operating system that uses a graphical user interface, abbreviated as **GUI** and pronounced "Gooey." When you first start your computer using Windows 95, a screen called the **desktop** appears. The desktop contains icons representing important applications that have been installed on your computer. You activate an application by double-clicking on the icon representing the application you want to use (Figure B.1).

If your computer has Windows 95 already installed, you may have already installed MSN. If you haven't, you can install it at any time. The user's manual that came with your computer contains easy-to-follow instructions for installing MSN. Once MSN has been installed on your computer, an icon representing MSN and another icon representing Microsoft's popular Web browser, **Internet Explorer,** are placed on the desktop. (Look again at Figure B.1.) After MSN is installed, you're ready to begin your voyages into cyberspace.

FIGURE B.1

Windows 95 Desktop Screen

When you start your computer using Windows 95, the desktop screen is automatically displayed. The desktop screen contains icons representing important applications. You activate an application by double-clicking on the icon representing the application you want to use. Internet Explorer 4.0 automatically creates "channels" (the vertical panel on right-hand-side) to the Web. You can also personalize your desktop. The one in this figure contains a photo of two professional basketball players, guards Gary Payton and Michael Jordan.

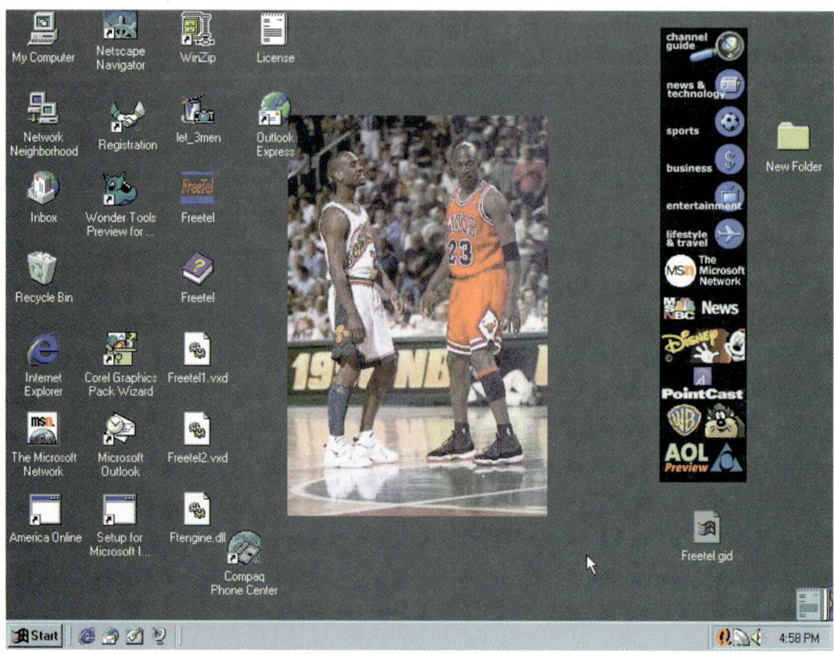

In this appendix, you will learn to use Microsoft's Internet Explorer 4.0 browser to visit interesting places. Space will not permit a complete explanation of all of Explorer's features. Our focus in this appendix is twofold. First, you will learn to use some of Explorer's main features, which will enable you to browse the World Wide Web. Later, you will learn to use Explorer's electronic mail function to send and receive electronic messages.

Starting Internet Explorer

On the desktop (Figure B.1), notice the icon representing Internet Explorer. This icon is an image of the Earth with a small magnifying glass and the words "The Internet" printed underneath the Earth. You start Internet Explorer by simply double-clicking on this icon. When MSN was first installed on your computer, you supplied requested information, including your user name, password, a phone number for contacting the service, and a phone number for the line to which your computer is connected. This information is stored so that you don't reenter it each time you use Explorer. If you want to see all the programs on this computer, click the **Start button** at the bottom left of your screen. You can also start Explorer from this menu. (See Figure B.2.)

After double-clicking on the Internet Explorer icon, a dialog box appears. The box shows your user name, but not your password. (The program remembers your password but does not display it for security). The dialog box also shows your phone number and the phone number for connecting to the service. On the dialog box is a Dial Properties button for entering or changing settings, a Connect button, and a Cancel button. To make a connection, you simply click on the **Connect**

FIGURE B.2

Windows 95 Desktop Screen Start Button and Menus

The Windows 95 desktop screen contains a Start button in the lower left corner that displays menus for selecting and activating specific applications.

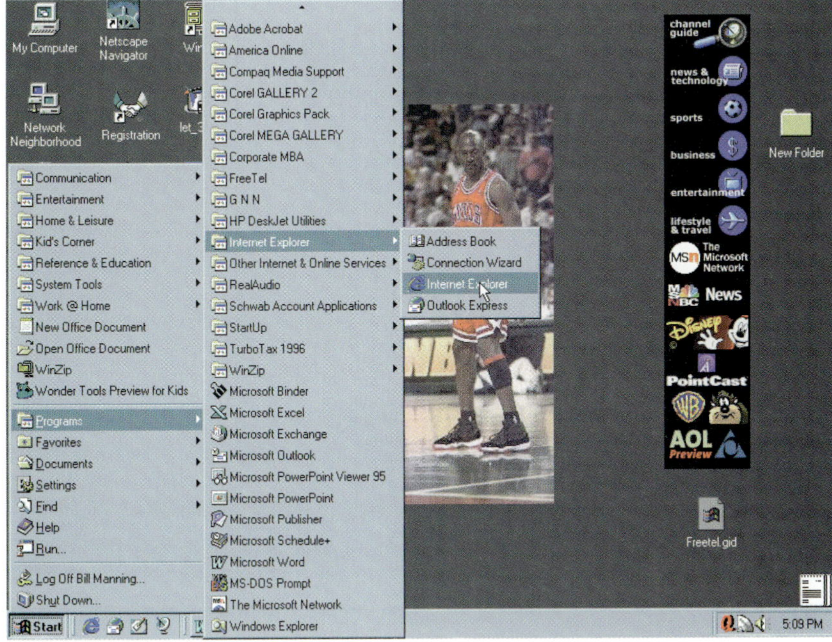

button. After you click on it, a message appears telling you that your modem is dialing the network service. Then a message appears saying that your account is being verified. After verification, the Microsoft Internet Explorer 4.0 start page is displayed on your screen (Figure B.3).

When Internet Explorer is activated and loaded into your computer, the first page you see is Microsoft's home page, shown in Figure B.3. Examine this figure carefully. The information in the following paragraphs is based on this figure.

FIGURE B.3

Internet Explorer Start Page

After clicking on the Internet Explorer icon on the desktop, Microsoft's home page will appear on your screen. This page contains a title bar, menu bar, toolbar, an Address text box, Explorer logo, status bar, hotlinks to other pages, and a display area where Web pages are displayed when you visit other Web sites and pages.

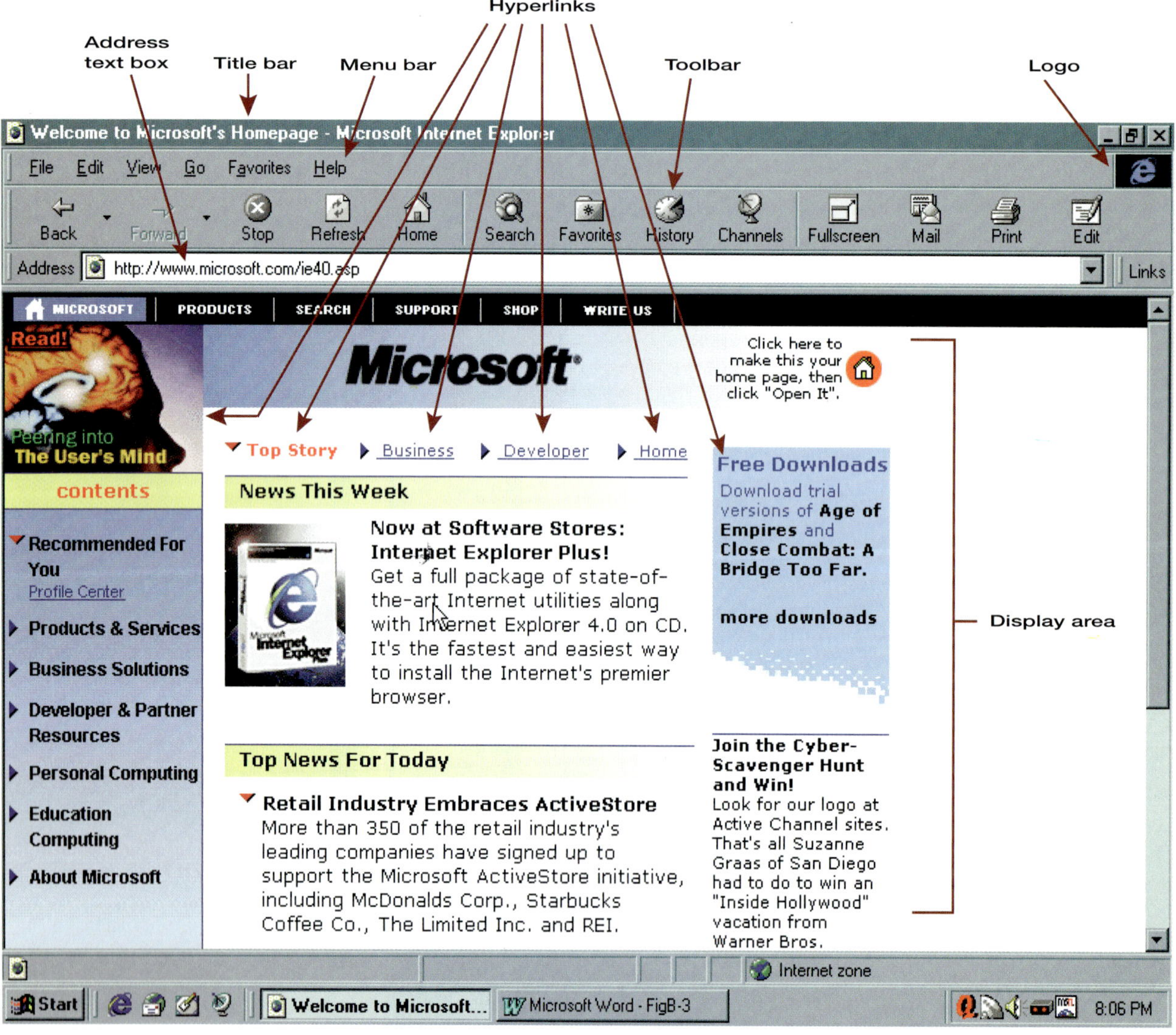

The Internet Explorer Start Page

The Explorer **start page** consists of features that make browsing easy. This is the page you use to browse the World Wide Web and to work with the information you retrieve.

The top bar is the **title bar.** It identifies the title of the Web page displayed.

Immediately below the title of the page is the menu bar. The **menu bar** includes available options, each with pull-down menus, and works like other menu bars, such as those in word processing and spreadsheet programs. For example, clicking the word **File** on the menu bar results in a drop-down menu containing several options. One option is Print. By clicking on **Print** and supplying appropriate information in the dialog box, the user can print a Web page.

Below the menu bar is the **toolbar** (Figure B.4), which allows the user to perform tasks more quickly by simply clicking one of the buttons. For example, clicking on the Refresh button delivers the most current content of a retrieved document. Updating stock quotations would be a good example of how the Refresh button is used. Figure B.4 shows the Internet Explorer 4.0 toolbar and identifies the purpose of each button.

Below the toolbar is the **Address text box** for entering the Internet address, or URL, for the Web site or page you want to visit. To go to the desired site, type the Uniform Resource Locator (URL) in the box and then press the Enter key. The URL is updated automatically as the user goes from page to page at that site.

The large area where Web pages are shown is the **display area.** When Explorer is first activated, Explorer's start page is displayed in this area. When various Web sites are visited, pages from these sites are displayed in this area.

At the lower left beneath the display area is the **status line.** The status line shows the current status of a Web page being retrieved.

In the following sections, you will use the menu bar, Address text box, and toolbar buttons to browser the Internet and Web. The more you browse the Internet and Web, the more proficient you will become.

FIGURE B.4

Internet Explorer 4.0 Toolbar

The Internet Explorer 4.0 toolbar contains buttons that allow you to perform specific actions easily and quickly, such as moving to the previous page or printing a document.

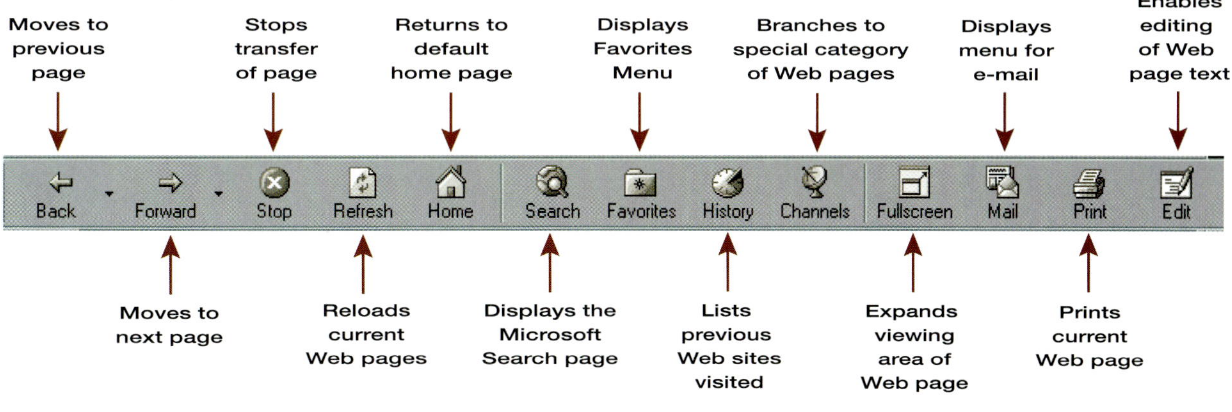

Browsing the Web

When you "browse" the World Wide Web, you move from one Web site (location) to another. The purpose of browsing is to visit various Web sites to learn what is available. Recall from Chapter Three that you can go to a Web site by typing the Internet address, or URL, for the site in the Address box. Also, recall that an URL uses the format shown in the example below, although some sites do not require you to include www in the address:

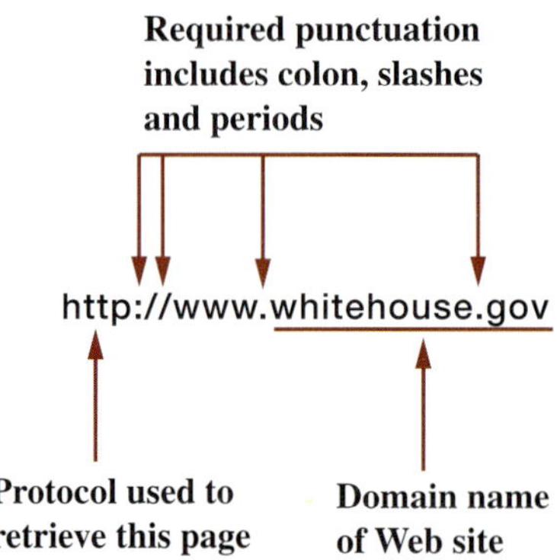

Suppose you want to visit the White House Web site in Washington, D.C., to learn about the White House, its rooms, history and more. Using Explorer, type the Internet address for the White House as shown in Figure B.5. After typing the URL, press the Enter key.

After you've typed the Internet address (URL) for the White House Web site and pressed the Enter key, the White House home page will appear on your screen. (See Figure B.6.) Notice on the White House home page the title *Welcome to the White House.* A picture of the White House is on this page. The page also contains links to other pages with information about the White House and its occupants. If you position the pointer on a link to another location, the pointer (arrow) will change to a hand. You can go directly to the linked page by clicking the left mouse button on that link.

Remember that Explorer allows you to move from one Web site to another and that many pages contain links to other pages and sites. Practice moving around the Web and using available links to view other pages and sites. You will discover many interesting sites containing useful information.

FIGURE B.5

Typing an URL in the Address Box

To visit a particular Web site you must type the Internet address (URL) for the site in the Address text box as shown and then press the Enter key.

FIGURE B.6

White House Home Page

The White House home page contains a picture of the White House and links to other pages that provide information about the White House, its rooms, history, and so on. You can also send a message to the president.

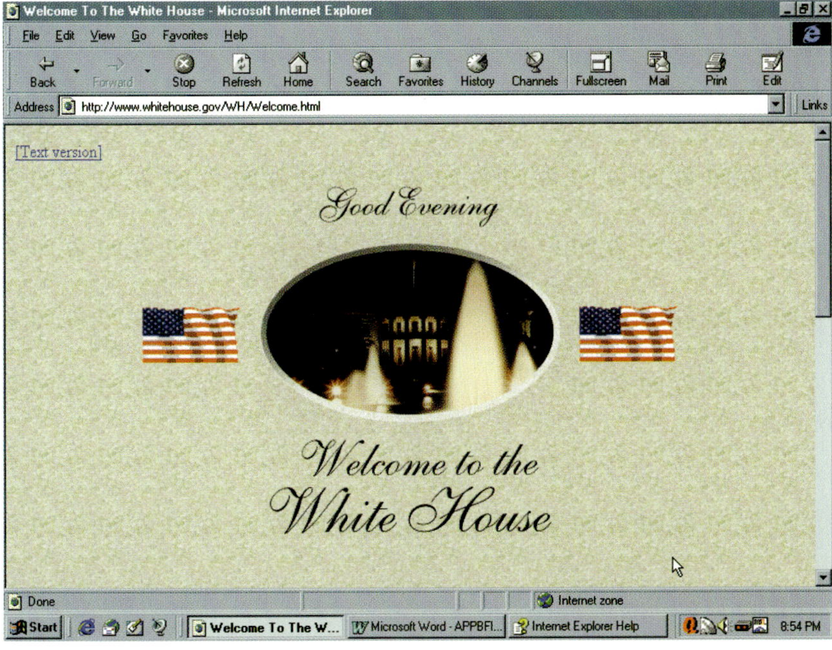

Using a History List

As you move around the Web from site to site and page to page, Internet Explorer keeps track of the sites and pages you visit in a special place called a **history list.** When you first start Explorer, the history list is empty because you have not yet visited any sites. As you visit various sites, Explorer stores the URLs of the sites in the order they are visited. You can return to a previous page by clicking on the **Back button** on the toolbar. If you have returned to previous pages, you can move forward to the next page by clicking on the **Forward button** on the toolbar.

The Go menu contains a list of sites previously visited. You can quickly return to any site on the list. To return to a specific site listed on the list, click on Go on the menu bar and then click on the site on the list you wish to visit.

Internet Explorer stores sites you have visited for a period of five days. You can, however, reconfigure your system to store URLs of previously visited sites for a longer period. If you want to keep track of important sites indefinitely, you can do so by saving your favorite Web pages on a special list called the Favorites list.

Saving and Using Favorite Web Pages

Typing a long URL for a favorite Web page can sometimes be tedious, and typing errors may occur. Fortunately, Internet Explorer offers a special feature that allows you to permanently save the URLs of pages you may want to go to later.

Adding a Favorite Web Page to a Favorites List

Using Internet Explorer's Favorites feature, you can save page titles and the URLs of those pages to a permanent favorites list. You can then save those lists in folders on a floppy disk and can arrange lists of related pages in separate folders.

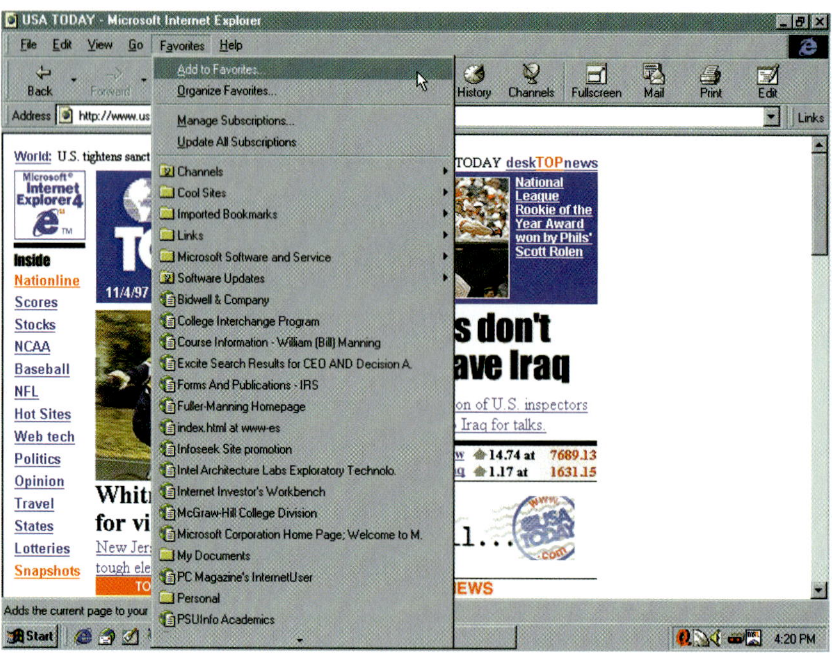

A **favorite** consists of the title of the Web page and the URL of that page. A **favorites list** is a list of permanently saved favorites. Explorer uses a favorites list to quickly identify and find a Web page. You can add new favorites and delete favorites you no longer want to keep.

Adding a Favorite Web Page

Adding a favorite to a list is easy. With the Web page you want to add to the list displayed on your screen, click on the Favorites tool on the toolbar. When the Favorites drop-down menu appears, click on Add To Favorites (see Figure B.7). After you've added a site to this list, you can check to see if it was added by clicking again on the Favorites tool on the toolbar.

Deleting a Favorite

There may be several reasons for wanting to delete a favorite. With the changing nature of the World Wide Web, you may discover that some Web pages no longer exist. You may have added pages you no longer want to keep. Your list may become too cumbersome to use. Whatever the reason, you may need to delete some favorites.

Deleting a favorite page is a simple procedure. Click on the Favorites button on the toolbar. Then click on Organize Favorites to display the Organize Favorites dialog box. The dialog box contains a list of your favorite pages, as shown in Figure B.8. On the list, highlight the page you want to delete by clicking it. Click

FIGURE B.8

Deleting a Favorite Web Page

You can delete favorite Web pages you no longer want.

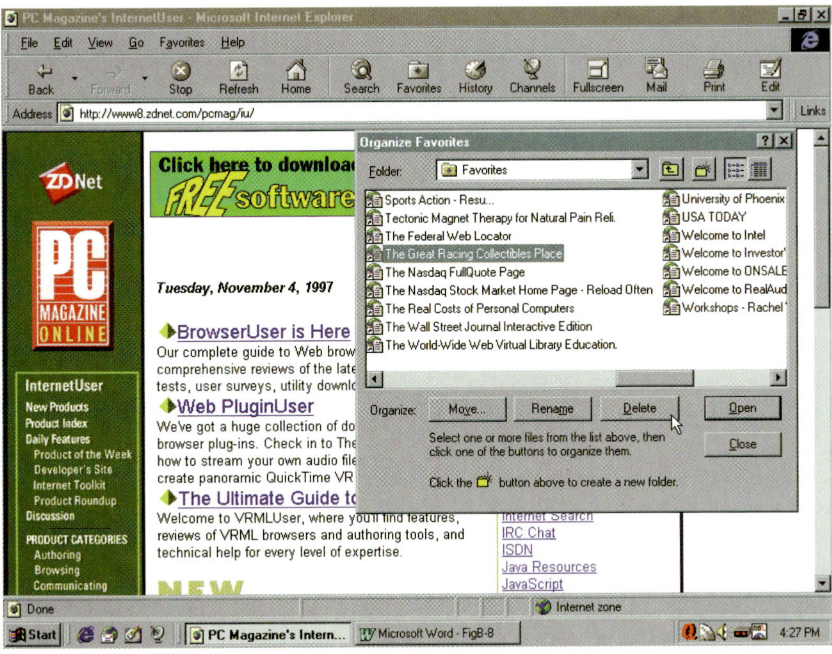

the Delete button. Another dialog box appears asking you to confirm that you want to delete the page. Click the Yes button to delete the page. Click the Close button to close the dialog box. You can verify that the page has been deleted by clicking on the Favorites button on the toolbar. If you successfully deleted the page, the site title no longer appears on the list.

The Organize Favorites dialog box also allows you to perform other actions. Look again at the buttons shown in Figure B.8. You can move a page to a different folder, rename a page, or create a new folder.

Retrieving a Favorite Web Page

You can use a Favorites list to retrieve Web pages quickly and easily. To retrieve a favorite Web page, click on the Favorites button to display the Favorites menu. The menu contains a list of favorites below the Organize Favorites option. Point to and click on the title of the page you want to see. Within a few seconds, the page you selected will appear on your screen.

Saving Information with Explorer

As you travel the Internet and World Wide Web, you may find information you want to save for use later. Internet Explorer allows you to save documents, pages, and pictures you find at various Web sites on a floppy disk or hard disk. In the following sections, you will learn how to save important information, including pictures you can insert into a word processing document such as a letter or report.

Saving a Web Page

On the World Wide Web there are almost 20 million Web sites containing useful information. You may find pages you want to save for use later use. With Explorer you can easily do this.

With the page you want to save displayed on your screen, insert a floppy disk in your floppy disk drive (for example, drive A if drive A is your floppy disk drive). Click on File on the menu bar to display the File drop-down menu. Click on the Save As command. The Save As dialog box will appear. Near the bottom of the dialog box is the File name box. In the File name box, type the letter designation for your floppy disk drive and the file name you want to use. For example, if your floppy disk drive is drive A, and you want to name the file "apples," you should type *A:apples.* In the Save as type box, you can specify the type of file you want the page saved as. To select a file type click on the small arrowhead at the right to display file types. Then click on the type you want and click on the Save button or press the Enter key or to save the page. The page or document is now saved on a floppy disk and can be retrieved later.

Saving a Picture

As you view various Web documents and pages, occasionally you may see a picture you want to save and perhaps insert into a word processing or other application. Internet Explorer allows you to save these pictures.

FIGURE B.9

Save As Dialog Box

Using Internet Explorer you can save a picture you find on a Web page to a storage medium such as a floppy disk. The saved picture can be inserted into other Web page application. Be sure you do not violate copyright laws if you do this.

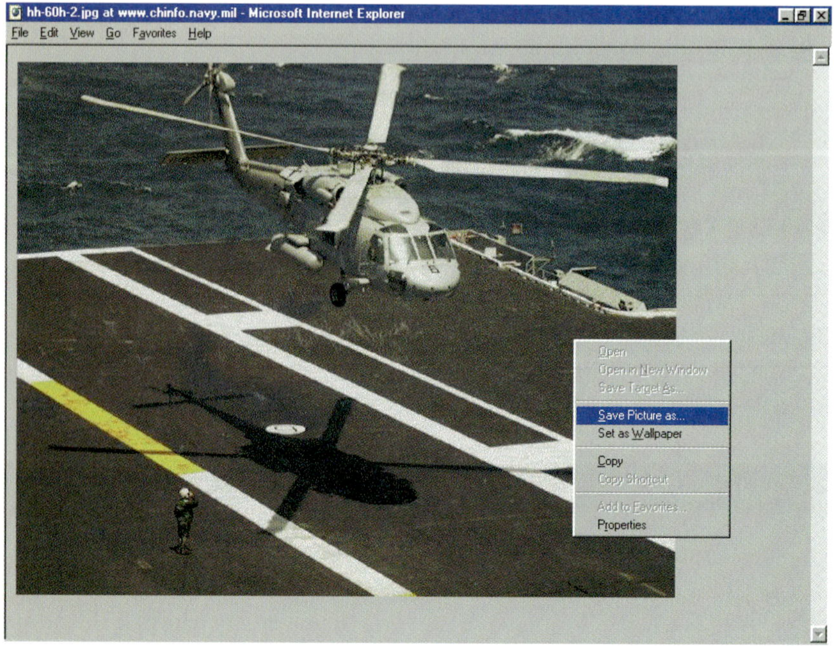

Suppose you want to save a picture of the U.S. Navy's SH-H60 *Seahawk* helicopter contained on a page. With the page containing a picture you want to save displayed on your screen, point to the picture and press the *right* mouse button. (Do not press the left button because a picture is often a link to another document or page.) A menu will appear on your screen (Figure B.9). On the menu, click on Save Picture As… to display the Save As dialog box. In the File name field of the dialog box, type the filename (for example, Viper) for the picture and click the Save button or press the Enter key. The picture will be saved on your floppy disk.

Inserting a Picture

A saved picture can be inserted into other applications, such as a Microsoft Word document or a Microsoft PowerPoint slide. The following steps are for inserting a saved picture in a Microsoft Word document. If you are using another program, the steps may be somewhat different and you will need to consult with your instructor or refer to the user's manual.

With a Microsoft Word document page displayed on your screen, click on Insert on the menu bar to see the Insert drop-down menu. Click on Picture. Click on From File. In the Look in box, type the letter for your floppy disk drive and press the Enter key. A list of files will be displayed. Click on the file name of the picture saved on your floppy disk. Click on Insert to insert the picture into the document. In a few seconds the picture will appear in the document.

FIGURE B.10

Searching the Internet Using Internet Explorer 4.0

The Internet Explorer toolbar contains a Search button that allows you to search for information on the Internet. After clicking the Search button, a window is displayed in which you enter a word or phrase for your search and choose a search engine. Your search is initiated when you click the Search button.

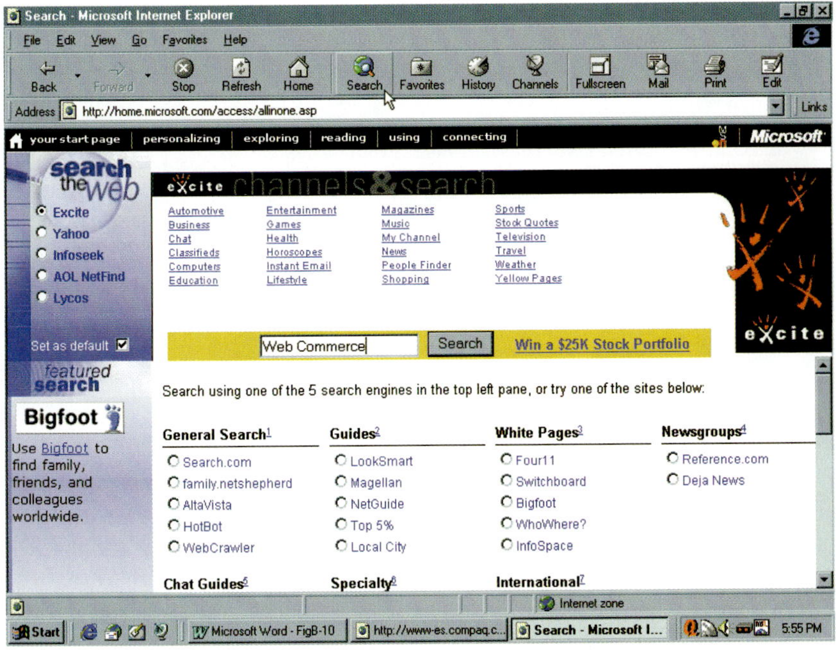

Printing a Web Page or Document

Internet Explorer contains a feature that allows you to print Web documents. Printing a Web page is simple. First, make sure your printer is ready.

With the document you want to print displayed on your screen, click on the Print button. The Print dialog box will appear on your screen. In the dialog box, enter your print specifications, such as the number of copies or the range of pages to be printed. Then, click OK to print the document.

Another printing method is to click on File on the menu bar to get the File drop-down menu. Click on Print to display the Print dialog box. In the dialog box, enter your print specifications, such as the number of copies or the range of pages to be printed. Then, click OK to print the document. Either method will result in the document or page being printed.

Using Internet Explorer for Searches

In Chapter Four you learned to use search engines to search for information on the Internet. You may find it useful to review that information.

Internet Explorer contains links to several search engines you can use to search the Internet. Click on the Search button on the toolbar. A window titled *MSN.COM, Find—Microsoft Internet Explorer* will soon appear on your screen (Figure B.10).

FIGURE B.11
The MSN Central Screen

After signing in to the Microsoft Network, a default home page is displayed. Here that page is the Microsoft home page. In the menu shown across the top of the page, you will see an icon labeled Mail. To use the e-mail function, you simply click on this icon. Four options now appear in the drop-down menu. To send a message, click on the New Message bar. A dialog box named Untitled Message will appear. Now you are ready to compose your new message to another person.

This window contains a field with the heading *Enter what you are searching for.* It is here that you enter a word or phrase to identify what you are looking for. Several search engines are displayed in the window. Select a search engine by clicking on the search engine of your choice. Then, click on the **Search button** to begin your search.

Getting Started with MSN Mail

Electronic mail, or **e-mail,** is the single most popular service on the Internet. Using electronic mail you can send and receive messages to anyone in the world who has an Internet address. E-mail represents the fastest and cheapest way to converse with other people. You can prepare and send messages, receive and read messages sent to you, save your messages, print messages, and delete messages you no longer want to keep.

There are some preliminary steps you must take before using the Microsoft Explorer mail function. In order to send a mail message over the Internet, you need to know the recipient's e-mail address. A person's e-mail address consists of an account name followed by the @ symbol and the Internet address (domain name) of the computer where the person's account is located. Also, to send and receive messages you must supply your Internet account name to the Microsoft Network so that the service can deliver the messages. (This was probably done when Microsoft Network was first installed on your computer.) Now, you can begin sending and receiving e-mail messages.

FIGURE B.12

Inbox Screen

After signing in to the Microsoft Network and clicking on the Mail icon, the program does not yet know whether you want to send or receive electronic mail. Thus, the Inbox containing all messages you have received appears. You can read any message on the list by double-clicking on that message.

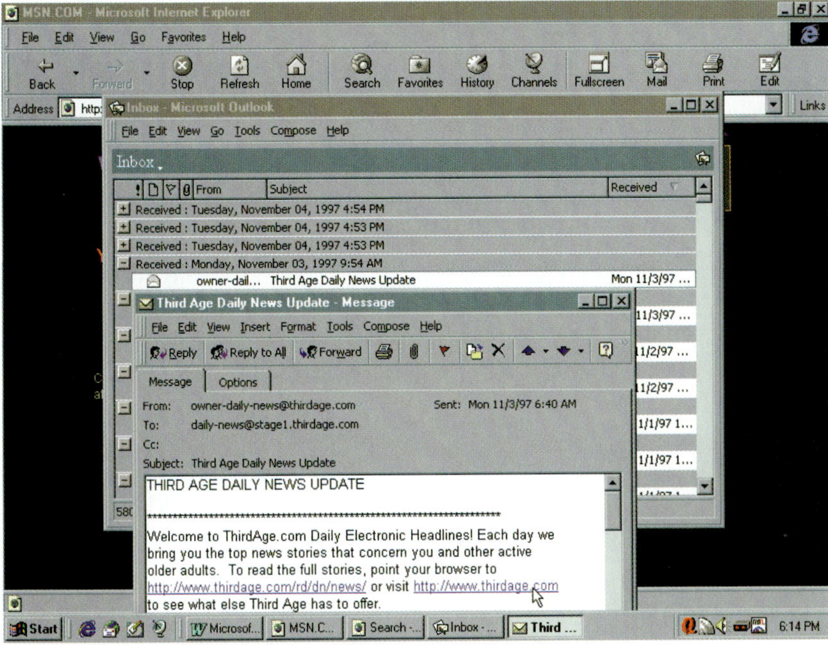

Accessing MSN Mail

Before you can use the e-mail function, you must first start Internet Explorer. After signing in to the Microsoft Network, your default home page is displayed. In Figure B.11, this is the Microsoft home page. In the Menu section, you will see an icon labeled Mail. To open the e-mail function, click on this icon. Four options appear in a drop-down menu. For new messages, click on the New Message bar. This leads you to a dialog box named Untitled Message (see below). Here is where you enter your new message to another party.

The **Inbox** contains all messages you have received. (See Figure B.12.) If you want to reread a previous message, simply click on that message bar and it will appear on the screen. You can even forward previous messages to another person or group of people. Can you begin to see how e-mail might improve personal and organizational efficiency?

FIGURE B.13

The New Message Dialog Box

You use the New Message dialog box to send a new message. In the To… box, you need to type the Internet address of the recipient and type the message you want to send.

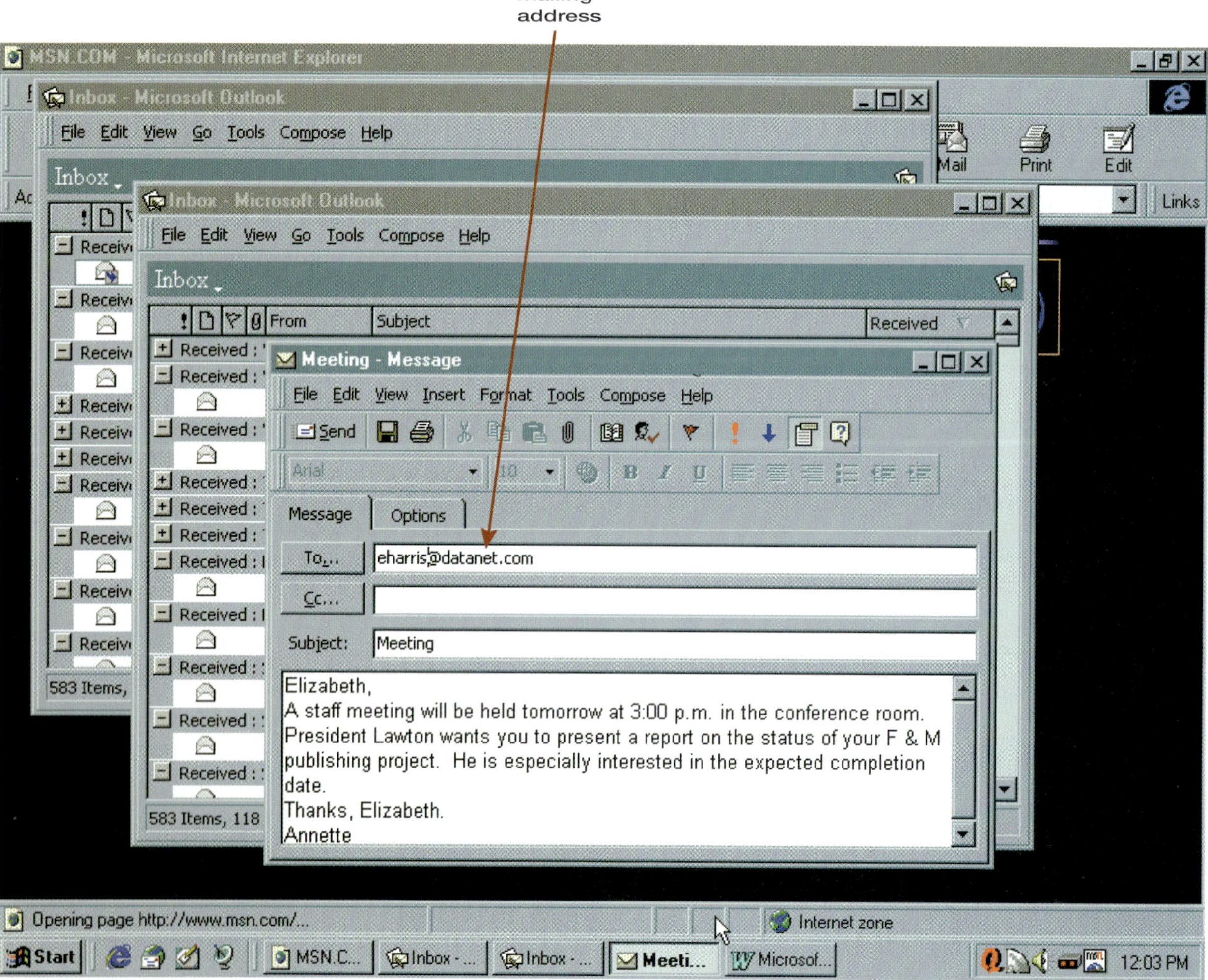

Preparing and Sending Mail Messages

On the menu bar is a button labeled Compose. Click on the Compose button to display the Compose drop-down menu. Click on New Mail Message at the top of the drop-down menu. A dialog box called New Message appears. To send a message, you need to type the Internet address of the recipient and the message you will send (Figure B.13).

Before proceeding, you need to familiarize yourself with the menu bar and the toolbar on the New Message dialog box. Take a few minutes to learn the menu bar. A drop-down menu accompanies each item on the menu bar. Click on each item to view the options on the item's drop-down menu. The menu bar contains items similar to menu bars of other programs, such as Microsoft Word. Situations will arise when you will need to select items from this menu bar.

The toolbar, located beneath the menu bar, contains several useful buttons that make it easier for you to send and receive messages. Figure B.14 shows the toolbar. Take time to familiarize yourself with it.

The **Send button** is used to send a message. When you've finished typing a message, clicking the Send button will cause your message to be sent immediately to the recipient. The floppy disk icon allows you to save a message displayed on your screen.

The printer icon lets you print a copy of a message. The cut icon (scissors) allows you to highlight and cut text from a message or to remove text from its present location and paste it to a different location, using the clipboard icon. The copy icon lets you copy information to the clipboard, possibly for pasting into other applications. The insert file icon (paperclip) enables you to attach one or more files to an e-mail message. The address book icon is used to store and retrieve Internet addresses. The question mark icon (?) displays helpful information. Other icons represent actions taken less often.

To send an e-mail message the New Message dialog box must be displayed on your screen. In the To... field you must type the Internet address for the recipient. You can send a copy of your message to other persons by typing the Internet address for each person in the cc... field. If you want others to receive a copy of the message, press the Tab key to move the cursor to the text box labeled cc. Type the Internet addresses. Then, press the Tab key to move to the text Subject box and type a subject for the message. After you've typed a subject, press the Tab key to move to the text Message window and begin typing the message. After you've

FIGURE B.14

New Message Toolbar

The toolbar contains several important and useful buttons. Clicking on one of the buttons will result in an action being taken.

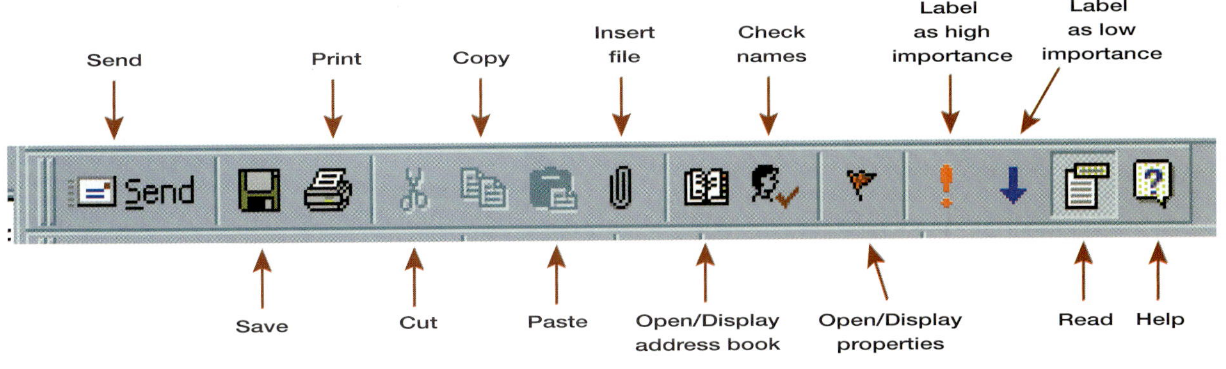

finished typing the message, press the Send button on the toolbar and your message will be sent over the Internet to the recipient.

You can practice by sending an e-mail message to yourself. Just type your Internet address in the To… box, along with a subject and the message. When you click on the Send button, your message will be sent to you as the recipient.

Personalized Address Book

Over a long period you are likely to send mail messages to many people, each having a different Internet address. Microsoft's address book feature makes it easier to keep track of Internet addresses, and you can use it anytime you send a message. An **address book** is a file containing the names and Internet addresses of persons to whom you frequently send messages. You can create a personalized

Storing Addresses in the Personalized Address Book

You can use the personalized address book to store e-mail addresses of persons with whom you often communicate.

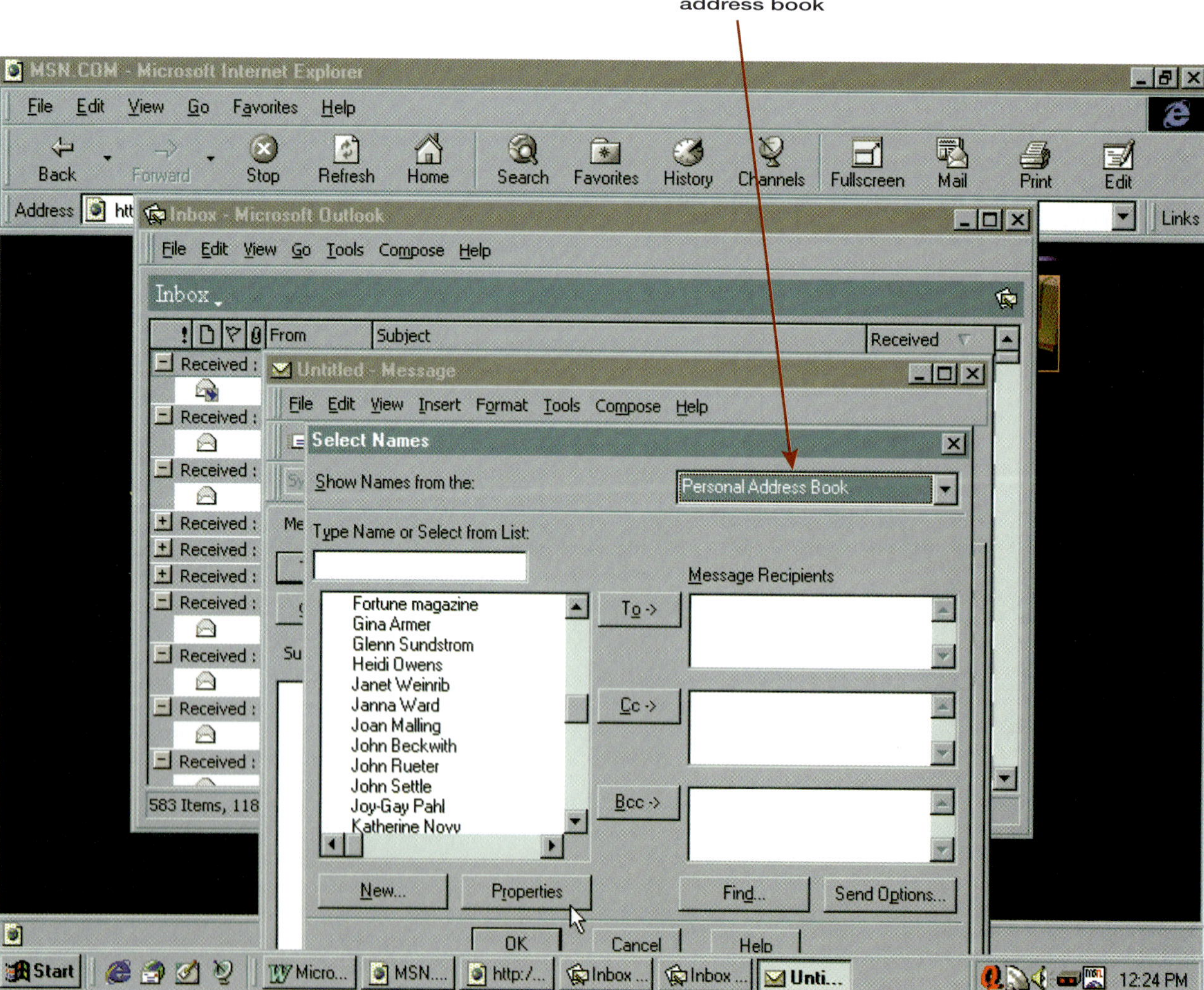

address book with names of other people to whom you often send messages. You can add and remove addresses at any time.

To access the personalized address book you must first display the Inbox. Click on Compose to display the New Message window. On the toolbar, click on the address book icon to display the address book window. Click on File. Click on New Entry to display the New Entry window. Choose the option New Internet over The Microsoft Network. Click OK. The New Internet over the Microsoft Network window will be displayed. Type the name (the first part of the person's Internet address) of the person whose address you will save in the address book, as shown in Figure B.15. Tab to the Domain Name field and type the domain. Tab to the Name field and type the person's name. Click OK to save the person's address in the personalized address book.

The personalized address book identifies the Internet address of the person you will send a message to. To select a name from the personalized address book, the New Message window should be displayed on your screen. On the menu bar, click on the address book icon. In the box at the top of the window, click on Personal Address Book. A list of names will appear. Highlight the recipient's name. Click the To button. Click OK. The Internet address of the person you selected will appear in the To field on the New Message window.

Reading Mail Messages

When you first sign on to the Microsoft Network, you will be notified if you have new e-mail waiting. A small dialog box appears asking if you want to read the message now. By clicking the Yes button, the sender and subject of the new message appears in your Inbox, along with other messages that are still in your Inbox. New unread messages appear in bold print. Just click on any message to display the message on your screen for you to read.

After reading a message, click on the Close button to close the message and return to the Inbox. This indicates that you have read the message. You can then read another message by clicking on the message you want to read.

Saving a Mail Message on a Floppy Disk

With the Inbox displayed on your screen, you can save an important message on a formatted floppy disk inserted in your floppy disk drive. To save a message, highlight the message. Click on File. Click on Save As to display the Save As dialog box. In the File name box, type the letter identifying your floppy disk drive, a colon, and a file name (for example: *A:Memo*). Finally, click on the Save button to save the message on a floppy disk.

Deleting a Mail Message

In the Inbox, you can delete mail messages you no longer need. To delete a message listed in the Inbox, first highlight the message. With the message highlighted, click on File to get the File drop-down menu. On the Filer menu, click on Delete. The listed message will disappear from the Inbox, indicating it has been deleted.

Printing a Mail Message

There may be an occasion when you want to have a printed copy of a mail message. It's easy to print a mail message on your printer. Before attempting to print a message, make sure your printer is turned on and ready to print.

To print a mail message, select the message to be printed the same way you select a message to be save—by highlighting the message's subject in the Inbox. Click on the Print button on the toolbar. The message will be printed on your printer.

Exiting Electronic Mail

With the Inbox displayed on your screen, you can leave Microsoft's mail function by completing two steps. First, click on the Inbox icon in the upper left corner of the screen. Then, click the close button (the square button in the top right corner marked with an X) to close the mail program.

Exiting the Microsoft Network

When you have finished using the Microsoft Network, you should close MSN before turning your computer off or before using a different application. To close MSN, point to and click on the MSN icon in the upper left corner of the screen to display a drop-down menu. Then click on Close.

Internet Explorer 4.0 is your window to the Web. Take time to learn its features and capabilities. These efforts will improve your understanding and efficiencies in using this new and powerful resource. The rewards are well worth the effort.

Active link indicator   An area at the bottom of Navigator in which the URL of a Web page is displayed when the pointer is positioned on an object linked to the page.

Add-on board   An electronic board that can be inserted into a personal computer to provide additional capabilities. An add-on is designed to complement other products. (Also called expansion board or plug-in board.)

Address book   A file containing the names and Internet addresses of persons to whom you frequently send messages.

Address book icon   An icon that is used to store and retrieve Internet addresses.

Address text box   A rectangular box for entering the Internet address (URL) of the desired location or URL for the Web site or page you want to visit when using Internet Explorer.

Advanced search   A search that provides the user with more control over a search by displaying only Web pages containing the word or phrase specified by the user.

AltaVista   A search engine developed by Digital Equipment Corporation capable of searching through various Web resources. AltaVista is one of the largest and most popular search engines on the Web, with more than 30 million entries.

Animations   Images that move about on a computer screen or Web page.

Antivirus program   A program that can detect the presence of viruses and eradicate them. You should install an antivirus program on your computer and update the program periodically to safeguard against the potential for a new virus infecting your computer.

ARPANET   An experimental network created in 1969 by the U.S. Department of Defense's Advanced Research Projects Agency (ARPA) to allow military scientists to use computers to share data files and research findings. ARPANET is recognized as the beginning of the Internet.

ASCII file   A human-readable file in which the data is in the form of text.

Asynchronous communications   A time gap exists between the time a message is sent and the time it is received. Voice mail and e-mail are examples of asynchronous communications modes. The process may take longer, but it does accommodate differences in time schedules between the sender and receiver.

Automotive Network eXchange (ANX)   An extranet being developed by Chrysler Corporation, General Motors Corporation, and Ford Motor Company for the purpose of coordinating and scheduling the delivery of materials to the companies as the materials are needed. The system also routes deliveries and even helps coordinate design and manufacturing efforts.

Backbone   A private network that is owned by an Internet provider and that handles Internet operations.

Back button   A browser button that, when selected, returns the user to the previous page that was viewed.

Bandwidth   Refers to the ability of a communications medium to carry a message. It also refers to the speed at which information can be transmitted.

Information-intensive media such as graphics and animation require large bandwidths and thus travel more slowly than does text through the communications medium.

Bar graphs Charts that show relative levels of a key variable, such as the amount of sales by each salesperson in a retail store.

Binary file A machine-readable-only file in which data is in the form of only two numbers (zeroes and ones).

BITNET An early network that allowed messages and data to be transmitted among computers over the network.

Bookmark A Web page's title and its URL that a user has saved for later use while using Netscape Navigator.

Bookmark feature A browser feature that allows a user to permanently save the URLs of pages the user may want to return to.

Bookmark list A feature of Netscape Navigator that provides a user with a way to keep track of favorite or frequently visited Web pages by permanently storing the titles and addresses of Web pages the user wants to save and access later.

Browser A navigational software tool (program) that makes it easy to find and display Web pages by interpreting the complex commands used to create the pages. A browser enables a user to browse the Web easily and quickly, like browsing through library stacks or stores in a shopping mall.

Browser icon A small image (icon) on the desktop that a user can select to activate a browser.

Business chains A linkage in which information about a company's products and services is shared with various departments and with suppliers, distributors, channels, retailers, markets, and consumers. (Also called Value chains.)

Chat room An Internet feature that enables a user to discuss life, current events, or common interests with other people who share similar interests.

Client-server model A special type of network in which personal computers (clients) are connected to a larger computer (server). The server uses special software to find and deliver requested Web documents to the client computer requesting the document.

Clip art Consists of electronically stored figures, cartoons, and images that can be added to a Web page or other document. Clip art libraries are available that contain thousands of images that can be pasted onto a Web page, including animals, shapes, buildings, people, cartoons, signs, maps, and computers.

Clock speed The speed at which a microprocessor executes instructions.

Collaboration Working together to accomplish a specific goal or group of goals.

Collaborative system A type of work environment in which team members share ideas, resources, and friendships. It provides individuals who are physically separated with the ability to work together using the Web and Internet. Electronic communication tools may include personal computers, shared whiteboards, conferencing software, and voice and video conferencing.

Commercial online service A private company that provides a wide range of information and services to subscribers willing to pay a regular subscription fee. In addition to providing access to the Internet, commercial online services typically provide special kinds of information, such as timely news items, information arranged into groupings, newsgroups, e-mail, and business information. By providing online links to information, the service allows subscribers to easily locate information they are seeking.

Communications protocols   Protocols used in writing communications software that allow the computer you are using to communicate with other computers.

Communications software   Software that allows you to send and receive information over telephone lines through a modem. Without communications software, you cannot connect your computer to another computer, such as a Web server.

Communications system   A system consisting of a sender, communications medium (such as a telephone), and receiver that allows persons to send and receive messages.

Compatibility   The ability of one computer hardware or software product to work with another hardware or software product. For example, a computer and printer are said to be compatible if they are connected and work together. Software products are compatible if they use the same data formats.

Competitive upgrade   A program or product that can be purchased at a discount if you can prove that you own a competing product.

Computer cracker   An individual who tests his (or her) computer skills by breaking into computer systems. This definition suggests that computer crackers do not cause damage or steal information. However, they may view information stored in computer systems.

Computer hacker   A derogatory term that most often refers to a person who tries (and sometimes succeeds) to gain unauthorized access to computer systems for the purpose of altering, damaging, or stealing information.

Connect button   A special button that allows a user to make a connection to an internet service provider or an online service such as the Microsoft Network.

Copy icon   An icon that, when selected, lets you copy information to the clipboard, possibly for pasting into other applications.

Critical inflection points   Opportunity points in the life of an individual, organization, or industry where growth either ramps up to achieve even greater successes or turns down to eventual difficulties.

Cut icon (scissors)   When selected, this icon allows you to highlight and cut text from a message or to remove text from its present location and paste it to a different location, using another icon, called the clipboard icon.

Cyber portfolio   A personal Web site that displays an individual's employment qualifications, including education, experience, and skills.

Cyberspace   A term that refers to the invisible realm of the Internet universe.

Cyberteams   A work or study environment in which team members at various geographical locations use the Internet to share ideas, resources, and friendships. A student cyberteam, for example, might study a specific problem, make recommendations, and prepare a group report. Team evaluations can be done online.

Data   Random, unorganized measurements of activities related to a problem that are entered into a computer for processing.

Decision making   The process of identifying and selecting the best solution to a particular problem.

Decryption   The conversion of encrypted data back into a readable form. The receiver of encrypted data must have access to a secret key or password to decrypt (decode) and thus read the data.

Design cycle   A series of steps followed in designing a Web page.

Design phase   Step in Web page development that combines content with images and perceptions to achieve a desired outcome or action. Clear thought and quality time spent in this phase is well worth it.

Design template   A carefully planned and structured outline showing what is to be included and presented on a Web site.

Desktop   A computer screen on which icons representing various applications or groups of applications are displayed.

Dial-up networking   A program that allows a user to easily establish a connection to another computer, such as a network or the Internet.

Digital camera   A specialized camera that takes pictures and stores them in an electronic format in the camera without using standard film. After a picture has been taken, it can be inserted into a document.

Digital highway   A system consisting of hardware, software, and communications channels that allow information to be electronically sent and received in digital form.

Directory   The manner in which files and subdirectories at FTP sites are stored. Files in your computer are also stored in directories.

Display area   The large area used by a Web browser to display pages of a Web document being viewed.

Domain   Element used in an Internet address to show the type of site. Typical Internet domains include commercial companies, departments or agencies of the government, or educational institutions.

Download   To receive the new program via your modem and store the program on your computer.

Downloading   The process of retrieving files from another computer, such as a computer on the Internet.

Electronic commerce (EC)   The use of computer networks to conduct business— the buying and selling of goods and services—with one's suppliers, customers, and competitors electronically. (Also called Internet Commerce [IC].)

Electronic data interchange (EDI)   Technology that allows the exchange of information between individuals and organizations. EDI systems use computers to automatically transfer inventory, delivery, and billing information between organizations.

Electronic funds transfer (EFT)   A technology that allows for the electronic exchange of payments, payment-related information, and financial documents between an organization's customers, suppliers, and financial institutions.

Electronic mail (e-mail)   A software program that allows a user to send and receive messages across the Internet. E-mail messages can be saved, printed, and even routed to others.

Electronic malls (e-Malls)   Virtual marketplaces on the Internet in which consumers use their computers to access an Internet-based, interactive, online system to browse catalogs of products and services at a large number of different stores. (Also called electronic marketplaces.)

Electronic marketplaces   See electronic malls.

e-mail   See electronic mail.

Empowering agents   Resources that allow persons to do things that were not possible before.

Encryption   The process of converting information into a coded form that prevents it from being read by unauthorized people. Once data has been encrypted, it can be transmitted with little concern that it can be intercepted and read by another person.

Espionage   The use of the Internet to commit the act of spying. An example is an unauthorized person using the Internet to gain access to government and private computer systems for the purpose of spying; that is, to view confidential information.

Ethics   A body of principles relating to right and wrong behavior. Rules and practices that ask us all to make every effort to be fair, honest, and courteous.

Etiquette   Social rules for acceptable behavior in society.

Excite   One of the most comprehensive search engines available on the Web. It offers a reference section and online maps for locations across the U.S. and around the world in addition to its more than 50 million Web pages.

External modem   A modem contained in a small box that is plugged into one of the computer's ports.

Extranet   A computer network used between organizations.

Favorite   A Web page's title and its URL that a user has saved for later use while using Microsoft's Internet Explorer.

Favorites List   A feature of Microsoft's Internet Explorer that provides a user with a way to keep track of favorite or frequently visited Web pages by permanently storing the titles and addresses of Web pages the user wants to save and access later.

Fiber-optic cable   A cable containing tiny glass fibers through which data can be transmitted in digital form.

File   An option available on a menu bar that allows a user to work with a file by performing such actions as opening, closing, or saving it.

File specification   The name of a particular file or file folder. At some Web sites a vast amount of information is available for retrieval and viewing. At these sites, information is often arranged and stored in folders, just as you might store information in folders in a file cabinet. If you know the name of the particular file you are seeking, or the name of the folder containing the information, accessing the information is easier and faster.

File Transfer Protocol (FTP)   A protocol that allows you to upload (transmit) files over telephone lines to another computer and to download (retrieve) files stored on another computer.

Firewall   Computer hardware and/or software that provides protection and security for the Intranet. Only authorized users can access information stored on a computer or network. Users gain access through assigned passwords.

Floppy disk icon   When selected, the Floppy disk icon allows you to save a message displayed on your screen.

Forward button   A browser button that, when selected, displays the next page of a document.

Frame   A rectangular area of your screen in which text or graphics can appear. Many Web pages are segmented into frames so that information can be displayed in a meaningful fashion.

Fraud   A false representation of a material fact, made with knowledge of its falsity and with the intent to mislead or defraud. If the respresentation is relied upon by the receiver, and results in injury, there may be legal grounds for damages.

FTP client software   A software program installed on a personal computer that allows for the transfer of files between computers such as client computers and server computers.

FTP daemon   A program installed on an FTP server that enables you to transfer (upload or download) files.

Get Msg   A special button that enables the user to retrieve e-mail messages when using Netscape Navigator.

Graphical user interface A special part of an operating system that allows a user to take advantage of the computer's graphics capabilities.

Graphics Pictorial representations of reality. Examples include tables, charts, illustrations, photos, and animations.

Graphics board An electronic board installed inside a personal computer that enables the user to capture and display vivid pictures and images.

History list A feature of the Internet Explorer and Navigator browsers whereby Explorer and Navigator keep track of the sites and pages visited. When you first start either browser, the history list is empty because you have not yet visited any sites. As you visit various sites, the browser stores the URLs of the sites in the order they are visited.

Hit A visit to a Web site.

Home button A browser button that, when selected, returns the user to the browser's home page.

Home page The first page that you will likely see displayed on your screen when you go to a particular Web site. A home page typically contains basic information the company, organization, or agency wants you to see first.

Home shopping Using a computer and the Internet to locate, evaluate, and purchase products and services.

Hooks Special eye-catching effects included in a Web site to of catch and retain a user's attention.

Hypermedia Additional media dimensions added to hypertext, including sounds, images, and movies. The images can also be selected to link to sounds or images in other documents.

Hypertext Traditional text that, in addition to the text, contains connections to other documents.

Hypertext link A link included with Web pages that enables a user to jump from place to place on the Web. (Usually referred to simply as link.)

Hypertext Markup Language (HTML) A language used by creators of Web pages that allows the user to view Web pages.

Hypertext Transfer Protocol (HTTP) A protocol for transferring data from the host computer to the user's computer.

Icon A picture displayed on a computer screen to represent an activity or an object such as a printer, trashcan, or software program.

Ideate To think creatively and objectively about ways to create an impressive Web site.

Inbox A special place containing all messages you have received.

Information Small, refined, high-quality, relevant inputs to the solution of a problem that have been processed into a useful form.

Information appliance Special limited-purpose electronic devices such as WebTV.

Information terminals A combination of hardware and software utilized for specialized applications with the Internet. These terminals can send, receive, and process signals traveling on the Internet.

Information theft Using the Internet to steal information. Thieves use the Internet to steal all kinds of information, ranging from corporate secrets to individuals' credit card numbers.

Infoseek A highly rated search engine from Infoseek Corporation located in Santa Clara, California. Using Infoseek, you can search a database containing a large number of magazines and more than 19 million Web pages.

Insert File   An icon that, when selected, enables you to attach one or more files to an e-mail message.

Intelligent shopping agent   Unique software that can be programmed to perform for the purchaser a variety of search and analysis functions at electronic marketplaces or electronic malls. Intelligent agents can do continuous comparison shopping across several electronic marketplaces by periodically scanning new products or close-out items.

Intercast   A new technology being developed by some major computer manufacturers and television networks that will make the Internet available via television sets.

Internal clock   An electronic clock inside a computer that produces pulses at a fixed rate (like a ticking clock) to synchronize all computer operations.

Internal modem   A modem that is contained on a circuit board installed inside the computer.

Internaut   An accomplished Internet explorer or user.

Internet   A collection or network of networks. The Internet is comprised of thousands of smaller, regional computer networks scattered throughout the globe connecting millions of users in hundreds of countries.

Internet access provider (IAP)   A company that offers only access to the Internet but not to other services typically provided by Internet service providers. IAP subscribers typically do not have access to electronic mail or other services.

Internet commerce (IC)   See electronic commerce (EC).

Internet Explorer   A popular Web browser produced by Microsoft Corporation.

Internet Relay Chat (IRC)   An Internet activity that allows Internet users all over the world to communicate (chat) with each other by typing messages on their keyboards. The typed words are immediately relayed to people's computers throughout the world and displayed on their screens for them to see and read.

Internet router   A special computer that examines a request by an Internet user to determine the specific Web server to which the request is to be sent. The Web server receives the request and determines which page, file, or object is being requested.

Internet service provider (ISP)   A private commercial company that provides basic Internet services. Services provided typically include access to the Internet, electronic mail, links to browsers and search engines, and the opportunity to communicate with other individuals and groups.

Internet telephone   A recent Internet development that allows a user to make telephone calls using the Internet. The technology is free except for the Internet connection and the hardware and software you need for making Internet phone calls. (Also called telephony.)

Intranet   A computer network capable of sending information to other computers and networks and receiving information from other computers and networks. Typically, Intranets operate inside an organization and are protected from unauthorized users by a firewall or protective shield.

IRC server   A type of server used for Internet Relay Chat. IRC servers are located throughout the world and are connected together in a network so they can send messages to one another.

ISDN (Integrated Services Digital Network)   A special digital telephone line that allows you to connect to the Internet at very high speeds. ISDN speeds range from 64 Kbps to 128 Kbps. To use an ISDN line you need a special ISDN modem and an Internet provider that offers ISDN access.

Java   A special programming language by Sun Microsystems for creating Web sites and providing links to other sites and pages. Java enables pages containing animation, sound, and video to be created and displayed.

Just-in-Time (JIT) inventory systems   Manufacturing inventory systems that use computers and networks to reduce the need to maintain large inventories. Inventory arrives at each location just in time to be used in the manufacturing process.

Keyboard   A typewriter-like device used to enter data. The data is then temporarily stored in the computer's primary storage and displayed on the screen.

Keywords   Words or phrases that represent topics a user wants to search for on the Internet and Web.

Knowledge   The processes a person uses to convert data into useful information.

Line graphs   Graphs that portray trends or direction of a variable over time. For example, a line chart can be used to show the increase in a person's earnings over a period of years.

Location text box   A rectangular box for entering the address of a desired location. To go to the desired site, the user types the Uniform Resource Locator (URL) in the box and then either presses the Enter key or clicks on the Open button on the tool bar. The URL in the location text box is updated automatically as the user goes from page to page at a particular site.

Location toolbar   A toolbar that contains a Bookmarks button for working with bookmarks and a rectangular box called the location text box for entering the Internet address for the Web site the user wants to visit.

Lycos   A search engine that searches both titles and Web pages for keywords entered by a user. The Lycos search form contains several options for controlling a search of the Web.

Mailing list   A list of addresses of those individuals who can receive electronic mail messages sent to members of the group. You can subscribe to, or withdraw from, a mailing list by sending an e-mail message to the mailing list administrator of the group.

Megahertz (MHz)   A measurement of the clock speed of a computer. One megahertz represents one million cycles per second.

Menu bar   A group of available options, each with pull-down menus, usually located near the top of a program screen.

Messenger   Electronic mail (e-mail) application available with Netscape Navigator and Netscape Communicator.

Microsoft Network (MSN)   One of the newest and fastest-growing online services, by Microsoft Corporation.

Microsoft's SiteBuilder   A service offered by Microsoft Corporation promoting Internet Explorer. By agreeing to exhibit its logo on your site, Microsoft allows you to join its SiteBuilder Network. This service helps you to stay current with new Web technologies and ideas and to receive tips and ideas to make your site more appealing and effective. Your site also gets highlighted when it is listed as a hit on a search done through the Microsoft search site.

Misinformation   Information that is inaccurate, incomplete, misleading, deceptive, or confusing.

Modem   An electronic device that enables a computer to transmit (send and receive) data over telephone lines.

Moore's Law   A trend in the computer industry that suggests the speed of computers doubles every eighteen months, while the cost of that same computer drops by half, due to technology improvements. The law is named after Roger Moore, a co-founder of Intel.

Mosaic   The first Web browser that provided command icons and a more user-friendly graphical look, created in 1994 by professors and students at the University of Illinois.

Mouse   A pointing device used to select options or other information displayed on the screen.

Multimedia computer   A computer with add-on boards installed inside that allow a user to create and receive text, audio, video, and animation effects.

Multitasking   An operating system feature that allows you to perform multiple operations in parallel. For example, with multitasking you can be conducting a library search while a file is being downloaded to your computer from an FTP site.

National Information Infrastructure (NII)   A proposed high-speed, digital communications system that will deliver information, education, health resources, and government services to all sectors of our society.

National Information Superhighway   See National Information Infrastructure

Navigation Toolbar   Located below the menu bar when using the Navigator browser, the Navigation Toolbar allows the user to perform tasks quickly by clicking on one of the buttons.

NetFind   America Online's new search engine that offers a user an easy and comprehensive way to find information on the World Wide Web. With NetFind, you can find people, businesses, organizations, phone numbers, e-mail addresses, a variety of newsgroups, and even Web sites for children.

Netiquette   Rules for acceptable behavior on the Internet.

Netizen   A term that refers to being a good citizen when using the Internet.

Netscape Communicator   A powerful and versatile Internet product from Netscape Communications Corporation that includes several useful applications in addition to the Netscape Navigator browser.

Netscape Navigator   A popular Web browser produced by Netscape Communications Corporation.

Netsite   The Internet address of the Web site currently being viewed when using Netscape Navigator.

Network Wizards   A company located in Menlo Park, California, that specializes in products related to computers and communications.

NSFNET   A network operated by the National Science Foundation between 1989 and 1995 that individuals were permitted to use.

Open Systems Interconnection (OSI)   A set of communications protocols developed by the International Standards Organization based in Geneva, Switzerland. The ISO model has been adopted by the United Nations.

Operator   Words and special symbols used with most search engines to limit a search to specific information.

People-to-people systems (PPSs)   Systems in which individuals or groups are connected so they can collaborate on common problems or communicate with each other about specific issues. The connections allow for simultaneous discussions and exist long enough to complete the task.

People-to-system-to-people systems (PSPSs)   An extension of a people-to-people system in which a computer is added to the network to provide support, storage, or mediation for users. The central computer allows all participants to communicate with each other at different times. An example is electronic mail.

Personal toolbar   A special Navigator toolbar that contains an Internet button for activating Navigator, a What's New button that displays a page containing links to newer Web pages, and a What's Cool button that displays a page containing links to unique and interesting Web pages.

Personalized computer   A computer capable of recognizing the user, talking to the user, and recognizing and reacting to moods and unusual user behavior.

Pie graphs   Charts that visually show the percentage of each part of a whole. For example, a pie chart can be used to show the percentage of students in a class that earn A's, B's, C's, and so on.

Pointer   A small symbol usually resembling an arrowhead which, when a mouse is moved horizontally about the desktop, allows a user to select an item displayed on the computer screen. The procedure of moving the mouse so that the pointer is touching an object is called pointing.

Portfolio   A collection of personal and professional highlights bound together for display.

Print   An option available on a menu bar that allows a user to print a file.

Printer icon   An icon in the form of a printer that, when selected, allows you to print a copy of a message.

Privacy   A major issue regarding electronic mail over whether an employer, or someone else, has a right to intercept and read messages sent by employees.

Problem solving   The process of seeking the best solution to a specific problem.

Programs command   A menu choice that appears immediately when the user clicks on the Start button. Clicking on the Programs command displays a menu of programs, any of which can be activated by clicking on the name of the program.

Progress indicator   A rectangular box to the left of the mail icon on the Navigator browser that shows the progress of the transfer of a Web page or document.

Progressive graphics capability   A browser feature that allows a low-resolution version of images to be displayed quickly while more data needed to sharpen the images is being downloaded to your computer. This allows you to get an idea of what the final image will look like while you're waiting for the remainder of the data to be downloaded.

Protocol   A set of rules and procedures for exchanging information between computers. Protocols are software programs that define how computers interact, or communicate, with each other and how errors are detected.

Puffing   Preparing information for posting on the Internet in such a way as to sensationalize the information to make it more appealing to viewers.

Pull technologies   Using the Internet and Web to retrieve (pull) desired information into the user's computer for viewing.

Push technologies   Using Internet technologies and resources to send (push) information to a user's computer. For example, a commercial company might "push" an advertisement about a specific product that has not been requested to other computers on the Internet.

Query   A keyword or phrase that enables a search engine to systematically search the World Wide Web for documents on a specific topic.

Question mark icon (?)   An icon that, when selected, displays helpful information.

Random Access Memory (RAM)   Temporary storage capacity inside a computer. Any information entered into, or received by, your computer is temporarily stored in RAM. (Also called primary storage.)

Registration agents   Web services or individuals authorized to register a Web site.

Sabotage   The willful and illegal destruction of property. On the Internet, saboteurs try to gain entry into computer systems to destroy information. The work of saboteurs can be devastating. Because of the potential seriousness of acts of sabotage, penalties for these offenses are often severe.

Scanners   Electronic devices similar to copiers that are capable of capturing text and graphics, displaying them on a computer screen, and storing them for future use in documents such as word processing programs or Web pages.

Schematics   Illustrations used to show process flow or relationship levels. An example is a diagram showing the flow of electricity through a house or a computer.

Search button   A button on the Navigator toolbar which, when selected, displays a search screen containing one or more search engines a user can select to search for information on the Internet.

Search Engine   A software service that facilitates queries by allowing a user to enter search criteria to locate Web sources. A search engine allows a user to search for, locate, and retrieve information on the World Wide Web. Search engine sites often display advertisements for other popular Web sites and supply links to those sites.

Searching   Using a search engine to locate and retrieve information on the Internet.

Search program   A software program that enables the user to search the Web for information by topic, rather than by location. Search programs are useful for those who perform frequent Web searches and are available for purchase from computer stores and by downloading from the manufacturer.

Secondary storage   A type of permanent information storage. Examples include floppy disks and hard disks.

Send button   A button which, when selected, causes a message you have typed to be sent to the recipient.

Server software   Special software that runs on a host (server) computer that allows the server to communicate with client and other computers.

Set-up package   A software package used to set up or enable a user's computer to communicate with a service provider's computer. The package contains an instruction manual together with a diskette or CD-ROM containing installation software.

Simple search   A search that is executed by typing words separated by a space or a phrase surrounded by quotation marks.

Site registration process   A process whereby a Web site is registered with a search service by the owner or promoter of the Web page.

Software piracy   The distribution of software—by copying, loaning, or renting—to people who have not legally purchased it.

Sound board   An electronic board installed inside a personal computer that allows you to hear sounds available at some Web sites, as well as sounds available on many CD-ROM disks.

Spam mail   Worthless and useless messages received via the Internet that are similar to "junk mail" delivered by the U.S. Postal Service.

Spamming   A term that refers to any advertising in an inappropriate location on the Internet. For example, posting an advertisement to a newsgroup that is not involved in advertising is called a spam.

Standard   A definition or format that has been approved by a recognized standards organization such as the American National Standards Institute (ANSI), or a definition or format accepted as a de facto standard by the industry. A de facto standard is a standard only because a large number of companies have agreed to use it. Standards exist for computer programming languages, operating systems, data formats, and communications protocols. Without standards, only hardware and software from the same company would likely be compatible.

Start button   A small button located in the lower left corner of the desktop screen. Clicking on the Start button displays a menu of commands.

Start Page   The first page that appears when Internet Explorer is activated. The page contains features that make browsing easy.

Status line   A line that shows the current status of a Web page being retrieved. When a Web page has been retrieved and displayed, the message "Document: Done" or a similar message is displayed.

System-to-system systems (SSSs)   Systems in which computers at different organizations are connected. The systems operate autonomously with little or no direct human involvement. They replace paper-oriented communications processes such as inventory ordering, invoicing, payroll, shipping, and so on. Electronic information flows throughout the organization and to suppliers and customers.

Synchronous communications   A method of communication where there is no time lapse between sending and receiving a message. A telephone conversation is an example of synchronous communications. Synchronous communications allow for simultaneous, real-time, send/receive responses.

T1 Line   A leased telephone line that can carry data at speeds up to 1.544 megabits of data per second. Like ISDN, to be able to use a T1 line you need a special modem and a provider that offers T1 access.

Telecommuting   The activity of employees performing their work at home by being connected to the office via the Internet.

Telnet   A technology based on a client-server model that allows you to use your computer to access programs and information from another computer anyplace in the world. With Telnet software installed on your client computer, you can access any of many host computers around the world. The host allows many clients access at the same time.

Title bar   The top bar of the Navigator and Explorer browsers. It identifies the page displayed on the computer screen.

Toolbar   A group of icon buttons that allow a user to perform tasks faster than when using the menu bar. For example, selecting the Print button causes the displayed page to be printed. Some buttons have a printed word or icon on them that identifies the button's function.

Top-level domain   A part of an Internet address (URL) that indicates the type of domain, such as a commercial company, a department or agency of the government, or an educational institution.

Trojan horse   A concealed program within a file that, when the file is opened, can retrieve information from the user's computer or harm the user's computer system in some way. It might, for instance, collect a subscriber's account name and password and return them to the thief. With access to a subscriber's account, the thief can impersonate the subscriber and purchase products and services online that will be charged to the subscriber. The term Trojan horse is from the Greek story about a wooden horse filled with marauding soldiers.

Uniform Resource Locator (URL)   An Internet address for locating Web sites and links to Web pages. A Web site or page is usually located by entering its URL in the designated box.

Upgrade   A new version of a hardware or software product designed to replace an older version of the same product.

Uploading   The process of transferring files from your computer to another computer.

UUencode   A popular encoding scheme that contains instructions for both encoding and decoding large multimedia files.

Value chains   See Business chains.

Video Cameras   A device capable of capturing images and their movements on film. The images can then be downloaded into a specially equipped computer, processed, and inserted into a Web page or another document.

Videoconferencing   An Internet technology that allows for the simultaneous broadcast of audio and video signals to multiple locations, enabling individuals to use computers to participate in a conference.

VIEWnet   Internet technology that facilitates communications over the Internet by such capabilities as allowing employers to interview prospective employees online. With VIEWnet, employers and job applicants can see and hear each other.

Virtual reality (VR)   A new technology that provides for the creation of pages containing sound and lifelike 3-D images, graphics and movement.

Virtual Reality Modeling Language (VRML)   A special language that makes it possible to create Web pages in three-dimensional form.

Virtual teams   Organizations that collect a group of experts together on the Internet to study specific problems. Team members from multiple disciplines and multiple locations are convened in the problem-solving process.

Virus   A program that can disrupt or even destroy the normal operations of a computer. A virus can cause a variety of problems, ranging from the appearance of messages on the screen to the actual destruction of files stored on the computer's hard drive.

Virus hoax   False information (from any source) that a computer or computer system has been, or will be, infected by a virus.

Warez   Illegally copied software that is sent out over the Internet.

Web browser   A client software program your computer uses to display Web pages. Browsers are available for IBM-compatible PCs, Apple's Macintosh computers, and computers using the UNIX operating system. Your browser displays information on your screen by interpreting the Hypertext Markup Language (HTML) that was used to create pages containing text, sound, and multimedia files that were placed on the Web.

Webcasters   A computer professional whose job is to broadcast the contents of a particular Web site to computers connected to the Web.

WebCrawler   A search engine developed by Brian Pinkerton as a research project at the University of Washington and later bought by America Online. It is easy to learn and use. It maintains an index with information on more than 275,000 different documents that its staff has reviewed. The remainder of its database contains data on nearly 2 million documents.

Webmaster   A computer professional having the knowledge and skill to design, construct, and maintain Web sites and pages.

Web media   Media such as sight and sound that add interest to a Web site.

Web site   A destination on the World Wide Web that contains useful information. The Web allows a user to connect from one place to another.

Web TV   A limited-feature, information device that combines with a normal television set to access the Internet and send and receive e-mail. The system is inexpensive, but cannot store programs or data or do word processing or spreadsheet analysis.

Whiteboards   A technology that allows users at remote sites to share a common work area on their PCs through a modem or a network. The software tools include electronic pointers, markers, and text that participants use to draw and share information over the Internet. Each participant sees the same board and reacts to the drawings and comments of the team members.

Wisdom   An understanding of the value and implications of that which has been found.

World Wide Web   A wide-area hypermedia information retrieval initiative to give universal access to a large number of documents. The World Wide Web (WWW) provides users on computer networks with a consistent means to access a variety of media in a simplified fashion using popular graphical software interfaces.

WS_FTP   A File Transfer Protocol client computer application designed to take full advantage of the point-and-click capabilities of the Windows 3.1 or Windows 95 environment. Many Internet providers include a WS_FTP program on an installation disk or CD-ROM supplied to subscribers together with a manual explaining its use for accessing files stored on other computers. WS_FTP enables a user to access files available from computers around the world.

Yahoo!   One of the most popular and widely used search engines available. Yahoo! was created at Stanford University by two students as a means of keeping a list of Web sites they liked and might want to revisit.

INDEX

A

Active link indicator, 238
Add-on boards, 38
Add-ons, 37
Address box, 74
Advanced Research Projects Agency (ARPA), 5
Advanced search, 96
Advertisements, Web addresses in, 17
Advertising, 175, 195
AltaVista, 95-97
Amazon.com, 125
America Online (AOL), 101, 103, 173, 193, 211, 212
Anonymous access, 107
Antivirus programs, 189
ARPANET, 5, 6
Art, 125
ASCII file, 40
Asynchronous communications, 134
ATM, 65
Automotive Network eXchange (ANX), 219

B

Backbone, 48
Bandwidth, 166
Bar charts, 162
Basic computer system, 35
BITNET, 6
Boeing Company, 11, 12, 105, 214, 219, 220
Bookmark list, 77, 78, 241
Bookmarks, 77, 241, 242
Brainstorming, 153
Browser icon, 71
Browser windows, 71-75
Browsers, 67, 69. *See also* Web browsers
    defined, 41
    ease of use, 42
    framing capability, 43
    functions, 42
    Internet Explorer. *See* Internet Explorer
    multimedia support, 43, 44
    Netscape Navigator. *See* Netscape Navigator
    publishing capability, 44
    security, 45
    speed, 42, 43
    starting, 70, 71
Browsing the Web, 239, 240
Building a Web site. *See* Web site creation
Busch Gardens home page, 239
Business applications. *See* Internet commerce (IC)
Business chains, 207
Buttons, 72, 74
Buying a car, 139-141

C

Career guidance, 27
Career Mosaic, 138
Careers and opportunities
    data communications specialist, 92, 93
    Internet service representative, 47
    researching professional opportunities, 136-139
    Web page designer, 69, 70
CarMax, 140, 141
CarPoint, 139, 140
Censorship, 23
Charles Schwab, 221-223
Chat rooms, 14, 15
Chicago Bulls, 128
Chicago Museum of Natural History, 60
Classroom 2000 research program, 26
Clicking, 62
Client-server model, 23, 61, 62
Clip art, 163
Clock speed, 35
Collaboration, 120, 130
Collaborative systems, 130
Commercial online services, 47, 48
Commercial Superhighway, 227
Communications process, 3, 4
Communications protocols, 37, 65
Communications software, 40
Communications system, 3
Compatibility, 37
Competitive upgrades, 39
CompuServe, 173
Computer crackers, 193
Computer ethics, 185
Computer games, 197
Computer hackers, 193
Computer hardware, 34-39
Computer software, 39-47
Concerns. *See* Issues/concerns
Conferencing software, 130
Connect time, 49
Connecting to the Internet, 8-12, 47-50
Consumer's commerce propensity grid, 227
Copyright laws, 198
Crackers, 193
Create and Share Internet phone, 15
Creating a Web site. *See* Web site creation
Critical inflection points, 206
Cryptology, 188
Cyber Chef, 179
Cyber football leagues, 124
Cyber portfolio, 151
Cyber Promotions, 135
Cyberspace, 60
Cyberteams, 120, 121, 123, 130-134

D

Data, 114
Data communications specialist, 92, 93
De facto standard, 37
Debit cards, 225
Decision making, 114
Decrypt, 188
Design cycle, 148
Design template, 157
Desktop, 235
Dial-up networking, 40
Digital cameras, 166, 167
Directories, 107
Directory buttons, 73
Discount stock brokerage, 221-223
Display area, 73, 75, 238
Distance learning, 25-27, 123
Domain, 66, 67
Double clicking, 71
Downloading, 39, 106
Driving Directions, 130

E

e-mail, 42, 80
    MSN mail, 261-266
    Netscape Messenger, 244-248
    reading, by phone, 191, 192
e-mail filtering, 136
E-Meals, 179
Earth-to-sky theory, 160, 161
EDI, 214
Educational institutions/programs, 189, 190
EFT, 214, 225
Electronic commerce (EC), 93, 206. *See also* Internet commerce (IC)
Electronic data interchange (EDI), 214
Electronic funds transfer (EFT), 214, 225
Electronic mail. *See* e-mail
Electronic malls (e-malls), 223
Electronic marketplaces, 223
Electronic telephone, 81, 82
EMail Reader, 192
Empowering agents, 119
Encryption, 16, 45, 188
Entertainment, 15
Espionage, 193
Ethernet, 65
Ethics, 185
Etiquette, 185
Europe through the Back Door, 130
Excite, 90, 93, 97-99
Expansion board, 38
External modem, 36
Extranets, 217-220

F

Favorite, 77
FDDI, 65
Federal Express, 218
Fiber-optic cable, 116, 117
File specification, 66
File transfer, 12
File transfer protocol (FTP), 40, 42, 106-108
Firewall, 192, 214
5/24 systems team, 121
Flame, 186
Frame, 43
Framing capability, 43, 45
Fraud, 190
FTP, 40, 42, 106-108
FTP client software, 107
FTP daemon, 107
FTP main directory page, 108
Furlong, Mary, 123
Future Computing Environments, 27

G

Games, 197
Gates, Bill, 2, 12
Getting connected, 8-12, 47-50
Government, 126
Graphic, Visualization, and Usability Center
  (GVU), 21
Graphical user interface (GUI), 39, 40
Graphics, 161, 162
Graphics board (card), 38
Grocery shopping, 179, 225, 226
Grove, Andrew, 206
GUI, 39, 40
GVU, 21

H

Hackers, 193
Hardware, 34-39
Hewlett Packard, 120
History list
  Internet Explorer, 255
  Netscape Navigator, 240
Hit, 58
Home grocery shopping, 179, 225, 226
Home page design template, 157
Home pages, 76
Home shopping, 16, 121, 126-128
Hooks, 155, 157
Hopper, Grace, 92
HTML, 78, 168, 169
HTTP, 65, 66
Hypermedia, 23, 77
Hypertext, 22-24
Hypertext link, 77
Hypertext markup language (HTML), 78,
  168, 169
HyperText Transfer Protocol (HTTP), 65, 66

I

Icon, 62
Ideate, 153
Information, 114
Information processing, 114

Information retrieval, 12
Information terminal, 118, 119
Information theft, 192, 193
Infoseek, 91, 100, 101
Inserting a picture
  Internet Explorer, 259
  Netscape Navigator, 244
Instant messaging, 123
Intel, 15
Intelligent shopping agents, 223, 224
Intercast, 8, 9
Intermind, 136
Internal clock, 35
Internal modem, 36
International Telecom conference, 5
Internaut, 60
Internet. *See also* World Wide Web (WWW)
  applications/users, 12-16
  censorship, 23
  content, 13
  current status, 6-8
  defined, 4
  getting connected, 8-12, 47-50
  history, 5, 6
  issues/concerns. *See* Issues/concerns
  money-making ideas for use at home, 121
  scope/size, 5
  service providers, 47-50
  services available, 13
  set up, 50, 51
  student use, 14
Internet access providers (IAPs), 48
Internet addresses, 64-67
Internet commerce (IC), 205-231
  commerce system configurations, 212-215
  electronic marketplaces, 223
  extranets, 217-220
  financial services/electronic payments, 224,
    225
  growth projections, 207, 208
  intelligent shopping agents, 223, 224
  intranets, 215-217
  local Web shopping, 225, 226
  motivation for customer/business, 226, 227
  organization-consumer connections,
    220, 221
  organizational value chain, and, 208, 209
Internet Explorer, 41, 74, 75
  browsing the Web, 254
  favorite Web pages, 255-257
  history list, 255
  inserting a picture, 259
  printing, 260
  saving a picture, 258, 259
  saving a Web page, 258
  searching, 260, 261
  start page, 253
  starting, 251, 252
Internet fraud, 190
Internet host sites, 18
Internet Mall, 223, 224
Internet Phone, 82
Internet relay chat (IRC), 81
Internet routers, 61
Internet service providers (ISPs), 36, 48-50

Internet service representative (ISR), 47
Internet shopping malls, 127
Internet telephone (telephony), 81, 82
Intranets, 215-217
IRC (Internet relay chat), 81
IRC server, 81
ISDN line, 49
ISO model, 63, 64
Issues/concerns, 109, 183-203
  advertising, 195
  censorship, 23
  control of Internet, 184
  cryptology, 188
  espionage/sabotage, 193, 194
  ethics/etiquette, 185, 186
  fraud, 190
  games, 197
  hackers/crackers, 193
  information theft, 192, 193
  mailing lists, 186, 187
  misinformation, 195, 196
  overburdened resources, 196, 197
  pornography/obscenity, 190, 191
  privacy, 187, 188
  security, 192
  software piracy, 197-199
  useless sites, 194
  viruses, 188-190
  Year 2000 dilemma, 194, 195

J

Java, 20
Jobs. *See* Careers and opportunities
Junk mail, 135, 136
Just-in-time (JIT) inventory systems, 219

K

Keyboard, 62, 63
Keywords, 94
KN Energy, 36
Knowledge, 114

L

Learning, 123, 178
Leisure, 124
Library computerized card catalog, 88
Lifelong learning, 123, 178
Line graphs, 162
Link, 77
Local Web shopping, 225, 226
Location text box, 72
Lycos, 99, 100

M

Mailing lists, 80, 186, 187
MASIE Company Web site, 178
McCaw, Craig, 12
Megahertz (MHz), 35
Menu bar, 72, 74
Messenger, 244-248
Microsoft, 217
Microsoft Corporation, 105
Microsoft Network (MSN)
  desktop, 250, 251

exiting, 266
    Internet Explorer. *See* Internet Explorer
    MSN mail, 261-266
Microsoft SiteBuilder, 176, 177
Microsoft's Office 97, 41, 170
Millennia Software, 192
Mirror sites, 59
Misinformation, 195, 196
Modems, 36, 37
Moore, Gordon, 116
Moore's law, 116
Mosaic, 19
Mouse, 62, 63
MSN. *See* Microsoft Network (MSN)
MSN mail, 261-266
Multimedia capability, 43, 44
Multimedia computers, 38
Multimedia Marketing Group, 173, 175, 176
Multitasking, 43

N

NASA home page, 63
National Information Infrastructure (NII),
    115-117
Navigation toolbar, 72
Navigational software. *See* Browsers
Navigator. *See* Netscape Navigator
NET TV computers, 10, 11
NetFind, 103, 104
Netiquette, 177, 185
Netizen, 186
Netscape Communicator, 69, 234
Netscape home page, 236-238
Netscape Navigator, 41, 233-248
    bookmarks, 241, 242
    browsing the Web, 239, 240
    e-mail, 244-248
    exiting Netscape, 248
    history list, 240
    inserting a picture, 244
    Navigator 4.0, 61
    Netscape home page, 71-74, 236-238
    printing, 244
    saving a Web page, 243
    saving an image, 243, 244
    starting Netscape Communicator, 235, 236
Network Wizards, 18
NSFNET, 6

O

Obscenity, 190, 191
Older Web users, 122, 123
Online games, 197
Online learning, 178
Online Web page builder tutorial, 174
Only the Paranoid Survive, 206
Open systems interconnection (ISO), 63, 64
Operators, 106
Overburdened resources, 196, 197

P

PacifiCorp., 36
PC Pantry, 179
Peapod, 225, 226
People-to-people systems (PPSs), 213

People-to-system-to-people systems (PSPSs),
    213, 214
Personal shopper, 223, 224
Personalized computers, 2
Picture, inserting. *See* Inserting a picture
Pie charts, 162
Pinkerton, Brian, 101
Plug-in board, 38
Plug-ins, 37
PointCast Network, 136
Pointer, 62
Police officers, 118
Pornography, 190, 191
Portfolio, 150
Portfolio development process, 152
Potomac Electric Power Company, 36
PowerPoint 97 Graphic, 170, 172
PowerTalk, 65
Primary storage, 37
Principles of Real Estate Law, 190
Privacy, 187, 188
Problem solving, 114
Problems. *See* Issues/concerns
Prodigy, 173
Progress indicator, 238
Progressive graphics capability, 43, 44
Protocol, 63
Pub, 108
Publishing capability, 44
Puffing, 196
Pull technologies, 134
Push technologies, 134-136
Pyramid of wisdom, 114

Q

Query, 94

R

RAM, 33, 37
Random-access memory (RAM), 33, 37
RealAudio Web site, 178
Registration agents, 175
Research, 90, 91
Rinaldi, Arlene, 185

S

Sabotage, 194
Satellite dishes, 10, 11
Saving a Web page
    Internet Explorer, 258
    Netscape Navigator, 243
Saving an image/picture
    Internet Explorer, 258, 259
    Netscape Navigator, 243, 244
Scanners, 167
Schematics, 163, 164
Search box, 97
Search engines, 45, 46
    AltaVista, 95-97
    Excite, 90, 93, 97-99
    Infoseek, 91, 100, 101
    list of top search services, 173, 175
    Lycos, 99, 100
    NetFind, 103, 104
    WebCrawler, 101-103

Yahoo! 104, 105
Search programs, 106
Searching, 87-106
    defined, 88
    Internet Explorer, 260, 261
    keywords/symbols, 105, 106
    reasons for, 89
    search engines. *See* Search engines
    search programs, 106
Secondary storage, 33
Security, 45
Senior citizens, 122, 123
Server software, 61
Service providers, 47-50
Setup package, 50, 51
Shared whiteboards, 130, 131
Shopping services, 179, 225, 226
Shouting, 186
Simple search, 96
Site hooks, 155, 157
Site registration process, 173
Skills 2000 program, 217
Smithsonian Institute, 125, 126
SNA, 65
Software, 39-47
Software piracy, 197-199
Software Publishers Association, 198, 199
Sound Blaster, 38
Sound board, 38
Spam, 186
Spam-filtering program, 136
Spam mail, 135
Spamming, 186
Speed
    browsers, 42, 43
    microcomputer (clock), 35
    modems, 37
    service providers, 49
Sports, 128
Standards, 37
Status line, 238
Steves, Rick, 129, 130
Streamline, 179
Students, 14, 124. *See also* Careers and oppor-
    tunities
    art and leisure, 125
    cyberteams, 123
    government, 126
    home shopping, 126-128
    Internet/Web opportunities, 25-27
    portfolio, 151
    researching professional opportunities,
        136-139
    sports, 128
    travel, 128-130
Sun Microsystems, 20
Surfing the Net, 60
Surplus Direct, 127
Synchronous communications, 134
System-to-system systems (SSSs), 213, 214

T

T1 line, 49
TCP/IP, 65
Teams, 120, 121, 123, 130-134

Telecommuting, 121
Teledesic, 11, 12
ThirdAge, 123
3-D virtual reality, 165
Token Ring, 65
Toolbar, 72, 74
Top-level domain, 67
Travel, 128-130
Tripod, 137, 173
Trojan horse, 193
Typical computer system, 35

U

Uniform resource locator (URL), 66, 173
University of Phoenix, 26
Upgrades, 38, 39
Uploading, 106
URLs, 66, 173
Useless Web sites, 194
Utility companies, 36
UUencode, 108

V

Value chains, 207, 208
Video cameras, 167, 168
Vidoeconferencing, 130, 131
VIEWnet, 138
Virtual reality (VR), 78, 165
Virtual reality modeling language (VRML),
  78, 79
Virtual teams, 132
Virtual universities, 123
Virus hoax, 189
Viruses, 188-190
VRML, 78, 79

W

Wal-Mart, 16, 126, 128, 209
Watauga County Schools, 189, 190
Web browsers, 75, 76, 79, 80. *See also*
  Browsers
Web media, 160
Web page designer, 69, 70
Web pages, 77-79
Web-publishing capabilities, 44
Web site capacities, 59
Web site creation, 147-182
    advertising, 175
    clip art, 163
    color/emotion, 160, 161
    construction options, 168-170
    content, 157-160
    continuous refinement, 177, 178
    customer, 156, 157
    HTML, 168, 169
    maintaining the site, 177, 178
    organizational sites, 149, 150
    personal sites, 148, 149
    promotion options, 175-177
    registration process, 173-175
    schematics, 163, 164
    site structure, 159
    sound, 164, 165
    specialized media hardware devices,
      166-168
    step 1 (ideate), 153
    step 2 (formulate), 154
    step 3 (construct), 154
    storage of site, 171-173
    text, 160, 161
    3-d virtual reality, 165
    timely/current information, 177
    user equipment considerations, 165, 166
Web sites, 58, 76, 77
Web TV, 117, 119
Webcasters, 134
WebCrawler, 101-103
Webmaster, 27
WebPhone, 82
WebTalk, 82
Whiteboards, 130, 131
Windows 95 desktop screen, 234
Windows 95 desktop screen start
  buttons/menus, 235
Windows 95 dial-up connection, 41
Wireless microwave transmissions, 9, 10
Wisdom, 114
Women users, 122, 123
Woods, Tiger, 128, 129
Work, 91, 92, 120, 121
World Wide Web (WWW), 16-21. *See also*
  Internet
    defined, 17
    hyptertext/hypermedia, 22-24
    implications, 20, 21
    improvements, 19, 20
    issues/concerns, 23
    services/opportunities, 25
    user demographics, 21
    uses, 21, 22
    Web addresses in advertisements, 17
WS_FTP, 108

Y

Yahoo! 104, 105
Year 2000 dilemma, 194, 195

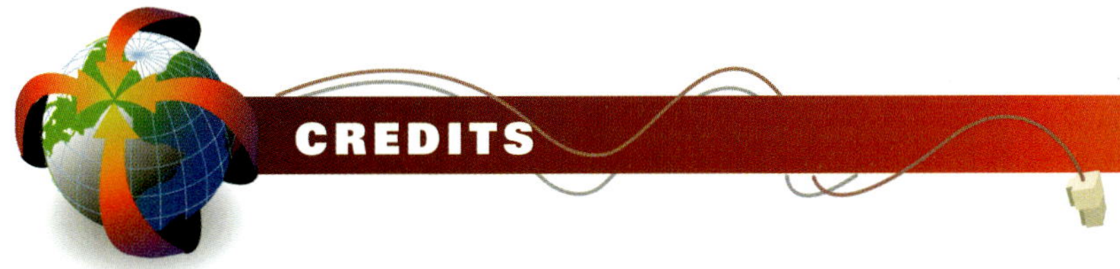

Fig. 1.01, 1.06, 5.05b, 6.19—Photo courtesy of Hewlett-Packard Company

Fig. 1.07, 1.08—Photo courtesy of Direct TV

Fig. 1.11, 4.01—Photo courtesy of Floyd Fuller

Fig. 1.12, 1.13—Photo courtesy of Amelia Hill

Fig. 2.04, 2.05, 3.13, 3.19, 3.20, 4.18, 4.19, 5.26, 6.25a, 6.25b, 6.29, A.01, A.02, B.01, B.02, B.03, B.04, B.05, B.11, B.12, B.13, B.14, B.15—Screen shot reprinted with permission of Microsoft Corporation

Fig. 2.07—Copyright 1998, The Nasdaq Stock Market, Inc.

Fig. 2.09—Copyright, USA TODAY. Reprinted with permission.

Fig. 2.12, 4.16—Copyright 1997-98, America Online, Inc. All Rights Reserved.

Fig. 3.03—The Field Museum in Chicago (http://www.fmnh.org)

Fig. 3.11c—Screen shot courtesy of PBS ONLINE®

Fig. 2.06, 3.14, 3.15, 3.16, 3.17, 3.18, 3.22, 4.09, 4.17, A.03, A.04, A.05, A.06, A.07, A.08, A.10, A.11, A.14, A.15, A.16—Portions © Netscape Communications Corporation 1997. All rights reserved. Netscape, Netscape Navigator and the Netscape N logo are registered trademarks of Netscape in the United States and other countries.

Fig. 4.02a, 4.02b, 4.06, 4.10, 4.15, B.10—Excite, Excite Search, and the Excite Logo are trademarks of Excite, Inc. and may be registered in various jurisdictions. Excite screen display copyright 1995-1998 Excite, Inc.

Fig. 4.03, 4.13, 4.14, 6.27—Reprinted by permission. Infoseek, Infoseek Ultra, Ultrasmart, Ultraseek, Ultraseek Server, Infoseek Desktop, ISeek, Quickseek, Imageseek, Ultrashop, the Infoseek logos and the tagline "Once you know, you know." are trademarks of Infoseek Corporation which may be registered in certain jurisdictions. Other trademarks shown are trademarks of their respective owners. Copyright © 1994-1998 Infoseek Corporation. All rights reserved. © 1998 EarthLink Network, Inc., EarthLink Network, the EarthLink logo and EarthLink Network Total Acess are trademarks of EarthLink Network, Inc. All Rights Reserved.

Fig. 4.04—The Computer Museum History Center

Fig. 4.05—Ski Utah/Network Publishing

Fig. 5.03, 6.18—Sony Electronics Inc.

Fig. 5.04—Copyright 1998 Steve Cowden/Oregonian Newspaper. Used with permission.

Fig. 5.05a, 5.05c, 5.05d, 6.17—Courtesy of International Business Machines Corporation. Unauthorized use not permitted.

Fig. 5.08—Copyright, Los Angeles Times. Reprinted by permission.

Fig. 5.18—Photo courtesy of Intel

Fig. 5.12a—Internet Shopping Network

Fig. 5.12b—L.L.Bean, Inc.

Fig. 5.21a—© 1998 PointCast Inc. PointCast is a registered trademark of PointCast Incorporated

Fig. 5.21b—© 1997 Intermind

Fig. 5.23—Tripod, Inc.

Fig. 5.25, 8.11—The Boeing Co.

Fig. 5.27—Car Max, The Auto Superstore, a subsidiary of Circuit City Stores, Inc., Richmond, Va.

Fig. 6.7—© Scott Barrow/International Stock

Fig. 6.19b—Artec (Newark, Calif., *www.artecusa.com*) ViewScan Home 1 is a compact portable color scanner. Its auto stitch feature merges multiple scans into a single image, and allows users to scan text and pictures from hard-to-reach places such as large books and odd surfaces. It offers resolution of 100-2400dpi and it scans up to 16.8 million colors and 256 shades of gray as well.